The Collected Courses of the Academy of European Law

Series Editors: Professor Marise Cremona,
Professor Bruno de Witte,
Professor Francesco Francioni
European University Institute, Florence
Assistant Editor: Anny Bremner
European University Institute, Florence

VOLUME XXI/1
Human Rights and Immigration

The Collected Courses of the Academy of European Law
Edited by Professor Marise Cremona,
Professor Bruno de Witte, and Professor Francesco Francioni
Assistant Editor: Anny Bremner

Each year the Academy of European Law in Florence, Italy, invites a group of outstanding lecturers to teach at its summer courses on Human Rights law and European Union law.

A 'general course' is given in each of the two fields by a distinguished scholar or practitioner, who examines the field as a whole through a particular thematic, conceptual, or philosophical lens, or looks at a theme in the context of the overall body of law. In addition, a series of 'specialized courses' brings together a group of highly qualified scholars to explore and analyse a specific theme in relation to Human Rights law and EU law.

The Academy's mission, to produce scholarly analyses which are at the cutting edge of these two fields, is achieved through the publication of this series, the Collected Courses of the Academy of European Law.

Human Rights and Immigration

Edited by
RUTH RUBIO-MARÍN

OXFORD
UNIVERSITY PRESS

OXFORD
UNIVERSITY PRESS

Great Clarendon Street, Oxford, OX2 6DP,
United Kingdom

Oxford University Press is a department of the University of Oxford.
It furthers the University's objective of excellence in research, scholarship,
and education by publishing worldwide. Oxford is a registered trade mark of
Oxford University Press in the UK and in certain other countries

First Edition published in 2014

Published in the United States of America by Oxford University Press
198 Madison Avenue, New York, NY 10016, United States of America

British Library Cataloguing in Publication Data
Data available

Library of Congress Control Number: 2014930236

ISBN 978–0–19–870117–0

Contents

List of Abbreviations

ACFC	Advisory Committee on the Framework Convention on National Minorities
ACHR	American Convention on Human Rights
CAT	Committee Against Torture
CBA	Canadian Bar Association
CEACR	ILO Committee of Experts on the Application of Conventions and Recommendations
CEDAW	Convention to Eliminate All Forms of Discrimination Against Women
CERD	Committee on the Elimination of Discrimination
CESCR	Committee on Economic, Social and Cultural Rights
CFA	Committee on Freedom of Association
CIC	Citizenship and Immigration Canada
CIR	Comprehensive Immigration Reform
CMW	UN Committee on the Protection of the Rights of all Migrant Workers and Members of their Families
CPT	Council of Europe Committee for the Prevention of Torture and Inhuman or Degrading Treatment or Punishment
ECHR	European Convention on Human Rights
ECSMA	European Convention on Social and Medical Assistance
ECSR	European Committee of Social Rights
ECtHR	European Court of Human Rights
ECmHR	European Commission on Human Rights
ECLSMW	European Convention on the Legal Status of Migrant Workers
ESC	European Social Charter
FCNM	European Framework Convention on National Minorities
FGM	female genital mutilation
H&C	Humanitarian and Compassionate application
IACtHR	Inter-American Court of Human Rights
ICCPR	International Covenant on Civil and Political Rights
ICJ	International Court of Justice
ICESCR	International Covenant on Economic, Social and Cultural Rights
ICRMW	International Convention on the Protection of the Rights of Migrant Workers and their Families
IIRIRA	Illegal Immigration Reform and Immigrant Responsibility Act of 1996
ILO	International Labour Organization
NATO	North Atlantic Treaty Organization
OSCE	Organization for Security and Co-operation in Europe
PRRA	pre-removal risk assessment
RAD	Refugee Appeal Division
UDHR	Universal Declaration of Human Rights
UNCLOS	United Nations Convention on the Law of the Sea
UNHCR	United Nations High Commission for Refugees

Notes on Contributors

Vincent Chetail is Professor of Public International Law at the Graduate Institute of International and Development Studies, Geneva, where he is also Director of the Programme for the Study of Global Migration. He is a Board Member of the Geneva Academy of International Humanitarian Law and Human Rights and, from 2004 to 2012, was the Research Director of the Geneva Academy. Professor Chetail is Editor-in-Chief of the *Refugee Survey Quarterly*, member of the founding editorial board of *Oxford Bibliographies in International Law* and General Editor of the series *Organisation internationale et relations internationales* (Bruylant, Brussels). He is also Senior Research Associate at the Refugee Law Initiative (University of London), as well as member of the Academic Network for Legal Studies on Immigration and Asylum in Europe, and the General Assembly of the International Institute of Human Rights (Strasbourg).

Michael J. Churgin is the Raybourne Thompson Centennial Professor in Law at the University of Texas at Austin. A graduate of Brown University and the Yale Law School, he joined the Texas faculty in 1975 and also teaches in the Mental Health Clinic. Professor Churgin teaches and writes in the fields of immigration and refugee law, criminal procedure (including juvenile justice), and mental health law. He has been a visiting fellow at Wolfson College and Clare Hall, and most recently, the Quatercentenary Visiting Fellow at Emmanuel College, University of Cambridge.

Alessia Di Pascale is currently a research fellow in EU law at the University of Milan. She was Jean Monnet Lecturer in international migration law (2011–2013) at the University of Bergamo. She has been a visiting fellow at the Université Libre de Bruxelles and at the University of Nijmegen. Dr Di Pascale has carried out extensive research in the field of human rights, with a special focus on migrants' rights and asylum and corporate social responsibility. She is deputy member for Italy of the Odysseus Network (EU Academic network on migration and asylum law) and is also a lawyer qualified with the Milan Bar.

Virginia Mantouvalou is Reader in Human Rights and Labour Law in the Faculty of Law at University College London (UCL), where she is also Co-Director of the Institute for Human Rights. She is joint Editor of *Current Legal Problems.* Dr Mantouvalou is the author of *Debating Social Rights* (with Conor Gearty, Hart, 2011), as well as articles, book chapters and essays in human rights, labour law and European law. In 2010 she was Dean's Visiting Scholar at Georgetown University Law Center in Washington DC. She holds a PhD in law from the London School of Economics, an LLM in human rights from the London School of Economics, and an LLB from the University of Athens. She has received several scholarships and awards for her research, including an Arts and Humanities Research Council grant to work on theoretical aspects of social and labour rights. She has also worked as a consultant for projects of the International Labour Organization and the Equal Rights Trust.

Siobhán Mullally is Professor of Law at University College Cork and Director of the Centre for Criminal Justice and Human Rights. She is joint Editor of the *Irish Yearbook of International Law* and has published widely in the fields of human rights, gender and migration law. She is an elected member of the Council of Europe monitoring body, the

Group of Experts on Action against Trafficking (GRETA). Professor Mullally has held visiting fellowships at several universities, including a Fulbright scholarship at Columbia University and a Fernand Braudel senior fellowship at the European University Institute. She has worked as an advisor and consultant to UN bodies and NGOs, including UNDP, UNIFEM, International Bar Association and International Crisis Group.

Ruth Rubio-Marín is Professor of Comparative Public Law at the European University Institute in Florence, Italy. She was previously Professor of Constitutional Law at the University of Seville, Spain, and a member of the Faculty of the Hauser Global Law School Program at New York University. Her interests include comparative constitutional law, transitional justice, human rights, migration, minority rights and feminist theory. She is the author and editor of several books, including *Immigration as a Democratic Challenge* (2000); *The Gender of Constitutional Jurisprudence* (edited with B. Baines, 2004); *What Happened to the Women? Gender and Reparations for Human Rights Violations* (ed., 2006), *The Gender of Reparations: Subverting Sexual Hierarchies while Redressing Human Rights Violations* (ed., 2009) and *The Battle for Female Suffrage in the EU: Voting to Become Citizens* (edited with B. Rodriguez Ruiz, 2012).

Bernard Ryan is Professor of Migration Law at the University of Kent, where he teaches and researches all aspects of migration law and policy. His most recent publications have concerned extraterritorial immigration control, integration tests in British migration law and legal aspects of labour migration. In 2010, he was a Fernand Braudel Senior Research Fellow in the Law Department of the European University Institute. He is the co-chair of the Migration and Law Network, which promotes the field of migration law in British universities.

Tullio Scovazzi is Professor of International Law at the University of Milano-Bicocca, Milan, Italy. He occasionally acts as legal advisor for Italy or for international secretariats in negotiations or meetings relating to human rights, the international law of the sea, and the law of cultural properties.

Daniel Thym is Professor of Public, European and International Law at the University of Konstanz, where he is also Co-Director of the Research Centre Immigration & Asylum Law (FZAA). Professor Thym obtained his PhD at Humboldt-University, Berlin in 2004, and completed his *Habilitation* on 'Administrative Migration Governance (*Migrationsverwaltungsrecht*)' in 2009. He was Assistant Professor at Humboldt-University from 2005 to 2009. Since 2006 he has served as a member of the Editorial Board of the *European Law Journal*. Since 2012 he has been a Principle Investigator of the interdisciplinary Centre of Excellence 'Cultural Foundations of Social Integration' in Konstanz. His research interests include migration law at the national, European and international level as well as European constitutional developments, including foreign affairs.

Table of Cases

INTERNATIONAL AND REGIONAL JURISDICTIONS

European Court of Justice

Human Rights Committee (United Nations)

Inter-American Commission of Human Rights

Inter-American Court of Human Rights

International Court of Justice

International Criminal Tribunal for the Former Yugoslavia

International Labour Organisation

Refugee Status Appeals Authority (United Nations)

NATIONAL JURISDICTIONS

Australia

United States

Introduction: Human Rights and the Citizen/Non-citizen Distinction Revisited

Ruth Rubio-Marín

I. The Context

The coexistence of citizens and non-citizens has become a permanent feature in contemporary societies. The share of international migrants in the world's population has remained stable in the past fifty years at an approximate rate of 3 per cent of the world population. In 2009, the total population of international migrants was estimated at around 214 million. If one asks who these migrants are, the answer is that 48 per cent of total international migration is composed of women, most of whom now migrate on their own rather than as family members of other migrants. They do so to respond to the increase in demand for paid domestic work, as women in more developed societies join the paid labour force while care support from the welfare state is in retreat. Also, the ILO has established that around 90 per cent of international migration is composed of economically active migrants and members of their families whereas only 7–8 per cent of migrants are refugees and asylum seekers. Moreover, in 2009 an estimated 50 million people were living or working in a foreign country with irregular status.[1]

In spite of migration having become a structural feature in Western democracies, the last two decades have witnessed an almost generalized restrictive turn among countries of destination, signalling a marked deterioration in migrants' status. A general climate of socio-economic uncertainty conditioned by rising unemployment, labour market deregulation, decreasing resources for social security and welfare programmes, political populism, as well as fears surrounding globalization and terrorism, lies behind rising levels of racism, xenophobia, and discrimination rendering solidarity from nationals towards the precarious living and working conditions of migrants unlikely.[2] A neoliberal economic environment in which

[1] Data taken from International Commission of Jurists, *Migration and International Human Rights Law: Practitioners Guide No. 6* (2011).

[2] See P. De Guchteneire and A. Pécoud, 'Introduction: The UN Convention on Migrant Workers' Rights', in P. De Guchteneire, A. Pécoud, and R. Cholewinski, (eds), *Migration and Human Rights: The United Nations Convention on Migrant Workers' Rights* (2009) 3.

states play an ever-decreasing role in labour market regulation favours irregularities and abuse, especially when it comes to low-skilled economic sectors in which migrants are active.[3]

Within this wider socio-economic context, and aggravated by the political impact of terrorist attacks since 2001, migration policies around the world have increasingly shifted towards law enforcement, and migration issues are increasingly addressed as a problem of law and order.[4] This is also evident in the new immigration rules introduced by the European Union over the past decade, rules which show that the EU's common migration approach is much less driven by human-rights considerations than by economic concerns and a desire to stop illegal migration.[5] Many national laws and practices also show a process of securitization in relation to migration matters,[6] a phenomenon illustrated by the discussion of the recent immigration law reforms and policies in Italy in Di Pascale's contribution to this book (Chapter 8). In the minds of an increasing number of states, the perceived links between international migration, irregular migration, and international crime have come to dominate the discourse; and the focus has been placed on effective border control and the increasing reliance on criminal means to fight the trafficking and smuggling of migrants,[7] but also against the presence of undocumented migrants. Little does it matter that undocumented migration is taking place against the background of an unequal global distribution of resources, services, and opportunities.

Looming large is not only the anxiety around protecting territorial sovereignty, control over borders, and employment for nationals, but also a growing anti-Islamic feeling amongst a population which perceives Muslim immigrants as a threat to the

[3] See De Guchteneire et al. (n 2) at 21.

[4] C. Fernandez, A. Manavella, and J. M. Ortuno, 'The Effects of Exceptional Legislation on Criminalization of Immigrants and People Suspected of Terrorism' (Challenge Report 9, 2009), available at: <http://www.libertysecurity.org/article2496.html>. See also A. Edwards, 'Back to Basics: The Right to Liberty and Security of Person and "Alternatives to Detention" of Refugees, Asylum-Seekers, Stateless Persons and Other Migrants' (2011), PPLA/2011/01.Rev.01; available at: <http://www.unhcr.org/refworld/pdfid/4dc935fd2.pdf>; V. Türk and A. Edwards, 'Introductory Note to the Summary Conclusions of the Global Roundtable on Alternatives to Immigration Detention', 23 *Int. J. Refugee Law* (2011) 873.

[5] R. Cholewinski, 'The Criminalisation of Migration in EU Law and Policy', in A. Baldaccini, E. Guild, and H. Toner (eds), *Whose Freedom, Security and Justice? EU Immigration and Asylum Law and Policy* (2006), at 301. See also M. Merlino and J. Parkin, 'Irregular Migration in Europe: EU Policies and the Fundamental Rights Gap' (CEPS Report, 2011) available at: <http://migration.etuc.org/en/docs_en/1%20Irregular%20Migration%20in%20Europe_%20EU%20policies%20and%20the%20Fundamental%20Rights%20Gap.pdf>.

[6] See J. Huysmans, 'The European Union and the Securitization of Migration', 38 *JCMS* (2000) 751; D. Bigo, 'Security and Immigration: Toward a Critique of the Governmentality of Unease', 27 *Alternatives* (2002) 63; T. Balzacq, 'The Three Faces of Securitization: Political Agency, Audience and Context', 11 *EJIR* (2005) 2, at 171–201; D. Bigo, 'Globalized (in)Security: the Field and the Ban-opticon', in D. Bigo and A. Tsoukala (eds), *Terror, Insecurity and Liberty: Illiberal Practices of Liberal Regimes after 9/11* (2008) 5.

[7] In 2000, states agreed to two new treaties to criminalize migrant trafficking and migrant smuggling: the Protocol to Prevent, Suppress and Punish Trafficking in Persons, especially Women and Children (Palermo Protocol) and the Protocol against the Smuggling of Migrants by Land, Sea and Air, supplementing the 2000 United Nations Convention against Transnational Organized Crime.

security of the state and its democratic stability. The expectation that immigrants, especially those of Muslim origin, will naturally embrace liberal values and human rights has been undermined, and the confidence that they will not pose any threat to the basic security of the state has also eroded, especially after terrorist attacks at the turn of the century. As I discuss in Chapter 2, it is in this context that a growing preoccupation with immigrant integration has arisen and integration contracts, courses, and tests have flourished all over Europe and been extended from naturalization procedures, where they were traditionally located, conditioning access to national citizenship only, to the different gates of migratory control, such as access to the territory, but also, tellingly, to the status of permanent residence. In other words, external territorial borders are affirmed, rendering access to the territory ever more difficult, at the same time as internal membership borders are built, leaving out of the domain of equal concern and protection not only those who came without authorization, but also those who have not yet shown their ability to pass newly defined membership qualifiers measured in terms of cultural affinity, civic virtue and, increasingly, economic self-sufficiency.

Parallel to this process of external and internal border affirmation is one, we believe, of externalization of migration control. Failing to live up to their collective responsibility in responding to the needs of those seeking to protect their life and livelihood, states have come to depend on the assistance of others to perform the dirty business of containing the unsolicited.[8] The practices vary and include cooperation for containment purposes (often relying on bilateral agreements and aid to countries of origin and transit of migrants), cooperation to facilitate reception in case of interception in international waters, and push-backs in case of collective removal of asylum seekers and undocumented migrants. The practices also include safe third-country agreements, such as those discussed in Chapter 7, binding Canada and the US, and forcing asylum seekers to have their case adjudicated in the first country reached.

Virtually all of the authors in this book are worried about the impact that the issue of security poses in terms of rights enjoyment in the migration discourse and the practices that such discourse helps to legitimize. Di Pascale (Chapter 8) denounces the increasingly common practice of countries which, in fighting against undocumented migration, have recourse to the restriction of their fundamental rights.[9] Like

[8] In this book, Scovazzi (Chapter 6) refers to the existence of asymmetrical rights in the international order, suggesting that they account for part of the difficulty in identifying an adequate system for allocating collective responsibility for migrants among existing states. Examples of such asymmetries include the obligations under the international law of the sea for a number of states to cooperate to deliver rescued people to a place of safety as soon as possible, which do not predetermine with precision where the place of safety is located; Article 13(2) of the 1948 Universal Declaration of Human Rights and Article 12(2) of the 1966 International Covenant on Civil and Political Rights, under which every individual has the right to leave any country, including his own, which is not complemented by a corresponding right to immigrate; or the recognition, under the Refugee Convention, of the right of the refugee not to be returned to a state, including his own, where he would be under threat for a number of specific reasons, which is not accompanied by a right of entry into a given state.

[9] See also B. Bogusz et al. (eds), *Irregular Migration and Human Rights: Theoretical, European and International Perspectives* (2004); C. Dauvergne, *Making People Illegal: What Globalisation Means for Migration Law* (2008). See also S. Palidda, *Racial Criminalization of Migrants in the 21st Century*

Scovazzi, she also denounces collective removals and interception in international waters and push-backs of undocumented migrants and asylum seekers in Italy, a practice both authors claim is hardly compatible with the principle of *non-refoulement*. Mullally (Chapter 4) compellingly discusses how migrant women's rights claims have been instrumentalized by states to legitimize the expansion of criminal laws in the context of human trafficking and irregular migration, and to restrict, instead of expand, pathways to safe and secure migration, failing to recognize the links between access to safe migration routes, application of human rights norms to immigration law and policy, and potentially reducing migrant women's vulnerability to trafficking.[10] In turn, Churgin (Chapter 7) describes how in Canada, the concern with illegal trafficking in persons has translated into the restriction of refugee rights, and how, in this context, recent legislation has been passed in Canada (the 2012 Protecting Canada's Immigration System Act), imitating some of the harsh provisions of the UK, US, and Australian refugee adjudicatory process and narrowing the distance between Canada, which had been praised internationally in the last quarter of the century for its progressive policies, and the US, which had passed draconian legislation in 1996.

These authors are not alone in expressing concern. Former UN Special Rapporteur for the human rights of migrants, Mr Bustamante, already denounced migration policies that aim to address solely security and border control concerns and that lack a human protection approach, affect the human rights of migrants detrimentally, and do not result in the deterrence of irregular immigration. He also pointed out the consequences of the criminalization of migration on the enjoyment of human rights by migrants and warned of the disproportionate use of the criminal justice system to manage irregular migration.[11] His successor, Mr Crépeau, has also expressed similar concerns and specifically warned against the dangers of the growing belief that there are two types of human rights, those held by citizens and those of a second-class category held by non-citizens.[12]

In spite of this, as in past historical periods of economic crises and rising nationalism, the prospect of states happily accepting wider international human rights obligations to protect the well-being of non-citizens are dim. Even to this

(2011); A. Leerkes, G. Engbersen, and J. Van der Leun, 'Crime Among Irregular Immigrants and the Influence of Internal Border Control', 58 *Crime Law and Social Change* (2012) 15.

[10] See also V. E. Munro, 'Stopping Traffic: A Comparative Study of Responses to the Trafficking in Women for Prostitution', 46 *Brit. J. Criminology* (2006) 318.

[11] See Report of the Special Rapporteur on the human rights of migrants, Mr Jorge Bustamante, 3 August 2010, UN Doc A/65/222.

[12] Statement by Mr François Crépeau, Special Rapporteur on the Human Rights of Migrants to the 66th session of the General Assembly, Third Committee—Item 69 (b), (c), 21 October 2011, para. 3; available at: <http://www.ohchr.org/EN/NewsEvents/Pages/DisplayNews.aspx?NewsID=11523&LangID=E>. Similarly, the UN Committee on the Rights of Migrant Workers has recently defended the view that qualifying migrants as 'illegal' contributes to the criminalization of migration and feeds into the stereotyping of this sector of the population as persons who disregard the law and the social arrangements of the society they transit or live in (see UN Committee on RMW, Draft General Comment No. 2 on the rights of migrant workers in an irregular situation and members of their families, December 2012, point I.3; available at: <http://www2.ochcr.orh/ensglish.bodies/CRMW/GC2.htm>).

day, the International Convention on the Protection of the Rights of All Migrant Workers and Members of Their Families, the most comprehensive international treaty in the field of migration and human rights which came into force in 2003, thirteen years since its adoption, has only been ratified by forty-six states, none of which is a major immigrant-receiving country, in spite of the European Parliament and a former UN Secretary-General urging European member states to adopt it.[13] The disinterest in migrants' rights affects other migration-related treaties.[14] Not surprisingly, this disinterest is being challenged via increased activism around migrants' rights by individuals and organizations outside formal government frameworks.[15]

II. The Central Question: The Lexical Priority of Human Rights?

For anyone approaching migration from a human rights perspective, one central question underlies all these debates. It is mostly uncontroversial that, as a matter of well-established international law and subject to their treaty obligations, states enjoy the right to control the entry, residence, and expulsion of aliens. With the exception of international refugee law, this prerogative has persisted until the present day. The central question thus becomes the extent to which human rights variations can be used as a legitimate tool for immigration policy purposes. In other words, can states deny or limit human rights as a way to achieve their immigration/asylum policy objectives? Does the determination of the treatment of aliens, as part and parcel of state sovereignty, include deciding what human rights obligations states have vis-à-vis non-citizen residents?[16] Or can we instead say that, with the narrow exceptions already embedded in the human rights system, the lexical priority of human rights and their pre-eminent link to personhood instead of national citizenship should be affirmed, and that this affirmation should severely constrain the realm of legitimate policy options in the immigration domain? As De Guchteneire and Pécoud state, what is basically at stake is whether rights can be

[13] See European Parliament, Resolution on Development and Migration, Doc. P6_TA (2006) 0319, 6 July 2006, and Address to the European Parliament upon receipt of the Andrei Sakharov Prize for Freedom of Thought (Brussels, 29 January 2004); available at: <http://www.europa-eu-un.org/artoicles/en/articles_3178_en.htm>.

[14] These include ILO Conventions Nos. 97 and 143, with 49 and 23 ratifications respectively. And although eleven developed industrialized nations have ratified one or both conventions, none did so after 1982, indicating a lack of interest in the last three decades. The same applies to the European Convention on the Legal Status of Migrant Workers; only eleven states have ratified it and all but three did so more than twenty years ago.

[15] Within the UN, the Commission on Human Rights appointed a Working Group of Intergovernmental Experts on the Human Rights of Migrants in 1997. In 1999 a Special Rapporteur on the Human Rights of Migrants was appointed. The Global Campaign for Ratification of the Convention on Rights of Migrants was launched in 1998, and this pushed the Convention over the 23 threshold so that it could enter into force in 2003.

[16] See also S. Grant, 'The Recognition of Migrants' Rights within the UN Human Rights System: the First 60 years', in M. Dembour and T. Kelly (eds), *Are Human Rights for Migrants? Critical Reflections on the Statue of Irregular Migrants in Europe and the United States* (2011) 25, at 30–1.

made to derive not from universal norms like those in human rights conventions, but rather from the supply-and-demand mechanism that determines migrants' value on the labour market.[17]

Granted, the human rights system in itself reflects the acceptance of the territorial state order and this has a bearing on the rights status of non-citizens.[18] Thus, although human rights instruments commonly link legal personality to personhood[19] and articulate the right to non-discrimination in broad terms,[20] they also specify that they apply to (but only to) all those persons subject to the state's jurisdiction.[21] Also, some human rights are typically reserved for nationals only—primarily core political rights, such as the franchise, the right to residential stability, or the right to enter and remain in one's country of residence.[22] Full legal equality between citizens and non-citizens is therefore not the assumption on which the human rights order rests regardless of the universal vocation of human rights. As Benhabib has written, there is thus 'an irresolvable contradiction, between the expansive and inclusionary principles of moral and political universalism, as anchored in universal human rights, and the particularistic and exclusionary conception of democratic closure' in the modern nation-state.[23] The question then is whether the exception to equality is to be understood as a narrow exception to the general principle of equal rights, or whether it falls primarily on the legislator to modulate the fundamental rights of migrants, citizenship being a priori a valid classification ground.[24]

[17] See De Guchteneire et al. (n 2) at 30.

[18] See C. M. Rodriguez and R. Rubio-Marín, 'The Constitutional Status of Irregular Migrants: Testing the Boundaries of Human Rights Protection of Irregular Migrants in Spain and the United States', in M. Dembour and T. Kelly (eds), *Are Human Rights for Migrants? Critical Reflections on the Statue of Irregular Migrants in Europe and the United States* (2011) 73, at 74–5.

[19] See, for instance, Art. 6 UDHR, Art. 16 ICCPR and Art. 3 ACHR, which all recognize that 'everyone has the right to recognition everywhere as a person before the law'.

[20] See Art. 2 UDHR; Art. 26 ICCPR; Art. 14 ECHR; and Art. 24 ACHR.

[21] Art. 2 ICCPR, for instance, declares: 'Each State Party to the present Covenant undertakes to respect and to ensure to all individuals within its territory and subject to its jurisdiction the rights recognized in the present Covenant'. Art. 1 ECHR and Art. 1 ACHR provide similarly.

[22] The UDHR recognizes that everyone has the right of equal access to public service, as well as to take part in the government of his or her country directly or through freely chosen representatives. Art. 25 ICCPR and Art. 23 ACHR refer to citizens as having the right to take part in the conduct of public affairs, to vote and be elected, and to access on equal terms the public service. Art. 3 Protocol 1 to ECHR (on political rights), 'Enforcement of Certain Rights and Freedoms not included in Section I of the Convention' refers to 'the people' when detailing the right to vote by secret ballot. Finally, regarding residential stability, the right to enter and not be expelled from a specific country is recognized only for nationals of a given country. See Art. 13 UDHR; Art. 12(4) ICCPR; Art. 3, Protocol 4 to ECHR, 'Protecting Certain Additional Rights'; and Art. 22(5) ACHR. For aliens legally in a territory, the most commonly acknowledged human right is the freedom of movement within the territory, or the freedom to choose one's residence once accepted into a country: Art 12(1) ICCPR; Art. 2(1) Protocol 4 to ECHR; and Art. 22(1) ACHR. Some human rights instruments also protect aliens from collective expulsions, ECHR Protocol 4, Art. 4; and ACHR Art 22.

[23] S. Benhabib, *The Rights of Others: Aliens, Residents, and Citizens* (2004) at 19.

[24] A regulatory source-related question is whether it makes sense for immigration legislation to try to cover in any systematic manner migrants' fundamental rights (as seems increasingly the practice in recent immigration countries), or whether it should be assumed that human rights and fundamental rights as enshrined in the constitution ought to remain the main regulatory sources limiting migratory

One increasingly recurring state practice whose legitimacy hinges primarily on the answer given to this question—a practice discussed in several chapters in this book—is that of connecting the exercise of various fundamental rights to the proof of legal presence and/or permanent residence status in the territory. Another practice concerns the increasing trend to subject resident aliens to integration tests as a condition of their enjoyment of certain rights either directly or indirectly, as when the enjoyment of rights is in turn attached to a specific residential/migration status. In Chapter 2, I argue that, in human rights terms, the regulatory transfer of integration policies away from citizenship policies to ensure equal rights, accommodate cultural differences, and remove obstacles to participation, and their insertion in migration policies[25]—where they often take the form of selectively imposed duties and obligations—entails an expansion of state sovereignty that defeats the lexical order embedded in the human rights system, and the notion of societal integration around which this order is inherently built. This turn-about all too often makes the conversation on immigrant integration about the search for (often short-sighted) national interest and the satisfaction of electoral needs. The key question, which is how to retain citizenship as a tool of equality and inclusion in immigrant, and increasingly diverse, societies, is thereby pushed aside.

In recent times, and partly as a reaction to the nativist turn described above, different actors have raised their voices to push for a principled affirmation of the idea that equality, attached to personhood, must indeed be affirmed as the general norm or principle, from which only narrowly justified departures, beyond those inherent in the system itself, can exist, departures which must in turn be duly justified.[26] Courts, in particular, both national and international, as well as quasi-judicial bodies, have played an active role in such affirmation. In Chapter 7, Churgin describes how the Supreme Court of Canada has continued to be solicitous of the rights of applicants for refugee status, for instance, by ordering that they should have the same detention review process as permanent residents. Also, Di Pascale (Chapter 8) discusses how, in reviewing the 2008 and 2009 security packages, the Italian Constitutional Court decided that whereas criminalizing the illegal entry of undocumented persons was not unconstitutional per se in view of the state's legitimate interest in controlling and managing migratory flows,

legislation to the specific aspects, such as entry, stay, and removal, which, by definition, apply only to non-citizens.

25 This phenomenon has adequately been described as a displacement from the 'politics of coexistence' to 'the politics of access'. See J. De Lucas, 'Sobre los Fundamentos de la Igualdad y del Reconocimiento. Un análisis crítico de las condiciones de las políticas europeas de integración ante la inmigración', in J. de Lucas et al. (eds), *Inmigración e integración en la UE. Dos retos para el s. XXI* (2012) 11.

26 This is, in essence, the position defended by Special Rapporteur David Weissbrodt in his influential Report on the rights of non-citizens, (Commission on Human Rights, UN Doc E/CN.4/Sub.2/2003/23, 26 May 2003). According to him, the architecture of international human rights law is built on the premise that all persons should by virtue of their essential humanity enjoy all human rights unless exceptional distinctions serve a legitimate state objective and are proportional to the achievement of that objective. States may draw narrow distinctions between citizens and non-citizens with respect to political rights explicitly guaranteed to citizens and freedom of movement (at 6).

the norm which sanctioned a general aggravating circumstance for crimes committed by undocumented migrants, as well as that which linked the possibility of marriage to the demonstration of the alien's regular position, were not in conformity with Italy's Constitution.[27] As for this Constitution, interestingly, Di Pascale notices that similar issues had been examined in France by the *Conseil Constitutionnel*, in Switzerland by the Federal Administrative Court, and by the ECtHR in relation to UK legislation. The same consensus was affirmed at every instance: a sham marriage could not simply be presumed from the illegality of residential status and the right to marriage, as a fundamental right, could not simply be categorically denied to undocumented aliens.

International courts have also contributed to the affirmation of the lexical priority of human rights and their link to personhood and to equal dignity. Most famously, in 2003 the Inter-American Court of Human Rights delivered its Advisory Opinion on the *Juridical Condition and Rights of Undocumented Migrants*, reaffirming the highest status of the principle of equality and non-discrimination in concluding that 'the principle of equality before the law, equal protection before the law and non-discrimination belongs to *ius cogens*, because the whole legal structure of national and international public order rests on it and it is a fundamental principle that permeates all laws'.[28] Over the last ten years, human rights treaty bodies have increasingly and consistently reaffirmed the applicability of human rights standards to migrant persons and the prohibition of discrimination based on national origin or immigration status. Paradigmatic of this affirmation is *General Recommendation No. 30*, on Discrimination against Non-Citizens of 2004, by the UN Committee on the Elimination of Racial Discrimination. Shifting away from its prior position expressed in *General Recommendation No. 11* in 1993,[29] in 2004 the Committee affirmed that the distinction citizen/non-citizen 'must be construed so as to avoid undermining the basic prohibition of discrimination; hence, it should not be interpreted to detract in any way from the rights and freedoms recognized and enunciated in particular in the UDHR, the ICESCR and the ICCPR'.[30]

In Chapter 5, Ryan and Mantouvalou give evidence of a particular emphasis on migrants' labour and social rights on the part of courts and supervisory bodies, including the Committee on Migrant Workers, the CESCR, the ILO Committee on Freedom of Association, the European Committee of Social Rights, the European Court of Human Rights, and the Inter-American Court of Human Rights. They argue that these committees and courts have been more prone to accept that *all* persons are eligible for key labour and social rights than have the political actors

[27] See Constitutional Court (Corte Costituzionale), Judgment no. 249 of 8 July 2010. According to Italy's Constitutional Court, an unreasonable aggravation of a penalty based on the unlawful presumption of undocumented migrants being more dangerous simply could not be accepted.

[28] *Juridical Condition and Rights of the Undocumented Migrants*, IACtHR (2003) Series A, No. 18, at 101.

[29] In 1993 the Committee had set forth that Article 1.2 of the Convention exempts from the definition of racial discrimination the actions by a State party which differentiate between citizens and non-citizens.

[30] See UN Committee on the Elimination of Racial Discrimination, *General Recommendation No. 30: Discrimination Against Non Citizens*, paras 14–15.

who negotiate migration-specific texts which often apply only to a limited group of migrants. Behind this evolution which, in their view, supports the presumption today in international law that all migrants are entitled to equal treatment in the labour market and in social provision, they see a fundamental evolution in the international law approach to the treatment of foreign nationals. According to them, the traditional view—that the treatment of foreigners is an aspect of the relationship between the two states in question—which characterized pre-1945 international law, has over the past twenty-five years given way to the principled affirmation of equal treatment as a norm, and regardless of reciprocity.

The application of human rights law to non-citizens has, to some extent, facilitated the expansion of the state's domain of responsibility, underscoring the importance of a territorial link. Examples are provided in this book. In Chapter 1, Chetail describes how Article 3 of the European Convention on Human Rights has in fact expanded beyond the reach of the Refugee Convention and now protects individuals against political persecution in the country of origin, covering also threats by non-state actors including with regard to severe violations of basic human rights. If Article 3 ECHR serves as the central guarantee against mistreatment in the country of origin which the European host state is asked to provide shelter from, Thym (Chapter 3) describes how Article 8 ECHR has been used by migrants against the European countries in which they live, without primary consideration of the situation in their country of origin, to challenge the states' attempt to deport settled migrants, and thus protect migrants' ties to their residential communities, including, in some rare instance, ties developed by those who are undocumented.

Expansive evolutions have however gone beyond the scope shaped by the territorial link. This is because in the context of human rights treaties, the term 'jurisdiction', which is often used to indicate the scope of application of human rights treaties, is sometimes understood as 'power or effective control', with the consequence that respect for human rights is due to any individual who is under the power or effective control of any agent of a state party, wherever he happens to act. The present jurisprudence of the European Court of Human Rights confirms that the ECHR binds states parties also beyond their territory and in particular on the high seas, which cannot be seen as an area outside the law.[31]

The impact of these expansions remains limited, however. The revolutionary character of the norm of *non-refoulement*, resulting from the application of the prohibition on torture and inhuman and degrading treatment in the immigration context under Article 3 ECHR, was celebrated as evidence of the possibility to break away from a territorial, state-centred conception of the interests involved in territorial sovereignty.[32] In fact, almost twenty years ago, the ECtHR's judicial

[31] See *Hirsi Jamaa and Others v. Italy*, ECHR (2012) Appl. No. 27765/09, judgment of 23 February 2012.

[32] See G. Cornelisse, 'A New Articulation of Human Rights, or Why the European Court of Human Rights Should Think Beyond Westphalian Sovereignty', in M. Dembour and T. Kelly (eds), *Are Human Rights for Migrants? Critical Reflections on the Statue of Irregular Migrants in Europe and the United States* (2011)100, at 112.

innovations were first identified as the manifestation of an emergent post-national society with an incipient form of transnational membership, which supersedes national citizenship.[33] At this point in time, though, the national citizenship construct does not seem to fade away; and although international law does, to date, not oblige states to support the gradual extension of citizenship rights to long-term residents, several international instances are indeed suggesting that this would be the preferred path to achieve full equality.[34]

III. Beyond the Citizen/Non-citizen Divide: Modulating Concepts

No matter how categorically one affirms personhood as the central concept in human rights law and territorial or simply state jurisdiction as the main triggering factor of state responsibility, unlike other discrimination grounds (such as race, sex, and disability) whose legal relevance can be said to be mainly culturally and socially constructed, for as long as the state order exists, it seems that the citizen/non-citizen distinction cannot be entirely put aside. As Chetail recalls, the very existence of an entire branch of international law, such as refugee law, is but the normative corollary to the absence of generalized freedom of movement, as a human right. Although ontologically grounded on the intrinsic equal worth of human beings, the human rights order is one that has affirmed itself not only in spite of, but also *through*, the recognition of a world order that accepts states as self-defining and self-determining political entities. In this order of things, states derive their legitimacy from the protection of human rights, but also from the pursuit of national self-interest and the well-being of the members of their bounded communities. In other words, the human rights-based order of states combines a statist and a universalist logic inevitably bound to be in tension with each other, especially in contemporary states with both increasingly porous boundaries and economic disparities.

If this is so, we are likely to find that the affirmation of principled equality is not sufficient. Rather, we will need to identify modulating concepts which, going beyond the citizen/non-citizen dichotomy or the common humanity principle, may be useful to assess where to draw the legitimate lines between different degrees of human rights protection.[35] None of these modulating concepts may by

[33] For a pioneering study, see Y. N. Soysal, *Limits of Citizenship: Migrants and Postnational Membership in Europe* (1994), chapters 8 and 9.

[34] In this volume, Thym's chapter suggests that although the ECtHR has no official position on this question, recent judgments endorse a growing consensus in Europe that long-term residents should have an option to become full and equal members of European societies through naturalization. Moreover, although the European Union cannot dictate due to a lack of competence in this area, it has invited European states to support naturalization through soft-law instruments. See J. Shaw, *The Transformation of Citizenship in the European Union: Electoral Rights and the Restructuring of Political Space* (2007) at 209–37.

[35] See also, along similar lines, the Final Report on the rights of non-citizens, (Commission on Human Rights, UN Doc E/CN.4/Sub.2/2003/23, 26 May 2003) by David Weissbrodt. In the Report it is argued that any approach to combating discrimination against non-citizens should take into account the varying state interests at stake in regard to categories of rights (eg political rights, right to education, social security, other economic rights, etc.) with respect to the various kinds of non-citizens

themselves provide a comprehensive answer, and, since they may intersect with one another, one would need to ponder the relative weight that must be given to each. In any event, conceptual clarity is increasingly required and will be essential if human rights law is to retain its power in setting limits to state sovereign discretion and allocating responsibility for human well-being.

A. Core human rights?

In Chapter 8, Di Pascale suggests that one way to approach this question is by identifying a certain core of basic rights which can be identified, a core that maps universally recognized values, for which the (citizenship) status of the individual should be irrelevant. To support this, she cites international jurisprudence identifying, among the list of essential rights, the right to life, safety, and personal freedom, but also, according to wider interpretations, the right not to be enslaved or to be subjected to torture or cruel, inhuman, or degrading treatment or punishment, the inviolability of private life, and freedom of thought and religion. In contrast to these rights, which are seen as truly fundamental, Di Pascale recalls that social and economic rights have often been regarded as aspirations or ideals rather than rights, and that this may better allow for citizenship-based distinctions.

Whereas the idea of reading a certain hierarchy into human rights law when it comes to the protection of non-citizens is not implausible in view of the fact that, even before the human rights law era, there was a principle that certain rights were recognized for aliens in accordance with minimum standards rules, even though at the time these were understood to be the rights of the state of nationality which could take diplomatic and other action to ensure that its citizens were protected.[36] However, in Chapter 5 Ryan and Mantouvalou provide ample evidence that the civil-political/socio-economic divide may no longer provide an adequate proxy. For instance, looking at the practice of the UN Committee on Economic, Social and Cultural Rights, we find that the Committee has drawn relevant distinctions among different so-called socio-economic rights. Thus, the Committee's strongest rejection of *all* discrimination on grounds of nationality or immigration status has been in relation to the right to education (Article 13 ICESCR).[37] The Committee has been somewhat less clear in relation to the right to health, affirming the universal application only of some types of health services and calling instead for

having distinct relationships to the country in which they are residing (eg, permanent residents, migrant workers, temporary residents, tourists, undocumented workers, etc.) and in proportion to the legitimacy of state interests or rationales for distinctions between citizens and non-citizens or among non-citizens (eg, issues of national reciprocity, promoting development, etc.).

36 That minimum standard of civilization comprised, in particular, the rights of personal liberty and, generally, the right to equality before the law. See H. Lauterpacht, *International Law and Human Rights* (1950) at 121.

37 See CESCR, *General Comment No. 13: The Right to Education* (1999), para. 34, in which both nationality and lack of legal status were ruled out as reasons to deny education to 'persons of school age residing in the territory of a State party'. The Committee has also taken the view that the freedom to set up educational institutions (Article 13(4) ICESCR) should not be restricted on grounds of nationality: CESCR, *General Comment No. 13*, para. 30.

access to 'adequate health care facilities, goods and services' for asylum seekers and irregular migrant workers and members of their families (Article 12 ICESCR).[38] An emphasis on adequacy is also evident in the CESCR's approach to the housing of non-nationals, probably because Article 11 ICESCR itself refers to 'the right of everyone to an adequate standard of living for himself and his family, including adequate... housing'. This suggests that within categories of rights, further distinctions may be needed, including, for instance and specifically, those regarding socio-economic rights, whether life or basic livelihood are at stake, or whether the deprivation of rights may produce serious negative externalities on the rest of society, as seems to be the case with the denial of education of basic health services.

B. Legal status and ties of membership

Another set of factors which the state and international practice are coming to recognize is the type of membership status and connection binding the non-citizen to the country of residence. Of all, the most frequently relied upon differentiating criterion to this day seems to be the legality of migrants' residential status. After all, irregular migration is the most obvious challenge to sovereignty. But other factors have also come to the fore, including short- or long-term residence, the actual ties developed during the stay in the country of residence, the acquisition or proof of membership-qualifying skills and virtues, and, finally, a legal status related to membership in a supra-national political entity, such as EU citizenship.

Both state practice and human rights documents have recognized a higher protection in favour of documented migrants, probably reflecting the fact that the former, but not the latter, are members the community has agreed to accept, and, in any event, persons who have respected membership rules of the community. Already in 1985, the Declaration on the Human Rights of Individuals Who are Not Nationals of the Country in Which They Live[39]—the first document responding to the need to clarify the subject matter—defined under Article 1 that 'the term alien shall apply, with due regard to qualifications made in subsequent article, to any individual who is not a national of the state in which he or she is present',[40] and yet stipulated that only 'aliens lawfully residing in the territory of a state' would enjoy the whole range of social rights.[41] Similarly, the UN

[38] CESCR, *General Comment No. 14: The Right to the Highest Attainable Standard of Health* (2000), para. 34. The CESCR stated that parties were obliged to '[refrain] from denying or limiting equal access for all persons, including... asylum seekers and illegal immigrants, to preventive, curative and palliative health services'. However limited, the threshold goes beyond that of the Migrant Workers Convention, which only required that those lacking an immigration status be granted equal access to health services of an urgent nature.

[39] UN Doc A/RES/40/144, 13 December 1985.

[40] G. S. Goodwin-Gill, 'International Law and Human Rights: Trends Concerning International Migrants and Refugees', 23 *IMR* (1989) 526.

[41] Pursuant to Article 8, only aliens lawfully residing in the territory of a state enjoy the right to safe and healthy working conditions, to fair wages and equal remuneration for work of equal value without distinction of any kind; the right to join trade unions and other organizations or associations of their choice and to participate in their activities; the right to health protection, medical care, social security, social services, education, rest and leisure.

Convention on Migrant Workers[42] contains a list which distinguishes the rights specifically applicable to undocumented migrants, reserving the rest only in favour of documented migrants.[43]

In spite of this, an increasing number of critical voices claim the need also to recognize core human rights for undocumented migrants, and to go beyond traditional reciprocity considerations.[44] For instance, the Council of Europe treaties concerning the status of foreign nationals are based on reciprocity, and generally require that a foreign national be lawfully resident. Faced with these limitations, the political organs of the Council of Europe have sought to provide for the position of migrants in an irregular situation through non-binding measures.[45] In 2006, the Council of Europe's Parliamentary Assembly adopted a resolution specifically on the human rights of irregular migrants,[46] urging member states to protect at least a 'core minimum' of rights of irregular migrants. This, then, is the most frequent context in which the core minimum thesis is discussed nowadays.[47]

In Chapter 3, Thym describes how, at least in Europe, long-term residents have been accorded a heightened human rights protection status, mostly through an expansive interpretation of Article 8 ECHR's right to family and private life which has enabled rights-based objections to the deportation of settled migrants and, under certain conditions, even brought about a potential right to regularize illegal stay. He rightly underscores the novelty of the recognition of a human right to be a resident of a country of which one does not possess nationality, as an additional

[42] Other relevant conventions are ILO Convention No. 143 of 1975 and the European Convention on the Legal Status of Migrant Workers, CETS No. 93.

[43] In spite of this, one of the main obstacles to a wider ratification of the ICRMW has been the claim that it endows irregular migrants with too many rights, and as a result would hinder both processes of social integration and the struggle against irregular movements of people. See E. MacDonald and R. Cholewinski, *The Migrant Workers Convention in Europe: Obstacles to the Ratification of the International Convention on the Protection of the Rights of All Migrant Workers and Members of their Families: EU/EEA Perspectives* (2007); available at: <http://unesdoc.unesco.org/images/0015/001525/152537e.pdf>.

[44] See, for instance, the Global Migration Group, listing the fundamental rights of all persons, regardless of their migration status, including not only rights such as the right to life, liberty, and security of the person, and to be free from arbitrary arrest or detention, and the right to seek and enjoy asylum from persecution, the right to be free from discrimination based on race, sex, language, religion, national or social origin, or other status, the right to be protected from abuse and exploitation, to be free from slavery, and from involuntary servitude, and from torture and cruel or inhuman or degrading treatment or punishment, the right to a fair trial and to legal redress, but also the right to protection of economic, social, and cultural rights, including the right to health, and adequate standard of living, housing, and education. (Cited from ICJ, *Migration and International Human Rights Law: Practitioners Guide No. 6* (2011) at 30).

[45] In 2000, the Committee of Ministers adopted a Recommendation on the Right to the Satisfaction of Basic Material Needs of All Persons in a Situation of Extreme Hardship. See Council of Europe, Committee of Ministers, Recommendation No. R (2000) 3.

[46] PACE Resolution 1509 (2006).

[47] Thus, regarding socio-economic rights, there is now clear support for the right of irregular migrant workers to the full protection of labour law, both in international texts and in the work of supervisory bodies. Similarly, there is clear support for the equal treatment of irregular migrants in respect of schooling. In the case of other social rights, meanwhile, the emerging consensus is for equal access to a basic level of social support and a basic level of health care, but not necessarily more than that.

element calling into question the conventional division between citizenship with equal rights and alien status without the full protection of the law. He also points to the fact that this evolution signalled the tacit recognition of migrants' societal membership in the early 1990s when it became evident that the 'guest workers' and other migrants in the industrialized societies of western Europe would remain in the host state indefinitely, and yet the host countries themselves were still strongly resisting their self-perception as immigrant societies. That it was societal membership, broadly understood, and not just the links with the nuclear family that was the object of protection, became increasingly clear as the Court developed its jurisprudence,[48] a jurisprudence that did not completely cancel out the state's power to deport long-term residents, but significantly raised the bar as to the kinds of public order threats that could outweigh the migrants' interests in remaining in the receiving society.

Interestingly, Thym describes how, in more recent times, the Court has become increasingly restrictive and may be in fact be changing somewhat its understanding of the kind of membership that triggers a right to stay, from one centred on de facto membership and ties with the society of residence, to one which tests social integration by carefully assessing the solidity of linguistic and civic integration though labour market participation and educational records. This trend towards a notion of 'meritocratic' or 'virtuous' membership is to be read in the context of a broader shift in European policies, described in Chapter 2, from a commitment to supporting the social, economic, and political integration of foreigners into European societies—exemplified by the EU's Common Basic Principles for immigrant integration policy[49]—to a new emphasis on testing integration. In other words, it is no longer the concern with defending the interests of the second generation of children who had been born in Europe while rarely visiting their parents' home country that dominates the conversation, but rather an increasing concern with securing cohesive and integrated societies.

As shown by Chetail, a regime which distinguishes different degrees of protection and rights entitlements to reflect the intensity of the territorial bond between a refugee and his/her state of asylum, is characteristic of refugee law also. In practice, the Geneva Convention recognizes core guarantees to any refugee, but then acknowledges additional entitlements which are subordinated to the existence of a territorial bond with the asylum state, the other two levels of applicability respectively requiring presence or stay of the refugee, with a further distinction then drawn between lawful stay and habitual residence.

Finally, stronger ties of membership, and privileged status of rights, can result also from the existence of bilateral treaties and reciprocity arrangements or the common belonging to a supranational entity, like the European Union. Ryan and

[48] This expansive reading was recognized by the Court in the 2000s, when it extended the protective reach of Article 8 ECHR to 'the network of personal, social and economic relations that make up the private life of every human being'.

[49] See Common Basic Principles (CBP) for Immigrant Integration Policy in the European Union, Council Document 14615/04 of 19 November 2004.

Mantouvalou's contribution exemplifies this. They explain how the European Union's own bilateral agreements with third countries have given extensive recognition to labour and social rights, as well as how a series of directives on migration since 2003 have addressed the labour and social rights of third-country nationals in the EU. Among these, the most extensive provisions are contained in the 2003 Long-term Residents Directive,[50] which applies to non-EU nationals who have been lawfully resident in a member state for five years, and who are not in temporary immigration categories, including—from 20 May 2013—persons who are refugees or beneficiaries of international protection. Extensive provision for labour and social rights has also been made by the Qualification Directives of 2004 and 2011, which concern both refugees and a wider category of humanitarian cases ('subsidiary protection'),[51] going beyond the Refugee Convention in several respects.

C. Special vulnerability

Since approximately the beginning of the new century, a relatively frequent call has been made to underscore categories of particularly vulnerable migrants as deserving a heightened degree of human rights protection. These include women and children, but also those undocumented or in an irregular situation, who, because of this, are prone to accept extremely precarious living and working conditions that favour discrimination and exploitation.[52] In some ways, this singling out of particularly vulnerable groups among non-nationals has been with us from the start. It was always the case that among the general category of migrants and non-citizens, asylum seekers/refugees and stateless persons were distinguished as requiring a particularly protected status, whereas it was assumed that regular migrants could be protected first by their countries of origin, and then by either general or migration-specific human rights treaties. This two-track system of protection, one for especially vulnerable non-citizens, and one for ordinary non-citizens, has increasingly come under attack both descriptively and normatively, especially as the development of general human rights standards is in fact promoting the highest standard of protection.

The earlier distinction in protection terms between poor refugees and stateless persons on the one hand, and migrant workers on the other, has been said to no

[50] Directive 2003/109, OJ 2004 L 16/44, concerning the status of third-country nationals who are long-term residents, as amended by Directive 2011/51, OJ 2011 L 132/1. These directives do not apply to Britain, Denmark, or Ireland.

[51] Directive 2004/83, OJ 2004 L 304/12, on minimum standards for the qualification and status of third country nationals or stateless persons as refugees or as persons who otherwise need international protection and the content of the protection granted, and Directive 2011/95, OJ 2011 L 337/9, on standards for the qualification of third-country nationals or stateless persons as beneficiaries of international protection, for a uniform status for refugees or for persons eligible for subsidiary protection, and for the content of the protection granted. The 2011 Directive applies to twenty-four states, Britain and Ireland are bound by the 2004 Directive alone, and Denmark is bound by neither.

[52] See Commission on Human Rights, Resolution 1999/44.

longer hold good. On the one hand, in recent years the number of vulnerable migrants has grown, taking the form of mixed flows of asylum seekers, and irregular migrants. As Grant rightly points out, this migration has been driven by a complex combination of factors, which include persecution, poverty, conflict, famine, and repression, as well as violations of economic and social rights, population pressure on scarce natural resources, and wage or income inequality between the poor and rich countries.[53] Yet, as Scovazzi (Chapter 6) recalls, the limitation of the current definition of refugee is that it only covers people who are persecuted for a number of specified reasons and does not include people who, without being persecuted in their countries, are trying to flee conflicts, either international or internal, natural disasters, or poverty.

Just as interestingly, Chetail (Chapter 1) compellingly shows how, over time, human rights law has radically informed and transformed the distinctive tenets of the Geneva Convention to such an extent that the normative frame of forced migration has been displaced from refugee law to human rights law, so much so that, he claims, human rights law should be understood today as *the* primary source of refugee protection, while the Geneva Convention is bound to play a complementary and secondary role. According to him, this phenomenon of appropriation is structurally grounded on the distinctive characteristics of human rights law regarding both its personal and material scope. Thus, while the Geneva Convention retains some symbolic relevance, the distinction between nationals and aliens which conditions the very content of refugee status has been largely marginalized and superseded by the general applicability of human rights to non-citizens. Both Mullally and Chetail exemplify the important impact of human rights law in gender-related asylum claims. Although gender is not explicitly listed among the grounds of persecution, human rights law has further played a crucial role in developing a gender-sensitive approach that mirrors its own evolution, so that gender-based claims, as well as those related to sexual orientation, are now commonly considered as being encapsulated within the broad and residual ground of membership of a particular social group.

In view of the paramount importance of general human rights law in standards setting, we must ask ourselves whether we should celebrate the return of 'special vulnerability' as a source of strengthened protection. Ryan and Mantouvalou (Chapter 5) describe how the vulnerability of new groups is indeed being foregrounded as a reason to expand the domain of concern of human rights law. Thus, they provide some examples of creative interpretations of the law to ensure that undocumented aliens, especially children, who are increasingly the beneficiaries of the principle of the protection of the best interest of the child under international human rights law, are duly protected. In particular, they explain how the European Committee on Social Rights has attempted to address the limitations on the personal scope of the European Social Charter in the context of collective complaints. Thus, in the case *International Federation of Human Rights Leagues (FIDH)*

[53] See Grant (n 16) at 40, citing data from International Labour Organization, *Towards a Fair Deal for Migrants Workers in the Global Economy* (2004).

v. France, the lack of access to healthcare of children of undocumented migrants was held to be in breach of the right of children and young persons to social, legal, and economic protection under Article 17 of the Revised ESC.[54] While that conclusion appeared contrary to the clear wording of the Annex in the Charter—limiting the personal scope of application to foreigners only insofar as they are nationals of other contracting parties or refugees and stateless persons lawfully staying in the territory of a contracting state—the Committee ruled that the exclusion of irregular migrants would be contrary to human dignity, as one of the document's most fundamental underlying values.[55]

There seem to be some risks nevertheless in highlighting the vulnerability of some subcategories of migrants in claiming a higher degree of protection. The risk is that this phenomenon may end up contributing to a narrow understanding of 'ordinary' migrants' rights and, in practice, to render invisible the multiple axes of vulnerability affecting and exposing migrants to human rights violations 'as non-nationals or people of foreign origin, as workers in what are often underprivileged sectors of the economy, as politically disempowered, and as carriers of foreign cultures/religion'.[56] While the need to protect women and children is uncontested, granting rights to migrants is not understood as a priority, even though migrants' labour is increasingly essential to the world economy.[57] According to De Guchteneire and Pécoud, this is because migrant workers are not recognized as a vulnerable group per se.[58] This, they claim, points to an almost ontological characteristic of migrants: migration, it is assumed, is not an immutable characteristic. It is migrants themselves who choose to come to their destination countries. Ultimately, if they are not happy, they can and should always go back home. Neither children nor women can escape their condition.

Moreover, the special vulnerability framing may also be disempowering for those intended to benefit from it. Let us take the example of women. CEDAW's *General Recommendation No. 26 on Women Migrant Workers*, of 2008, emphasizes migrant women's vulnerability, especially those who are undocumented migrants. According to the *Recommendation*, undocumented women migrant workers are particularly vulnerable to exploitation and abuse because of their irregular immigration status, which exacerbates their exclusion and the risk of exploitation. They may be exploited as forced labour, and their access to minimum labour rights may be

[54] *International Federation of Human Rights Leagues (FIDH) v. France*, ECSR (2004) Complaint No. 14/2003, Decision of 8 September 2004.

[55] This interpretation was confirmed in a subsequent ruling against the Netherlands, which held that the exclusion of children in an irregular position from access to housing was a breach of the specific right to housing in Article 31 of the Revised ESC, and the right of migrants to protection in Article 17. *Defence for Children International (DCI) v. Netherlands*, ECSR (2009) Complaint No. 47/2008, Decision of 20 October 2009. A provision in the Appendix to both the ESC and the Revised ESC on the 'Scope of the Social Charter in Terms of Persons Protected' confines Articles 1 to 17 to 'foreigners only insofar as they are nationals of other Contracting Parties'. The same limitation arises in the text of Articles 18 and 19. The Appendix to the Revised European Social Charter sets out exceptions, but only for refugees and stateless persons lawfully staying in the territory of a contracting state.

[56] See De Guchteneire et al. (n 2) at 2–3.

[57] See De Guchteneire et al. (n 2) at 28.

[58] See De Guchteneire et al. (n 2) at 28.

limited by fear of denouncement. They may also face harassment by the police. If they are apprehended, they are usually prosecuted for violations of immigration laws and placed in detention centres, where they are vulnerable to sexual abuse, and then deported.[59]

Yet, in Chapter 4, Mullally expresses particular scepticism about the law's framing of migrant women as vulnerable to abuse and in need of protection. According to her, this constructed vulnerability is presumed to justify the coercive interventions of the state which reacts with instruments primarily designed to fight against criminality.[60] Also, she claims, the normative re-emergence of protective categories does little to enhance women's autonomy, agency, or equality. Ultimately, the vulnerability approach is an invitation to focus primarily on the most extreme but not necessarily the most recurrent and daily forms of exploitation and subordination that should also be the concern of human rights law. For migrant women, these may include 'everyday' work-place exploitation, exclusion from employment protections, social security, and precarious migration status, which only now are starting to attract some attention.[61]

[59] See CEDAW, *General Recommendation No. 26 on Women Migrant Workers* (2008), para. 22.

[60] As an example, Mullally discusses the case *Siliadin v. France*, ECHR (2005) Appl. No. 73316/01, judgment of 26 July 2005, where the ECtHR recognized for the first time that Article 4 ECHR could give rise to positive obligations for states. In her critical view, however, it failed to recognize that such obligations could extend to regularization of a victim's migration status and positive obligations of rehabilitation. Rather, the Court's focus on the need for more effective criminal justice responses to problems of servitude fits within the predominantly prosecutorial model that has shaped international legal developments on human trafficking, but falls short of a response that would support recognition of the complex rights claims of trafficked persons, including children.

[61] See the landmark 2011 ILO Convention Concerning Decent Work for Domestic Workers, adopted at the 100th session of the International Labour Conference, Geneva, 2011.

1

Are Refugee Rights Human Rights? An Unorthodox Questioning of the Relations between Refugee Law and Human Rights Law

Vincent Chetail

Are refugee rights human rights? Such a question may appear provocative at a time when refugees are regularly victims of abuses in a context of restrictive asylum policies. While this sad reality is anything but new, it is further exacerbated by the current recession. The United Nations High Commissioner for Refugees (UNHCR), António Guterres, observes that 'the human rights agenda out of which UNHCR was born, and on which we depend, is increasingly coming under strain. The global economic crisis brought with it a populist wave of anti-foreigner sentiment, albeit often couched in terms of national sovereignty and national security'.[1] This difficult environment highlights the need to prevent the economic crisis from becoming a protection crisis at the expense of refugee rights.[2]

Against such a background, assessing the relations between refugee law and human rights law is essential in order to identify the full range of states' obligations and thereby inform their practice towards refugees and asylum seekers. Although refugee law and human rights law were initially conceived as two distinct branches of international law, their multifaceted interaction is now well acknowledged in both state practice and academic writing. The literature has schematically evolved around three successive narratives.

Originally, the relationship between the two has been approached as a causal link, the violations of human rights being acknowledged as the primary cause of refugee movements.[3] Since then, the conceptualization of their interrelationship

[1] A. Guterres, Remarks at the Opening of the Judicial Year of the European Court of Human Rights, Strasbourg, 28 January 2011, 2.

[2] V. Chetail and C. Bauloz, *The European Union and the Challenges of Forced Migration: From Economic Crisis to Protection Crisis?* Research Report, European University Institute (2011).

[3] See, in particular, P. Weis, 'Refugees and Human Rights', 1 *Israel Yearbook on Human Rights* (1971) 35, esp. at 48–9; O. Kimminich, 'Die Entwicklung des internationalen Flüchtlingsrechts—faktischer und rechtsdogmatischer Rahmen', 20 *Archiv des Völkerrechts* (1982) 369, 405; M. Moussalli, 'Human Rights and Refugees', *Yearbook of the International Institute of Humanitarian Law* (1984) 13; G. J. L. Coles, 'Human Rights and Refugee Law', *Bulletin of Human Rights* (1991/1) 63;

has gradually shifted from a preventive approach to an interactive one. This new impetus has mainly focused on the specific linkages between human rights standards and the distinctive tenets of international refugee law, such as the definition of 'refugee'[4] and the principle of *non-refoulement*.[5] More recently, this interactive approach has finally paved the way for a more integrative one, which concentrates on the complementary protection[6] to the refugee status under the 1951 UN Convention Relating to the Status of Refugees (Geneva Convention).

While this evolution largely echoes the practice and concerns of states, the abundant literature devoted to the interaction between human rights law and refugee law calls for two preliminary remarks. On the one hand, academic discussions remain very specific and refugee law-oriented, to the detriment of a more systemic analysis.[7] On the other hand, they are grounded on the premise that the

T. Stoltenberg, 'Human Rights and Refugees', in A. Eide and J. Helgesen (eds), *The Future of Human Rights Protection in a Changing World: Essays in Honour of Torkel Opsahl* (1991) 145.

[4] See, most notably, J. C. Hathaway, *The Law of Refugee Status* (1991); T. A. Aleinikoff, 'The Meaning of "Persecution" in United States Asylum Law', 3 *IJRL* (1991) 5; K. Musalo, 'Irreconcilable Differences? Divorcing Refugee Protections from Human Rights Norms', 15 *Mich. J. Int'l L.* (1994) 1179; J.-Y. Carlier, 'General Report', in J.-Y. Carlier et al. (eds), *Who is a Refugee?* (1997) 685; N. Sitaropoulos, *Judicial Interpretation of Refugee Status* (1999); M. J. Parrish, 'Redefining the Refugee: The Universal Declaration of Human Rights as a Basis for Refugee Protection', 22 *Cardozo L. Rev.* (2000) 223; H. Lambert, 'The Conceptualisation of "Persecution" by the House of Lords: *Horvath v. Secretary of State for the Home Department*', 13 *IJRL* (2001) 16; R. von Sternberg, *The Grounds of Refugee Protection in the Context of International Human Rights and Humanitarian Law* (2002).

[5] Among an abundant literature, see W. Suntinger, 'The Principle of Non-Refoulement: Looking Rather to Geneva than to Strasbourg?', *Austrian JPIL* (1995) 203; H. Lambert, 'Protection against *Refoulement* from Europe: Human Rights Law Comes to the Rescue', 48 *ICLQ* (1999) 515; B. Gorlick, 'The Convention and the Committee against Torture: A Complementary Protection Regime for Refugees' 11 *IJRL* (1999) 479; D. Weissbrodt and I. Hortreiter, 'The Principle of Non-Refoulement: Article 3 of the Convention Against Torture and Other Cruel, Inhuman or Degrading Treatment or Punishment in Comparison with the Non-Refoulement Provisions of Other International Human Rights Treaties', 5 *Buffalo HRLR* (1999) 1; P. Burns, 'United Nations Committee against Torture and its Role in Refugee Protection', 15 *Geo. Immigr. L.J.* (2001) 403; V. Chetail, 'Le droit des réfugiés à l'épreuve des droits de l'homme: bilan de la jurisprudence de la Cour européenne des droits de l'homme sur l'interdiction du renvoi des étrangers menacés de torture et de traitements inhumains ou dégradants', 37 *RBDI* (2004) 155; J. Doerfel, 'The Convention against Torture and the Protection of Refugees', 24 *RSQ* (2005) 83; V. Chetail, 'Le Comité des Nations Unies contre la torture et l'expulsion des étrangers: dix ans de jurisprudence', 26 *RSDIE* (2006) 63; J. Pirjola, 'Shadows in Paradise—Exploring Non-Refoulement as an Open Concept', 19 *IJRL* (2007) 639; A. Duffy, 'Expulsion to Face Torture? Non-refoulement in International Law', 20 *IJRL* (2008) 373; C. W. Wouters, *International Legal Standards for the Protection from Refoulement* (2009).

[6] See, in particular, W. Kälin, 'Temporary Protection in the EC: Refugee Law, Human Rights and the Temptation of Pragmatism', 44 *GYIL* (2001) 202; D. Bouteillet-Paquet (ed.), *Subsidiary Protection of Refugees in the European Union: Complementing the Geneva Convention?* (2002); G. Noll, 'International Protection Obligations and the Definition of Subsidiary Protection in the EU Qualification Directive', in C. D. Urbano de Sousa and P. De Bruycker (eds), *The Emergence of a European Asylum Policy* (2004) 183; R. Piotrowicz and C. Van Eck, 'Subsidiary Protection and Primary Rights', 53 *ICLQ* (2004) 138; R. Mandal, *Protection Mechanisms Outside of the 1951 Convention ('Complementary Protection')* (2005); M.-T. Gil-Bazo, *Refugee Status, Subsidiary Protection and the Right to be Granted Asylum Under EC Law* (2006) New Issues in Refugee Research, Research Paper No. 136; J. McAdam, *Complementary Protection in International Refugee Law* (2006); J. Pobjoy, 'Treating Like Alike: The Principle of Non-Discrimination as a Tool to Mandate the Equal Treatment of Refugees and Beneficiaries of Complementary Protection', 34 *Melb. U. L. Rev.* (2010) 181.

[7] For a more general overview of the interactions between refugee law and human rights law, see however: J. C. Hathaway, *The Rights of Refugees under International Law* (2005), esp. at 1–14; A. Edwards, 'Human Rights, Refugees and the Right "to Enjoy" Asylum', 17 *IJRL* (2005) 293;

Geneva Convention is a 'specialist human rights treaty'.[8] This assertion is generally accompanied by a poignant celebration of the Refugee Convention as opposed to the alleged drawbacks of general human rights treaties. For the community of refugee lawyers, the 'other' human rights instruments would be based on 'inappropriate assumptions'[9] and would 'not address many refugee-specific concerns'.[10] Slightly more radically, it is asserted that 'human rights law is often not sufficiently detailed' and 'as a whole lacks a coherent structure',[11] so that its invocation 'will either be largely rhetorical or it will promot[e] fragmentation'.[12] Even worse, reliance on this branch of law would be 'a dangerous option',[13] because 'international human rights law is strong on principle but weak on delivery'.[14]

These arguments are, however, not convincing for they can be applied equally to international refugee law itself. Indeed, the Geneva Convention has attracted similar criticisms on the ground that 'the Convention is redundant . . . or because it is functionally inefficient, overly legalistic, complex and difficult to apply'.[15] Another set of arguments for claiming the primacy of the Refugee Convention by opposition to general human rights treaties may be found in the maxim *lex specialis derogat lex generalis*.[16] However, while this reasoning may have some pedagogical

J. Bhabha, 'Internationalist Gatekeepers?: The Tension between Asylum Advocacy and Human Rights', 15 *Harv. HRJ* (2002) 155; J.-F. Flauss, 'Les droits de l'homme et la Convention de Genève du 28 juillet 1951 relative au statut des réfugiés', in V. Chetail and J.-F. Flauss (eds), *La Convention de Genève du 28 juillet 1951 relative au statut des réfugiés 50 ans après: bilan et perspectives* (2001) 91; B. Gorlick, 'Human Rights and Refugees: Enhancing Protection through International Human Rights Law', 69 *NJIL* (2000) 117; T. Clark and F. Crépeau, 'Mainstreaming Refugee Rights. The 1951 Refugee Convention and International Human Rights Law', 17 *NQHR* (1999) 389.

8 McAdam (n 6) at 14. Among a copious literature asserting the human rights nature of the Geneva Convention, see Hathaway (n 7) at 5; Edwards (n 7) at 306; L. Curran and S. Kneebone, 'Overview', in S. Kneebone (ed.), *The Refugees Convention 50 Years On. Globalisation and International Law* (2003) 1; Gorlick (n 7) at 122; F. Nicholson and P. Twomey, 'Introduction', in F. Nicholson and P. Twomey (eds), *Refugee Rights and Realities. Evolving International Concepts and Regimes* (1999) 2; Clark and Crépeau (n 7) at 391; A. C. Helton, 'Refugees and Human Rights', 15 *In Defense of the Alien* (1993) 142, 146–7; I. Jackson, 'The 1951 Convention Relating to the Status of Refugees: A Universal Basis for Protection', 3 *IJRL* (1991) 404; I. Khokhlov, 'The Rights of Refugees under International Law', *Bulletin of Human Rights* (1991/1) 85; P. Nobel, 'Blurred Vision in the Right World and Violations of Human Rights—A Critical Assessment of the Human Rights and Refugee Linkage', *Bulletin of Human Rights* (1991/1) 74. For a more conceptual and critical stance, see however: E. Haddad, 'Refugee Protection: A Clash of Values', 7 *IJHR* (2003) 1; P. Tuitt, 'Human Rights and Refugees', 1 *IJHR* (1997) 66.

9 Hathaway (n 7) at 121.

10 Hathaway (n 7) at 154. He however acknowledges that 'both in principle and in practice, refugee rights will in the overwhelming majority of cases consist of an amalgam of principles drawn from both refugee law and the [UN] Covenants'. Hathaway (n 7) 9. See also W. Kälin, 'The Legal Condition of Refugees in Switzerland', 7 *JRS* (1994) 82, 93–5.

11 K. Jastram, 'Economic Harm as a Basis for Refugee Status and the Application of Human Rights Law to the Interpretation of Economic Persecution', in J. C. Simeon (ed.), *Critical Issues in International Refugee Law: Strategies Toward Interpretative Harmony* (2010) 143, 166–7.

12 Jastram (n 11) at 171.

13 McAdam (n 6) at 203.

14 McAdam (n 6) at 202.

15 G. S. Goodwin-Gill, 'Editorial: Asylum 2001—A Convention and A Purpose', 13 *IJRL* (2001) 1, at 1.

16 '[T]he Refugee Convention functions as a form of *lex specialis* (specialist law) for all those in need of international protection, and provides an appropriate legal status irrespective of the source of the State's protection obligation': McAdam (n 6) at 1. See also A. Edwards, 'Crossing Legal Borders: The

virtues, resort to the *lex specialis* is flawed for three main reasons. First, general human rights norms cannot be totally dissociated from their subsequent interpretation by treaty bodies, with the result that they may appear more precise and even clearer than their refugee law counterparts. Second, *lex specialis* presupposes a conflict of norms between human rights law and refugee law that is extremely rare.[17] Third, the Geneva Convention itself provides the means for resolving any potential conflicts of norms, for its Article 5 preserves the continuing applicability of more favourable standards granted apart from this Convention without regard to the so-called speciality of the norms.[18]

Thus, the main rationale for arguing the centrality of the Refugee Convention should be explored elsewhere. Two putative factors may be asserted. First, the professional bias in favour of the Geneva Convention is probably a reaction against states' strategic manoeuvring under the banner of human rights law. To many observers, complementary protection schemes established at the regional and domestic levels constitute subtle tools for undermining the universal refugee regime. Second, one should not underestimate the weight of professional culture among refugee lawyers. International refugee law is traditionally understood within academic circles as a specialization in its own right primarily grounded in the Geneva Convention. Refugee lawyers are thus naturally inclined to perceive human rights law as a supplementary and therefore secondary source of law.

The present chapter argues that this professional posture is no longer tenable. Contrary to conventional wisdom, the Geneva Convention is not a human rights treaty in the orthodox sense, for both historical and legal reasons. However, human rights law has radically informed and transformed the distinctive tenets of the Geneva Convention to such an extent that the normative frame of forced migration has been displaced from refugee law to human rights law. As a result of this systemic evolution, the terms of the debate should be inversed: human rights law is *the* primary source of refugee protection, while the Geneva Convention is bound to play a complementary and secondary role. This assertion is grounded on a comparative assessment of applicable norms under both refugee law and human rights law. This normative inquiry into their respective scope and content is centred on the three major pillars of the refugee protection regime, namely the access to international protection (part I), the content of such protection (part II), and its implementation scheme (part III).

Interface Between Refugee Law, Human Rights Law and Humanitarian Law in the "International Protection" of Refugees', in R. Arnold and N. Quenivet (eds), *International Humanitarian Law and International Human Rights Law: Towards a New Merger in International Law* (2008) 429. See, *contra*, J. C. Hathaway, 'Leveraging Asylum', 45 *Texas ILJ* (2010) 502, 532–4; P. Mathew, 'Review: James Hathaway, The Rights of Refugees under International Law', 102 *AJIL* (2008) 206, 207.

[17] As will be shown later, the only possible conflict derives from the absolute character of the *non-refoulement* principle under human rights treaties and has been resolved in favour of the latter, thereby discarding the exceptions set out in the Refugee Convention.

[18] 'Nothing in this Convention shall be deemed to impair any rights and benefits granted by a Contracting State to refugees apart from this Convention'.

I. Access to International Protection: Towards a Gradual Merger between Refugee Law and Human Rights Law?

Access to protection is primarily conditioned by two parameters: the definition of 'refugee' (A), and the principle of *non-refoulement* (B). These two critical components express the very essence of the Geneva Convention. At the same time, their scope and content reflect the ambivalent relationship between refugee law and human rights law. Indeed, the refugee definition and the principle of *non-refoulement* crystallize both the idiosyncratic features of refugee law and the profound impact of human rights law on the Geneva Convention.

A. The changing meaning of the refugee definition

The refugee definition tells us more about the distinctive attributes of the Geneva Convention than any other provisions. Like any definition, it draws a delicate—and arguably restrictive—line of demarcation between the insiders and outsiders (this chapter, A.1). While selective by nature, the refugee definition has been critically reshaped by human rights law through a gradual process of pollination (this chapter, A.2).

1. The refugee definition and the original tenets of international refugee law

The scope of refugee law and human rights law represents the most palpable difference between the two branches of international law. Whereas human rights are applicable to everyone because of the dignity inherent in every human being, the benefit of refugee status depends on the identification of a predetermined category of protected persons. From the perspective of general international law, identifying foreigners who deserve protection is the normative corollary to the absence of a generalized freedom of movement. It is not by coincidence that the emergence of modern refugee law coincides with the generalization of migration controls during the interwar period.[19] International refugee law constitutes an exception to the migration control paradigm and, as such, the former legitimates the latter within a self-referential logic.[20]

Defining who is a refugee stands out as a prerequisite not only for identifying the persons in need of protection but also for determining the correlative extent of the international obligations assumed by states under the Geneva Convention. From the beginning, the refugee definition was accordingly considered to be the 'crux of the entire matter',[21] 'the cornerstone on which the entire edifice of

[19] C. M. Skran, *Refugees in Inter-War Europe. The Emergence of a Regime* (1995); J. C. Hathaway, 'The Evolution of Refugee Status in International Law: 1920–1950', 33 *ICLQ* (1984) 348.

[20] Hathaway (n 7) at 231.

[21] Mr Leslie of Canada, UN Doc E/AC.32/SR.2 (1950), 6.

the Convention rested'.[22] At the same time, state representatives stressed that they 'could not sign a blank cheque and assume unlimited and indefinite commitments in respect of all refugees'.[23] As a result of such anxiety, 'the Convention definition was tailored to fit an approximately foreseeable number of prospective beneficiaries who fell within acceptable categories'.[24] This reflects in turn the original premise of international refugee law. As observed by Bhabha, 'from the outset, the refugee protection regime was intended to be restrictive and partial, a compromise between unfettered state sovereignty over the admission of aliens, and an open door for non-citizen victims of serious human rights violation. It was always clear that only a subset of forced transnational migrant persecutes were intended beneficiaries'.[25]

The selectivity inherent in the refugee definition is reinforced by its very structure, which is composed of three different levels of requirements, commonly labelled as the inclusion, exclusion, and cessation clauses. Inclusion criteria in the refugee definition are cautiously spelled out in Article 1(A)(2) of the Geneva Convention on the basis of four cumulative conditions: first, a refugee is outside his/her country of origin; second, he/she is unable or unwilling to avail himself/herself of the protection of his/her country; third, such inability or unwillingness is attributable to a well-founded fear of persecution; and fourth, the persecution is based on five limitative grounds (race, religion, nationality, membership of particular social group, and political opinion).

Such a composite definition highlights the two essential specificities of international refugee law. On the one hand, it reveals the primary function of refugee law as a protection of substitution when the state of origin fails to fulfil its duty of protection towards its own citizens. As notably acknowledged by the House of Lords, 'the general purpose of the convention is to enable the person who no longer has the benefit of protection against persecution for a convention reason in his own country to turn for protection to the international community'.[26] On the other hand, such a principle of surrogacy was not conceived to obviate any failure of protection from the state of origin.[27] The cumulative effect of the various conditions required by Article 1(A)(2) underlines the selective nature of the refugee definition, which is not bound to cover all causes of forced migration. Such a

[22] Mr Giraldo-Jamarillo of Colombia, UN Doc A/CONF.2/SR.21 (1951), 8.

[23] Mr Mostafa of Egypt referring to the statement of the French representative, UN Doc A/CONF.2/SR.20 (1951), 5. This concern is also evidenced by the fact that the refugee definition was originally limited to persons fleeing events occurring before January 1951 and states parties were enabled to further restrict its scope to events occurring within Europe. These temporal and geographical limitations have been removed by the 1967 Protocol, thus giving the Geneva Convention universal coverage. See more generally: K. Bem, 'The Coming of a "Blank Cheque"—Europe, the 1951 Convention, and the 1967 Protocol', 16 *IJRL* (2004) 609.

[24] J. Sztucki, 'Who is a Refugee? The Convention Definition: Universal or Obsolete?', in Nicholson and Twomey (n 8) at 57.

[25] Bhabha (n 7) at 167.

[26] *Horvath v. Secretary of State for the Home Department* [2001] 1 AC 489, 497 (Lord Hope of Craighead).

[27] *Canada v. Ward* [1993] 103 DLR 4th 1, 67–8.

restrictive stance was clearly premeditated, for states were aware that the definition under the Geneva Convention would not include every refugee.[28]

The essential characteristics of refugee law as a surrogate but selective protection are further reinforced by the exclusion clauses. Even if a person duly satisfies all the conditions spelled out in Article 1(A)(2), he/she is excluded from the Geneva Convention under two different sets of circumstances. First, the protection of substitution offered by refugee status is excluded when a person already benefits from other international or national protection, whether he/she receives UN protection (Article 1(D)) or if he/she has the rights and obligations attached to the possession of the nationality in his/her country of residence (Article 1(E)). Second, the selectiveness of the refugee definition is patently reinforced by Article 1(F) which was introduced, according to the French delegate at the 1951 Conference, for the very purpose 'of separating the wheat from the chaff'.[29] In other words, 'the rationale . . . is that those who are responsible for the persecution which creates refugees should not enjoy the benefits of a Convention designed to protect those refugees'[30] in cases of serious crimes (crime against peace, war crime, crime against humanity, serious non-political crime, and acts contrary to the purposes and principles of the United Nations).

Finally, the cessation clauses enumerated in Article 1(C) reassert the dual nature of refugee status as a surrogate but selective protection. From that angle, refugee status is conceived of as a temporary protection, which is terminated as soon as the need for such protection is no longer justified.

2. The impact of international human rights law on the refugee definition

The selective approach permeating all the components of the refugee definition has been substantially informed—and to some extent mitigated—by the subsequent development of human rights law. Its impact on the refugee definition is primarily grounded in three main factors. First, as with any other conventional rules, Article 1 of the Geneva Convention must be construed and applied within the normative context prevailing at the time of its interpretation, including thus the human rights treaties adopted since its entry into force.[31] As exemplified below, such an *evolutive interpretation* has proved to be essential for adapting the Geneva Convention to the

[28] The Conference of Plenipotentiaries accordingly recommended in the Final Act that states parties should apply the Geneva Convention beyond 'its contractual scope' to other refugees 'who would not be covered by the terms of the Convention'.

[29] Mr Rochefort of France, UN Doc A/CONF.2/SR.19 (1951), 5.

[30] *Pushpanathan v. Canada (Minister of Citizenship and Immigration)* [1998] 1 SCR 982, para. 63.

[31] '[A]n international instrument has to be interpreted and applied within the framework of the entire legal system prevailing at the time of the interpretation'. *Legal Consequences for States of the Continued Presence of South Africa in Namibia (South West Africa) notwithstanding Security Council Resolution 276 (1970)*, ICJ Reports (1971) 16, at 31. Furthermore, human rights treaties constitute 'any relevant rules of international law applicable in the relations between the parties' under Art. 31(1)(c) of the Vienna Convention on the Law of Treaties.

ever changing reality of forced migration. Second, human rights law provides a universal and uniform set of standards which represents a particularly persuasive device for harmonizing the unilateral and frequently diverging interpretations of states parties. Third, given the subjectivity inherent in many key notions of the refugee definition, human rights standards offer a more predictable and objective normative framework for determining who is a refugee.

As the cornerstone of the refugee definition, the very notion of persecution clearly illustrates the permeation of human rights law within refugee law. This central concept has been left indeterminate by the Geneva Convention, probably because the lessons learned from the Nazi atrocities militated in favour of a concept flexible enough to encapsulate any possible future forms of mistreatment.[32] While its meaning has thus initially been relinquished to the subsequent interpretation of each state party, the need for a more principled and less subjective application has nevertheless prompted scholars to define persecution by reference to the new and growing body of human rights standards.

As early as 1953, Jacques Vernant 'equates "persecution" with severe measures and sanctions of an arbitrary nature, incompatible with the principles set forth in the Universal Declaration of Human Rights'.[33] Although this understanding was not commonly shared at the time,[34] it has progressively gained recognition with the unprecedented expansion of human rights law during the 1960s and the 1970s. In his pioneer study published in 1983, Goodwin-Gill framed the notion of persecution against the background of human rights.[35] This exercise was then further systematized by Hathaway in his seminal book *The Law of Refugee Status*, published in 1991. He defines persecution as a 'sustained or systemic violation of basic human rights demonstrative of a failure of state protection'.[36] Since then, defining persecution by reference to human rights has become conventional wisdom in legal doctrine.[37] More decisively, this understanding has been acknowledged in the subsequent practice of states parties to the Geneva Convention. It has notably

[32] P. Weis, 'The Concept of the Refugee in International Law', 87 *JDI* (1960) 928, 970; A. Grahl-Madsen, *The Status of Refugees in International Law* I (1966) 193.

[33] J. Vernant, *The Refugee in the Post-War World* (1953) 8, quoted in Grahl-Madsen (n 32) at 193.

[34] Grahl-Madsen (n 32) at 193–4.

[35] G. S. Goodwin-Gill, *The Refugee in International Law* (1983), 38–46. See also E. Lapenna, 'Le réfugié et l'émigrant dans le cadre des droits et libertés fondamentaux', 22 *AWR Bulletin* (1984) 50; G. Melander, *The Two Refugee Definitions* (1987).

[36] Hathaway (n 7) at 104–5.

[37] See, for instance, A. Zimmermann and C. Mahler, 'Article 1 A, para. 2 (Definition of the Term "Refugee")', in A. Zimmermann (ed.), *The 1951 Convention Relating to the Status of Refugees and its 1967 Protocol. A Commentary* (2011) 282, 345–58; M. Foster, *International Refugee Law and Socio-Economic Rights. Refugee from Deprivation* (2007) 27–86; von Sternberg (n 4) at 1–18; D. Alland and C. Teitgen-Colly, *Traité du droit de l'asile* (2002) 370–3; Lambert (n 4) at 19; F. Crépeau and D. Nakache, 'Une porte encore entrouverte: l'interprétation de la définition internationale du réfugié en droit canadien', in Chetail and Flauss (n 7) at 333–5; Parrish (n 4) at 223–67; C. J. Harvey, 'Refugee Law, the Judges and a "New" Human Rights Culture', 14 *Immigration and Nationality Law and Practice* (2000) 5; Sitaropoulos (n 4) at 215–45; J.-Y. Carlier, 'The Geneva Refugee Definition and the "Theory of the Three Scales"', in Nicholson and Twomey (n 8) at 41–5.

been restated by several domestic jurisdictions[38] and administrative authorities,[39] as well as in the EU Qualification Directive.[40]

The human rights-based approach to the refugee definition has resumed in turn with the underlying purpose of the Geneva Convention. The first paragraph of its preamble recalls in emphatic terms that 'the Charter of the United Nations and the Universal Declaration of Human Rights... have affirmed the principle that human beings shall enjoy fundamental rights and freedoms without discrimination'. This evasive but symbolic reference to human rights has been retrospectively interpreted by domestic jurisdictions as informing the whole rationale of the Geneva Convention: '[u]nderlying the Convention is the international community's commitment to the assurance of basic human rights without discrimination'.[41]

This human rights unction is not limited to the notion of persecution; it also shapes many other distinctive features of the refugee definition. As acknowledged by several domestic courts, the term 'refugee' is 'to be understood as written against the background of international human rights law, including as reflected or expressed in the Universal Declaration of Human Rights... and the International Covenant on Civil and Political Rights'.[42] The grounds of persecution provide one of the most obvious instances of the human rights filiation: the grounds of religion and political opinion are clearly based on freedom of thought[43] and that of opinion and expression,[44] while the other ones—race, nationality, and membership of a particular social group—are anchored within the principle of non-discrimination.[45]

Although gender is not explicitly listed among the grounds of persecution, human rights law has further played a crucial role in developing a gender-sensitive approach that mirrors its own evolution. Gender sensitivity is even a forerunner of the human rights approach of the refugee definition.[46] Hence,

[38] See, most notably, *Canada v. Ward* [1993] 103 DLR 4th 1; *Horvath v. Secretary of State for the Home Department* (n 26); *K. v. Refugee Status Appeals Authority* [2005] NZAR 441 (2004).

[39] See, for instance, *INS Basic Law Manual*, quoted in D. Anker, *Law of Asylum in the United States* (1999) 174; UK Asylum Policy Instructions, *Considering the Protection (Asylum) Claim and Assessing Credibility* (2010) 22–3.

[40] Art. 9 of Council Directive 2004/83/EC, OJ 2004 L 304/12, 29 April 2004, on minimum standards for the qualification and status of third country nationals or stateless persons as refugees or as persons who otherwise need international protection and the content of the protection granted.

[41] *Canada (Attorney-General) v. Ward* [1993] 2 SCR 689, 733 (Laforest J). The House of Lords acknowledges in the same vein: 'The relevance of the preambles is twofold. First, they expressly show that a premise of the Convention was that all human beings shall enjoy fundamental rights and freedoms. Secondly, and more pertinently, they show that counteracting discrimination, which is referred to in the first preamble, was a fundamental purpose of the Convention'. *Islam v. Secretary of State for the Home Department, R. v. Immigration Appeal Tribunal and another, ex parte Shah* [1999] 2 AC 629, at 639 (Steyn LJ).

[42] *Applicant A v. Minister for Immigration and Multicultural Affairs* [1997] 190 CLR 225, 296–7 (Kirby J). See also *Pushpanathan v. Canada (Minister of Citizenship and Immigration and Multicultural Affairs)* [1998] 1 SCR 982 1024 (Bastarache J).

[43] Arts 18 of the UDHR and ICCPR.

[44] Arts 19 of the UDHR and ICCPR.

[45] Arts 2 of the UDHR and ICCPR.

[46] D. Anker, 'Refugee Law, Gender, and the Human Rights Paradigm', 15 *Harv. Hum. Rts. L.J.* (2002) 133, at 138–9.

gender-based claims,[47] as well as those related to sexual orientation,[48] are now commonly considered as being encapsulated within the broad and residual ground of membership of a particular social group.

Human rights law has played a similar influence regarding non-state actors of persecution. While this issue has raised long-standing controversies among the refugee law community, the human rights theory of *Drittwirkung* has critically reshaped the terms of the debate in favour of an inclusive approach. Non-state actors of persecution have been eventually acknowledged by domestic courts[49] and the EU Qualification Directive,[50] the adoption of the latter obliging the most recalcitrant states (Germany and France) to change their previous practice.[51]

In sum, human rights law has become the ultimate benchmark for determining who is a refugee. The authoritative intrusion of human rights has proved to be instrumental in infusing a common and dynamic understanding of the refugee definition that is more consonant with and loyal to the evolution of international law. It thus prevents the Geneva Convention from becoming a mere legal anachronism by adapting it to the changing realities of forced migrations.

B. The principle of *non-refoulement*: a common ground of protection

The distillation of human rights norms within refugee law has been further deepened and reinforced through a similar evolution encapsulating the principle of *non-refoulement*. While this fundamental principle is at the very heart of the refugee protection regime (B.1), human rights law has overtaken it via a persuasive process of appropriation (B.2). The duty of *non-refoulement* has accordingly emerged as an overlapping ground of protection common to both branches of international law.

[47] See, most notably, *Islam v. Secretary of State for the Home Department* and *R. v. Immigration Appeal Tribunal and Secretary of State for the Home Department, ex parte Shah* [1999] 2 WLR 1015.

[48] See, for instance, Refugee Appeal No. 1312/93, Re GJ, 30 August 1995; *Hernandez-Montiel v. Immigration and Naturalization Service* [2000] 225 F.3d 1084 (US Court of Appeal for the 9th Circuit).

[49] In addition to the *Ward* and *Horvath* cases already mentioned, see for instance: *Arteaga v. Immigration and Naturalization* Service [1988] 836 F.2d 1227, 1231 (9th Cir.); *Minister for Immigration and Multicultural Affairs v. Ibrahim* [2000] HCA 55; Refugee Appeal No. 71427/99 [2000] INLR 608, para. 106.

[50] Art. 6(c).

[51] Long before the change of the French practice induced by the EU Directive, the Human Rights Committee expressed its concern with regard to 'the restrictive definition of the concept of "persecution" of refugee used by the French authorities as it does not take into account possible persecution by non-State actors'. UN Doc CCPR/C/79/Add. 80 (1997), para. 21. For further assessment of the French practice, see: V. Chetail, 'The Implementation of the Qualification Directive in France: One Step Forward and Two Steps Backwards', in K. Zwaan (ed.), *The Qualification Directive: Central Themes, Problem Issues and Implementation in Selected Member States* (2007) 87; V. Chetail, 'La réforme française de l'asile: prélude à la banalisation européenne du droit des réfugiés', 131 *JDI* (2004) 817.

1. The principle of non-refoulement*: the cornerstone of international refugee law*

The principle of *non-refoulement* is commonly regarded as 'the cornerstone of international refugee law'.[52] Its origins go back to extradition treaties concluded during the nineteenth century,[53] before it was explicitly endorsed for the first time in the 1933 Convention relating to the International Status of Refugees. Under contemporary refugee law, its primary source is Article 33(1) of the Geneva Convention: 'No Contracting State shall expel or return ("refouler") a refugee in any manner whatsoever to the frontiers of territories where his life or freedom would be threatened on account of his race, religion, nationality, membership of a particular social group or political opinion'. The cardinal importance of such an elementary principle is further endorsed by Article 42 which prohibits any reservation to Article 33. Since then, this founding principle of refugee law has been restated in a large body of interstate instruments,[54] to such an extent that it is now considered a customary norm of international law.[55]

Whatever its legal nature under general international law, the scope of the *non-refoulement* duty is relatively broad. The inclusive language of Article 33—through the generic expression 'in any manner whatsoever'—clearly indicates that the prohibition of *refoulement* applies to any act of forcible removal or rejection that puts the person concerned at risk of persecution. The legal nature of the act

[52] San Remo Declaration on the Principle of Non-Refoulement (September 2001). For an overview of the principle of *non-refoulement*, see W. Kälin, M. Caroni, and L. Heim, 'Article 33, para. 1 (Prohibition of Expulsion or Return ("Refoulement")/Défense d'expulsion et de refoulement)', in A. Zimmermann (ed.), *The 1951 Convention Relating to the Status of Refugees and its 1967 Protocol. A Commentary* (2011) 1327; Wouters (n 5); J.-Y. Carlier, 'Droit d'asile et des réfugiés: de la protection aux droits', 332 *RCADI* (2008) 76; G. S. Goodwin-Gill and J. McAdam, *The Refugee in International Law* (2007) 201–84; Hathaway, *The Rights of Refugees under International Law* (n 7) at 278–369; E. Lauterpacht and D. Bethlehem, 'The Scope and Content of the Principle of Non-Refoulement: Opinion', in E. Feller, V. Türk, and F. Nicholson (eds), *Refugee Protection in International Law, UNHCR's Global Consultations on International Protection* (2003) 87; V. Chetail, 'Le principe de non refoulement et le statut de réfugié en droit international', in Chetail and Flauss (n 7) at 3.

[53] V. Chetail, 'Théorie et pratique de l'asile en droit international classique: étude sur les origines conceptuelles et normatives du droit international des réfugiés', 114 *RGDIP* (2011) 625, at 634–50.

[54] See in particular: Agreement relating to Refugee Seamen, 23 November 1957, completed by the Protocol to the Agreement relating to Refugee Seamen of 12 June 1973, Art. 10; Organization of African Unity Convention Governing the Specific Aspects of Refugee Problems in Africa, 10 September 1969, Art. II(3); Protocol to Prevent, Suppress and Punish Trafficking in Persons, Especially Women and Children, supplementing the United Nations Convention against Transnational Organized Crime, 15 November 2000, Art. 14(1); Protocol against the Smuggling of Migrants by Land, Sea and Air, supplementing the United Nations Convention against Transnational Organized Crime, 15 November 2000; 2004 Qualification Directive, Recital 2 and Art. 21; Council Directive 2005/85/EC, OJ 2005 L 326/13 of 1 December 2005 on minimum standards on procedures in Member States for granting and withdrawing refugee status, Recital 2 and Art. 20(2); Council of Europe Convention on Action against Trafficking in Human Beings, 16 May 2005, Art. 40(4). Among soft law instruments, besides a wide number of resolutions from the General Assembly and the UNHCR ExCom, see, most notably, Declaration on Territorial Asylum, 14 December 1967, Art. 3(1); Resolution (67) 14 of the Committee of Ministers of the Council of Europe on Asylum to persons in Danger of Persecution, 1967; Cartagena Declaration on Refugees, 22 November 1984.

[55] Declaration of States Parties to the 1951 Convention and or its 1967 Protocol relating to the Status of Refugees, UN Doc HCR/MMSP/2001/09 (2002), para. 4.

(expulsion, deportation, extradition, non-admission at the border, interception, transfer, or rendition) is therefore not relevant. The decisive consideration is the consequence of this act, namely whether one's life or liberty would be threatened on account of a Convention reason. Following that stance, the principle of *non-refoulement* covers equally both asylum seekers and recognized refugees, provided that they are under the jurisdiction of a state party. Contrary to many other provisions of the Geneva Convention, Article 33 is not dependent on the presence—whether lawful or unlawful—of asylum seekers within the territory of a state party. It thus applies regardless of whether they enter the territory legally or illegally.

This basic protection is reinforced by Article 31(1) of the Geneva Convention, which prohibits the imposition of penalties on account of the illegal entry of refugees. This last provision is aimed at exempting asylum seekers from the entry requirements generally imposed on immigrants.[56] As acknowledged by domestic courts, the purpose of Article 31 is 'to provide immunity for genuine refugees whose quest for asylum reasonably involved them in breaching the law' of states parties to the Geneva Convention.[57]

The principle of *non-refoulement*, combined with this duty of non-penalization, considerably challenges the traditional prerogative of states in the field of migration control.[58] States no longer enjoy an unconditional and uncontrolled discretion to refuse admission to their own territory. However, this does not create an obligation of asylum per se but instead conditions, circumscribes, and ultimately constrains their margin of appreciation. Hence, 'the Convention represents a significant but qualified limitation upon the absolute right of the member states to admit those whom they choose'.[59]

From a conceptual and legal perspective, *non-refoulement* must be distinguished from asylum. At the conceptual level, *non-refoulement* is a negative notion, prohibiting states from sending back refugees to a country of persecution. As underlined during the drafting of the Geneva Convention, '[i]t imposed a negative duty

[56] The drafters of the Geneva Convention were indeed plainly aware that '[a] refugee whose departure from his country of origin is usually a flight, is rarely in a position to comply with the requirements for legal entry (possession of national passport and visa) into the country of refuge. It would be in keeping with the notion of asylum to exempt from penalties a refugee, escaping from persecution, who after crossing the frontier clandestinely presents himself as soon as possible to the authorities of the country of asylum and is recognized as a *bona fide* refugee'. Memorandum by the Secretary General, UN Doc E/AC.32/2 (1950), para. 3.

[57] *R. v. Uxbridge Magistrates' Court ex parte Adimi* [1999] 4 All ER 520, 527 (Simon Brown LJ). It also confirmed that 'Article 31 extends not merely to those ultimately accorded refugee status but also to those claiming asylum in good faith (presumptive refugees) is not in doubt. Nor is it disputed that Article 31's protection can apply equally to those using false documents as to those . . . who enter a country clandestinely'.

[58] One should stress that while illegal entry is utterly irrelevant for benefiting from the principle of *non-refoulement*, the prohibition of penalties is much more limited in scope. It does not apply to all asylum-seekers but only to those who satisfy the three following conditions imposed by Art. 31(1): they come directly from a country of persecution; they present themselves without delay to the national authorities; and show good cause for their illegal entry or presence.

[59] *Minister for Immigration and Multicultural Affairs v. Khawar* [2002] HCA 14, para. 68 (McHugh and Gummow JJ).

forbidding the expulsion of any refugee to certain territories but did not impose the obligation to allow a refugee to take up residence'.[60] By contrast, asylum is a positive concept, which entails admission to residence and lasting protection against the jurisdiction of another state. This conceptual distinction between asylum and *non-refoulement* is further grounded on their respective legal natures: *non-refoulement* is an obligation of states, whereas asylum is a right of states. As evidenced by a large body of law, 'it has long been recognised that, according to customary international law, the right of asylum is a right of States, not of the individual'.[61]

As a result of this normative distinction, although the exact content of refugee status is spelled out in considerable detail, the Geneva Convention does not contain any provision on asylum.[62] The silence on this crucial issue may be surprising, for 'to speak of refugees is to speak of asylum, the very condition of their existence'.[63] Such normative hiatus between the right of asylum and the obligation of *non-refoulement* was, however, anything but unintentional. The Geneva Convention was carefully drafted to make sure that no obligation to grant asylum was explicitly imposed on states parties. The UK delegation made clear at the 1951 Conference that '[t]he right of asylum . . . was only a right, belonging to the State, to grant or refuse asylum not a right belonging to the individual and entitling him to insist on its being extended to him'.[64] '[Nevertheless], the only article which had any bearing on that aspect of the matter was the article [33] prohibiting the expulsion of a refugee to a country where his life or freedom would be in danger'.[65]

As admitted by the UK representative, the principle of *non-refoulement* is bound to play a pivotal role in the absence of an individual right to be granted asylum. Furthermore, while conceptually and legally well grounded, the distinctive nature of *non-refoulement* and asylum appears highly artificial in practice.[66] Although *non-refoulement* is primarily an obligation of result, asylum is generally the only practical means to respect and ensure respect for Article 33. Indeed, how can a state remove

60 Statement of Mr Weis of the International Refugee Organization, E/AC.32/SR40 (1950), 33. For a recent acknowledgement, see: *M38/2002 v. Minister for Immigration and Multicultural and Indigenous Affairs* [2003] FCAGC 131, para. 39.

61 *Minister for Immigration and Multicultural Affairs v. Khawar* [2002] HCA 14, para. 42 (McHugh and Gummow JJ). See also among many other similar judicial statements: *R v. Immigration Officer at Prague Airport and another ex parte Roma Rights Centre and others* [2004] UKHL 55, paras 11–17 (Lord Bingham of Cornhill).

62 The only explicit reference to asylum can be found in the preamble of the Geneva Convention in rather pejorative terms: 'Considering that *the grant of asylum may place unduly heavy burdens on certain countries*, and that a satisfactory solution of a problem of which the United Nations has recognized the international scope and nature cannot therefore be achieved without international co-operation' (emphasis added).

63 Aga Khan, 'Legal Problems Relating to Refugees and Displaced Persons', I-149 *RCADI* (1976), 316.

64 UN Doc A/CONF.2/SR.13 (1951), 13.

65 UN Doc A/CONF.2/SR.19 (1951), 18.

66 Referring to the interaction between asylum and *non-refoulement*, the House of Lords has acknowledged that 'although a refugee has no direct right to insist on asylum, there are certain statutory restrictions on the Secretary of State's freedom of choice as to the destination to which a person refused permission to remain may be sent, which may in practice achieve the same result'. *T. v. Secretary of State for the Home Department* [1996] AC 742, 754 (Lord Mustill).

an asylum-seeker without, beforehand, granting temporary admission for assessing whether his/her life or liberty may be threatened in the country of destination? Such constructive ambiguity was probably the price to pay for preserving the appearance of state sovereignty with due regard to the most essential rights of refugees.

In practice, states have two options for complying with their duty of *non-refoulement*: granting temporary asylum in order to examine whether the asylum-seeker is a refugee under the Geneva Convention, or sending him/her to a country where there is no risk of persecution.[67] Even in the last case, removal to a safe third country requires some form of temporary admission for asserting that the third country is not a country of persecution and provides an effective protection against any subsequent *refoulement* in breach of Article 33. It further presupposes that the asylum-seeker would be admissible in the safe third country—a condition which is hardly completed in the absence of a specific obligation spelled out in re-admission agreements or other related schemes for allocating the responsibility of examining the asylum request (such as the Dublin Regulation). In sum, whatever the different options available to states for implementing Article 33, due respect for the principle of *non-refoulement* implicitly requires 'a de facto duty to admit the refugee'.[68]

Such a duty is, however, not absolute. Article 33(2) provides that the benefit of *non-refoulement* cannot be claimed by a refugee who represents a danger to the security of the country in which he is, or who has been convicted by a final judgement of a particularly serious crime, constituting a danger to the community of that country. As with any exceptions to a principle, 'it is clear that Article 33(2) exception must be interpreted restrictively'.[69]

While states retain a substantial margin of appreciation, the threshold of these two exceptions remains relatively high. Regarding the first, '[t]he wording of the provision... requires the person him or herself to constitute a danger to national security'.[70] That a person be able to threaten the security of a whole country confines such a hypothesis to highly exceptional circumstances (mainly limited to terrorism, military operations, espionage, and other related activities aimed at overthrowing its institutions). In any event, 'the threat must be "serious", in the sense that it must be grounded on objectively reasonable suspicion based on evidence and in the sense that the threatened harm must be substantial rather than negligible'.[71]

While the first exception is aimed at safeguarding the security of the state and its institutions, the second exception focuses on the protection of the host society against criminality. Here again the wording of Article 33(2) is particularly

[67] These alternatives are further confirmed by Art. 31(2), which provides that 'restrictions [to the movement of refugees] shall only be applied until their status in the country is regularized or they obtain admission into another country'.

[68] Hathaway (n 7) at 301. See also Carlier (n 52) at 85; Goodwin-Gill and McAdam (n 52) at 384.

[69] *Attorney General v. Zaoui* [2004] Dec. No. CA20/04, para. 136.

[70] *Attorney General v. Zaoui* (n 69) para. 148.

[71] *Suresh v. Canada (Minister of Citizenship and Immigration)* [2002] 1 SCR 3, para. 90. See also *Attorney General v. Zaoui* (n 69) paras 133 and 140; *NSH v. Secretary of State for the Home Department* [1988] Imm AR 410.

restrictive. This last exception is circumscribed by three cumulative conditions: first, the refugee must have been 'convicted by a final judgement' (presupposing thus the exhaustion of all judicial remedies); second, this conviction is for 'a particularly serious crime' (thereby requiring a case-by-case assessment of the nature of the crime, the gravity of the harm inflicted, and the circumstances surrounding its perpetration); and third, because of his/her criminal record and the risk of subsequent offence, the refugee represents 'a danger to the community' as a whole.[72]

As exemplified by these exceptions as well as by its ambivalent relations with asylum, the principle of *non-refoulement* operates as a pragmatic attempt to reconcile two competing values. It preserves a subtle—and sometimes insecure—compromise between, on the one hand, the inescapable right of states to control access to their territory and, on the other, the imperious protection of refugees whose lives and liberty are threatened. This balancing act constitutes the driving force of international refugee law and reveals the normative dynamic as well as contradictions inherent in this branch of law.

2. *The appropriation of* non-refoulement *by international human rights law*

Human rights law does not fundamentally challenge the normative mantra of refugee law. Despite several attempts to do so,[73] the Universal Declaration of Human Rights (UDHR) failed to enshrine an individual right to be granted asylum. Its Article 14 refers instead to a vague and permissive proclamation without any correlative obligation of admission. It declares in minimalist terms that '[e]veryone has *the right to seek and to enjoy* in other countries asylum from persecution'.[74] Lauterpacht described this formula as 'artificial to the point of flippancy', for 'there was no intention to assume even a moral obligation to grant asylum' and, accordingly, 'no declaration would be necessary to give an individual the right to seek asylum without an assurance of receiving it'.[75] Referring to the vigilant reluctance of states in this field, the High Court of Australia concluded that:

[72] See, in particular, *A. v. Minister for Immigration and Multicultural Affairs* [1999] FCA 227, para. 42.

[73] See the French proposal presented by René Cassin: UN Doc E/CN.4/AC.1/SR37 (1948), 8.

[74] Even formulated in such evasive terms, the right to seek and to enjoy asylum is further restricted by the traditional exception based on criminal behaviour and other related acts: '[t]his right may not be invoked in the case of prosecutions genuinely arising from non-political crimes or from acts contrary to the purposes and principles of the United Nations'.

[75] H. Lauterpacht, 'The Universal Declaration of Human Rights', 25 *BYIL* (1948) 354, 373–4. The 1967 Declaration on Territorial Asylum restates in the same vein as the Universal Declaration on Human Rights (UDHR) that '[a]sylum granted by a State, in the exercise of its sovereignty, to persons entitled to invoke article 14 of the UDHR, including persons struggling against colonialism, shall be respected by all other States' (Art. 1(1)) and '[i]t shall rest with the State granting asylum to evaluate the grounds for the grant of asylum' (Art. 1(3)). See also on the blatant failure of the 1977 UN Conference on Territorial Asylum: R. Plender, 'Admission of Refugees: Draft Convention on Territorial Asylum', *SDLR* (1977–1978) 45; P. Weis, 'The Draft United Nations Convention on Territorial Asylum', *BYIL* (1979) 151; A. Grahl-Madsen, *Territorial Asylum* (1980), 61–8.

> [T]his right 'to seek' asylum was not accompanied by any assurance that the quest would be successful. A deliberate choice was made not to make a significant innovation in international law which would have amounted to a limitation upon the absolute right of member States to regulate immigration by conferring privileges upon individuals... Nor was the matter taken any further by the International Covenant on Civil and Political Rights... Article 12 of the ICCPR stipulates freedom to leave any country and forbids arbitrary deprivation of the right to enter one's own country; but the ICCPR does not provide for any right of entry to seek asylum and the omission was deliberate.[76]

Although this may appear frustrating, the failure of human rights law to secure an individual right of asylum simply echoes the existential dilemma of refugee law. Both branches of international law revolve around the same dialectic between, on the one hand, the state obligation of *non-refoulement* and, on the other, its sovereign right of granting or refusing asylum. However, while adopting the same normative stance, human rights law has considerably impacted on the principle of *non-refoulement,* thus reinforcing and consolidating the cornerstone of refugee law as a common ground of protection. The principle of *non-refoulement* has been expressly endorsed, at the universal level, in the 1984 UN Convention against Torture (Article 3) and the 2006 UN International Convention for the Protection of All Persons from Enforced Disappearance (Article 16) as well as, at the regional level, the 1969 American Convention on Human Rights (American Convention) (Article 22(8)), the 1985 Inter-American Convention to Prevent and Punish Torture (Article 13(4)), the 2000 Charter of Fundamental Rights of the European Union (Article 19(2)), and—to some extent—the 2004 Arab Charter on Human Rights (Arab Charter) (Article 28).[77]

Beside these explicit endorsements, most general human rights treaties have been construed by their respective treaty bodies as inferring an implicit prohibition of *refoulement.* As early as 1961, the European Commission of Human Rights considered that the removal of aliens may raise an issue under Article 3 of the European Convention on Human Rights (ECHR).[78] This purposive interpretation was notably endorsed in 1965 by the Parliamentary Assembly of the Council of Europe,[79] before being finally confirmed in 1989 by the European Court of Human Rights in the landmark *Soering* case.[80] This implied duty of *non-*

[76] *Minister for Immigration and Multicultural Affairs v. Ibrahim* [2000] HCA 55, para. 138. The right of asylum shares the same fate as the right to property, being the only rights proclaimed in the UDHR that were not restated in the UN Covenants. Moreover, while some regional human rights instruments contain apparently more demanding language through the expression 'the right to seek and be granted asylum', any sense of obligation is further neutralized by subordinating its exercise to the respect for relevant domestic legislations and international conventions: American Convention on Human Rights, 22 November 1969 (American Convention), Art. 22(7); African Charter on Human and People's Rights, 27 June 1981 (African Charter), Art. 12(3). Other regional instruments are even more vague and permissive: Charter of Fundamental Rights of the European Union, 18 December 2000, Art. 18; Arab Charter on Human Rights (Arab Charter), Art. 28.

[77] Art. 28 refers to the prohibition of extradition instead of the more generic term of *refoulement.*

[78] *X v. Belgium*, EComHR (1961) Appl. No. 984/61, (1961) 6 CD 39.

[79] PACE, Recommendation 434 (1965) on the Granting of the Right of Asylum to European refugees, paras 3–4.

[80] *Soering v. The United Kingdom*, ECHR (1989) Series A, No. 161, paras 87–88.

refoulement deriving from the general prohibition of torture, inhuman and degrading treatment has been further endorsed, at the universal level, by the Human Rights Committee[81] and the Committee on the Rights of the Child[82] as well as, at the regional level, by the Inter-American and African Commissions of Human Rights.[83]

Despite this consensual acknowledgement, treaty bodies have remained surprisingly evasive about the exact basis of their praetorian construction. One could however argue that protection against *refoulement* is anchored within the theory of positive obligations. States not only have the negative obligation to refrain from violating human rights; they also have the positive obligation to prevent violations so as to ensure the effective enjoyment of the basic rights at stake.[84] This obligation of prevention is applicable to virtually all human rights provided there is a real risk of serious violation in the receiving state. The implied duty of *non-refoulement* has been notably acknowledged by the Human Rights Committee with regard to any rights under the Covenant.[85] The European Court is, however, more hesitant and obviously embarrassed by any further enlargement besides the right to life, freedom from arbitrary detention, and the right to a fair trial.[86] In any case, identifying the specific human rights triggering the principle of *non-refoulement* remains a largely academic and arguably sterile exercise. Serious violations of any human rights would prompt the correlative prohibition of *refoulement*, as soon as the gravity of the prospective violation amounts to degrading treatment.

Following that stance, the human rights principle of *non-refoulement* coincides in substance with its refugee law counterpart. While the notions of degrading treatment and of persecution retain their own autonomous meanings, defining them by reference to a serious violation of human rights significantly erodes

81 HRCttee, *General Comment No. 20: Replaces General Comment 7 Concerning Prohibition of Torture and Cruel Treatment or Punishment (Art. 7)*, UN Doc HRI/GEN/1/Rev.9 (Vol. I) (1992), para. 9.

82 CRC, *General Comment No. 6: Treatment of Unaccompanied and Separated Children Outside their Country of Origin*, CRC/GC/2005/6 (2005), para. 27.

83 *The Haitian Centre for Human Rights et al. v. United States*, IAComHR (1997) Case 10.675, Report No. 51/96, OEA/Ser.L/V/II.95 Doc. 7 rev., para. 167; *John K. Modise v. Botswana*, ACommHPR (2000) Comm. No. 97/93, para. 91.

84 Chetail, 'Le droit des réfugiés à l'épreuve des droits de l'homme' (n 5) esp. 160–70. For further discussions about the possible rationale underlying the implicit duty of *non-refoulement*, see also H. Battjes, 'The *Soering* Threshold: Why Only Fundamental Values Prohibit Refoulement in ECHR Case Law', 11 *EJML* (2009) 205; M. Foster, 'Non-Refoulement on the Basis of Socio-Economic Deprivation: The Scope of Complementary Protection in International Human Rights Law', *NZ L. Rev.* (2009) 257, at 265–79; M. Den Heijer, 'Whose Rights and Which Rights? The Continuing Story of Non-Refoulement under the European Convention on Human Rights', 10 *EJML* (2008) 277; W. Kälin, 'Limits to Expulsion under the International Covenant on Civil and Political Rights', in F. Salerno (ed.), *Diritti Dell'Uomo, Estradizione ed Espulsione* (2003) 143; G. Noll, *Negotiating Asylum* (2000), 453–74.

85 See, for instance, HRCttee, *Kindler v. Canada*, CCPR/C/48/D/470/1991 (1993), para. 13.2; *G.T. v. Australia*, CCPR/C/61/D/706/1996 (1997), paras 8.1–8.7; HRCttee, *General Comment No. 31: The Nature of the General Legal Obligation Imposed on States Parties to the Covenant*, CCPR/C/21/Rev.1/add.13 (2004), para. 12.

86 See, especially, *Z and T v. The United Kingdom*, ECHR (2006) Appl. No. 27034/05; *Tomic v. The United Kingdom*, ECHR (2003) Appl. No. 17387/03.

their distinctive character. Already in 1984, the European Commission acknowledged that:

Although the risk of political persecution, as such, cannot be equated to torture, inhuman or degrading treatment, ... it may, in a particular case, raise an issue under Art. 3 if it brings about a prejudice for the individual concerned which reaches such level of severity as to bring it within the scope of this provision e.g. an arbitrary sentence ... or inhuman detention conditions.[87]

Conversely, from the perspective of the Geneva Convention, degrading treatment equates with persecution under the refugee definition.[88] The same material convergence may be observed with regard to the assessment of the risk. Whether it is phrased as 'a well-founded fear of being persecuted' or 'a real risk of being subjected to torture, inhuman or degrading treatment', both are prospective in nature. Although the different formulae used by treaty bodies and refugee status decision-makers have raised a disproportionate attention among commentators, the difference of wording is largely semantic. The reality of the risk under the Refugee Convention and the human rights treaties requires a case-by-case assessment grounded on two prognostic factors: the personal circumstances of the applicant as well as the general situation prevailing in the destination country. In both cases, assessing the well-foundedness of the alleged risk is in essence a hypothetical prediction of what might happen if the applicant were returned to his/her country of origin.

Notwithstanding this substantial convergence between the two variants of the *non-refoulement* obligation, human rights law provides a broader protection than refugee law on three specific issues. First, the human rights principle of *non-refoulement* is not subordinated to the five grounds of persecution required by the refugee definition under the Geneva Convention. However, this divergence should not be overestimated, for it can be counterbalanced by a cogent interpretation of the grounds of persecution with due regard to the object and purpose of the Geneva Convention. The second distinctive feature is probably more straightforward: whereas the refugee definition exclusively applies to a person who is 'outside the country of his nationality',[89] no such geographical limitation is required under human rights law. As a result, the human rights principle of *non-refoulement* still applies to any person who is in a diplomatic mission, in an area controlled by

[87] *C. v. Netherlands* (1984) DR 38, 224. Beside the specific examples mentioned by the Commission, assessing whether the level of severity amounts to degrading treatment requires an *in concreto* examination of all the circumstances of each case. Moreover, an accumulation of human rights violations may cross the threshold under Art. 3: *Ireland v. The United Kingdom*, ECHR (1978) Series A, No. 25, para. 162; *M.S.S. v. Belgium and Greece*, ECHR (2011) Appl. No. 30696/09, para. 220; *Ireland v. The United Kingdom*, ECHR (1978) Series A, No. 25, para. 167.

[88] Among an abundant case law, see *Cheung v. Canada (Minister of Employment and Immigration)* [1993] 1 CF 314, 324; *SZ and JM (Iran CG) v. The Secretary of State for the Home Department* [2008] UKAIT 00082, paras 168–169.

[89] Art. 1(A)(2) of the Geneva Convention; *R v. Immigration Officer at Prague Airport and another ex parte Roma Rights Centre and others* [2004] UKHL 55, paras 16–18 (Lord Bingham of Cornhill).

peacekeeping and occupying forces, or is otherwise under the effective control of another state within the territory of his/her own country.[90]

The third and the most well-known characteristic relies on the absolute nature of the *refoulement* prohibition in a state where there is a real risk of torture, inhuman, or degrading treatment.[91] It thus applies to asylum seekers and refugees who have been excluded from the protection of the Geneva Convention under the exclusion clauses of the refugee definition or by application of Article 33(2).[92] This last feature has received most of the attention from both states and commentators in a context largely dominated by the fight against terrorism. In practice, though, one should observe that this feature appears more symbolic than real, for it concerns a highly marginal number of persons compared to the total population of refugees and other persons in need of protection.[93] It remains, however, emblematic of the impact of human rights law on refugee law. Indeed, the archetypal balance between state sovereignty and human rights has reached its breaking point in favour of the latter. This reveals in turn the distinctive rationale underlying each branch of law: whereas refugee law is bound to grant protection only to those who deserve it, human rights law is universal and inclusive in essence.

More specifically, the human rights principle of *non-refoulement* stands out as a practical and powerful means for ensuring effective respect for fundamental rights. It is an integral part of the broader enforcement device of human rights law. Schabas rightly observes in this sense that:

> it may be better to see it as a piece in the international struggle for the enforcement of fundamental rights. Approached in this way, States should not expel persons to a place where they may be threatened with torture, or the death penalty, or other serious abuses, because this is a method of promoting global observance of human rights.[94]

From a systemic perspective, the structural function of *non-refoulement* re-inforces the normative merger of the two branches of law, since effective respect for human rights also constitutes the ultimate finality of refugee law.[95]

[90] Curiously enough, despite its far-reaching effects, this last characteristic has not yet given rise to a substantial practice by treaty bodies. For the time being, the most relevant practice essentially relates to the rights to liberty and security rather than *non-refoulement* per se. See, in particular, *W.M. v. Denmark*, EComHR (1992) Appl. No. 17392/90 and implicitly at least: HRCttee, *Concluding Observations on the United States of America*, CCPR/C/USA/CO/3/REV.1 (2006), para. 16.

[91] The absolute nature of the *non-refoulement* duty also applies when there is a real risk of enforced disappearance under Art. 16 of the UN Convention for the Protection from Enforced Disappearance.

[92] See, most notably, *Saadi v. Italy*, ECHR (2008) Appl. No. 37201/06, paras 138–141; *Chahal v. The United Kingdom*, ECHR (1996) Reports 1996-V, para. 80; CAT, *Tapia Paez v. Sweden*, CAT/C/18/D/39/1996 (1996), para. 14.5.

[93] In France, for instance, exclusion from refugee status only represents around 0.25 per cent of the judicial decisions delivered each year on the basis of Art. 1 of the Geneva Convention: Alland and Teitgen-Colly (n 37) at 520.

[94] W. A. Schabas, 'Non-Refoulement', in *Expert Workshop on Human Rights and International Co-operation in Counter-Terrorism*, ODIHR.GAL/14/07 (2007) at 47.

[95] As acknowledged by Kälin, 'granting refugee status and asylum together with the scrupulous observance of the principle of non-refoulement is one of the most effective means of securing human rights protection in that it ensures that the violator can no longer reach the victim of persecution'.

This purposive convergence between human rights law and refugee law is further reasserted by their common impact on the traditional right of states to control access to their territory. Under both branches of law, due respect for the principle of *non-refoulement* requires admission, except for possible removal to a safe third country.[96] Hence, while acknowledging that 'the State party is not required to modify its decision(s) concerning the granting of asylum', the Committee against Torture (CAT) has insisted on the fact that:

> [I]t does have a responsibility to find solutions that will enable it to take all necessary measures to comply with the provisions of article 3 of the Convention. These solutions may be of a legal nature (e.g. decision to admit the applicant temporarily), but also of a political nature (e.g. action to find a third State willing to admit the applicant to its territory and undertaking not to return or expel him in its turn).[97]

Regarding the removal to a safe third country, the European Court of Human Rights has underlined in the same line of reasoning that the conclusion of an international agreement for allocating the responsibility of examining asylum requests (such as the Dublin Regulation) does not absolve states from their obligations under human rights law.[98] It concluded that:

> When they apply the Dublin Regulation, therefore, the States must make sure that the intermediary country's asylum procedure affords sufficient guarantees to avoid an asylum-seeker being removed, directly or indirectly, to his country of origin without any evaluation of the risks he faces from the standpoint of Article 3 of the Convention.[99]

This *obiter dictum* remarkably illustrates the inextricable intermingling between human rights law and refugee law: the former guarantees the effectiveness of the latter and vice versa.

W. Kälin, 'The Prohibition of Inhuman Return and its Impact upon Refugee Status Determination', in *Refugee and Asylum Law: Assessing the Scope for Judicial Protection* (1997), 139.

[96] The implied duty of admission has sometimes been labelled as an individual right to be granted asylum: R. Plender and N. Mole, 'Beyond the Geneva Convention: Constructing a De Facto Right of Asylum from International Human Rights Instruments', in Nicholson and Twomey (n 8) at 81; T. Einarsen, 'The European Convention on Human Rights and the Notion of an Implied Right to *De facto* Asylum', 2 *IJRL* (1990) 361; D. S. Nance, 'The Individual Right to Asylum Under Article 3 of the European Convention on Human Rights', *Mich. Y. B. Int'l Leg. Stud.* (1982) 477. Such an assertion is arguably not correct. Under both refugee law and human rights law, the principle of *non-refoulement* is conceived as a duty-driven norm addressed to states and not as a right of individuals per se. Moreover, the choice between admission and removal to a safe third country pertains to the state and not the individual. In sum, 'so far as a State's actions may expose an individual to risk of violation of fundamental human rights, its responsibility should be duty-driven, rather than strictly correlative to any individual "right"' Goodwin-Gill and McAdam (n 52) at 295. See also W. Kälin, *Grundriss des Asylverfahrens* (1990), 211.

[97] CAT, *Aemei v. Switzerland*, CAT/C/18/D/34/1995 (1997), para. 11.

[98] *T.I. v. The United Kingdom*, ECHR (2000) Reports 2000-III; *M.S.S. v. Belgium and Greece* (n 87) para. 342.

[99] *M.S.S. v. Belgium and Greece* (n 87) para. 342.

II. The Content of International Protection: From Conditionality to Universality

While access to protection has witnessed a gradual merging of human rights law and refugee law, one remaining distinctive feature relies on the legal consequences attached to the principle of *non-refoulement*. In line with other treaty bodies, the CAT has noted in straightforward terms that 'the legal status of the individual concerned in the country where he/she is allowed to stay is not relevant for the Committee',[100] since 'its authority does not extend to a determination of whether or not the claimant is entitled to asylum under the national laws of a country, or can invoke the protection of the Geneva Convention relating to the Status of Refugees'.[101]

By contrast, the principle of *non-refoulement* under the Geneva Convention is accompanied and finalized by the granting of refugee status. Such an attribute has been commonly heralded by commentators as establishing the Geneva Convention as *the* primary source of refugee protection, relegating human rights law to a secondary role. Following a similar assumption (but with clearly different objectives in mind), states have established at the regional and domestic levels more malleable and precarious regimes under the label of so-called complementary protection.

This self-referential dialogue between states and refugee lawyers is arguably grounded on false premises. Indeed, closer examination of the content of the protection granted by the Geneva Convention and the ICCPR reveals a completely different picture. From this angle, human rights law is not only broader than refugee law with regard to both its personal and material scope, but more fundamentally, the former supplants the latter even when their respective norms overlap.

A. Refugee status and the conditionality of protection

Compared to human rights law, the content of international protection provided by refugee status presents significant specificities. Although the Geneva Convention is commonly presented as 'an extraordinary "Bill of Rights" for refugees',[102] it substantially differs from the phraseology of human rights. Formally speaking, the Refugee Convention is framed on the mode of interstate obligations rather than those of individual rights. It primarily addresses contracting states by spelling out their obligations, while the term 'rights' directly pertaining to refugees is rarely mentioned as such in the text of the Geneva Convention.[103] Thus the refugee is not conceived of as a subject

[100] CAT, *M.B.B. v. Sweden*, CAT/C/22/D/104/1998 (1999), para. 6.4.

[101] CAT, *X v. Spain*, CAT/C/15/D/23/1995 (1995), para. 7.3.

[102] Gorlick (n 7) at 122.

[103] The vast majority of its provisions are worded in the following manner: 'The Contracting States shall accord to refugees . . . '. Among the rare examples of true rights or freedoms directly bestowed on refugees by the Geneva Convention, see Art. 12 referring to the 'rights previously acquired by a refugee and dependent on personal status' and Art. 26 on 'the right to choose their place of residence and to move freely within [contracting states'] territory'. Even Art. 15, although entitled 'right of association', is not written in the mode of an individual right but as a treatment accorded by contracting states.

of law in his or her own right but rather as a beneficiary of common standards regulating the conduct of states. Technically speaking, therefore, the Geneva Convention cannot be labelled as a human rights treaty as is so frequently asserted by the doctrine.[104] In other words, it is a duty-based rather than a human rights-based instrument.[105]

One should not, though, overestimate the difference between rights of individuals and obligations of states, given that the state remains the primary guarantor of human rights. From that angle, several human rights instruments mix obligations of states and rights of individuals.[106] Although such a distinction is still important at the conceptual level, on a more practical plane, obligations contracted under the Geneva Convention indirectly echo—but do not equate with—individual claims of refugees opposable to states parties. Such normative digression was inevitable in the light of the historical context in which the Geneva Convention was drafted. In 1951, the individual did not have human rights conventionally binding at the universal level.[107] One would have to wait for fifteen years after the adoption of the Geneva Convention for the UN Covenants to give a conventional basis to the rights identified in the UDHR.[108] Furthermore, any attempt to draft a true Bill of Rights for refugees would have impinged upon the ongoing negotiations on the forthcoming UN Covenants. Framing refugee status as involving obligations of states rather than rights of individuals thus emerged as a necessity in the absence of legally binding human rights.

From this particular normative context flows the key difference with human rights law, namely the conditionality of refugee status. Contrary to human rights

[104] Among the plethora of authors already referred to in n 9, Edwards considers that 'the United Nations Convention Related to the Status of Refugees is a rights-based and rights-granting instrument. Its coverage in Articles 3 to 34 is of the same nature as some rights granted under various human rights instruments', Edwards (n 7) at 306. This (mis)perception has also found an increasing echo among domestic courts. See Refugee Status Appeals Authority, *Refugee Appeal No. 71684/99* [2000] INLR 165, para. 61.

[105] Among the very rare authors acknowledging this distinctive feature, Goodwin-Gill recalls that 'the formal scheme of the Convention, however, remains one of *obligations between states*. The refugee is a beneficiary, beholden to the state, with a status to which certain standards of treatment and certain guarantees attach'. He adds that 'a number of key obligations nevertheless rapidly made the transition into the doctrine and into the developing and strengthening discourse of individual rights'. G. S. Goodwin-Gill, *Refugees and their Human Rights* (2004) 7. See also M. G. Wachenfeld and H. Christensen, 'Note: An Introduction to Refugees and Human Rights', 59 *Nordic JIL* (1990) 178, at 180.

[106] They notably include the International Convention on the Elimination of All Forms of Racial Discrimination, the Convention on the Rights of the Child, the International Convention for the Protection of All Persons from Enforced Disappearance and the Convention on the Rights of Persons with Disabilities.

[107] At the time, only the Charter of the United Nations (UN Charter) had proclaimed in its first Article 'respect for human rights and for fundamental freedoms for all without distinction as to race, sex, language, or religion', without identifying the rights and freedoms in question. The 1948 UDHR was adopted as a non-binding resolution of the General Assembly for the purpose of identifying such rights and fundamental freedoms 'as a common standard of achievement for all peoples and all nations'. At the regional level, only the European Convention on Human Rights for the Protection of Human Rights and Fundamental Freedoms (ECHR) was adopted in 1950 but it only entered into force after the adoption of the Geneva Convention in September 1953.

[108] The two UN Covenants finally entered into force in 1976, ten years after their adoption.

treaties adopted subsequently, the Convention does not simply enumerate rights without distinction as to their beneficiaries. On the contrary, the content of refugee status is subordinated by the superposition of two cumulative conditions governing, first, the criteria of entitlement (the applicability of the norm) and, second, the standard of treatment (the content of the norm).[109]

As far as the first set of conditions is concerned, entitlement criteria are determined by reference to three distinct levels of applicability. The first level refers to the term 'refugee' without any further qualification. This concerns a core set of basic guarantees which includes the prohibition of discrimination (Article 3), acquisition of movable and immovable property and other rights pertaining thereto (Article 13), free access to domestic courts (Article 16(1)), rationing (Article 20), primary education (Article 22(1)), fiscal equality (Article 29), transfer of assets (Article 30), and protection against *refoulement* (Article 33(1)).

While all refugees benefit from these core guarantees, additional entitlements are subordinated to the existence of a territorial bond with the asylum state, whose degree of intensity varies from one 'right' to another. The two other levels of applicability, respectively, require presence or stay of the refugee, further depending on its physical or lawful nature. Concerning the second level, on the one hand, mere *physical presence* within the territory triggers the benefit of freedom of religion (Article 4), the delivery of identity papers (Article 27), and the prohibition of penalties on account of illegal entry (Article 31(1)). On the other hand, *lawful presence* is further required for engaging in self-employment (Article 18), for freely moving within the host territory (Article 26), and for being protected against expulsion (Article 32).

As for the third level of applicability, the Convention envisions an additional subdivision based on the nature of residence that entails three variants. *Physical residence* entitles one to administrative assistance for civil status documents (Article 25). A *lawful stay* on the territory of the asylum state is required for the right of association and to form trade unions (Article 15), access to wage-earning employment (Article 17), liberal professions (Article 19), housing (Article 21), and public relief (Article 23), protection of labour legislation and social security (Article 24), as well as issuance of travel documents (Article 28).[110] Finally, *habitual residence* grants refugees access to legal assistance (Article 16(2)) and the protection of artistic rights and industrial property (Article 14). As a result of this progressive entitlement regime, the Geneva Convention provides for an incremental continuum of protection that depends on the intensity of the territorial bond between a refugee and his/her state of asylum. In sum, the longer the refugee remains in the territory of the state party, the broader the range of entitlements becomes.

[109] For other possible classifications, see Carlier (n 52) at 271–98; Goodwin-Gill and McAdam (n 52) at 506–27; Hathaway (n 7) at 154–200.

[110] Although the English version of the Geneva Convention refers to 'stay', the term 'residence' is perhaps closer to the intention of the drafters, especially because this last one is retained in the French version by opposition to a simple sojourn. This is, however, a descriptive term which does not coincide with the legal meaning of residence under private international law.

Once these entitlement criteria are fulfilled, the precise content of applicable norms is determined on the basis of the traditional distinction between nationals and aliens, as, at the time of the Geneva Convention's drafting, no other normative frame of reference existed. The nature and scope of the benefits attached to refugee status are accordingly dependent upon three standards of treatment identified by reference to nationals of the asylum state, most favoured foreigners, and ordinary aliens. First, refugees benefit from the *same treatment accorded to nationals* regarding freedom of religion (Article 4), protection of artistic and industrial property (Article 14), rationing (Article 20), elementary education (Article 22(1)), public relief (Article 23), labour legislation and social security (Article 24), and fiscal charges (Article 29).

Second, refugees are assimilated to the *most favourable treatment accorded to nationals of a foreign country in the same circumstances* concerning their rights of association and to form trade unions (Article 15), as well as their access to wage-earning employment (Article 17). Third, the Convention recognizes refugees as deserving a *treatment not less favourable than that accorded to aliens generally in the same circumstances* as regards their acquisition of movable and immovable property (Article 13), their right to engage in self-employment (Article 18) and liberal professions (Article 19), their right and access to housing (Article 21), to education other than elementary education (Article 22(2)), and their freedom of movement within the asylum state (Article 26).

Albeit striking at first sight in a treaty aiming at defining an international status, the recurrent referral back to states parties' domestic law is both a major specificity of the Geneva Convention and the guarantor of its effectiveness. This comes as no surprise as national law provides a normative support which international law of the time was unable to secure in the absence of legally binding human rights. Accordingly, and contrary to conventional wisdom, there exist as many refugee statuses as states parties to the Geneva Convention, insofar as the content of the applicable standards to aliens and nationals is primarily determined by the legislation of each individual state.[111]

The legal regime deriving from the superposition of various entitlement criteria with different standards of treatment remains extremely complex. The rationale underlying such a patchwork of standards is anything but obvious and one can doubt the practical interest of this sophisticated differentiation. The difficulty in finding a cogent rationale in such a byzantine gradation is epitomized by the fact that both entitlement criteria and standards of treatment may differ even for rights of a similar nature (such as, for instance, those related to gainful employment).[112]

[111] Only an indefeasible hard core of standards remains out of the contingency of domestic law. It essentially includes the prohibition of discrimination, access to courts, and the principle of *non-refoulement*. The importance of these core obligations is further asserted by the prohibition of any reservations to the relevant provisions as laid down in Art. 42 of the Geneva Convention.

[112] A lawful stay is required for both wage-earning employment (Art. 17) and liberal profession (Art. 19), while self-employment activities only depend on a lawful presence (Art. 19). In any case, there is no causal relation between the entitlement criteria and the standards of treatment, for refugees are assimilated to most favoured aliens for the purpose of wage-earning employment, whereas

However, one possible way to conceptualize the *ratio legis* of the gradual protection granted by the Geneva Convention is to equate refugee status to an 'assimilative path'.[113] Devising refugee status as an assimilation process within the asylum state proves to be instrumental for two purposes. First, it elucidates and justifies the conditionality inherent in the heteroclite juxtaposition of entitlement criteria with standards of treatment. Second, the progressive entitlement of rights and benefits provides a coherent normative continuum which encapsulates and determines the applicable law at the three essential stages of the refugee's life cycle.

At the starting point of such an incremental protection regime, the declaratory nature of refugee status[114] presupposes that asylum seekers are entitled at a minimum to the core benefits applicable to all refugees without further territorial qualification as well as, depending on the circumstances, those which are contingent on the physical and lawful presence within the state territory. As underlined by the UNHCR, 'the gradations of treatment allowed by the Convention . . . serve as a useful yardstick in the context of defining reception standards for asylum-seekers'.[115] Seen from that angle, the limited range of benefits is grounded in the assumption that the presence of asylum seekers is bound to be a temporary one for the sole purpose of examining their claims.

At the second stage, once a refugee is formally recognized as such, the incremental continuum of rights and benefits will then facilitate his/her progressive integration in the new country of residence through the granting of an additional range of entitlements. At the end of this assimilative process, Article 34—the last provision devoted to refugee status—envisages as a promise of a common future that '[t]he Contracting States shall as far as possible facilitate the assimilation and naturalization of refugees'. In line with the incremental structure of the Geneva Convention, the acquisition of a new nationality will accordingly ensure the full range of rights to which any national is entitled and justify by the same token the end of the interim protection provided by the refugee status.

Albeit attractive, this conceptualization of refugee status as an assimilative process remains an a posteriori and essentially doctrinal reconstruction.[116] Although some support may be found in the drafting history of the Geneva Convention, the position of plenipotentiaries was neither clear nor unanimous.[117]

self-employment and liberal profession are determined by reference to the minimum treatment accorded to ordinary aliens. More generally, the already complicated structure of entitlements provided by the Geneva Convention has been exacerbated by the substantial number of reservations formulated by states parties.

113 Hathaway (n 7) at 156.

114 As acknowledged by the UNHCR Handbook (para. 38), '[a] person is a refugee within the meaning of the 1951 Convention as soon as he fulfils the criteria contained in the definition. This would necessarily occur prior to the time at which his refugee status is formally determined. Recognition of his refugee status does not therefore make him a refugee but declares him to be one. He does not become a refugee because of recognition, but is recognized because he is a refugee'. See also 2004 Qualification Directive, Recital 14.

115 *Reception of Asylum-Seekers, Including Standards of Treatment in the Context of Individual Asylum Systems*, Global Consultations on International Protection, 3rd meeting, EC/GC/17 (2001), para. 3.

116 See, also in this sense, Carlier (n 52) at 288–9.

117 See, especially, UN Doc E/AC/32/SR.15 (1950) and UN Doc E/AC.32/SR.42 (1950).

Besides the limited utility of the *travaux préparatoires*, subsequent practice is not in line with the assimilative approach, as states are reluctant to acknowledge the plain applicability of refugee status to asylum seekers beyond Articles 31 and 33.[118]

Beyond any possible conceptualization of the rationale underlying refugee status, the historical normative context prevailing at the time of the drafting of the Geneva Convention played a decisive role in framing the refugee rights regime. From such a retrospective perspective, refugee status has emerged as a hybrid legal creation: it is grounded in the very notion of minimum standards inherited from the traditional international law of aliens, while its ultimate objective is to secure the exercise of fundamental rights in line with the new branch of international human rights law. As underlined in its preamble, the *raison d'être* of the Geneva Convention is 'to assure refugees the widest possible exercise of . . . fundamental rights and freedoms'.

B. Refugee status and the UN International Covenant on Civil and Political Rights

The subsequent development of international human rights law has dramatically changed the normative content of refugee status. Compared to international refugee law, human rights law presents two essential characteristics: it is both inclusive and universal. This distinctive feature is based on the premise that human rights are by definition inherent in the quality of human being. Therefore, 'the enjoyment of Covenant rights is not limited to citizens of States Parties but must also be available to all individuals, regardless of nationality or statelessness, such as asylum seekers [and] refugees . . . who may find themselves in the territory or subject to the jurisdiction of the State Party'.[119] The added value of human rights law is obvious with regard to asylum seekers who have been excluded from the benefit of most of the provisions of the Geneva Convention through a restrictive and disputable interpretation. But the impact of human rights law goes far beyond the legal status of asylum seekers. It also retains its centrality for asserting the rights of refugees duly recognized as such under the Geneva Convention.

The UN International Covenant on Civil and Political Rights (ICCPR) proves to be essential for supplementing and reinforcing refugee status. Although the Geneva Convention is not indifferent to the civil and political rights of refugees, it contains a fairly limited range of these fundamental rights (including non-discrimination, freedom of religion, freedom of association, access to court, freedom of movement, and due process guarantees governing expulsion). From the outset, the drafters of the Geneva Convention were aware of this apparent lacuna. During the *travaux préparatoires*, the Belgian delegation proposed an explicit reference to Articles 18 and 19 of the UDHR (respectively devoted to freedoms of thought and of expression) in the text of the Geneva Convention. This proposal

[118] See, for instance, *R v. Secretary of State for the Home Departement, ex parte Jammeh* [1998] INLR 701 (CA), 710–1; *Krishnapillai v. Minister of Citizenship and Immigration* [2002] 3(1) FC 74, para. 25.

[119] HRCttee, *General Comment No. 31* (n 85) para. 10. See also *General Comment No. 15: The Position of Aliens under the Covenant*, UN Doc HRI/GEN/1/Rev.1 at 18 (1986), para. 2.

was finally withdrawn after the UK representative explained that 'a Convention relating to refugees could not include an outline of all the articles of the UDHR; furthermore, by its universal character, the Declaration applied to all human groups without exception, and it was pointless to specify that its provisions applied also to refugees'.[120]

The continuing applicability of human rights law has been instrumental in ensuring an additional set of crucial rights. The range of human rights supplementing the Geneva Convention is both expansive and substantial. As far as the ICCPR is concerned, it includes the right to an effective remedy for any violations of the rights recognized in the Covenant (Article 2(3)), the equal right of men and women to the enjoyment of all civil and political rights set forth in the Covenant (Article 3), the right to life (Article 6), the prohibition of torture and cruel, inhuman, or degrading treatment or punishment (Article 7), freedom from slavery and forced labour (Article 8), the right to liberty and security of person (Article 9), the right of detainees to be treated with humanity (Article 10), the prohibition of detention on the ground of inability to fulfil a contractual obligation (Article 11), the right to a fair trial (Article 14), the prohibition of retrospective application of criminal law (Article 15), the right to recognition as a person before the law (Article 16), the right to private and family life (Article 17), the right to hold opinions and freedom of expression (Article 19), the right of peaceful assembly (Article 21), the protection of children (Article 24), the right to equality before the law (Article 26), and the cultural rights of persons belonging to ethnic, religious, or linguistic minorities (Article 27).

This long list of fundamental rights and freedoms substantially enriches the paucity of civil and political rights in the Geneva Convention and proves to be particularly relevant in a refugee-specific context. While acknowledging the ICCPR as a 'critical source of rights for refugees',[121] Hathaway has, however, argued that:

> even where the subject matter of the Civil and Political Covenant is relevant to refugees, the Covenant often formulates rights on the basis of inappropriate assumptions. For example, the Civil and Political covenant sets guarantees of fairness in judicial proceedings, but does not deal with the more basic issue of access to a court system.[122]

This last example is not the most relevant one, for access to court is implicit in the right to a fair trial.[123] Besides this specific case, alleging that rights under the

[120] UN Doc E/AC.32/SR11 (1950), 8. [121] Hathaway (n 7) at 121.

[122] Hathaway (n 7) at 121. Among many other similar assertions, see also McAdam (n 6) at 203; Jastram (n 11) at 166–7.

[123] The Human Rights Committee has confirmed in line with the interpretation prevailing among other treaty bodies that 'Article 14 encompasses the right of access to the courts in cases of determination of criminal charges and rights and obligations in a suit at law.... The right of access to courts and tribunals and equality before them is not limited to citizens of States parties, but must also be available to all individuals, regardless of nationality or statelessness, or whatever their status, whether asylum-seekers, refugees, migrant workers, unaccompanied children or other persons, who may find themselves in the territory or subject to the jurisdiction of the State party'. *General Comment No. 32, Article 14: Right to equality before courts and tribunals and to a fair trial*, CCPR/C/GC/32 (2007), para. 9.

Covenant are based on inappropriate assumptions is arguably misconceived for two primary reasons.

First, the substance of the rights proclaimed in human rights instruments cannot be dissociated from their subsequent interpretation, which contributes to refining their scope and content in more specific contexts. Such a contextual interpretation of human rights has been essential for the purpose of ensuring to refugees two particularly critical rights—the right to family unity and the right to return—which, oddly, are not guaranteed by the Geneva Convention. As regards the right to family unity, the general obligation to protect the family under Article 23 of the ICCPR has been interpreted as including 'the adoption of appropriate measures... to ensure the unity or reunification of families, particularly when their members are separated for political, economic or similar reasons'.[124] A refusal of family reunification can also be considered an 'arbitrary or unlawful interference' with the right to family life under Article 17 of the ICCPR.

> [E]ven interference provided for by law should be in accordance with the provisions, aims and objectives of the Covenant and should be reasonable in the particular circumstances... [I]n cases where one part of a family must leave the territory of the State party while the other part would be entitled to remain, the relevant criteria for assessing whether or not the specific interference with family life can be objectively justified must be considered, on the one hand, in light of the significance of the State party's reasons for the removal of the person concerned and, on the other, the degree of hardship the family and its members would encounter as a consequence of such removal.[125]

Although states retain a broad margin of appreciation for assessing such a balancing act, denying family reunification to a refugee who has been duly recognized as such is clearly disproportionate to the alleged purpose, for, by definition, he cannot return to his own country and accordingly his family has no realistic prospects of enjoying the right to family life elsewhere.[126]

[124] HRCttee, *General Comment No. 19: Protection of the Family, the Right to Marriage and Equality of the Spouses (Art. 23)*, UN Doc HRI/GEN/1/Rev. 5 (1990), para. 5. The Committee has restated later that 'Article 23 of the Covenant guarantees the protection of family life including the interest in family reunification'. *Ngambi v. France*, CCPR/C/81/D/1179/2003 (2004), para. 6.4.

[125] HRCttee, *Byahuranga v. Denmark*, CCPR/C/82/D/1222/2003 (2004), para. 11.7 (this case, however, concerned a removal decision, reunification cases being rarely submitted to the Human Rights Committee).

[126] Such a conclusion is clearly in line with the predominant interpretation of the Human Rights Committee, although to the author's knowledge, it has not yet dealt with a refusal of family reunification by an asylum country. In a case concerning a Libyan refugee recognized in Switzerland, the Committee considered that the confiscation of passport and refusal of Libya to permit the departure of his wife and children constituted a violation of Art. 17 in so far as 'the State party's action amounted to a definitive, and sole, barrier to the family being reunited in Switzerland'. It further underlined that 'the author, as a person granted refugee status under the 1951 Convention, cannot reasonably be expected to return to his country of origin'. *El Dernawi v. Libyan Arab Jamahiriya*, CCPR/C/90/D/1143/2002 (2007), para. 6.3. In another particularly complex case concerning a person initially recognized as a refugee under the Geneva Convention (although the decision was later cancelled and was still under review at that time), the Committee concluded that the removal of his wife and children breached Art. 17: 'Taking into account the specific circumstances of the case, namely the number and age of the children..., the difficulties that Mrs Bakhtiyari and her children would face if returned to Pakistan without Mr Bakhtiyari and the absence of arguments by the State

The right to return also illustrates the normative potential offered by a contextual interpretation of human rights for filling the vacuum of the Geneva Convention. Such an essential right of refugees wishing to return to their countries of origin is based on the right to enter one's own country as notably enshrined in Article 12(4) of the Covenant. The Human Rights Committee hence underlines that 'the right of a person to enter his or her own country . . . includes . . . the right to return after having left one's own country' which 'is of the utmost importance for refugees seeking voluntary repatriation'.[127] While voluntary repatriation is commonly referred to as 'the ideal solution to refugee problems',[128] the human right to return proves to be crucial for ensuring both the voluntary nature of repatriation and the correlative obligation of states of origin to admit their nationals.[129]

Such contextual framing of the human right to enter one's own country has been further developed by the Committee on the Elimination of Racial Discrimination. Echoing the longstanding practice developed under the auspices of the UNCHR, the Committee on the Elimination of Racial Discrimination restates in its *General Recommendation No. 22* that:

> (a) All such refugees and displaced persons have the right freely to return to their homes of origin under conditions of safety;
>
> (b) States parties are obliged to ensure that the return of such refugees and displaced persons is voluntary and to observe the principle of *non-refoulement* and non-expulsion of refugees;
>
> (c) All such refugees and displaced persons have, after their return to their homes of origin, the right to have restored to them property of which they were deprived in the course of the conflict and to be compensated appropriately for any such property that cannot be restored to them. Any commitments or statements relating to such property made under duress are null and void;
>
> (d) All such refugees and displaced persons have, after their return to their homes of origin, the right to participate fully and equally in public affairs

party to justify removal in these circumstances, the Committee takes the view that removing Mrs Bakhtiyari and her children without awaiting the final determination of Mr Bakhtiyari's proceedings would constitute arbitrary interference in the family of the authors'. *Bakhtiyari v. Australia*, CCPR/C/79/D1069/2002 (2003), para. 9.6. One should nevertheless add that the proportionality test would probably be in favour of the state's interest when the whole family is able to live in a safe third country or when one of its members has been subjected to a final conviction for a serious criminal offence.

127 HRCttee, *General Comment No. 27: Freedom of Movement*, CCPR/C/21/Rev.1/Add.9 (1999), para. 19.

128 UN Doc A/RES/39/169 (1994). Since then, the General Assembly has constantly referred to voluntary repatriation as 'the preferred solution' by contrast to the other possible solutions provided by local integration or resettlement in a third country. See also among the numerous and somewhat repetitive Excom Conclusions: No. 109 (LXI)—2009, 16th preambular paragraph; No. 108 (LIX)—2008 (l); No. 104 (LVI)—2005, first preambular paragraph; No. 95 (LIV)—2003 (i); No. 90 (LII)—2001 (j); No. 87 (L)—1999 (r); No. 85 (XLIX)—1998 (g); No. 81 (XLVIII)—1997 (q); No. 79 (XLVII)—1996 (q).

129 For further discussion, see V. Chetail, 'Voluntary Repatriation in Public International Law: Concepts and Contents', 23 *RSQ* (2004) 1, with the bibliographical references mentioned therein.

at all levels and to have equal access to public services and to receive rehabilitation assistance.[130]

Accordingly, human rights law provides an indispensable yardstick for framing the legal content of return and reintegration of both refugees and internally displaced persons in their own countries. Although much remains to be done to ensure their basic rights in peace-building processes,[131] the predominant contextual approach of human rights has been further refined through *The Principles on Housing and Property Restitution for Refugees and Displaced Persons*, endorsed by the UN Sub-Commission on the Promotion and Protection of Human Rights in 2005.[132]

A second reason also contradicts the alleged inappropriateness of the Covenant for tackling refugee-specific contexts. Besides granting additional rights to refugees and asylum seekers, general human rights instruments prove to be more adequate and more protective even when the rights in question are already covered by the Geneva Convention. The minimum standards prescribed by refugee status have been increased—and in some instances superseded—by human rights law. The plain relevance of this last branch of international law is apparent in many common subjects of concern, such as freedom of movement, expulsion, and detention, insofar as the general provisions of the Geneva Convention have been refined by subsequent human rights instruments.[133]

The most promising avenue for enhancing refugee protection through human rights law relies on the principle of non-discrimination. The non-discrimination clause contained in Article 3 of the Geneva Convention is limited by three substantial qualifications. First, this provision only prohibits discrimination between and among refugees, thereby excluding any other discrimination between refugees and aliens or nationals. Second, the prohibited grounds of discrimination are restricted to 'race, religion or country of origin'. Third, the scope of Article 3 is limited to the application of the provisions of the Geneva Convention. By contrast, the principle of non-discrimination under human rights law is much more inclusive, insofar as state parties are bound to guarantee the exercise of the rights recognized in the relevant instruments 'without distinction of any kind, such as race, colour, sex, language, religion, political or other opinion, national or social origin, property, birth or other status'.[134]

130 CERD, *General Recommendation No. 22: Article 5 and Refugees and Displaced Persons*, UN Doc A/51/18 (1996).

131 See generally V. Tennant, 'Return and Reintegration', in V. Chetail (ed.), *Post-Conflict Peacebuilding: A Lexicon* (2009) 307, and the special issue on Displacement, Peace Processes and Post-Conflict Peacebuilding in 28 *RSQ* (2009).

132 UN Doc E/CN.4/Sub.2/2005/17 (2005). The Pinheiro Principles elaborate key human rights relating to the equitable restitution of housing and property and provide guidelines to states and international actors for ensuring access to these rights. One should recall in this regard that, contrary to the UDHR and the Geneva Convention, the two UN Covenants do not contain an explicit provision on the right to property because of the diverging conceptions prevailing at the time of the Cold War. However this difference between human rights law and refugee law remains marginal. As will be shown later, the equal protection before the law under Art. 26 of the ICCPR prohibits discrimination in access to property rights. Moreover, all regional human rights instruments guarantee the right to property.

133 See III.A, this chapter.

134 Art. 2(1) ICCPR.

Moreover, the principle of equality before the law as notably enshrined in Article 26 of the ICCPR provides a free-standing autonomous protection against discrimination which is not limited to the rights provided for in the ICCPR.[135] Likewise, the reference to 'national origin' and 'other status' among the non-exhaustive list of prohibited discriminatory grounds presumably includes both discrimination between refugees as such and other discriminatory treatments between refugees and nationals. Article 3 of the Geneva Convention has thus largely—if not totally—been neutralized by Article 26 of the Covenant.[136]

Obviously, this general prohibition of discrimination does not mean that any difference of treatment should be banned. The Human Rights Committee has recalled in line with all the other treaty bodies that 'not every differentiation of treatment will constitute discrimination, if the criteria for such differentiation are reasonable and objective and if the aim is to achieve a purpose which is legitimate under the Covenant'.[137] This requires a subtle case-by-case assessment for determining the proportionality of the differential treatment with the alleged purpose. For instance, requiring citizenship for property restitution of refugees[138] has been considered as discrimination prohibited under the Covenant.

The overarching duty of non-discrimination under Article 26 of the ICCPR has two further significant consequences which enhance to a great extent the protection under the Geneva Convention. On the one hand, the principle of equality before the law may require states parties to take affirmative action in favour of refugees for the purpose of guaranteeing them an effective and equal enjoyment of human rights.[139] On the other hand, the general applicability of human rights to non-citizens coupled with the prohibition of discrimination based on nationality substantially erode the traditional distinction between nationals and aliens which conditions most of the benefits attached to refugee status. In other words, human rights law cogently requires the assimilation to nationals even for rights which are determined by reference to the treatment accorded to aliens under the Geneva Convention.[140]

A typical illustration can be found in the freedom of association. While Article 15 of the Geneva Convention only requires 'the most favourable treatment

135 HRCttee, *General Comment No. 18: Non-discrimination*, UN Doc HRI/GEN/1/Rev.6, at 146 (1989), para. 12.

136 See *contra* Hathaway (n 7) at 258–9.

137 HRCttee, *General Comment No. 18* (n 135) para. 13. Among other similar statements, see CESCR, *General Comment No. 20, Non-Discrimination in Economic, Social and Cultural Rights (art. 2, para. 2)*, UN Doc E/C.12/GC/20 (2009), para. 13; CERD, *General Recommendation No. 30: Discrimination against Non Citizens*, CERD/C/64/Misc. 11/rev.3 (2004), para. 4.

138 *Kríž v. Czech Republic*, CCPR/C/85/D/1054/2002 (2005), para. 7.3.

139 '[T]he principle of equality sometimes requires States parties to take affirmative action in order to diminish or eliminate conditions which cause or help to perpetuate discrimination prohibited by the Covenant'. HRCttee, *General Comment No. 18* (n 135) para. 10. See also Arts. 1(4) and 2(2) of the International Convention on the Elimination of All Forms of Racial Discrimination and CERD, *General Recommendation No. 32: The Meaning and Scope of Special Measures in the International Convention on the Elimination of Racial Discrimination*, CERD/C/GC/32 (2009).

140 One should add that, even for rights assimilated to those of nationals, human rights law ensures that such treatment cannot be below the minimum assigned by human rights treaties.

accorded to nationals of a foreign country, in the same circumstances', freedom of association is granted by the ICCPR to 'everyone' and is therefore equally applicable to nationals and aliens.[141] Furthermore, this fundamental freedom applies to any kind of association and not only 'non-political and non-profit-making associations' as referred to in the Refugee Convention.[142] Nevertheless, as acknowledged by Article 20 of the Covenant, any propaganda for war and any advocacy of national, racial, or religious hatred that constitutes incitement to discrimination, hostility, or violence shall be prohibited by law. Hence, asylum states must ban a refugee organization that incites violence and any other national, racial, or religious hatred, whether such propaganda or advocacy is directed towards these states or their states of origin.[143] By contrast, refugee organizations campaigning for the right of peoples to self-determination or for any other democratic changes in their countries of origin are permitted under Article 22 of the Covenant.

III. The Implementation Scheme of Refugee Law and Human Rights Law: The Ultimate Test

The implementation scheme is another way to comprehend the relations between refugee law and human rights law. This shows more contrast in this field than in any other. Refugee law traditionally distinguishes between the content of international protection as enshrined in the Geneva Convention and an essentially decentralized implementation entrusted to each individual state party. This decentralization scheme is based on two levels of implementation. First, at the domestic level, states retain a particularly broad margin of appreciation in the means of implementing refugee law, since very few procedural guarantees are imposed to them by the Geneva Convention (III.A, this chapter). Second, at the international level, this decentralized regime is reinforced by the absence of a proper monitoring mechanism (III.B, this chapter).

These two distinctive features of refugee law have, however, been considerably counterbalanced and sometimes neutralized by human rights law. This leverage is primarily due to the control-oriented nature of human rights law. States are not

[141] HRCttee, *General Comment No. 15* (n 119) para. 7: 'Aliens receive the benefit of the right of peaceful assembly and of freedom of association . . . there shall be no discrimination between aliens and citizens in the applications of these rights'.

[142] Some regional instruments have adopted a more restrictive—though rarely applied—stance with regard to the political activity of aliens: Art. 16 ECHR and Art. 24 Arab Charter. However, states parties to both the Covenant and one of these regional instruments are bound to apply the most favourable treatment enshrined in the Covenant.

[143] At the regional level, the African Charter specifically prohibits 'any individual enjoying the right of asylum' from engaging in 'subversive activities' (Art. 23(2)). See also Art. 3(1) of the OAU Convention. As any exception to a right (ie, freedoms of expression, of association and of peaceful assembly), the very notion of 'subversive activities' must be interpreted restrictively and must not impair the essence of the rights in question. In any case, the prohibition of subversive activities has to be compatible with the lawful restrictions provided in the other relevant provisions (Arts. 8 to 11 of the African Charter).

only bound by procedural guarantees to ensure effective respect for human rights within their domestic orders, but the concrete implementation of their conventional obligations is also monitored by international bodies especially established for this purpose.

A. The implementation of international refugee law and international human rights law at the domestic level

Refugee law and human rights law reveal two opposite conceptions of their respective implementation schemes. Notwithstanding their divergence, human rights law has been instrumental in encapsulating and conditioning the implementation of the Geneva Convention at the domestic level. It has greatly detailed and refined the comparative paucity of the latter instrument by spelling out procedural guarantees on three decisive issues: the refugee status determination procedure (III.A.1), the detention of asylum seekers (III.A.2), and the expulsion process (III.A.3).

1. The refugee status determination procedure and the right to an effective remedy

Following the traditional international law perspective, the Geneva Convention draws a clear-cut distinction between the *international norms* enshrined therein and their *national implementation* entrusted to each individual state party. While both the refugee definition and status are internationally grounded, the functional link between these two components is constituted by domestic procedures for the very purpose of identifying who is entitled to refugee status. States accordingly recapture, at the implementation level, a portion of the sovereignty they have given up at the normative level, by agreeing to a relatively detailed regime. Domestic asylum procedures thus appear as privileged tools for determining the concrete extent of the obligations subscribed to under the Geneva Convention.

As a result of this premise, the Geneva Convention does not formally require a refugee status determination procedure nor explicitly regulate its content and functioning. However, both in principle and in practice, the refugee definition presupposes some kind of identification process, although no specific procedure is explicitly mentioned in the Geneva Convention.[144] Otherwise, states would be bound to apply the refugee status to all persons claiming to be refugees. This implicit duty is also confirmed by several other provisions, such as Articles 9 and 31(2).[145] It is further

[144] For a similar account see notably F. Crépeau, *Droit d'asile. De l'hospitalité aux contrôles migratoires* (1995), 123; P. Hyndman, 'The 1951 Convention and Its Implications for Procedural Questions', 6 *IJRL* (1994) 246; R. Marx, 'Non-Refoulement, Access to Procedures, and Responsibility for Determining Refugee Claims', 7 *IJRL* (1995) 401. See however Hathaway (n 7) at 180–1.

[145] Art. 9 allows states to take provisional measures in times of war and other exceptional circumstances 'pending a determination by the Contracting State that that person is in fact a refugee'. Art. 31(2) governing restrictions to the movements of refugees also mentions that 'such restrictions shall only be applied until their status in the country is regularized . . . ', presupposing thus a refugee status determination procedure.

required by the effective implementation of the principle of *non-refoulement* under Article 33. Nevertheless the exact content and modalities of these procedures is supposed to be determined by each contracting state with due regard to its own constitutional and administrative structure.[146]

Despite this considerable margin of appreciation, Article 16(1) of the Geneva Convention retains its relevance, for it ensures free access to courts in particularly inclusive and unconditional terms. The broad material scope of this provision presumably includes access to asylum courts for reviewing any refusals of refugee status.[147] This is confirmed by the personal scope of Article 16(1), for the term 'refugee' without any further qualification is plainly apt to include asylum seekers as a result of the declaratory nature of refugee status recognition.[148] Despite the clear and compulsory meaning of the Geneva Convention, states parties have nonetheless remained astonishingly inconsistent in their interpretation of Article 16(1).

This can possibly be mitigated by the right to a fair trial notably enshrined in Article 14(1) ICCPR. As is apparent from the wording of this provision, its applicability is conditional on the criminal or civil nature of the rights involved in the relevant proceedings. Such a requirement is, however, plainly in line with the very nature of the rights at stake in an asylum procedure. Indeed, the refugee status determination procedure inherently aims at determining the civil rights of the claimant, for its sole purpose is to establish whether an asylum-seeker is entitled to refugee status, which precisely includes a relatively broad range of civil rights and social benefits.[149] While considering that the right to a fair trial does not apply to 'extradition, expulsion and deportation procedures',[150] the Human Rights Committee has tended to presume its applicability to asylum procedures.[151] Its position is nevertheless far from crystal clear. It even gives the impression of deliberately avoiding settling this issue by generating a certain level of confusion between asylum and deportation proceedings.[152] Although the former may have an impact on the latter, they remain in fact as well as in law two distinct procedures. However, this is precisely the confusion between the two types of procedure which led the

[146] In practice, Western states have established sophisticated national procedures for determining who is a refugee. But the identification process may take other forms. States parties to the Geneva Convention—including those from the global south—may delegate such a task to the UNHCR and/or resort to *prima facie* basis group determination of refugee status notably in cases of massive influx.

[147] For a similar interpretation, see Hathaway (n 7) at 645; Carlier (n 52) at 320.

[148] See, in this sense, *R v. Secretary of State for the Home Departement, ex parte Jahangeer et al.* [1993] Imm AR 564, per Jowitt J., 566. See *contra*, *Krishnapillai v. Minister of Citizenship and Immigration* (2002) 3(1) FC 74, paras 31–32, per Décary JA.

[149] See, in this sense, Hathaway (n 7) at 649; S. Persaud, *Protecting Refugees and Asylum Seekers under the International Covenant on Civil and Political Rights* (2006), 15.

[150] HRCttee, *General Comment No. 32, Article 14: Right to Equality Before Courts and Tribunals and to a Fair Trial*, CCPR/C/GC/32 (2007), para. 17.

[151] *Adu v. Canada*, CCPR/C/60/D/654/1995 (1997), para. 6.3. In this case, the Committee implicitly admitted the applicability of the right to a fair trial in a refugee status determination procedure by assessing the fairness of the asylum procedure. See also *Dranichnikov v. Australia*, CCPR/C/88/D/1291/2004 (2006), paras 6.7–7.2.

[152] A typical illustration of such confusion may be found in *Kaur v. Canada*, CCPR/C/94/D/1455/2006 (2007), paras 7.4–7.5.

European Court of Human Rights to deduce that none of them is covered by the right to a fair trial.[153]

Whatever the controversies surrounding the applicability of the right to fair trial to asylum procedures, the right to an effective review offers a solid avenue for ensuring procedural guarantees to asylum seekers. As restated by the Human Rights Committee, 'Article 2, paragraph 3, requires that . . . individuals . . . have *accessible, effective and enforceable remedies* to vindicate those rights'.[154] Nevertheless, 'article 2 can only be invoked by individuals in conjunction with other articles of the Covenant'.[155] As a result of this requirement, although the right of asylum is not set forth in the ICCPR, other provisions triggering the prohibition of *refoulement* can be invoked in connection with the right to an effective remedy.[156] Asylum seekers must thus be entitled to challenge their removals to any country where there is a real risk of violation of their rights under the Covenant.

From this angle, the substantial overlap between the principle of *non-refoulement* under refugee law and human rights law has a critical impact by compensating for the absence of procedural guarantees in the Geneva Convention. Moreover, except for the ECHR, all the other regional instruments explicitly endorse the right to seek asylum, which must accordingly be exercised with due respect to the right to an effective remedy.[157]

The right to an effective remedy, combined with the human rights principle of *non-refoulement* and/or the right to seek asylum, ensures three main guarantees. First, non-respect of procedural requirements—such as the late submission of an asylum request—cannot be an obstacle to the examination of the merits of the claim by national authorities.[158] The European Court of Human Rights has underlined that:

> It should be borne in mind in this regard that in applications for recognition of refugee status it may be difficult, if not impossible, for the person concerned to supply evidence within a short time, especially if . . . such evidence must be obtained from the country from which he or she claims to have fled. Accordingly, time-limits should not be so short, or applied so inflexibly, as to deny an applicant for recognition of refugee status a realistic opportunity to prove his or her claim.[159]

153 According to the Grand Chamber, 'decisions regarding the entry, stay and deportation of aliens do not concern the determination of an applicant's civil rights or obligations or of a criminal charge against him, within the meaning of Article 6 § 1 of the Convention'. *Maaouia v. France*, ECHR (2000) Reports 2000-X, para. 40. The Court then transposed its conclusion *mutatis mutandis* to asylum procedures. *Çiçek v. Netherlands*, ECHR (2001) Appl. No. 49866/99, para. 2; *IN v. Sweden*, ECHR (2009) Appl. No. 1334/09, para. 40.

154 HRCttee, *Kazantzis v. Cyprus*, CCPR/C/78/D/972/2001 (2003), para. 6.6 (emphasis added).

155 HRCttee, *Kazantzis v. Cyprus* (n 154) para. 6.6.

156 See, for instance, *Maksudov and others v. Kyrgyzstan*, CCPR/C/93/D/1461, 1462, 1476, and 1477/2006 (2008), para. 12.7; *Al Zery v. Sweden*, CCPR/C/88/D/1416/2005 (2006), para. 11.8.

157 See Arts. 22(7) and 25(1) American Convention, Arts. 7(1)(a) and 12(3) African Charter, as well as Arts. 23 and 28 Arab Charter.

158 See, in particular, *Jabari v. Turkey*, ECHR (2000) Reports 2000-VIII, paras 40 and 49. In this case, the European Court held that the refusal of an asylum request on the sole ground that it was not submitted within five days after the arrival of the asylum-seeker is a violation of the right to an effective remedy.

159 *Bahaddar v. The Netherlands*, ECHR (1998) Reports 1998-I, para. 45.

Second, the right to an effective remedy 'requires independent and rigorous scrutiny'[160] of the claim that substantial grounds exist to fear a real risk of inhuman or degrading treatment. As restated by the European Court, 'such scrutiny need not be provided by a judicial authority but, if it is not, the powers and guarantees which it affords are relevant in determining whether the remedy before it is effective'.[161] To be considered an effective remedy, the relevant domestic authority must have two essential characteristics. It must be empowered to take a binding decision and grant appropriate relief, excluding thus any form of consultative procedure.[162] Moreover, the domestic authority must offer sufficient procedural safeguards for ensuring its independence and basic rights of the claimant, including equality of arms and legal representation.[163]

Third, the effective nature of the domestic remedy requires that any removal must be suspended during the examination of the claim: 'in view of... the irreversible nature of the damage which may result if the risk of torture or ill-treatment materialises,... Article 13 requires that the person concerned should have access to a remedy with automatic suspensive effect'.[164] In any case, the risks of overloading and abuse of process frequently alleged by states do not exempt them from their duty to provide an effective remedy against any refusals of asylum requests.[165]

2. *The procedural guarantees governing the detention of asylum seekers*

As exemplified earlier, human rights law plays a crucial role by filling the procedural gap of the Geneva Convention. These guarantees are further strengthened when asylum seekers are deprived of their liberty during the asylum procedure or pending their removal. Article 31(2) of the Geneva Convention addresses this issue in general and arguably vague terms. While permitting states to apply some restrictions to the movement of asylum seekers, any restrictions must fulfil two conditions: they must be 'necessary and such restrictions shall only be applied until their status in the country is regularized or they obtain admission into another country'. Considerable detail has been added to these general guidelines by human rights law regarding the grounds of detention, its legal basis, and other related procedural guarantees.

The grounds of detention have been refined by human rights law through the prohibition of arbitrary detention notably restated in Article 9 of the ICCPR. The Human Rights Committee has recalled in the leading case *A. v. Australia* that

> the notion of 'arbitrariness' must not be equated with 'against the law' but be interpreted more broadly to include such elements as inappropriateness and injustice. Furthermore,

160 *Jabari v. Turkey* (n 158) para. 50.

161 *Chahal v. The United Kingdom* (n 92) para. 152.

162 *Chahal v. The United Kingdom* (n 92) paras 145 and 154.

163 *Chahal v. The United Kingdom* (n 92) paras 145 and 154.

164 *Gebremedhin v. France*, ECHR (2007) Appl. No. 25389/05, para. 66. See also *Conka v. Belgium*, ECHR (2002) Reports 2002-I, paras 81–85; *Jabari v. Turkey* (n 158) para. 50.

165 *Conka v. Belgium*, ECHR (2002) (n 164) para. 84.

remand in custody could be considered arbitrary if it is not necessary in all the circumstances of the case, for example to prevent flight or interference with evidence: the element of proportionality becomes relevant in this context.[166]

While considering that the detention of asylum seekers is not arbitrary per se, it observed that

every decision to keep a person in detention should be open to review periodically so that the grounds justifying the detention can be assessed. In any event, detention should not continue beyond the period for which the State can provide appropriate justification. For example, the fact of illegal entry may indicate a need for investigation and there may be other factors particular to the individuals, such as the likelihood of absconding and lack of cooperation, which may justify detention for a period. Without such factors detention may be considered arbitrary, even if entry was illegal.[167]

In sum, detaining individuals requesting asylum cannot be systematic or mandatory but must be duly justified on the basis of the particular circumstances of each case, assessing the likelihood of absconding and lack of cooperation. These grounds should persist during the whole period of detention, otherwise the deprivation of liberty is no longer justified.

The principle of proportionality further requires that states examine whether there are other measures they could use to achieve their objectives without interfering with the right to liberty and security. As underlined by the Human Rights Committee, states must demonstrate that

in the light of the author's particular circumstances, there were not less invasive means of achieving the same ends, that is to say, compliance with the State party's immigration policies, by, for example, the imposition of reporting obligations, sureties or other conditions which would take account of the author's . . . condition.[168]

Moreover, any detention must be in accordance with and authorized by law. This last requirement has been authoritatively illuminated by the European Court of Human Rights in the landmark case *Amuur v. France*. As restated by the Court, the legal basis in domestic law must be not only predictable and precise, but it must also be applied with due respect to other applicable norms of international law, including the Geneva Convention:

[C]onfinement, accompanied by suitable safeguards for the persons concerned, is acceptable only in order to enable States to prevent unlawful immigration while complying with their

166 HRCttee, *A v. Australia*, CCPR/C/59/D/560/1993 (1997), para. 9.2. For similar statements at the regional level, see *Gangaram Panday Case*, IACtHR (1994) Series C, No. 16, para. 47; *Organisation Mondiale Contre La Torture v. Rwanda*, ACHPR (1996) Comm. Nos. 27/89, 46/91, 49/91, 99/93; *Annette Pagnoulle (on behalf of Abdoulaye Mazou) v. Cameroon*, ACHPR (1997) Comm. No. 39/90. See however *Saadi v. United Kingdom*, ECHR (2008) Appl. No. 13229/03, para. 45.

167 HRCttee, *A v. Australia* (n 166) para. 9.4.

168 HRCttee, *C. v. Australia* (2002), CCPR/C/76/D/900/1999, para. 8.2. For similar restatements, see *D. and E. v. Australia*, CCPR/C/87/D/1050/2002 (2006), para. 7.2; *Baban v. Australia*, CCPR/C/78/D/1014/2001 (2003), para. 7.2.

> international obligations, particularly under the 1951 Geneva Convention Relating to the Status of Refugees and the European Convention on Human Rights. States' legitimate concern to foil the increasingly frequent attempts to circumvent immigration restrictions must not deprive asylum-seekers of the protection afforded by these conventions... In that connection account should be taken of the fact that the measure is applicable not to those who have committed criminal offences but to aliens who, often fearing for their lives, have fled from their own country... Above all, such confinement must not deprive the asylum-seeker of *the right to gain effective access to the procedure for determining refugee status.*[169]

This last assertion may surprise, for the European Court is not formally empowered to review the application of the Geneva Convention and the European Convention on Human Rights does not explicitly enshrine such a right to effective access to the refugee status determination procedure. However, for the purpose of assessing the arbitrariness of the detention, the Court is entitled to consider compliance with national law, including international norms incorporated into domestic law. Moreover, although not explicitly mentioned in the Geneva Convention, effective access to the refugee status determination procedure is implicitly required by a good faith implementation of the Geneva Convention and in particular of its cornerstone principle of *non-refoulement*. Such acknowledgement by the European Court reflects the mutually supportive nature of human rights law and refugee law through a contextualised interpretation by treaty bodies. The Strasbourg Court even adds that the right to gain effective access to the asylum procedure presupposes adequate 'legal and social assistance—particularly with a view to completing the formalities relating to an application for political refugee status'.[170]

In parallel to the implicit duties deriving from the Geneva Convention, human rights instruments provide two other essential procedural guarantees to any person deprived of their liberty. First, 'anyone who is arrested shall be informed, at the time of arrest, of the reasons for his arrest and shall be promptly informed of any charges against him'.[171] Whilst the content and promptness of this information is to be assessed according to the particular circumstances of each case,[172] notifying the reasons after 76 hours in detention has been held not to be compatible with the requirement that such reasons be given 'promptly'.[173] Moreover, the reasons for the detention must be given 'in simple, non-technical language that he can understand' and they must specify both 'the essential legal and factual grounds for his arrest, so as to be able, if he sees fit, to apply to a court to challenge its lawfulness'.[174]

Second, as restated by all human rights treaties, 'anyone who is deprived of his liberty by arrest or detention shall be entitled to take proceedings before a court, in order that that court may decide without delay on the lawfulness of his detention

[169] *Amuur v. France*, ECHR (1996) Reports 1996-III, at para. 43 (emphasis added).

[170] *Amuur v. France* (n 169) at para. 45.

[171] Art. 9(2) ICCPR. See also Art. 7(4) American Convention; Art. 5(2) ECHR; Art. 14(3) Arab Charter.

[172] *Conka v. Belgium* (n 164) para. 50.

[173] *Saadi v. The United Kingdom* (n 166) para. 84.

[174] *Conka v. Belgium* (n 164) para. 50.

and order his release if the detention is not lawful'.[175] Here again treaty body practice has refined and specified the guarantees inherent in such a right to judicial review. As notably underlined by the European Court, 'the person concerned should have access to a court and the opportunity to be heard either in person or through some form of representation'.[176] Although states parties may impose time limits on the applications of detainees for exercising their right to a judicial review, the brevity of such time limits should not impair the accessibility and the effectiveness of the judicial remedy.[177] For instance, a 24-hour period for submitting an application before a court is not compatible with the right to judicial review.[178] Regarding the prompt intervention of the court for reviewing the lawfulness of the detention, the Court considered that six days for delivering a judicial decision was acceptable,[179] whereas a delay of thirty-six days was held to be excessive.[180]

Besides access to court, the scope and content of the judicial review has been spelled out in similar terms by the Human Rights Committee and the European Court of Human Rights. The domestic review must be effective and the lawfulness of the detention should take into account both domestic law and the applicable international instrument.[181] Among the other procedural safeguards, legal representation represents 'an important guarantee' especially when 'the detainee is, by definition, a foreigner in the country in question and therefore often unfamiliar with its legal system'.[182] More generally, conditions of detention must ensure that 'all persons deprived of their liberty shall be treated with humanity and with respect for the inherent dignity of the human person'.[183] While such a provision is restated in all human rights treaties with the exception of the ECHR, similar protection can be offered through the general prohibition of torture, inhuman, and degrading treatment.

For instance, among its abundant case law devoted to the conditions of detention of asylum seekers in Greece, the European Court has held that 'a period of

[175] Art. 9(4) ICCPR; Art. 7(6) American Convention; Art. 5(4) ECHR; Art. 7(1) African Charter; Art. 14(6) Arab Charter.

[176] *Al-Nashif v. Bulgaria*, ECHR (2002) Appl. No. 50963/99, para. 92. See also *Sanchez-Reisse v. Switzerland*, ECHR (1986) Appl. No. 9862/82, para 51.

[177] *Farmakopoulos v. Belgium*, EComHR (1990) Appl. No. 11683/85, para. 51.

[178] *Farmakopoulos v. Belgium* (n 177) para. 53.

[179] *Muskhadzhiyeva and others v. Belgium*, ECHR (2010) Appl. No. 41442/07, para. 83.

[180] *Sanchez-Reisse v. Switzerland* (n 176) para. 60.

[181] 'In the Committee's opinion, court review of the lawfulness of detention under article 9, paragraph 4... is not limited to mere compliance of the detention with domestic law. While domestic legal systems may institute differing methods for ensuring court review of administrative detention, what is decisive for the purposes of article 9, paragraph 4, is that *such review is, in its effects, real and not merely formal.* By stipulating that the court must have the power to order release "if the detention is not lawful", article 9, paragraph 4, requires that the court be empowered to order release, if the detention is incompatible with the requirements in article 9, paragraph 1, or in other provisions of the Covenant'. HRCttee, *A. v. Australia* (n 166) para. 9.5 (emphasis added). With regard to the European Court, see especially *Chahal v. The United Kingdom* (n 92) para. 127 *Dougoz v. Greece*, ECHR (2001) Reports 2001-II, at para. 55, para. 61.

[182] *Sanchez-Reisse v. Switzerland* (n 176) para. 47. See also HRCttee, *A. v. Australia* (n 166) para. 9.6; *Chahal v. The United Kingdom* (n 92) para. 130; *Mohammed Zamir v. United Kingdom*, EComHR (1983) Appl. No. 9174/80, para. 113.

[183] Art. 10(1) ICCPR.

detention of six days, in a confined space, with no possibility of taking a walk, no leisure area, sleeping on dirty mattresses and with no free access to a toilet is unacceptable with respect to Article 3'.[184] A similar conclusion has been drawn with regard to the detention of asylum seekers in a Belgian transit zone[185] and a Turkish police headquarters.[186] Likewise, detaining an unaccompanied five-year-old child in a transit centre for adults 'demonstrated a lack of humanity to such a degree that it amounted to inhuman treatment'.[187] The European Court came to the same conclusion with regard to the detention of four children with their mother during more than one month despite serious signs of psychological distress.[188] It recalled on this occasion that, according to Article 22 of the UN Convention on the Rights of the Child, 'States Parties shall take appropriate measures to ensure that a child who is seeking refugee status . . . shall, whether unaccompanied or accompanied by his or her parents or by any other person, receive appropriate protection and humanitarian assistance'.[189]

3. The procedural guarantees governing expulsion

The intermingling of international refugee law and human rights law is further reinforced by the procedural guarantees governing expulsion. In contrast to the absence of provisions on the refugee status determination procedure, Article 32 of the Geneva Convention spells out in a relatively detailed manner the conditions governing expulsion. It has been restated almost verbatim by Article 13 ICCPR.[190] The convergence between international refugee law and human rights law in the field of expulsion comes as no surprise, for Article 32 was inspired by an early draft of the Covenant which was then remodelled on the basis of the Geneva Convention.[191] However, Article 32 appears more specific than Article 13 on three main issues.

First, the grounds of expulsion are explicitly mentioned in the Geneva Convention, whereas the ICCPR contains no similar specification. This difference is nevertheless negligible, because national security and public order are relatively broad notions capable of encapsulating a great diversity of situations and they constitute the traditional grounds of expulsion in domestic law and practice. From this angle, the expression 'in accordance with law' as interpreted by the Human Rights Committee means that 'Article 13 requires compliance with both the substantive and the procedural requirements of the law'.[192] Thus, although 'the interpretation of domestic law is essentially a matter for the courts and authorities of the State

184 *S.D. v. Greece*, ECHR (2009) Appl. No. 53541/07, para. 51.

185 *Riad and Idiab v. Belgium*, ECHR (2008) Appl. No. 29787/03 and 29810/03, paras 106–110.

186 *Abdolkhani and Karimnia v. Turkey*, ECHR (2010) Appl. No. 50213/08, para. 31.

187 *Mayeka and Mitunga v. Belgium*, ECHR (2006) Appl. No. 13178/03, para. 58.

188 *Muskhadzhiyeva and others v. Belgium*, ECHR (2010) Appl. No. 41442/07, paras 60–63.

189 *Muskhadzhiyeva and others v. Belgium* (n 188) para. 62. See also, with regard to Art. 24 ICCPR, HRCttee, *Bakhtiyari v. Australia* (2003) (n 126) para. 9.7.

190 See also, with regard to regional human rights treaties, Art. 1 Protocol No. 7 to the ECHR; Art. 22(6) American Convention; Art. 12(5) African Charter; Art. 26(2) Arab Charter.

191 See, respectively, UN Doc E/AC.32/5 (1950), para. 60; UN Doc E/2256 (1952), para. 199.

192 HRCttee, *Maroufidou v. Sweden*, CCPR/C/OP/1 (1981), para. 9.3.

party concerned', the Human Rights Committee is bound to review the grounds of expulsion when 'they have not interpreted and applied it in good faith or that it is evident that there has been an abuse of power'.[193]

Second, the Geneva Convention explicitly enshrines a right to appeal against any expulsion decision, whereas the ICCPR only refers to the right to have the 'case reviewed by . . . the competent authority'. This difference is, however, largely neutralized by the right to an effective remedy under Article 2(3) of the ICCPR. Indeed, this provision can be invoked in connection with Article 13 and, accordingly, ensures that any expulsion order must be reviewed by an independent authority with all the guarantees inherent in the effectiveness of such remedy. The Human Rights Committee has further confirmed in its *General Comment 15: The Position of Aliens under the Covenant* that '[a]n alien must be given full facilities for pursuing his remedy against expulsion so that this right will in all the circumstances of his case be an effective one'.[194]

Third, Article 32(3) of the Geneva Convention specifically requires that, before carrying out the expulsion order, states parties shall allow a reasonable period within which refugees can seek legal admission into another country. Here again, although this last indication is not explicitly mentioned in the ICCPR, the subsequent interpretation of Article 13 has contributed to neutralizing the difference from the Geneva Convention. Indeed, the Human Rights Committee has considered that '[n]ormally an alien who is expelled must be allowed to leave for any country that agrees to take him'.[195] In *V. M. R. B. v. Canada*, it accordingly dismissed any risk to the life of an asylum-seeker in the case that he would be deported to his country of origin, after observing that 'the Government of Canada has publicly stated on several occasions that it would not [deport] the author to El Salvador and has given him the opportunity to select a safe third country'.[196]

In the absence of a safe third country, refugees and asylum seekers can be subjected to restrictions of movement. In such a case, Article 12 of the ICCPR and Article 26 of the Geneva Convention governing internal freedom of movement coincide in substance. However, the freedom granted by the Geneva Convention is 'subject to any regulations applicable to aliens generally' without any further qualifications, whereas the ICCPR is more specific by delimiting permissible restrictions to freedom of movement. According to its Article 12(3), any restrictions

[193] HRCttee, *Maroufidou v. Sweden* (n 192) para. 10.1. See also: HRCttee, *Hammel v. Madagascar*, CCPR/C/29/D/155/1983 (1987), para. 19.3; *Giry v. Dominican* Republic, CCPR/C/39/D/193/1985 (1985), para. 5.5.

[194] HRCttee, *General Comment No. 15* (n 119) para. 10. Curiously enough, the Committee does not explicitly refer to Art. 2(3) for deducing the right to an effective remedy. It even considers that the right to appeal is implicit in Art. 13 after stating that '*the principles of article 13 relating to appeal against expulsion* and the entitlement to review by a competent authority may only be departed from when "compelling reasons of national security" so require'. HRCttee, *General Comment No. 15* (n 119) para. 10 (emphasis added). In *Ahani v. Canada*, it stressed in the same vein that 'article 13 . . . incorporates notions of due process also reflected in article 14 of the Covenant'. HRCttee, *Ahani v. Canada*, CCPR/80/D/1051/2002 (2004), para. 10.9.

[195] HRCttee, *General Comment No. 15* (n 119) para. 9.

[196] HRCttee, *V.M.R.B. v. Canada*, CCPR/C/333/D/236/1987 (1988), para. 6.3.

of movement are only permissible when the three following conditions are duly fulfilled by the state: restrictions must have a legal basis; they must be necessary to protect national security, public order, public health, morals, or the rights and freedoms of others; and they must be consistent with the other rights recognized in the Covenant.[197]

While the added value of the Geneva Convention has been largely neutralized by the subsequent interpretation of the ICCPR, the latter instrument offers more comprehensive protection in both personal and material scope. Its personal scope not only includes refugees, but also asylum seekers and any other persons in need of protection. Provisions in both the Geneva Convention and the ICCPR nevertheless subordinate their applicability to those who are 'lawfully' within the territory of the state concerned. The Human Rights Committee has underlined, on this last requirement:

> The particular rights of article 13 only protect those aliens who are lawfully in the territory of a State party. This means that national law concerning the requirements for entry and stay must be taken into account in determining the scope of that protection, and that illegal entrants and aliens who have stayed longer than the law or their permits allow, in particular, are not covered by its provisions. However, *if the legality of an alien's entry or stay is in dispute, any decision on this point leading to his expulsion or deportation ought to be taken in accordance with article 13*.[198]

Although the Human Rights Committee has not yet had the opportunity to further clarify this last assertion, it may have a substantial impact on the refugee status determination procedure. Indeed, it presupposes that asylum procedures must conform to the guarantees spelled out in Article 13 as soon as eligibility to refugee status conditions the lawful presence of an asylum-seeker and the refusal of refugee status leads to his/her removal.[199]

Whatever the uncertainties surrounding the applicability of Article 13 to asylum procedures, another substantial and less controversial added value of human rights law lies in the prohibition of collective expulsion. Although not explicitly mentioned in the ICCPR, the Human Rights Committee considers that this prohibition is implicit in Article 13, because 'it entitles each alien to a decision in his own case and, hence, article 13 would not be satisfied with laws or decisions providing for collective or mass expulsions'.[200] Moreover, the prohibition of collective expulsion has been explicitly acknowledged in all regional human rights treaties.[201]

[197] See also HRCttee, *General Comment No. 27* (n 127) paras 14 and 18; *Karker v. France*, CCPR/C/70/D/833/1998 (2000), para. 9.2; *Celepli v. Sweden*, CCPR/C/51/D/456/1991 (1993).

[198] HRCttee, *General Comment No. 15* (n 119) para. 9 (emphasis added).

[199] See also, in this sense: 'That article is applicable to all procedures aimed at the obligatory departure of an alien, whether described in national law as expulsion or otherwise'. HRCttee, *General Comment No. 15* (n 119) para. 9.

[200] HRCttee, *General Comment No. 15* (n 119) para. 10. Although a similar interpretation could be argued with regard to Art. 32 of the Geneva Convention, it still lacks official endorsement in state practice.

[201] Art. 22(9) American Convention, Art. 12(5) African Charter, Art. 4 Protocol No. 4 of ECHR; Art. 26(b) Arab Charter.

In each of these instruments, it is conceived as an absolute prohibition without any possible exceptions. The main difficulty, however, lies in the definition of the term 'collective expulsion'. The African Charter on Human and People's Rights (African Charter) is the only treaty which attempts to define it. According to its Article 12 (5), 'mass expulsion shall be that which is aimed at national, racial, ethnic or religious groups'. It accordingly requires two cumulative conditions regarding the purpose of the expulsion and the characteristics of the group concerned which, taken together, reveal its discriminatory nature.

The European Court of Human Rights privileges a more empirical definition based on the decision-making process, which requires an individual examination of the particular situation of each alien.[202] In the *Andric* case, the deportation of Bosnian and Croatian asylum seekers was not considered a collective expulsion, because their asylum requests were examined on an individual basis by administrative and judicial authorities. The prohibition of collective expulsion thus has a considerable impact on the refugee status determination procedure, by requiring a case-by-case assessment of each asylum application.

The European Court further added in *Conka v. Belgium* that, even when asylum claims have been individually examined by the competent authorities, the implementation conditions of the expulsion orders must also afford 'sufficient guarantees demonstrating that the personal circumstances of each of those concerned had been genuinely and individually taken into account'.[203] In sum, the individual situation of every asylum seeker must be assessed at each stage of the process: during the refugee status determination procedure, and then, following a refusal of asylum request, when the expulsion decision is ordered and carried out.

B. The supervisory mechanism under international refugee law and international human rights law

As demonstrated, procedural guarantees granted by human rights law at the domestic level prove to be vital to compensate the lacunae of the Geneva Convention. In the meantime, the contextual and dynamic interpretation of treaty bodies has been so instrumental that the two branches of international law are now intimately interdependent. Both in principle and in practice, human rights law and refugee law are bound to work in tandem.

The primary reason for this cross-fertilization process can be found in the very existence of the human rights treaty bodies. They have played a decisive role in the propagation of human rights law within refugee law. Obviously this does not mean

[202] '[C]ollective expulsion is to be understood as any measure compelling aliens, as a group, to leave a country, except where such a measure is taken on the basis of a reasonable and objective examination of the particular case of each individual alien of the group. Moreover, the fact that a number of aliens receive similar decisions does not lead to the conclusion that there is a collective expulsion when each person concerned has been given the opportunity to put arguments against his expulsion to the competent authorities on an individual basis'. *Andric v. Sweden*, ECHR (1999) Appl. No. 45917/99, para. 1.

[203] *Conka v. Belgium* (n 164) para. 63.

that there is a hierarchical relation between the two branches, since each regime retains its conventional autonomy. Human rights treaty bodies have constantly reiterated that 'it is not [their] function to examine asylum claims or to monitor the performance of Contracting States with regard to their observance of their obligations under the Geneva Convention on Refugees'.[204] However, from the perspective of the content of their respective norms, the border between the two regimes has been steadily blurred. Both in substance and essence, treaty bodies have—whether consciously or not—counterbalanced the normative and institutional weaknesses of the Geneva Convention.

1. Nature and limits of the supervisory mechanism under the Geneva Convention

Compared to human rights law, the supervision mechanism provided by the Refugee Convention is rather traditional and rudimentary. This is fairly apparent from the final clause on settlement of disputes, which envisages the International Court of Justice (ICJ) as the primary means for settling disputes regarding the Convention.[205] The insertion of such a clause arguably 'corresponds to a trend of the time, which still focused essentially on States as subjects of international law even if the obligations at stake concerned primarily individuals'.[206] One should add, however, that several human rights treaties contain a similar provision.[207] Furthermore, every state party to the Geneva Convention is entitled to refer any violation to the ICJ, even if it is not specifically affected by particular damage.[208] This *actio popularis* highlights in turn a key common characteristic of the very nature of the Geneva Convention and human rights treaties. Both kinds of instruments enshrine *erga omnes partes* obligations, that is, those which all states parties have an interest to protect.[209]

Similar to human rights treaties, the Geneva Convention does not create purely interstate obligations concluded on a contractual basis. It establishes instead a collective regime of objective obligations in favour of a particular category of individuals who are threatened in their life and liberty. The peculiar legal nature of the Geneva Convention was acknowledged from the outset. Already during its

[204] *T.I. v. United Kingdom* (n 98); *M.S.S. v. Belgium and Greece* (n 87) para. 286.

[205] Art. 38 Geneva Convention and Art. IV of the 1967 Protocol.

[206] K. Oellers-Frahm, 'Article 38 of the 1951 Convention/Article IV of the 1967 Protocol', in A. Zimmermann (ed.), *The 1951 Convention Relating to the Status of Refugees and its 1967 Protocol. A Commentary* (2011) 1550.

[207] Art. 22 of the International Convention on the Elimination of All Forms of Racial Discrimination; Art. 29 of the 1979 Convention on the Elimination of All Forms of Discrimination Against Women; Art. 30 of the Convention Against Torture; Art. 42 of the International Convention for the Protection of All Persons from Enforced Disappearance.

[208] W. Kälin, 'Supervising the 1951 Convention Relating to the Status of Refugees: Article 35 and Beyond', in Feller, Türk, and Nicholson (n 52) 632. See also C. Tams, *Enforcing Obligations Erga Omnes in International Law* (2005), at 75.

[209] Although they may overlap, *erga omnes partes* obligations are by definition limited to the states parties to a particular treaty and must be distinguished from the broader notion of *erga omnes* obligations enshrined in general international law towards the international community as a whole.

drafting history, state representatives agreed that 'the text of the Convention was not a treaty under which the Contracting States assumed certain obligations in exchange for certain advantages; it was rather a form of solemn declaration made in order to benefit a third party'.[210] This statement echoes the *obiter dictum* of the ICJ made a few months before with regard to the Genocide Convention. It explained in emphatic terms that can be transposed *mutatis mutandis* to the Geneva Convention that

> [t]he Convention was manifestly adopted for a purely humanitarian and civilizing purpose. It is indeed difficult to imagine a convention that might have this dual character to a greater degree, since its object on the one hand is to safeguard the very existence of certain human groups and on the other to confirm and endorse the most elementary principles of morality. In such a convention the contracting States do not have any interests of their own; they merely have, one and all, a common interest, namely, the accomplishment of those high purposes which are the *raison d'être* of the Convention. Consequently, in a convention of this type one cannot speak of individual advantages or disadvantages to States, or of the maintenance of a perfect contractual balance between rights and duties. The high ideals which inspired the Convention provide, by virtue of the common will of the parties, the foundation and measure of all its provisions.[211]

In parallel to their common underlying philosophy, the Geneva Convention and other related human rights instruments are thus grounded on the very notion of collective interests, which transcends the traditional principle of reciprocity. However, the similarity of their normative pattern should not be overestimated, for *erga omnes partes* obligations are not peculiar to human rights treaties. They may be found in other multilateral treaties, such as those related to environmental law or diplomatic relations, to mention but a few instances.

Moreover, while the *erga omnes* nature of these kinds of treaties clearly informs their application and interpretation, experience has shown that referral to the ICJ remains the exception rather than the rule. It, accordingly, offers a limited avenue for defending collective interests. In practice, Article 38 has never been invoked by states parties to the Geneva Convention, thus highlighting the limits inherent in such interstate means of dispute settlement for ensuring the effective protection of individuals.

As a compromise to this state-centred mechanism of implementation, UNHCR has been conceived of as the guardian of the Geneva Convention. Article 35(1) of the Geneva Convention requires states parties to 'cooperate with the Office of the United Nations High Commissioner for Refugees... in the exercise of its functions, and [shall] in particular facilitate its duty of supervising the application of the provisions of the Convention'.[212] Although the duty of cooperation is a rather

210 UN Doc A/CONF.2/SR.19 (1951).

211 *Reservations to the Convention on the Prevention of and Punishment of the Crime of Genocide, Advisory Opinion*, ICJ Reports (1951), 23.

212 The same conventional obligation is laid down in Art. II(1) of the 1967 Protocol and restated in several other instruments, such as in the Preamble to the 1957 Agreement relating to Refugee Seamen, Art. 8 of the OAU Convention, recommendation (e) of the Cartagena Declaration and Art. 21 of the EU Asylum Procedures Directive.

vague and indefinite notion, it establishes a crucial link between the state's obligation to respect the Geneva Convention and the correlative institutional responsibility of UNHCR for supervising its proper application.[213]

As a concrete tool for ensuring its supervisory function, Article 35(2) further requires states parties to 'provide in the appropriate form with information and statistical data requested concerning: (a) the conditions of refugees, (b) the implementation of this Convention, and (c) laws, regulations and decrees which are, or may hereafter be, in force relating to refugees'. This reporting duty is curiously not accompanied by a proper monitoring mechanism for examining periodical reports of states parties on the implementation of the Geneva Convention.[214] In this area as in many others, the Geneva Convention probably paid the price for being the forerunner of the subsequent human rights treaties. As observed by Zieck, 'whilst innovative at the time, Art. 35, para. 1, in particular the supervisory role of UNHCR, appears to suffer the drawbacks of being one of the first external supervisory mechanisms in that it is of a rather rudimentary nature... when compared to the supervisory mechanisms of human rights treaties'.[215] Seen from this perspective, the absence of an independent supervisory mechanism for monitoring the implementation of the Geneva Convention is clearly 'an historical anomaly'.[216]

There is, however, nothing irremediable nor insurmountable in this situation. The dual obligation enshrined in Article 35 to cooperate with UNHCR and provide relevant information on the implementation of the Geneva Convention constitutes an adequate legal basis to establish a reporting and evaluation procedure. More generally, the very notion of international supervision includes by definition an enforcement component for the purpose of monitoring state compliance and asserting violations.[217] However, the primary responsibility entrusted to UNHCR in this field has been denatured to nothing more than an advisory rather than a truly supervisory function.

While the Refugee Agency plays a key role by providing interpretative guidance on the Geneva Convention and encouraging a harmonized application of its provisions by states parties,[218] enforcement-related activities still remain the weakest

[213] 'The primary purpose of Article 35(1) of the 1951 Convention and Article II(1) of the 1967 Protocol is thus to link the duty of States Parties to apply the Convention and the Protocol with UNHCR's task of supervising their application by imposing a treaty obligation on States Parties (i) to respect UNHCR's supervisory power and not to hinder UNHCR in carrying out this task, and (ii) to cooperate actively with UNHCR in this regard in order to achieve an optimal implementation and harmonized application of all provisions of the Convention and its Protocol'. Kälin (n 208) at 617. See also V. Türk, 'UNHCR's Supervisory Responsibility', 14 *RQDI* (2001) 135.

[214] Information gathering from states parties is carried out by UNHCR on an informal and confidential basis. Kälin (n 208) at 624–5.

[215] M. Zieck, 'Article 35 of the 1951 Convention/Article II of the 1967 Protocol', in A. Zimmermann (ed.), *The 1951 Convention Relating to the Status of Refugees and its 1967 Protocol. A Commentary* (2011), 1508.

[216] Hathaway (n 7) at 995.

[217] T. Chowdhury, *Legal Framework of International Supervision* (1986), at 181, quoted in Türk (n 213) 146.

[218] V. Türk, 'The Role of UNHCR in the Development of International Refugee Law', in Nicholson and Twomey (n 8) 153; C. Lewis, 'UNHCR's Contribution to the Development of International Refugee Law: Its Foundations and Evolution', 17 *IJRL* (2005) 67.

side of its mandate. Its inability to assume the monitoring tasks inherent in its supervisory responsibility is commonly attributed to two interrelated reasons.[219] First, UNHCR is both politically and financially dependent on states. It is governed by an intergovernmental body—the Executive Committee of the High Commissioner's program (ExCom)—and is therefore 'not even nominally independent of the political will of states'.[220] Its dependence is further exacerbated by the fact that the UNHCR budget is primarily funded by voluntary contributions of states. Second, the enlargement of its initial mandate by the General Assembly has dramatically transformed the very nature of UNHCR. It is becoming the most prominent UN operational agency for delivering humanitarian relief on the ground. While its 'operationality'[221] represents a unique characteristic compared with other human rights agencies, the effectiveness of such assistance programmes requires a close cooperation with states, impeding thus a more critical stance towards them to the detriment of its supervisory responsibility. The schizophrenic position of UNHCR has contributed in turn to the isolation of refugee law from the other branches of international law.

2. The palliative function of human rights treaty bodies

The lack of an independent mechanism for monitoring the Geneva Convention sharply contrasts with the control-oriented paradigm of human rights law. Both universal and regional human rights treaties are supported by their own treaty bodies specifically mandated to monitor state compliance with their conventional obligations. Within the UN, most treaty bodies are entrusted with three core functions: the promotion of interpretative standards (through the adoption of general comments), the processing of interstate and individual petitions on alleged violations, and the examination of states parties' periodic reports. As abundantly exemplified by this chapter, the two first functions have played a critical role in ensuring the protection of refugees and asylum seekers through a contextual interpretation of general human rights treaties. The vital importance of treaty bodies can be further asserted by the fact that between 80 and 90 per cent of all individual complaints submitted to the Committee against Torture are based on Article 3.[222]

[219] See Hathaway (n 7) at 995–8; Kälin (n 208) at 627–8 and 633–4; Türk (n 213) at 153; T. Glover and S. Russell, *Coordination with UNHCR and States* (2001); S. Takahashi, *Effective Monitoring of the Refugee Convention* (2001).

[220] Takahashi (n 219) at 3.

[221] Türk (n 213) at 138.

[222] Chetail, 'Le Comité des Nations Unies contre la torture' (n 5) at 65–6; M. Nowak and E. McArthur, *The United Nations Convention Against Torture: A Commentary* (2008), at 159. For a general overview of the role of treaty bodies in refugee protection, see C. Beyani, 'The Role of Human Rights Bodies in Protecting Refugees', in A. F. Bayefsky (ed.), *Human Rights and Refugees, Internally Displaced Persons and Migrant Workers. Essays in Memory of Joan Fitzpatrick and Arthur Helton* (2006) 270; N. Poynder, '"Mind the Gap": Seeking Alternative Protection under the Convention against Torture and the International Covenant on Civil and Political Rights', in Kneebone (n 8) 173; S. Takahashi, 'Recourse to Human Rights Treaty Bodies for Monitoring of the Refugee Convention', 20 *NQHR* (2002) 53; O. Andrysek, 'Gaps in International Protection and the Potential for Redress through Individual Complaints Procedures', 9 *IJRL* (1997) 392.

Beyond giving rejected asylum seekers a chance to submit their claims of *non-refoulement* to a supranational organ, examination of state reports provides a unique opportunity to assess states' human rights records towards refugees and asylum seekers.[223] Among the most recurrent issues, treaty bodies have notably addressed the principle of non-discrimination,[224] the specific needs of children and women refugees,[225] as well as adequate standard of living,[226] and integration of long-term refugees.[227] Further reinforcing the interface between refugee law and human rights law, they also frequently call on states to ratify the Geneva Convention[228] and to cooperate more closely with UNHCR.[229] While human rights treaty bodies are not a panacea,[230] they contribute within their own mandates to filling the institutional deficit of the Geneva Convention.

UNHCR's position towards these newcomers has gradually evolved from a reluctant stance to a more collaborative—albeit selective—approach. This is fairly apparent from its policy paper on *UNHCR and Human Rights* adopted in 1997 where the office states:

> Extreme caution traditionally marked UNHCR's approach to any suggestion that it should cooperate and collaborate with established mechanisms for the promotion and protection of general human RIGHTS principles... Motivating this approach was the fear that greater activism would lead to politicisation of UNHCR activities which would compromise our capacity to work with our government counterparts. Over recent years, however, this 'hands off' approach has given way to a policy of more constructive engagement with selected human rights bodies... The approach now is increasingly one of cooperation based on complementarity but respect for and maintenance of differences in mandates and approaches.[231]

[223] For a comprehensive account of the UN treaty bodies' activities in this field until 2000, see Gorlick (n 7) at 147–75.

[224] See, for instance, CERD, *Concluding Observations: Congo*, CERD/C/COG/CO/9 (2009), para. 18; *Nepal*, CERD/C/64/CO/5 (2004), par. 19; *Japan*, CERD/C/304/Add.114 (2001), para. 19; *Denmark*, CERD/C/60/CO/5 (2002), para. 17; CESCR, *Concluding Observations: Nepal*, E/C.12/1/Add.66 (2001), paras 29 and 54.

[225] Concerning refugee children, see, for instance, CRC, *Concluding Observations: Armenia*, CRC/C/15/Add.119 (2000), para. 47; *Central African Republic*, CRC/C/15/Add.138 (2000), para. 6; *Portugal*, CRC/C/15/Add.162 (2001), paras 46–47; *Niger*, CRC/C/15/Add. 179 (2002), para. 60; *Indonesia*, CRC/C/15/Add.223 (2004), para. 65; *Nigeria*, CRC/C/NGA/CO/3–4 (2010), para. 73. See also regarding women refugees: CEDAW, *Concluding Comments: Malawi*, CEDAW/C/MWI/CO/5 (2006), paras 35–36; *India*, CEDAW/C/IND/CO/3 (2007), paras 50–51; *Lebanon*, CEDAW/C/LBN/CO/3 (2008), para. 40.

[226] See, notably, CERD, *Concluding Observations: Bangladesh*, CERD/C/304/Add.118 (2001), para. 12; CRC, *Concluding Observations: Georgia*, CRC/C/GEO/CO/3 (2008), para. 58.

[227] See, among others, CERD, *Concluding Observations: Iceland*, CERD/C/304/Add.111 (2001), para. 10; *Zambia*, CERD/C/ZMB/CO/16 (2005), para. 14.

[228] CESCR, *Concluding Observations: Nepal*, CESCR E/2002/22 (2001) para. 30; CRC, *Concluding Observations: Lebanon*, CRC/C/SR.751–2 (2002), para. 53; CERD, *Concluding Observations: India*, CERD/C/IND/CO/19 (2007), para. 16; CAT, *Conclusions and Recommendations: Uzbekistan*, CAT/C/UZB/CO/3 (2008), para. 24.

[229] CERD, *Nepal* (n 224) para. 19; CAT, *Uzbekistan* (n 228) para. 24; CAT, *Conclusions and Recommendations: Costa Rica*, CAT/C/CRI/CO/2 (2008), para. 9.

[230] Beside the non-binding nature of their observations, treaty bodies are victims of their own success, with increased petitions concerning removal decisions to the extent that the few resources at their disposal are not adequate for addressing their caseload. Moreover, many state reports are overdue.

[231] UNHCR, *UNHCR and Human Rights* (1997), at 1.

However, asserting the 'complementarity but difference between the refugee specific mandate of UNHCR and the broader human rights mandates of other concerned organs and institutions'[232] simply appears as another—albeit more subtle—way to insist on the distinctive nature of the two protection regimes. The ExCom steadily reaffirms in this sense that

> [t]he need to maintain the mutually supportive but separate character of respective mandates is particularly clear in the area of monitoring. While human rights monitoring missions must investigate and encourage prosecution of human rights violations, action in support of refugees and returnees is essentially humanitarian, involving confidence-building and creation of conditions conducive to peace and reconciliation.[233]

To many observers, maintaining the two distinctive protection regimes appears ineluctable for preserving the vital operational function carried out by UNHCR on the ground. Hence, despite the growing normative convergence between the two bodies of international law, monitoring and enforcement-related measures represent the core—and perhaps irreducible—difference between refugee law and human rights law.

The prevailing dichotomy between their respective implementation schemes may nevertheless be largely attenuated provided that all the stakeholders are willing to do so. This would require the concerted adoption of a complementary set of practical measures at three distinct levels. First, at the UNHCR level, periodical examination of states' reports on the implementation of the Geneva Convention could be undertaken either by UNHCR within its ExCom or by an independent body of experts appointed by the High Commissioner.[234] Each alternative has its own merits and limits. On the one hand, the former option would be a peer-review process more easily acceptable to states but its intergovernmental nature presents obvious risks of politicization and confrontations. On the other hand, the latter option would present the advantage of being an independent and objective assessment and it would preserve UNHCR from being involved in any conflict of interests. For these reasons, establishing an independent monitoring process is both more credible and more appropriate.

Second, at the Human Rights Council level, a Special Rapporteur on the human rights of refugees and asylum seekers should be established with a view to promoting better awareness and application of the human rights norms applicable to these particularly vulnerable groups. Undoubtedly, a new special procedure cannot be considered an antidote to the absence of a monitoring process of the Geneva Convention. It would nevertheless considerably enrich and strengthen the current

[232] ExCom, *Note on International Protection*, UN Doc A/AC.96/989 (1998), para. 47.

[233] ExCom, *Note on International Protection* (n 232) para. 47. This cautious and arguably conservative tone was reiterated in 2003. Although acknowledging that 'the refugee experience, in all its stages, is affected by the degree of respect by States for human rights and fundamental freedoms', the ExCom simply took note of 'the possible role of the United Nations human rights mechanisms in this area' and 'suggest[ed] that these bodies may, in turn, wish to reflect, within their mandates, on the human rights dimensions of forced displacement'. ExCom, *General Conclusion on International Protection*, No. 95(LIV) (1993), para. (l).

[234] For further discussion, see A. Hurwitz, *The Collective Responsibility of States to Protect Refugees* (2009), at 275–81; Kälin (n 208) at 657–61; Türk (n 213) at 154–8.

UN institutional framework for dealing with basic rights of refugees and other persons in need of protection. It would also ensure by the same token a more holistic approach within the Human Rights Council in complementing the work carried out by the Special Rapporteur on the human rights of migrants established in 1999 and the Special Rapporteur on the human rights of internally displaced persons created in 1992.

Third, at the treaty body level, a more cogent and comprehensive approach could be further reinforced within the bodies' own mandates. With this aim in mind, each treaty body should adopt a general comment specifically devoted to the rights of refugees and asylum seekers under their respective treaties. While the Committee on the Elimination of Racial Discrimination (CERD) has already adopted a comment on the right to return, this exercise should be undertaken in a more systematic way by all the nine UN treaty bodies so as to clarify the scope and the content of the relevant human rights instruments.

These three proposals would not only ensure a more consistent approach between the two protection regimes, they would also improve to a large extent due respect for refugee rights.

IV. Conclusion

The interaction between human rights law and refugee law is extremely dense. As a result of a gradual normative process, they have become so intimately interdependent and imbricated that it is now virtually impossible to separate one from the other. Notwithstanding this impressive convergence, the conceptualization of their interrelation still diametrically diverges when seen from the standpoints of different observers. In the refugee lawyers' community, human rights law is generally understood as a safety net, a secondary source for supplementing the primary one (that is, the Geneva Convention). On the contrary, for others, the terms of this relation should be reversed: the accessory is the principal. As argued by Schabas, '[a]lthough this is known as "complementary protection", the human rights regime governing non-refoulement has largely taken over that of the Refugee Convention, which is gradually becoming virtually superfluous'.[235] This kind of assertion is not confined to the principle of *non-refoulement*, but it also concerns refugee status as such. Indeed, several commentators have asserted that '[h]uman rights conventions... eclipse whole sections of the U.N. Refugee Convention concerning the treatment of refugees, even in areas of equal levels of treatments'.[236] Following this last stance, but in slightly less categorical terms, 'a more appropriate way of expressing this relationship is to say that the provisions of international human rights law are more extensive than the specific tenets of refugee law, but the latter is really in essence a subset of the former'.[237]

[235] Schabas (n 94) at 23. [236] Wachenfeld and Christensen (n 105) at 183.

[237] T. Maluwa, 'Human Rights and Refugees in Southern Africa: Some Perspectives on Recent Legislative Developments in Malawi', 53 *ZaöRV* (1993) 88, at 92. Helton acknowledged in the same

One could be tempted to say that each conception is right. On the one hand, a closer examination of their respective norms clearly demonstrates that human rights law has become the primary source of refugee protection. The Geneva Convention has been accordingly relegated to a supporting role. Treaty bodies have been instrumental in developing a contextual interpretation of general human rights norms, which—intentionally or not—counterbalances restrictive interpretations carried out by individual states parties to the Geneva Convention in the absence of a proper monitoring mechanism.

Furthermore, this phenomenon of appropriation is structurally grounded on the distinctive characteristics of human rights law regarding both its personal and material scope. Its personal scope is obviously broader, since it includes not only refugees but also asylum seekers and any other persons in need of protection. On the contrary, the Geneva Convention is essentially applicable to recognized refugees, whereas asylum seekers have been consciously excluded from its scope (except for a few elementary provisions, such as penal immunity and the principle of *non-refoulement*). The centrality of human rights law is further reinforced by its material scope, for it sets out a wide range of rights which are not covered by the Geneva Convention. This concerns an extensive number of civil, political and cultural rights for refugees and, under rare exceptions, all human rights of asylum seekers.

By contrast, extremely few rights remain exclusively governed by the Geneva Convention. This primarily concerns very technical and specific matters, such as equality in fiscal charges (Article 29) and transfer of assets (Article 30). One could still argue that, from a conceptual and normative perspective, these two provisions are practical derivatives of the general principle of equality before the law and of the broader human right to property. The same reasoning can be applied with regard to identity papers (Article 27) and travel documents (Article 28), which are frequently heralded as the distinctive advantages of refugee status. Although these two provisions do not have exact human rights equivalents, delivering identity papers to refugees can be considered as a positive obligation deriving from the right to recognition everywhere as a person before the law.[238] The same contextual interpretation of the right to leave any country should further include the granting of travel documents to refugees who have no other possibility to obtain such documents from their country of origin.[239] In fact, the only truly specific right granted by the Geneva Convention concerns penal immunity under Article 31(1). However, as

vein that '[h]uman rights law thus serve refugees, asylum seekers, and displaced persons in way that refugee... law cannot, by providing them with broad principles upon which to establish an entitlement to protection'. A. C. Helton, 'The Role of Refugee, Humanitarian and Human Rights Law in Planning for the Repatriation of Kampuchean Asylum Seekers in Thailand', 3 *IJRL* (1991) 546, at 559.

[238] Art. 16 ICCPR; Art. 8 Convention on the Rights of the Child; Art. 3 American Convention; Art. 22 Arab Charter.

[239] Art. 12(2) ICCPR; Art. 5(d)(ii) International Convention on the Elimination of All Forms of Racial Discrimination; Art. 10(2) Convention on the Rights of the Child; Art. 22(2) American Convention; Art. 2(2) Protocol No. 4 to the ECHR; Art. 12(2) African Charter; Art. 27(1) Arab Charter.

already noted, the scope of this provision is circumscribed by three substantial limitations and it does not prohibit the administrative detention of undocumented asylum seekers. In any event, the human rights principle of *non-refoulement* does apply to everyone whether he/she enters legally or otherwise the territory of a state. In sum, compared to human rights law, the Geneva Convention has much more to receive than to give.

On the other hand, one could nevertheless argue that, despite its marginal added value, the Geneva Convention still remains a primary source of protection, not only because it is considered as such by states but, more fundamentally, because human rights law has considerably refined, reinforced, and sustained its normative frame. As noted above, refugee status is primarily structured by the traditional distinction between citizens and non-citizens. In the absence of any other normative frame of reference, the content of the applicable standards was supposed—initially at least—to be determined by the domestic law of each state party. Against such a background, human rights law has given a second life to the Geneva Convention by internationalizing its frame of reference. It provides a vital baseline for determining the minimum standard which domestic legislation cannot go beyond without breaching international human rights law.

The cumulative application of the two branches of international law reinforces the international refugee protection regime through a mutually supportive process of normative sedimentation. As a result of such intermingling, refugee law is now indissociable from human rights law, each branch of international law being part of the same normative continuum. Following such a stance, one can even argue further that refugee law has been absorbed by human rights law. While the Geneva Convention retains some symbolic relevance, the distinction between nationals and aliens which conditions the very content of refugee status has been largely marginalized and superseded by the general applicability of human rights to non-citizens.

The transformation of refugee law by human rights law has far-reaching effects largely beyond the content of its norms. The gravitational force of human rights law has attracted the Geneva Convention into its orbit and anchored it as a satellite within the constellation of other applicable human rights treaties. As a result of this centripetal force, the conception of the Geneva Convention as a whole has been revisited and reframed through the lens of human rights law. The single and evasive reference to human rights in its preamble has been retrospectively viewed as the ultimate evidence of its human rights origin. The Geneva Convention has thus been reconstructed as a human rights treaty in its own right. This is rather ironic, given that the Refugee Convention is not a human rights treaty per se simply because it is a duty-driven—and not a human rights-based—instrument. Clearly perception counts more than reality. In a normative environment largely dominated by human rights, all observers are now convinced of the human rights nature of the Geneva Convention. Both in principle and in practice, human rights law has thus become the new orthodoxy of refugee law.

From a systemic perspective, human rights law considerably informs the very function of refugee law. It appears as 'a remedial or palliative branch of human rights law'.[240] Its *raison d'être* is to ensure effective respect for human rights, when victims of abuses have no other option than to leave their own country and ask for the substitute protection of another state. From this stance, refugee law cogently constitutes 'a right to have rights' following Arendt's terminology.[241] Echoing the most prominent philosopher of the last century, Lord Clyde acknowledges:

> [w]hat [the Geneva Convention] seeks to achieve is the preservation of those rights and freedoms for individuals where they are denied them in their own state. Another state is to provide a surrogate protection where protection is not available in the home state. The convention assumes that every state has the obligation to protect its own nationals. But it recognises that circumstances may occur where that protection may be inadequate. The purpose of the convention is to secure that a refugee may in the surrogate state enjoy the rights and freedoms to which all are entitled without discrimination and which he cannot enjoy in his own state.[242]

Although the reverse has not always been true, human rights law *is* refugee law. One question still remains to be addressed: does the ubiquitous stance of state sovereignty in refugee law affect its human rights nature? Undoubtedly, state sovereignty is more visible in refugee law than in many other fields of international law. Territorial sovereignty is both the foundation and the limit of international refugee law. On the one hand, refugees are protected against persecution from their own countries, as a consequence of the territorial jurisdiction of asylum states. The duty of every state to respect the territorial integrity of others means that countries of origin can no longer exercise any act of authority upon their nationals who found asylum abroad. On the other hand, asylum states do not have the correlative obligation to grant protection within their own territory. However, such a normative dilemma is not specific to refugee law, since human rights law is framed by the same dialectic. Under both branches of international law, the sovereign right of granting or refusing asylum is mitigated and sometimes neutralized by the obligation of *non-refoulement*. In short, while state sovereignty influences the content of the applicable norms, its does not fundamentally affect the very nature of refugee law.

More generally, as recalled by Lord Bingham, 'like most international conventions, [the Geneva Convention] represented a compromise between competing interests, in this case between the need to ensure humane treatment of the victims of oppression on the one hand and the wish of sovereign states to maintain control over those seeking entry to their territory on the other'.[243] This existential compromise does not radically diverge from other branches of international law. Humanitarian law is grounded on a precarious balance between military necessity

240 Hathaway (n 7) at 5. 241 H. Arendt, *The Origins of Totalitarianism* (1958), at 296–7.

242 *Horvath v. Secretary of State for the Home Department* (2001) (n 4) at 508.

243 *R v. Immigration Officer at Prague Airport and another ex parte Roma Rights Centre and others* (n 61) para. 15 (Lord Bingham of Cornhill).

and considerations of humanity, while human rights law encapsulates national security concerns within the delimitation of individual entitlements.[244]

Twenty years ago, Aleinikoff reminded us that 'refugee lawyers must be human rights lawyers'.[245] Refugee lawyers are clearly on the right path and they have made substantial steps forward during the last decades. But there are still some obstacles to overcome before they will truly become human rights lawyers. The last step is perhaps the most difficult one. It requires a cultural revolution in the profession, not only in recognizing the centrality of human rights law, but also by accepting all its consequences. While the fetishism of the Geneva Convention is no longer tenable, human rights law requires a holistic approach of refugee protection. This may ultimately revive the ancestral function to asylum: asylum is not only an act of protection; it is also an act of affirmation against another subject of law which is deemed unable to hold its primary function. In essence, granting asylum reflects the judgment that the state of origin has failed to fulfil its duty of protection and has, accordingly, lost its legitimacy.[246]

Whereas the Geneva Convention exclusively focuses on the obligations of asylum states, human rights law provides a broader avenue for encapsulating the correlative responsibility of states of origin. This presupposes in turn that the so-called neutral and humanitarian character of asylum is abandoned to assume the political nature of human rights. Although this dilemma is anything but new, it may represent another motive of dissidence for the refugee lawyers' community. As rightly emphasized by Bhabha, '[i]n the process of using [human rights] norms, however, advocates and decision-makers have had to navigate the delicate path between the Scilla of human rights enforcement and the Charybdis of what one might polemically call human rights imperialism'.[247] Besides the obvious risks of manipulations carried out under the banner of human rights, one cannot fail to notice that assuming refugee law as an integral part of human rights law has both legal and political implications which are intrinsically interconnected. Acknowledging the multifaceted intermingling between refugee rights and human rights paves the way towards a radical change in perception. It calls for revisiting the international regime of refugee protection as a whole, while forcing both states of origin and of asylum to face their responsibilities. As illuminatingly synthesized by Henkin, '[i]n sum, and in a few words: Not only compassion but responsibility; not only individual state responsibility but collective responsibility; not only the Refugee Convention but the International Covenants and the U.N. Charter; not only UNHCR but the Human Rights Committee and, if necessary, the U.N. Security Council'.[248]

[244] Most human rights are not absolute and they can accordingly be subjected to restrictions on the ground of public order and security considerations. Several human rights treaties also allow states parties to derogate from their obligations in time of public emergency threatening the life of the nation.

[245] T. A. Aleinikoff, 'The Refugee Convention at Forty: Reflections on the IJRL Colloquium', 3 *IJRL* (1991) 617, at 625.

[246] For further discussion, see M. E. Price, *Rethinking Asylum: History, Purpose, and Limits* (2009); Chetail (n 53).

[247] Bhabha (n 7) at 168–9.

[248] L. Henkin, 'Introduction. Refugees and Their Human Rights', 18 *Fordham Int'l L.J.* (1994–1995) 1079, at 1081.

2

Integration in Immigrant Europe: Human Rights at a Crossroads

*Ruth Rubio-Marín**

I. Introduction

Concern about immigrant integration has been on the rise in Western Europe for the last fifteen years at least. Outbursts of violence in the periphery of urban centres where immigrants often concentrate, the persistent gap between nationals' and immigrants' levels of socio-economic performance, and the rising electoral success of new right-wing and xenophobic parties, have coalesced to fuel a new common sense among politicians of different political colours and countries with different immigration policies and citizenship traditions. According to this common sense, which has spread since the late 1990s and was most famously articulated through lapidary statements uttered by both German Chancellor Angela Merkel and British Prime Minister David Cameron, a retreat from multiculturalism is required. Social cohesion, common values, and unitary citizenship must be reaffirmed; and stronger integrationist policies are required. Right-wing and left-wing forces have joined in the proclamation of the death of immigrant multiculturalism, but have done so on different accounts. Whereas nativist and populist right-wing forces have placed some of the emphasis on the need to rescue the well-being of society and autochthonous culture from the threat posed by the floods of immigrants, the forces of the centre-left have criticized the overemphasis on cultural accommodation and its role in ensuring immigrants' interests to the detriment of policies which would arguably tackle the real causes underlying the social isolation of immigrants and the increasing fragmentation of society more effectively.

Looming large in the background is an increasing anti-immigrant and anti-Islamic feeling amongst a population which perceives migrants as unwanted and uncontrolled, and sees Muslim immigrants as a threat to the security of the state and its democratic stability. The trust that immigrants, especially of Muslim origin, will naturally embrace liberal values and human rights has been undermined and

* I would like to express my deepest gratitude to Dorothy Estrada-Tanck for her invaluable research assistance throughout the process of elaboration of this piece. Thanks also to Bruno de Witte for his generous comments.

the confidence they will not pose any threat to the basic security of the state has also been eroding, especially after terrorist attacks occurred early this century. This has prompted scholars to point out that it is not so much the normative appeal of multicultural citizenship, but its preconditions which have gradually been eroding in a context where immigrants are perceived as predominantly 'illegal, carriers of illiberal practices, or movements'.[1] This has happened precisely at a juncture where European countries were barely used to their new identities as immigrant societies, with the end result that a number of issues that used to be part of the 'normal democratic politics box' have been placed into the 'state security box'.[2]

In this context of 'securitization of immigration', aggravated by the economic crisis, rising levels of unemployment, and the growing perception in many European countries that immigrants are no longer needed, an increasing preoccupation with immigrant integration has come to light. Integration contracts, courses, and tests have flourished all over Europe, rhetorically justified by their potential to contribute to the solution of several proclaimed social evils, including social disintegration, violence, racism, socio-economic stratification, and the undermining of national identity and cohesion. These have rendered immigrants' access to the different layers of membership—including access to the territory, permanent residence status, or naturalization—dependent on the acquisition of a certain level of language proficiency, and/or a certain degree of familiarity with, and commitment to, the legal system, political institutions, history, traditions, and culture of the majority in the host society, as well as on (signs of) economic self-sufficiency.[3]

As integration tests proliferate, they are being extended from naturalization procedures—where they were traditionally located, conditioning access to national citizenship only—to the different gates of migratory control, such as access to the territory, but also, tellingly, to the status of permanent resident. This increase in integration tests means, on the one hand, that Europe is coming to terms with the fact that immigrants 'come and come to stay', that is, that European countries have become immigrant societies. At the same time, they reflect the belief that integration cannot simply be seen as a condition for political citizenship, and must instead be seen as a condition for an entitlement to societal membership.

Two risks ensue from the joint proclamation of the death of multiculturalism as a normative aspiration, and the generalized belief that the challenge of keeping immigrant societies integrated can be meaningfully approached by inserting

[1] W. Kymlicka, 'The Rise and Fall of Multiculturalism? New Debates on Inclusion and Accommodation in Diverse Societies', 199 *International Social Science Journal* (2010) 97, 108; P. De Guchteneire and A. Pécoud, 'Introduction: The UN Convention on Migrant Workers' Rights', in R. Cholewinski, P. De Guchteneire, and A. Pércoud, *Migration and Human Rights: The United Nations Convention on Migrant Workers' Rights* (2009) 1, at 33.

[2] W. Kymlicka, *Multicultural Odysseys, Navigating the New International Politics of Diversity* (2007) 124.

[3] S. Carrera and A. Wiesbrock, *Civic Integration of Third-Country Nationals: Nationalism versus Europeanisation in the Common EU Immigration Policy* (2009); E. Guild, K. Groenendijk, and S. Carrera (eds), *Illiberal Liberal States: Immigration, Citizenship and Integration in the EU* (2009); R. van Oers, E. Ersboll, and D. Kostakopolou, *A Re-definition of Belonging? Language and Integration Tests in Europe* (2010).

integration *conditions and tests* in immigration policies. The first is the risk that the problems which are taken as expressions or symptoms of disintegration in immigrant societies come to be attributed to an excess in cultural accommodation towards immigrants, thereby supporting the view that the recognition of policies to accommodate immigrants' cultural identities must necessarily come at the expense of policies geared towards ensuring their socio-economic, or even their political inclusion, suggesting a false 'either/or' logic. The second risk is that of removing the debate about integration from the domain of citizenship, and anchoring it, instead, in that of immigration in what has been described as a displacement from the 'politics of coexistence' to 'the politics of access'.[4] This turnaround all too often makes the dialogue on immigrant integration about the search for (often short-sighted) national interest—frequently defined by promoting electoral politics—instead of about how to retain citizenship as a tool of equality and inclusion in immigrant, and increasingly diverse, societies.

The true potential of these integration tests and conditions to facilitate integration in immigrant societies will have to be assessed over time. There are, however, indications of some scepticism, especially for those who have for years been arguing that integration must be approached from theories which place *recognition* from a juridical-political and a social-cultural perspective centre stage.[5] If, following these theories, one believes equality of rights and a culturally inclusive conception of rights to be the truly necessary conditions for integration, the move to disconnect integration policies from citizenship policies and attach integration policies to immigration policies has the potential to be inherently disintegrative, for it means that the politically enfranchised citizenry will come to define the conditions and requirements of a 'right to belong and enjoy rights' of those who in fact are often already in their midst (and thus, in a sociological sense, already belong), and, by doing so, if anything, inefficiently delay, rather than facilitate, their integration. Beyond efficiency considerations, by acting in this way states may be wrongfully transferring onto immigrants the state's own duties regarding the provision of enabling conditions which must supplement the recognition of rights. They may be imposing culturally hegemonic views of an imagined shared national identity in ways incompatible with the demands of socio-cultural recognition and pluralism. Or at best, they may be selectively and unilaterally demanding and testing that non-citizens exhibit the civic virtues that the system would arguably require from all its residents for its overall long-term sustainability.[6]

I share these concerns, and will now cast my gaze towards human rights law in order to assess its relevance in defining the parameters for immigrant integration

[4] J. de Lucas, 'Sobre los Fundamentos de la Igualdad y del Reconocimiento. Un análisis crítico de las condiciones de las políticas europeas de integración ante la inmigración', in J. de Lucas et al. (eds), *Inmigración e integración en la UE. Dos retos para el s. XXI* (2012) 11.

[5] See, for all, A. Honneth, *The Struggle for Recognition: The Moral Grammar of Social Conflicts* (1995); A. Honneth, *Disrespect: The Normative Foundations of Critical Theory* (2007); C. Taylor, *Sources of the Self: The Making of the Modern Identity* (1989).

[6] S. Carrera, *In Search of the Perfect Citizen? The Intersection between Integration, Immigration and Nationality in the EU* (2009).

policies, especially in Europe. Indeed, the area of human rights law seems particularly fruitful for exploring the question of immigrant integration in general, and in Europe, in particular. In general, because although ontologically grounded on the intrinsic equal worth of human beings, the human rights order is one that has affirmed itself not only in spite of, but also *through*, the recognition of a world state order that accepts states as self-defining and self-determining political entities, deriving their legitimacy from the protection of human rights, but also from the pursuit of national self-interest and the well-being of the members of their bounded communities. In other words, the human rights-based order of states combines a statist and a universalistic logic which are inevitably bound to be in tension with each other, especially in contemporary states with both increasingly porous boundaries and economic disparities. Additionally, in Europe, the post-Second World War human rights revolution has coincided with the transformation of the self-perception of several of its countries into immigrant societies. Because the tensions between axiological universalism and statist-nationalist particularism are intrinsic to the human rights state order system, I do not expect a neat picture to come out of this analysis. What I am mostly interested in is identifying where the tensions are, and where human rights law currently stands—at a crossroads pointing to alternative paths for future evolution. For those who believe that ultimately the universalist logic is, in the long run, the only just and sustainable one, and who defend, on the basis of this, the need to gradually de-nationalize the concept of citizenship so as to preserve its democratic relevance in immigrant societies (but also for those who do not share this premise), identifying points of inflection might be crucial at a European juncture which finds states under stress.

This chapter addresses four specific issues which I deem relevant to the discussion of integration in immigrant Europe from a human rights angle. First comes the discussion of the protection of the cultural identity of migrants under human rights law, in section II. Part III analyses migrants' equality of rights under human rights law, whereas part IV fleshes out the vision of immigrants' integration and integration preconditions as enshrined in human rights law. Part V raises the question of the connection between human rights and citizenship virtues with the understanding that respect for the former requires nurturing of the latter in increasingly pluralistic societies. Part VI concludes with remarks to guide further discussion in this field.

II. Multiculturalism, Human Rights, and Immigrants' Cultural Identity

The trend towards liberal immigrant multiculturalism since the late 1960s in Western democracies translated into modest policies, including the adoption of multiculturalism in school curriculums; the inclusion of ethnic representation and sensitivity in the mandate of public media or media licensing; exemptions from dress codes and from Sunday-closing legislation; the allowing of dual citizenship;

the funding of ethnic group organizations to support cultural activities and bilingual education or mother-tongue instruction; and affirmative action measures for disadvantaged immigrant groups.[7] In European countries, multicultural policies regarding immigrants were very modest from the start—with the possible exception of Belgium, the Netherlands, Sweden, and the United Kingdom—mainly because many European countries simply did not see themselves as countries of immigration, assuming immigration to be a temporary phenomenon.

Far from a deviation from a human rights paradigm, it has been argued that these multicultural policies, to the extent that they existed at all, expressed a new stage in the gradual consolidation of the ethos of racial and ethnic equality intrinsic to the human rights project and to the idea of democratic citizenship.[8] If we approach the question of immigrants' cultural identity by taking a look at human rights law and practice, we can indeed identify expressions of principled rejection of ethno-cultural hierarchies, and the recognition of the essential importance of cultural identity for the individual. However, visible also are signs of caution on the part of states unwilling to bind themselves to rigid positions that maximize the protection of migrants' cultural identity, which might precipitate potentially disintegrative processes through the violent cultural disestablishment of majorities, the unsettling of delicate balances negotiated among what are considered autochthonous ethno-cultural or religious groups, or the overstretching of public spending in an effort to ensure pluralist integration.

Migrant-focused human rights instruments have not been numerous or particularly successful in achieving wide ratification, but they express a clear principle: the need to respect migrants' cultural identity. However, they remain almost silent on concrete state obligations regarding cultural accommodations due to migrants. This is not surprising, especially for those crafted in Europe at a time when many European countries still expected migration to be a temporary, rather than a structural, phenomenon in their societies. Minority rights instruments, which flourished in the 1990s, especially in the context of ethno-cultural violent conflicts in former Communist Europe, made important advances in spelling out (mostly non-justiciable) state obligations to accommodate and protect the cultural identity of national minorities. However, in the absence of general consensus, they have remained declaratory at the international level, and vague or ambiguous at the European level, about the extent to which they cover migrants as opposed to autochthonous or traditional minorities only, allowing wide interpretive discretion for member states. Finally, general human rights instruments have from the start framed both basic obligations of cultural tolerance, and the limits thereof, in ways that are obviously relevant to this dialogue. The extent to which they have been, or could be, read as grounding positive obligations on the state of cultural accommodation from which migrants could specifically benefit, has so far been rather modest. Let us take a closer look in reverse order.

[7] Kymlicka (n 1) at 101. [8] Kymlicka (n 2) at 96–7.

A. General human rights law

To a certain extent, general human rights treaties define the scope of valid expression and limits of cultural affirmation of everyone, migrants included. After all, these general human rights treaties, with territorially defined spheres of application, came to substitute minority-specific rights treaties predominant in the interwar period under the League of Nations, the underlying philosophy being that basic civil and political rights would allow all individuals to express their cultures and group life, while putting aside fears of disloyalty and irredentism.[9] Freedom of expression, freedom of association, freedom of education (encompassing the freedom to choose the kind of education to be given to one's children, and the freedom to establish educational centres), and freedom of religion, are some of the most obvious examples. Human rights treaties have invariably articulated them as rights of universal application, citizenship being, in principle, irrelevant regarding their enjoyment or protection.[10] They all lend themselves to collective and culturally relevant forms of exercise. Moreover, at least one human rights provision, Article 27 ICCPR, was explicitly framed to recognize non-discrimination and non-interference vis-à-vis members of ethnic, religious, or linguistic minorities wishing to enjoy their own culture, to profess and practise their own religion, or to use their own languages.[11] Tellingly, in 1994, this provision was explicitly interpreted as applying to migrant workers as well through *General Comment No. 23* of the Convention's supervisory mechanism, the UN Human Rights Committee.[12]

Similarly, the general human rights order also expresses the limits to the kind of cultural practices that can be accommodated.[13] Cultural diversity cannot, for

[9] Kymlicka (n 2) at 29–30.

[10] See, for example, Arts 18, 19, and 20 of the Universal Declaration of Human Rights (UDHR); Arts 18, 19, 21, and 22 International Covenant on Civil and Political Rights (ICCPR); Arts 9, 10, and 11 European Convention on Human Rights (ECHR), and Art. 2 of its First Protocol; but also Arts 10, 11, 12, and 14 of the European Charter of Fundamental Rights (EUCFR). These instruments generally consider 'everyone' or 'all' as the right-holders of such entitlements.

[11] Literally, 'in those States where ethnic, religious or linguistic minorities exist, persons belonging to such minorities *shall not be denied* the right, in community with the other members of their group, to enjoy their own culture, to profess and practise their own religion, or to use their own language' (emphasis added). The same provision is included with regard to children who are members of these minorities in Art. 30 of the UN Convention on the Rights of the Child (CRC).

[12] 'Article 27 confers rights on persons belonging to minorities which "exist" in a State party. Given the nature and scope of the rights envisaged under that article, it is not relevant to determine the degree of permanence that the term "exist" connotes. Those rights simply are that individuals belonging to those minorities should not be denied the right, in community with members of their group, to enjoy their own culture, to practise their religion and speak their language. Just as they need not be nationals or citizens, they need not be permanent residents. Thus, *migrant workers* or even visitors in a State party constituting such minorities are entitled not to be denied the exercise of those rights. As any other individual in the territory of the State party, they would, also for this purpose, have the general rights, for example, *to freedom of association, of assembly, and of expression.* The existence of an ethnic, religious or linguistic minority in a given State party does not depend upon a decision by that State party but requires to be established by objective criteria' (emphasis added). HRCttee, *General Comment No. 23: The rights of minorities (Art. 27)*, CCPR/C/21/Rev.1/Add. 5 (1994), para. 5.2.

[13] The UNESCO Universal Declaration on Cultural Diversity states that '[n]o one may invoke cultural diversity to infringe upon human rights guaranteed by international law, nor to limit their

instance, be an excuse to disrespect sexual or racial non-discrimination, religious freedom, or basic due process principles. It has therefore been said that human rights contain the guidelines for drawing a balance between conflicting interests arising from diversity and cohesion through a shared legal order.[14] This is to say, cultural *tolerance,* broadly understood, has become a defining feature of the human rights-based order put into place after the Second World War, setting clear limits to both straightforward, assimilation-driven, nation-building agendas and claims which, in the language of cultural relativism, may contest the foundational political culture of liberal democracies.

Furthermore, from a cultural point of view, human rights are likely to remain an exercise in the making. For beyond those rights which are most obviously relevant for the promotion of culture, human rights provisions in general—including those carving out a sphere of autonomy and non-interference—inevitably open paths for cultural affirmation, and must be subject to interpretive processes which simply cannot be culturally neutral. This means that, in confronting cultural pluralism, human rights implementers, including courts, will decide—more, or less, self-reflectively—the range of acceptable forms of expression of basic interest or human capability underlying a certain rights provision, other than those traditionally accepted. Being subject to negotiation and interpretation, human rights norms are simply not free of the influence of what Iris Young defined as domination through the universalization of a dominant group's experience and culture, meaning the establishment of norms through which dominant groups project their own experience as representative of humanity as such.[15] The right to property, for instance, can be, and has been, creatively interpreted to accommodate indigenous notions of collective land tenure.[16] The right to marriage and family life begs the question about what cultural forms of marriage and family are encompassed. The mainstream, or conventional, understanding of the family (in many European societies: marriage-based, nuclear, heterogeneous, and monogamous) has been challenged by groups whose cultural forms of intimacy, solidarity, and lifestyle, differ from the mainstream.[17] Similarly, the question of what amounts to private

scope' (Art. 4). The same idea is reflected in Art. 8(2) of the UN Declaration on Minority Rights, and can be derived from Art. 34 of the UN Convention on the Rights of Migrant Workers (ICRMW). Forced marriages would, for instance, be contrary to Art. 23(2) ICCPR. More broadly, Art. 24 CRC obliges states to take effective measures against traditional practices affecting the health of minors (such as, arguably, female genital mutilation), where the protection of the needs of the child against serious dangers of physical or psychological abuse justify a state's intervention, or where adults are involuntarily endangered by serious physical or psychological harm (for example when they are not allowed to leave a particular group).

[14] R. Medda-Windischer, *Old and New Minorities: Reconciling Diversity and Cohesion: a Human Rights Model for Minority Integration* (2009).

[15] I. M. Young, *Justice and the Politics of Difference* (1990), 59.

[16] See, for instance, *Case of the Mayagna (Sumo) Awas Tingni Community v. Nicaragua*, IACtHR (2001) Series C, No. 79, judgment of 31 August 2001.

[17] For instance, under Art. 8 ECHR, the Court has absorbed changes in mainstream society, separating the concept of family ties from that of marriage, and no longer requiring cohabitation for a stable relationship to constitute a family life. See *Marckx v. Belgium*, ECHR (1979) Series A, No. 31, para. 31; *Johnston and Others v. Ireland*, ECHR (1986) Series A, No. 112, para. 55; *Keegan v. Ireland*,

life and home is inevitably culturally loaded.[18] Even the drawn-out headscarf debate, usually coined in terms of religious freedom and gender equality,[19] lends itself to interesting, and in my view under-explored, questions regarding notions of bodily privacy which are culturally specific. Immigration, to the extent that it increases cultural diversity in society, will in the long run contribute to bringing such issues to the fore, forcing courts to identify proper and consistent hermeneutic tools to deal with the challenges that increasing cultural pluralism presents to the human rights project. Human rights law stands at a crossroads.[20]

An obvious difficulty in relying on generically worded human rights to derive specific cultural protections for immigrant minorities is that these protections have the potential to subvert national and often constitutionally articulated systems, reciprocal accommodations between several 'traditional' or 'autochthonous' groups with competing claims over the state, or parts of its territory, as expressive, and protective of certain specific cultures. The ECHR, and its treatment of linguistic diversity, offers a paradigmatic illustration of the limitations of general human rights provisions when deriving linguistic protections. Indeed, the European Court of Human Rights (ECtHR) and European Commission on Human Rights (ECmHR) have obviously taken the position that the Convention's generically expressed freedom of expression (Article 10 ECHR) does not protect the right to express oneself in one's mother tongue or usual language in any specific given context, such as voting in a municipal council by an elected representative,[21] or in administrative matters[22]—including the registration of a political party for

ECHR (1994) Series A, No. 290, para. 44; and *Al-Nashif v. Bulgaria*, ECHR (2002) Appl. No. 50963/99, para. 112. See also *Muñoz Díaz v. Spain*, ECHR (2010) Appl. No. 49151/07, validating a woman's pension entitlement ensuing from her Roma rite marriage on antidiscrimination grounds. On the other hand, the European Commission has held that priority must be given to the protection of the majority culture over respect for an individual's right to family life or cultural identity when upholding immigration rules which did not approve of polygamous unions (see, for instance, *Bibi v. The United Kingdom*, ECmHR (1992) Appl. No. 19628/92, 29 June 1992). Also, in the case of *Şerife Yiğit v. Turkey*, ECHR (2010) Appl. No. 3976/05 (GC) (decided only a few months after the judgment in *Muñoz Díaz v. Spain*), the Court analysed a similar case involving the denial of a woman's claim for pension and health insurance as the surviving partner from a non-civil marriage—in this instance, a religious marriage celebrated under Islamic rite, which lasted for twenty-six years until the man's death and from which six children were born—quite disturbingly resolving that there had been no discrimination.

[18] Several 'new' rights have been derived from Art. 8 ECHR, including the right to respect for a particular lifestyle, private life, family life, or home, all of which have acted as vessels for the protection of minority cultures and lifestyle. See, for example, *Chapman v. the United Kingdom*, ECHR (2001-I) Appl. No. 27138/95 (GC), paras 92 and 96 and *Connors v. the United Kingdom*, ECHR (2004) Appl. No. 66746/01, deriving state obligations to respect the gypsy lifestyle under Art. 8.

[19] See *Leyla Şahin v. Turkey*, ECHR (2005) Appl. No. 44774/98 (GC) and *Dogru v. France*, ECHR (2009) Appl. No. 27058/05.

[20] Given the wide range of approaches to human rights interpretation in plural societies, it may be queried whether greater consistency might be achieved by resorting to an overarching constitutional value or principle, such as recognition or even promotion of multiculturalism, like the one contained in the Canadian Charter of Rights and Freedoms. See P. Bosset, A. Gamper, and T. Öhlinger, 'Multicultural Societies and Migration', in M. Tushnet, T. Fleiner, and C. Saunders (eds), *Routledge Handbook of Constitutional Law* (2013) 450, at 451.

[21] *Clerfayt, Legros et al. v. Belgium*, ECHR (1985) Appl. No. 10650/83, decision of 17 May 1985.

[22] ECmHR, *A Group of Inhabitants of Sint-Pieters-Leeuw v. Belgium* (1968) Appl. No. 2333/64, *Recueil* 28, 1, 16 December 1968.

elections, when this entails unsettling the rules of official use of languages.[23] Similarly, in the educational context, a number of cases under Article 2 of the First Protocol (recognizing the right to education) have brought up the issue of minority languages in education, but the Court has ruled that this provision, while requiring the respecting of parents' religious and philosophical convictions in education, does not require states to respect parents' linguistic preferences in the sphere of education or teaching, even when read in conjunction with the equality principle under Article 14.[24]

B. A close look at religious accommodation

Because of the salience of religion as a cultural identity marker, and Europe's growing Islamophobia, religious accommodation is a particularly interesting area for exploration. It is also an area which shows both the potential and the shortcomings of relying only on general human rights law for the protection of migrants' identities. The issue is directly relevant to the integration debate given the integrative potential of measures of exemption and reasonable accommodation vis-à-vis normalized state norms, such as those pertaining to dress code, official holidays, business hours, and animal slaughter. Because these norms typically reflect the cultural and religious features of the majority society, they are likely to have a disparate impact on religious minorities, both of immigrant and non-immigrant origin. By shaping the opportunities for minorities to live out their religion fully while participating unencumbered in the different public domains—including work life, public function, and civil service and institutions—these general norms and the existence of exemptions and accommodations affect the possibility of societal integration through the sharing of common institutions.

Because of the generic and negative framing of human rights religious freedom clauses, which fail to spell out which are, beyond non-interference and non-discrimination, the state's obligations toward ensuring the meaningful enjoyment of the right to religious freedom, what we find is that there is ample room for discretion by courts and adjudicatory bodies, and that, doctrinally, much will depend on how broadly or narrowly one interprets limitation clauses typically included in religious freedom provisions, including those that refer to 'public safety', 'order', 'health', 'morals', and 'the rights of others'.[25] More specifically, much can hinge on how strictly the proportionality test is applied when seeking to

[23] ECmHR, *Fryske Nasionale Partij and Others v. the Netherlands* (1985), DR 45, 240, 12 December 1985. Notice however that the Court has held in a recent judgment that freedom of expression protects the right to use a particular language (such as Kurdish) in political campaigning—but in a context which does not refer to the 'official' use of language (see *Case of Sükran Aydin and others v. Turkey*, 22 January 2013, Appl. No. 49197/06).

[24] In the case *'relating to certain aspects of the laws on the use of languages in education in Belgium' v. Belgium* (*Belgian Linguistic* Case), ECHR (1968) Series A, No. 6, judgment of 23 July 1968.

[25] See, for instance Art. 18(3) ICCPR and Art. 12(3) of the ICRMW. See also Art. 9(2) ECHR and Arts 10 and 14(3) of the EUCFR. In the case of the ECHR, ICCPR, and ICRMW, freedom of religion may be subject to limitations as are prescribed by law and are necessary in a democratic society to protect public safety, order, health, or morals, or the fundamental rights and freedoms of others.

identify the least restrictive means to serve the alleged public interests or to respect the rights of others. Finally, it will also be relevant whether impact-based or indirect discrimination are the chosen doctrines to interpret equality and non-discrimination in the religious domain, as this may allow screening out norms with no discriminatory intent, but with clear discriminatory impact. These are all doctrinal choices with important consequences. Human rights law indeed stands at a crossroads.

At the UN level, from the outset, the intention was to draft a declaration first and then a convention dealing specifically with religion and belief. Indeed, hand in hand with the proposal of a binding instrument on racial discrimination, the General Assembly suggested one on religious intolerance, which never saw the light of day.[26] Although there was a general agreement on protecting the freedom of religion or belief, the determination of the specific content of the right, and corresponding state obligations, were highly contentious, and the issue of freedom of conversion or change of religion was also a major obstacle to consensus. In the end, the most that could be achieved was the adoption of a Declaration on the Elimination of All Forms of Intolerance and of Discrimination Based on Religion or Belief[27] by the General Assembly in 1981, after a long process of drafting, confirming the wording of Article 18 of the ICCPR, and specifying the principle of non-discrimination on grounds of religion or other beliefs (Articles 1 and 2(1)).

Against this background, the Human Rights Committee clarified, in 1993 (through its *General Comment No. 22, Article 18: The Right to Freedom of Thought, Conscience and Religion*), that in interpreting the scope of permissible limitation clauses under the ICCPR, states parties should proceed from the need to protect the rights guaranteed under the Covenant, including the right to equality and non-discrimination. Permissible limitations, under Article 18(3), are only those 'as are prescribed by law and are necessary to protect public safety, order, health, or morals or the fundamental rights and freedoms of others'. According to *General Comment No. 22*, restrictions should not be allowed on grounds not specified in the provision, even if they would be permitted as restrictions to other rights protected in the Covenant, such as national security. Limitations may only be applied for those purposes for which they were prescribed, and have to be directly related, and proportionate to, the specific need on which they are predicated. They may not be imposed for discriminatory purposes, or applied in a discriminatory manner.[28] This framing has the potential to accommodate adequately the religious practices of minorities, as shown by the evolution in the way the Committee has been dealing with religious accommodation claims, and its most recent doctrine.[29]

[26] UNGA Res 1781 (XVII), 7 December 1962.

[27] UN Declaration on the Elimination of All Forms of Intolerance and of Discrimination Based on Religion or Belief, UNGA Res 55 (XXXVI), UN Doc A/36/684 (1981).

[28] HRCttee, *General Comment 22: The right to freedom of thought, conscience and religion (Art. 18)*, CCPR/C/21/Rev.1/Add.4 (1993), para. 8.

[29] See, as an example of an earlier case, HRCttee, *Karnel Singh Bhinder v. Canada*, CCPR/C/37/D/208/1986 (1989), denying a turban-wearing Sikh an exemption from the obligation under national legislation to wear a 'hard hat' in his work as a maintenance electrician at the Canadian National Railway Company, a denial that ultimately resulted in the termination of his labour contract. The complaint was based on Arts 18 (religious freedom) and 26 (non-discrimination) ICCPR. The

Interestingly, however, the closer we get to the state level, the more reticent we find adjudicatory bodies to interfere with the state's judgment about the scope of required accommodations for religious minority practices, especially when security concerns are raised, no matter how generically. At the European level, so far, the record shows an unpromising evolution from non-recognition (where minority claims are simply not recognized as valid expressions of religious exercise claims) to one of non-accommodation (where the claim is a priori recognized, but the practice not accommodated), on the basis of loosely interpreted limitation clauses and proportionality tests not strictly applied, often recognizing a wide margin of discretion owed to states to set the limitations they deem necessary to sustain a democratic society and, especially, the defence of secularism.[30] Article 9 ECHR certainly protects everyone's freedom to manifest their religion or belief, in worship, teaching, practice, and observance, either alone or in community with others, and in public or private. In addition, Article 2 of the First Additional Protocol guarantees the rights of parents to ensure the education of their children in conformity with their own religious and philosophical convictions.[31] Moreover, some of the crucial doctrinal instruments for a pluralist interpretation of these provisions have by now been recognized. This is in particular the case with the notion of indirect discrimination.[32] Still, an overall assessment of the case law so far shows a strong reluctance

Committee considered the requirement of wearing safety headgear 'reasonable and directed towards objective purposes that are compatible with the Covenant' (paras 6.2 and 7). However, in *Raihon Hudoyberganova v. Uzbekistan*, CCPR/C/82/D/931/2000 (2004), the Committee found that excluding a woman from university due to her refusal to remove the *hijab* (following a national law forbidding the wearing of religious dress in public places) was in violation of Art. 18 (see paras 6.2 and 7). Also, in the recent 2011 case of *Ranjit Singh v. France*, the Committee backed the claim of a Sikh with refugee status in France, who was denied renewal of his permanent residence permit because his photographs failed to meet the requirements set in a French decree stipulating that for these purposes foreign individuals must appear full face and bareheaded. The applicant's request for an exemption from this provision, on the basis of the use of a Sikh turban as part of his religious belief, had been rejected by French authorities, but the UN Human Rights Committee concluded that the measure was unnecessary and disproportionate to the aim of guaranteeing public order and safety put forward by France, and thus violated Art. 18(3). See *Ranjit Singh v. France*, CCPR/C/102/D/1876/2009 (2011), paras 8.4 and 10.

30 On the backlash against policies of accommodation, especially of religious differences and the emergence of a so-called post-multiculturalism, see C. McCrudden, 'Multiculturalism, Freedom of Religion, Equality and the British Constitution: The *JFS* Case Considered', 9 *International Journal of Constitutional Law* (2011) 200, at 201–5.

31 Similarly, the EUCFR includes a general statement in the sense that '[t]he Union shall respect cultural, religious and linguistic diversity' (Art. 22), and it does not foresee any restriction on the exercise of the right to freedom of religion (Art. 10). Also, the Organization for Security and Cooperation in Europe (OSCE) included as a priority in Principle VII of the Helsinki Final Act (1975) that the participating states 'will recognise and respect the freedom of the individual to profess and practice, alone or in community with others, religion or belief, acting in accordance with the dictates of his own conscience'. States also pledge to respect the freedom of religion and belief of persons belonging to *national minorities* living in their territory (paras 3 and 4 of Principle VII, at 6).

32 In *Thlimmenos v. Greece*, ECHR (2000) Appl. No. 34369/97, the ECtHR appreciated that discrimination may exist whenever neutral rules hinder cultural or religious practices in their application, if they are not accompanied by due exceptions. In *Hoogendijk v. Netherlands*, ECHR (2005) Appl. No. 58461/00, decision of 6 January 2005, the Court accepted that statistics alone could be enough to shift the burden of proof to the respondent state to provide an objective explanation of apparently neutral policies resulting in de facto differential treatment, in this case, involving discrimination

to accommodate minority religious practice. In many cases where applicants' claims of religious exemptions have been refused, the Commission and Court have not even felt the need to balance the religious claims against general interests and other individual rights. Instead, interference has been denied outright.[33] In others, where interference in the sphere of religious freedom has been acknowledged, the Court has promptly accepted that states had a wide margin of appreciation and that restrictions of religious practices were proportionate for a legitimate purpose, being readily satisfied with rather generic expressions of alleged public interest, and systematically failing to look for less restrictive means to satisfy this alleged public interest, paying only lip-service to a proportionality analysis, and dismissing many of the claims as simply inadmissible.[34] This has been particularly the case when

affecting women on the grounds of sex and/or marital status. More recently, in *D.H. and Others v. the Czech Republic*, ECHR (2008) Appl. No. 57325/00 (GC), the Court also admitted the concept of indirect discrimination in relation to access of Roma children to the general education system.

[33] See ECmHR, *Tuomo Konttinen v. Finland* (1996), DR 87-A, 68 (where the Commission validated for freedom of contract-related reasons the dismissal of a member of the Seventh-day Adventist Church in Finland for leaving his Friday shift earlier in order to respect the Sabbath, even when he had expressed willingness to work longer shifts on other days. The Commission declared his claim inadmissible, adding that 'having found his working hours to conflict with his religious convictions, the applicant was *free to relinquish his post*', at 7, emphasis added).

[34] See *Phull v. France*, ECHR (2005) Appl. No. 35753/03, decision of 11 January 2005, in which the Court justified the forceful removal of the turban of a British Sikh during a security check at a French airport, accepting that security checks were necessary for public security and that the modalities of the check fell within the margin of appreciation of the member states, whilst failing to address the possibility of less restrictive means to achieve the alleged state aims. See also *El Morsli v. France*, ECHR (2008) Appl. No. 15585/06, decision of 4 March 2008, involving a Muslim woman who was denied entrance to the French consulate at Marrakesh in Morocco because she did not take off her headscarf for an identity check in front of male personnel, although the claimant expressed readiness to show her face and hair to a female security agent. In *Mann Singh v. France*, ECHR (2008) Appl. No. 24479/07, decision of 13 November 2008, the Court once again declared inadmissible the claim of a Sikh man who refused to provide a photograph without his turban in order to obtain a driver's licence on the grounds of his religious belief, accepting generic public safety reasons and law and order considerations linked to the need for identification. Finally, see also the cases of *Aktas v. France*, ECHR (2009) Appl. No. 43563/08; *Bayrak v. France*, ECHR (2009) Appl. No. 14308/08; *Gamaleddyn v. France*, ECHR (2009) Appl. No. 18527/08; *Ghazal v. France*, ECHR (2009) Appl. No. 29134/08; *Jasvir Singh v. France*, ECHR (2009) Appl. No. 25463/08, and *Ranjit Singh v. France*, ECHR (2009) Appl. No. 57325/00 (all of them declared inadmissible by decisions rendered on 30 June 2009), concerning the placing in separate study rooms, followed by expulsion from school of Muslim girls wearing a headscarf and Sikh boys wearing a *keski* or under-turban, in application of the 2004 French Education Code, accepting that the legal prohibition from wearing *conspicuous* religious symbols to school implies a restriction on their freedom to manifest religion, but a restriction which is based on the constitutional principle of secularism and furthers the aim of protecting the rights and freedoms of others and public order. Some recent cases provide modest reasons for optimism. In *Eweida and Others v. the United Kingdom*, ECHR (2013) Appl. Nos. 48420/10, 59842/10, 51671/10, and 36516/10, judgment of 15 January 2013, which integrated four joined cases related to freedom of religion and non-discrimination, the ECtHR found a violation of freedom of religious expression (Art. 9) of Nadia Eweida, a practising Coptic Christian, due to the prohibition by her employer, British Airways, seconded by the UK authorities, to wear a Christian cross at work. However, it denied the claim of Shirley Chaplin, a nurse from Exeter, also alleging discrimination when she was not allowed to wear a cross at her work in a state hospital, on the grounds that the protection of *health and safety* in a hospital ward was inherently of a greater magnitude than that which applied in respect of Ms Eweida, referring also to the wide margin of appreciation that states must enjoy in this domain (para. 99). Celebrating the decision as a valuable step in the Court's moving away from the 'freedom to resign' doctrine as a poor guarantee of the freedom of religion, see L. Peroni, 'Eweida and Others v. the United Kingdom

reasons concerning security have been put forward. In the context of the increasing focus on security on matters surrounding immigration and Islam relations, this is not surprising but regrettable. However, seen from the perspective of the excluded 'other', a failure to provide concrete reasons and serious justifications for limiting one's human rights (through a strict application of the proportionality test) amounts to a severe form of non-recognition, especially because this way of proceeding does not allow for distillation of those cases in which non-accommodation is the expression of outright bias, prejudice, and bigotry.[35]

C. Migrant- and minorities-targeted human rights instruments

Given the limitations of general human rights provisions, one must look at migrant- and minority-specific human rights instruments to assess the potential of human rights as vessels for the affirmation of migrants' cultural identity. Regarding the former, beyond provisions reiterating the rights already recognized under general human rights treaties for migrants,[36] we find a clear expression of the direction to take, the general rejection of ethno-cultural domination, but little in terms of specific state obligations to ensure the protection of migrants' cultural identity, nor explicit endorsement of multiculturalism. ILO Migrant Workers (Supplementary Provisions) Convention No. 143, adopted in 1975, for instance, mentions equality of opportunity with respect to cultural rights (Article 10), and—more importantly—recognizes that 'each Member shall, by methods appropriate to national conditions and practice... take all steps to assist and encourage the efforts of migrant workers and their families to preserve their national and ethnic identity and their cultural ties with their country of origin, including the possibility for children to be given some knowledge of their mother tongue' (Article 12 (f)).[37]Adopted around the same time, the Council of Europe's 1977 Convention on the Legal Status of Migrant Workers (ECLSMW) sets forth a state obligation regarding freedom of religion 'to *ensure* that migrant workers and members of their families can worship freely, in accordance with their faith; each Contracting Party shall *facilitate* such worship, within the limit of available means' (Article 10(3), my emphasis), but fails to specify how, exactly. Even less compelling is the wording of the state's positive duties under the 1990 International Convention on the

(Part I): Taking Freedom of Religion More Seriously', 17 January 2013, *Strasbourg Observers*; available at: <http://strasbourgobservers.com/2013/01/17/eweida-and-others-v-the-united-kingdom-part-i-taking-freedom-of-religion-more-seriously/>.

[35] To contrast this *modus operandi* with that of a careful application of a proportionality analysis which is not satisfied with generic security concerns, see the Canadian Supreme Court decision *Multani v. Commission scolaire Marguerite-Bourgeoys* [2006] 1 SCR 256, ruling that an absolute prohibition on wearing a Sikh *kirpan* (sword) in public schools would contradict the promotion of multiculturalism, and allowing the child to bring the kirpan to school as long as some basic safeguards and precautions were taken as a way of satisfying the principle of proportionality.

[36] See, eg, Art. 12 ICRMW recognizing migrants' religious freedom.

[37] Emphasis on the teaching of the migrant workers' mother tongue for their children is also placed by the ECLSMW: Convention on the Legal Status of Migrant Workers, 24 November 1977, CETS No. 93, Art. 45.

Protection of the Rights of Migrant Workers and their Families (ICRMW), which, with regard to cultural identity, only indicates that 'States Parties shall ensure respect for the cultural identity of migrant workers and members of their families and shall not prevent them from maintaining their cultural links with their State of origin' (Article 31(1)); and that they *may* take 'appropriate measures to assist and encourage efforts in this respect' (Article 31(2)). Moreover, few European states, and none of the EU member states or immigration-receiving countries, have become party to the ICRMW to this day, and only a handful ratified the ECLSMW shortly after signature. Given the current strength of anti-immigrant feelings in Europe, neither the ratification of the ECLSMW or the ICRMW by European countries of immigration, nor the creation of further migrant-specific norms can now be reasonably expected,[38] even though the Parliamentary Assembly of the Council of Europe recommended that at some point a minority rights document be drafted specifically targeting immigrants.[39]

Inevitably, one must then look at human rights norms, which since the 1990s have recognized positive, cultural rights for minorities. The greatest shortcoming of such norms has been that the international community has mostly refused to turn them into judicially enforceable rights. Additionally, it has failed to take a firm position on whether immigrants should also benefit from them, or whether these minority protections should be kept for so-called 'old minorities', or 'autochthonous groups' instead.[40] Thus, while monitoring bodies, advocacy organizations, and—for the most part—scholars, have almost consistently pushed for an expansive interpretation of the concept of national minorities that would encompass migrants, states have been unwilling to give up their wide margin of discretion. The UN Declaration on Rights of Persons Belonging to National or Ethnic, Religious, and Linguistic Minorities, adopted in 1992, did not limit itself to autochthonous or traditional minorities when recognizing an obligation on the part of the state 'to encourage conditions for the promotion of [the] identity [of minorities]' (Article 1); to 'take measures to create favourable conditions to enable persons belonging to minorities to express their characteristics and to develop their culture, language, religion, traditions and customs' (Article 4(2)); as well as 'to take appropriate measures so that, wherever possible, persons belonging to minorities may have adequate opportunities to learn their mother tongue or to have instruction in their mother tongue' (Article 4(3)).[41] The UN Working Group on Minorities has also

[38] In spite of the low numbers of ratifications of both the UN and the European Conventions on the rights of migrants, in this chapter I have chosen to treat them as human rights law, because they embody the clearest standards of what states thought was right to do at a certain point in time to specifically address migrants' concerns through human rights law. The norms thus express a direction that the law could be taken in in the future, but can also be seen as relics of a past in a changed world. As they stand, these standards can probably be invoked even in countries which have not ratified them as a sort of soft law expressing normative aspirations.

[39] Council of Europe, Parliamentary Assembly Recommendation 1492 (2001), Rights of National Minorities, Assembly debate on 23 January 2001 (3rd Sitting).

[40] For an in-depth analysis of the issue, see Medda-Windischer (n 14) at 42.

[41] UN Doc A/RES/47/135 (1992).

supported this broad interpretation.[42] However, tellingly, the Declaration never reached the consensus level needed to be turned into a binding Convention.[43]

Similarly, at a European level, in the mid-1990s, minority rights protections started to flourish to provide a point of reference for the resolution of ethnic minority tensions in the former Communist states of Central and Eastern Europe. These encompass the Recommendations relating to minority rights, including in the sphere of education (1996), language (1998), effective participation (1999), and broadcasting (2003), issued by the High Commissioner on National Minorities, established by the OSCE in 1993. Most importantly, 1995 saw the adoption of the European Framework Convention on National Minorities (FCNM), which entered into force in 1998, and has come furthest as far as human rights law is concerned in articulating concrete, positive obligations for the promotion of cultural minority rights. Thus, besides the general freedoms replicated in general instruments,[44] the Convention spells out guarantees for the public use of minority languages, foreseeing the use of minority language in relations with administrative authorities 'in areas inhabited by persons belonging to national minorities traditionally or in substantial numbers, if those persons so request and where such a request corresponds to a real need' (Article 10); the right to use surname and name (patronymic) in the minority language (Article 11); and 'adequate opportunities to be taught the minority language or to receive instruction in this language, if there is sufficient demand in areas inhabited by persons belonging to national minorities traditionally or in substantial numbers' (Article 14). Moreover, Article 5(2) of the Convention explicitly recognizes that 'without prejudice to measures taken in pursuance of their general integration policy, the Parties shall refrain from policies or practices aimed at assimilation of persons belonging to national minorities against their will and shall protect these persons from any action aimed at such assimilation'.

Although the provisions in the Framework Convention are only indirectly justiciable,[45] and some hard-core objectors—including Belgium, France, Greece, and Turkey—have failed to ratify it, the drafters of the Convention purposefully did not define the concept of national minority, thereby not limiting its application

[42] See Commission on Human Rights, Sub-Commission on Promotion and Protection of Human Rights, Working Group on Minorities, Commentary to the Declaration on the Rights of Persons Belonging to National or Ethnic, Religious and Linguistic Minorities, Working paper submitted by Asbjørn Eide Sixth session, 22–26 May 2000, UN Doc E/CN/.4/Sub.2/AC.5/2000/WP.1 (2000).

[43] Notice also that Art. 27 ICCPR, which was initially crafted as an anti-discrimination provision, has since been read as possibly requiring the adoption of positive measures partly thanks to the jurisprudence of the UN's Human Rights Committee. See HRCttee, *General Comment No. 23, The rights of minorities (Art. 27)*, CCPR/C/21/rev.1/Add.5 (1994), paras 5.1–5.2.

[44] This includes freedom of assembly, association, thought, and religion (Art. 7); the right to establish their own private educational institutions (Art. 13), and the right to the manifestation of religion and establishment of religious institutions and organizations (Art. 8).

[45] The Convention is not internationally justiciable. However, many of the Convention provisions can be judicially enforceable by national courts. See, on this question, F. Palermo, "Domestic Enforcement and Direct Effect of the Framework Convention for the Protection of National Minorities", in A. Verstichel, A. Alen, B. De Witte, and B. Lemmens (eds), *The Framework Convention for the Protection of National Minorities: a Useful Pan-European Instrument?* (2008) 187.

to autochthonous or traditional minorities.[46] Since the actual rights codified in the FCNM and OSCE Recommendations do not arise from historic settlement and territorial concentration, but instead refer to the generic right to enjoy one's own culture, there is no obvious reason why they should not be recognized for new minorities. Both the Council of Europe[47] and the OSCE[48] have in fact tried to have a wider range of groups benefit from existing standards. Moreover, the Convention has gained authority and efficacy thanks to the dynamic monitoring practice of its Advisory Committee, which has been successful in putting pressure on the states concerned, whilst taking different countries' economic, and social conditions into account.[49] In terms of the actual minorities covered by the FCNM, the approach therefore has been flexible and state practice has varied. In particular, whereas in Central Europe the protection has been limited to old minorities with lasting ties to a particular territory, in several north-western European countries, like the UK, immigrant communities have been included as well.[50] In spite of this, looking ahead, the hope of turning the FCNM into a justiciable part of the ECHR is certainly not likely to be realized in the near future. One can also wonder whether the AFCF's expansive interpretation is indeed appropriate. It was certainly not the intention of the drafters of the Framework Convention to make it applicable to

[46] This is in contrast to the European Charter for Regional or Minority Languages which explicitly excludes migrants from its sphere of application, specifying that the definition of languages foreseen in the Charter 'does not include either dialects of the official language(s) of the State *or the languages of migrants*' (Art. 1(a), emphasis added). European Charter for Regional or Minority Languages, 5 November 1992, CETS No. 148.

[47] For the expansive interpretation pushed by the Advisory Committee on the Framework Convention on National Minorities (ACFC), see, among others, ACFC, Opinion on Austria, 16 May 2001, ACFC/INF/OP/I/009, paras 19–20, at 34; ACFC, Opinion on Germany, ACFC/INF/OP/I/008, 1 March 2002, paras 17–18; ACFC, Opinion on Ukraine, ACFC/INF/OP/I/010, 1 March 2002, para. 18. For the European Commission for Democracy Through Law (Venice Commission) see Report on Non-Citizens and Minority Rights, CDL-AD (2007)001, 18 January 2007. On the expansive interpretation adopted by the ACFC see A. Verstichel, 'Personal Scope of Application: An Open, Inclusive and Dynamic Approach—The FCNM as a Living Instrument' in Verstichel, Alen, De Witte, and Lemmens (n 45).

[48] The OSCE High Commissioner on National Minorities in fact extended his mandate to new minority groups stemming from migration. See OSCE High Commissioner on National Minorities, Policies on integration and diversity in some OSCE participating States. Exploratory study prepared by the Migration Policy Group, HCNM.GAL/6/06, 3 July 2006. See also, Rolf Ekeus, Statement to the OSCE Parliamentary Assembly, Fifth Annual Winter Meeting, Vienna, 23 February 2006, HCNM.GAL/3/06, 24 February 2006.

[49] P. Keller, 'Re-thinking Ethnic and Cultural Rights in Europe', 18 *Oxford Journal of Legal Studies* (1998) 29, at 58.

[50] Some states have adopted rather narrow views firmly opposing the extension of minority provisions to new minorities. See, among others, FCNM, List of Declarations, status as of 30 June 2008, Declaration by Germany, dated 11 May 1995, and renewed on 10 September 1997, and Declarations by Estonia, dated 6 January 1997; available at: <http://www.conventions.coe.int>. Others have instead pragmatically applied some provisions to new groups: ACFC, Opinion on the United Kingdom, ACFC/INF/OP/I(2002)006, 30 November 2001, para. 14. ACFC, Second Report submitted by Finland, ACF/SR/II(2004), 10 December 2004 (Art. 3). Finally, others have not yet taken an official position. Those which have limited the personal scope of application have done so by either requiring that members of the group concerned be citizens of the state in order to constitute a minority or that they have long-established or historical ties with the country. See Medda-Windischer (n 14) at 42.

immigrant groups, and many of its core provisions (especially those on language rights) really do not seem to be appropriate.

It may be that for now the conditions have not yet been met for a normatively binding, and universally applicable instrument, and that, as with socio-economic rights, the norm should be a principle of progressive realization which takes into account local conditions and variations, allowing the gradual recognition of different rights.[51] General criteria could be identified, referring to numbers of potential beneficiaries, geographical concentration, and the expressed will of migrants,[52] but also concerning the social and economic conditions in the receiving societies with an eye to determining its feasibility and preventing foreseeable backlashes. However, a specific problem in this regard is that such general conditions might actually play out very differently depending on the racial, religious, or national extraction of different groups. Yet one guideline in the application of the progressive realization principle, as consolidated in the area of socio-economic rights, is precisely the principle of non-discrimination.

In brief, universal, regional, general, migrant- and minority-specific human rights norms have set up the normative framework for the affirmation of cultural tolerance, and arguably placed limits on the range of legitimate integration policies that states may want to pursue, ruling out options in the pursuit of unitary and homogeneous nationhood, which may be straightforwardly coercively assimilationist. Also, some human rights norms have explicitly recognized that migrants have a right to preserve their cultural identity, and some have gone far in imposing specific obligations on the state to protect immigrant cultures actively. However, the more specific the protections, the less willing states have been to bind themselves to judicially enforceable norms. On the other hand, most international bodies dealing with minority treaties have pushed for an inclusive reading. Given the current backlash, we are unlikely to see an increase in the number of states willing to ratify some of the existing treaties, or the proliferation of further treaties spelling out state obligations to protect migrants' cultural identities. Therefore, general human rights treaties are likely to retain an important role. Their actual potential is determined by several conditions, including the extent to which the specific axis of cultural identity (for example, religious identity) has deserved explicit recognition through a rights or a non-discrimination provision; the scope given to equality and non-discrimination clauses linked to culturally relevant identity features; and the willingness of judicial, or quasi-judicial, bodies' enforcement mechanisms to adopt pluralist hermeneutics in a self-aware manner, and rigorously apply proportionality analysis when assessing limitation clauses. The experience so far is only modestly promising. Again, we can see that human rights stand at a crossroads.

[51] Kymlicka (n 1) at 110–11.

[52] R. Rubio-Marín, 'Exploring the Boundaries of Language Rights: Insiders, Newcomers, and Natives' in S. Macedo and A. Buchanan, *NOMOS XLV: Secession and Self-Determination* (2003) 136.

III. Immigrants' Equality of Rights under Human Rights Law

While the scope of the protection of cultural identity under human rights law deserves serious attention, it cannot obscure broader issues of redistribution, participation, and access, all of which are relevant to the discussion of integration in immigrant societies. A human rights perspective on the immigrant integration debate must therefore give due consideration to respecting (non-cultural) human rights of immigrants as *preconditions* for, or *vessels* of, the integration of immigrants, including by assisting in the removal of obstacles to participation, some of which may in fact have cultural roots. Economic, social, and cultural rights are particularly relevant, as they address issues such as education, labour, housing, or health that, together with the protection of family life, are of utmost importance for the integration of migrants.[53] One of the perverse effects of placing the debate about integration in immigrant societies within the immigration/membership domain instead of the citizenship domain is that it conveys the perception that states enjoy unfettered discretion. This framing in turn legitimizes states in their imposition of requirements, conditions, and duties, turning on its head what could otherwise be articulated as either rights-based entitlements on the part of resident migrants, or, arguably, civic duties applicable to both nationals and non-national residents for the preservation of a healthy democratic environment.

Elsewhere, I have explored how despite the promise of a universal human rights ethos privileging personhood as a source of rights claims, the human rights system, put into place after the Second World War, has not meant the displacement of either the state order system or national sovereignty as an organizing concept.[54] Rather, a delicate balance has been struck whereby bound national communities have retained wide discretion in deciding whom to accept on their territory, or as to the status of national citizenship.[55] On the other hand, for those who are physically

[53] W. Kälin, 'Human Rights and the Integration of Migrants', in T. A. Aleinikoff and V. Chetail (eds), *Migration and International Legal Norms* (2003) 271, at 279. On migrants' socio-economic rights, see Ryan and Mantouvalou in this volume. On the need for states to avoid different standards of treatment with regard to citizens and non-citizens, which might lead to racial segregation and the unequal enjoyment of economic, social, and cultural rights, see also Commission on Human Rights, Sub-Commission on the Promotion and Protection of Human Rights, The rights of non-citizens: Progress report of the Special Rapporteur, Mr David Weissbrodt, UN Doc E/CN.4/Sub.2/2002/25/Add. 1 (2002), para. 8, as well as Commission on Human Rights, Sub-Commission on the Promotion and Protection of Human Rights, The rights of non-citizens: Final report of the Special Rapporteur, Mr David Weissbrodt, UN Doc E/CN.4/Sub.2/2003/23 (2003), at 30.

[54] See C. M. Rodríguez and R. Rubio-Marín, 'The Constitutional Status of Irregular Migrants: Testing the Boundaries of Human Rights Protection in Spain and the United States', in M.-B. Dembour and T. Kelly (eds), *Are Human Rights for Migrants? Critical Reflections on the Status of Irregular Migrants in Europe and the United States* (2011) 73.

[55] There is no international law requirement that a state extends citizenship to the children of immigrants (international instruments do, however, urge steps to avoid statelessness, eg, Convention on the Rights of the Child, Art. 8). The 1961 Convention of the Reduction of Statelessness mandates that states parties grant nationality to persons born in their territories who would otherwise be stateless, and not deprive of their nationality persons born in their territories who would otherwise be stateless. There are no international conventions of universal application significantly regulating acquisition of

present, the territorially delimited jurisdictional domain of application of human rights ensures that *equality of rights* is the norm. This guarantees that horizontal and vertical relations remain—to a large extent—egalitarian, avoiding the generation of a cast-based society.

There are some exceptions, however. Under human rights law, residential security (understood as the right to enter and remain within the national territory) and core political rights, such as national voting, have been awarded to citizens only.[56] These exceptions are not insignificant, and some scholars concerned with legitimacy deficits have supported the need to extend full political rights or automatic access to national citizenship to migrants after a period of residence, in order to live up to the democratic challenge posed by immigrant societies.[57] There are also modest expressions in human rights law that this should be the direction to take, such as the adoption of the Convention on the Participation of Foreigners in Public Life at Local Level by the Council of Europe in 1992.[58] But even if we accept that national membership remains a reality, setting clear limits on immigrants' sense of agency and recognition through participation, the existence of a human rights regime anchored in personhood, much more than citizenship, has significantly constrained the capacity of states to commodify non-citizens in their midst when advancing national self-interest.

This delicate balance is now under stress. In a context where social rights are generally being undermined, some states have started to target migrants selectively, taking advantage of their political disenfranchisement. This targeting can proceed in more or less subtle ways, including selectively focusing on the most

citizenship; under customary international law, states are generally free to decide upon whom to confer citizenship. See K. Hailbronner, 'Nationality', in T. A. Aleinikoff and V. Chetail (eds), *Migration and International Legal Norms* (2003) 75. At a European level, we must refer to the European Convention on Nationality (1997), CETS No. 166, which several European states have ratified, but this Convention does not significantly limit signatory states' discretion in deciding the conditions upon which they ought to grant nationality to resident migrants.

[56] The UDHR recognizes that everyone has the right of equal access to public service, as well as to take part in the government of his country directly or through freely chosen representatives. Art. 25 of the ICCPR and Art. 23 of the American Convention on Human Rights (ACHR) refer to *citizens* as having the right to take part in the conduct of public affairs, to vote and be elected, and to access on equal terms the public service. Art. 3 of Protocol No. 1 to the ECHR (on political rights) refers to 'the people' when detailing the right to vote by secret ballot. Finally, regarding residential stability, the right to enter and not be expelled from a specific country is recognized only for nationals of a given country. See, eg, Art. 13 UDHR; Art. 12(4) ICCPR; Art. 3 Protocol No. 4 to the ECHR; and Art. 22(5) ACHR. For aliens legally in a territory, the most commonly acknowledged human right is the freedom of movement within the territory, or the freedom to choose one's residence once accepted into a country. See, eg, Art. 12(1) ICCPR; Art. 2(1) Protocol No. 4 to the ECHR; and Art. 22(1) ACHR. Some human rights instruments also protect aliens from collective expulsions. See Art. 4 Protocol No. 4 to the ECHR, and Art. 22 ACHR.

[57] R. Rubio-Marín, *Immigration as a Democratic Challenge: Citizenship and Inclusion in Germany and the United States* (2000); De Lucas (n 4); J. H. Carens, *Immigrants and the Right to Stay* (2010).

[58] CETS No. 144. The Convention grants foreigners the right to vote in local elections, provided that they fulfil the same legal requirements as apply to nationals and have been lawful and habitual residents in the state concerned for the five years preceding the elections. The Convention came into force in 1997, after the fourth ratification. As of 2010, the Convention has been ratified by eight member states. Five more states have signed it.

disenfranchised of all (that is, undocumented migrants), but also, indirectly, through integration and citizenship tests which make economic self-sufficiency and the lack of reliance on social services a condition for access to a secure residential or citizenship status, thus in fact 'punishing' or 'inhibiting' the exercise of rights. The question is consequently whether human rights law will evolve in ways which will help to narrow the 'inequality of rights' gap further, or instead further entrench the nationalist-statist logic by legitimating the gradual carving out of exceptions to the 'equality of rights' principle. Much will therefore depend on how the principle of equality and non-discrimination is defined and interpreted under human rights law, and the extent to which it helps shape migrants' legal status. It will fall to national courts and human rights adjudicatory bodies to decide, when interpreting human rights norms and constitutional fundamental rights, how narrowly or broadly to accept citizenship-based restrictions on the enjoyment of social rights and benefits, but also whether to allow states free rein by disguising the rights restrictions, clothing them as immigration/integration policies.

Looking back, we certainly find that the basic notion of equality of rights as covering resident migrants has been systematically confirmed since the coming into force of human rights instruments. Because national citizenship does make a difference in the enjoyment of some human rights (even though this is the exception), the non-discrimination mandate crafted under human rights law typically does not cite 'citizenship' as a prohibited ground for discrimination, but many of the grounds which are commonly mentioned as proscribed differentiation criteria—such as race, language, religion,[59] and of course national origin[60]—are obviously most relevant to the forms of discrimination that migrants experience. The basic notion of equality of rights as regards immigrants has been reaffirmed on several occasions. In 1985, when the UN Declaration on the human rights of individuals who are not nationals of the country in which they live was adopted,[61] it was already recognized that states have the right to enact laws regarding nationality and citizenship on the condition that 'such laws and regulations shall not be incompatible with the international legal obligations of that State, including those in the field of human rights' (Article 1). Similarly, in 2004, the Committee in charge of supervising the application of the Convention on the Elimination of Racial Discrimination[62] devoted its *General Recommendation No. 30* to discussing discrimination against non-citizens. It seized the opportunity to state that the distinction between citizens and non-citizens 'must be construed so as to avoid

[59] Arts 1(3) and 55 of the Charter of the United Nations.

[60] Art. 2 UDHR; Art. 2(1) ICCPR as well as Art. 2(2) ICESCR.

[61] Declaration on the Human Rights of Individuals Who are not Nationals of the Country in which They Live, UNGA Res 40/144, 13 December 1985.

[62] Worth underscoring is also the broad definition of racial discrimination under the Convention. Indeed, Art. 1 of the International Convention on the Elimination of All Forms of Racial Discrimination provides that the term 'racial discrimination' shall mean 'any distinction, exclusion, restriction or preference based on race, colour, descent, or *national or ethnic origin* which has the purpose or effect of nullifying or impairing the recognition, enjoyment or exercise, on an equal footing, of human rights and fundamental freedoms in the political, economic, social, cultural or any other field of public life' (emphasis added).

undermining the basic prohibition of discrimination', hence as 'not detracting from the rights and freedoms recognized' by international human rights instruments, enunciating in particular the Universal Declaration of Human Rights, the International Covenant on Economic, Social and Cultural Rights and the International Covenant on Civil and Political Rights (paragraph 2). Additionally, the Committee explained, in paragraphs 3 and 4 of the same recommendation, that, although some rights—such as the right to participate in elections, to vote, and to stand for election—may be confined to citizens, human rights are, in principle, to be enjoyed by all persons. In other words, equality is the norm, and 'differential treatment based on citizenship or immigration status will constitute discrimination if the criteria for such differentiation, judged in the light of the objectives and purposes of the Convention, are not applied pursuant to a legitimate aim, and are not proportional to the achievement of this aim'.[63] Once again, we confront the possibility of limitations subject to proportionality. However, the whole point of the General Recommendation seems to be that immigration-defined membership status cannot be taken as a self-evident justification for the restriction of rights otherwise universally recognized because human rights enjoy a lexical priority.

Relevant for our discussion is also the evolution under human rights law of the type of duties which fall to states and others to ensure the proclaimed equality of rights. In particular, it is important to prevent the undue transformation of 'rights and entitlements' relevant for immigrants' successful integration—some of which could arguably be claimed on equality grounds—into 'duties and conditions' for the acknowledgement of rights and membership status, under the purported justification of integration goals. For this, it is essential to recall that human rights law typically does not only oblige the state to *protect* rights, but also to *ensure* them (see Article 2(1) ICCPR), something which has been read as imposing positive action obligations on the state. In other words, the notion of substantive equality, or equality of opportunities, has increasingly gained force.[64] Worth mentioning, because of its explicitness, is the European Framework Convention on National Minorities, which includes an obligation of state parties 'to guarantee to persons

[63] Committee on the Elimination of Racial Discrimination, *General Recommendation No. 30: Discrimination Against Non Citizens*, 1 October 2004, available at Compilation of General Comments and General Recommendations adopted by Human Rights Treaty Bodies: Addendum, UN Doc HRI/GEN/1/Rev.7/Add.1, 4 May 2005.

[64] International and regional judicial and quasi-judicial bodies have addressed the nature of states' obligations to ensure equality and non-discrimination. They have specified that state actors must refrain from discriminatory actions that undermine the enjoyment of rights (duty to respect); prevent and protect against certain forms of discrimination by private actors (duty to protect), and take positive proactive steps to ensure the equal enjoyment of human rights (obligation to fulfil). See CESCR, *General Comment, No. 16*, paras 17–18; CESCR, *General Comment No. 20*, para. 8(b); CEDAW, *General Recommendation No. 25*, paras 4, 7–8; CERD, *General Comment No. 32*. They have affirmed that a state must ensure both de facto and de jure equality (CESCR, *General Comment No. 16*, para. 7; CEDAW, *General Recommendation No. 25*; para. 4; CERD, *General Comment, No. 32*, para. 6; CESCR, *General Comment No. 20*, para. 8.) and eliminate both direct and indirect discrimination, ensuring that seemingly neutral measures do not have a discriminatory effect in real terms (see CEDAW, *General Recommendation No. 25*, para. 7; CESCR, *General Comment No. 16*, paras 5, 12–13; CESCR, *General Comment No. 20*, para. 10; *General Comment No. 14*; CERD, *General Comment No. 32*, para. 7).

belonging to national minorities the right of equality before the law and of equal protection of the law', and to adopt, where necessary, 'adequate measures in order to promote, in all areas of economic, social, political and cultural life, *full and effective equality* between persons belonging to a national minority and those belonging to the majority', taking 'due account of the specific conditions of the persons belonging to national minorities' (Article 4(2)).

It must be granted that in case of social, economic, and cultural rights, this obligation has been subject to the maxim of progressive realization according to available resources. Nevertheless, in principle, this limitation allows for different, and changing, degrees of fulfilment, but not automatically for citizenship-based differentiations. Independent of resource availability, the two minimum obligations for states, which are immediately enforceable under the International Covenant on Economic, Social and Cultural Rights (ICESCR), are that of realizing these rights, observing the principles of *progressivity* and *non-regressivity,* on the one hand,[65] and that of *non-discrimination,* on the other.[66]

Some treaties go further in spelling out some of the domains which are in need of particular attention to ensure equality of opportunities. The 1977 European Convention on the Legal Status of Migrant Workers contains a strong obligation of state parties to ensure *equal treatment* to their own nationals regarding work conditions and the matter of social security (Articles 16 and 18). And, more recently, the ICRMW set forth an 'umbrella obligation' of non-discrimination with regard to all human rights (Article 7). It also explicitly recognized the obligation of state parties to promote conditions to ensure *effective equality* of treatment for migrant workers, explicitly referring to access to educational institutions, vocational guidance and placement services, housing schemes, social and health services, and participation in cultural life (Article 43), all of which are arguably of utmost importance for successful migrant integration.[67] In other words, it falls to the state to undertake those measures as may be needed to ensure that migrants can enjoy their human rights effectively.

From all of the above, two consequences follow. Both are important in present times, where direct, open discrimination on racial and ethnic grounds is—for the most part—no longer in the books, but prejudice, stigma, and xenophobia are on the rise. One, states are under the obligation not only not to discriminate, but also actively to fight against societal forces of discrimination which may be responsible

[65] On these principles, see C. Courtis, 'La prohibición de regresividad en materia de derechos sociales: apuntes introductorios', in C. Courtis (ed.), *Ni un paso atrás: La prohibición de regresividad en materia de derechos sociales* (2006) 3; and V. Abramovich and C. Courtis, *Los derechos sociales como derechos exigibles* (2002).

[66] See CESCR, *General Comment No. 20, Non-Discrimination in Economic, Social and Cultural Rights (art. 2, para. 2),* UN Doc E/C.12/GC/20, 10 June 2009, especially paras 7 and 9.

[67] Interpreting Art. 25 of the ICRMW, the UN Committee has also emphasized that labour protections in national law should be extended to migrant domestic workers to ensure equal protection under the law as well as additional provisions specific to the circumstances of domestic work. See UN Committee on the Protection of the Rights of all Migrant Workers and Members of their Families (CMW), *General Comment No. 1 on Migrant Domestic Workers*, CMW/C/GC/1, 23 February 2011, para. 38.

for the unsuccessful integration of migrants. Two, states may also be under an obligation to undertake explicit measures to help migrants overcome barriers related to their cultural background. It is precisely these barriers which may, in real-life scenarios, account for migrants' difficulties in the enjoyment of rights as crucial to their personal well-being and chances of successful integration as the right to education, to employment, and even to good health. Linguistic facilitation, allowing migrants to learn the majority language, but also, if needed, to express themselves and be understood in their own language, is certainly a case in point.[68]

Regarding the fight against discrimination, there is an increasing number of human rights provisions affirming the state obligation to prohibit and eliminate discrimination by third parties.[69] Moreover, as one would expect, migration-specific international instruments have made reference to some of the most common sources of societal discrimination and exploitation against which migrants deserve state protection, such as, for instance, exploitation in respect of rents (Article 43(1)(d) ICRMW). An explicit recognition of the importance of fighting discrimination is also to be found in the European Framework Convention on National Minorities, which includes an obligation of state parties to prohibit any discrimination based on belonging to a national minority (Article 4(1)), and to adopt 'measures to protect persons who may be subject to threats or acts of discrimination, hostility or violence as a result of their ethnic, cultural, linguistic or religious identity' (Article 6(2)). Finally, since the Treaty of Amsterdam introduced Article 13 EC Treaty, grounding the basis for the development of Community action to combat discrimination in the employment domain, new European paths to fight against discrimination have been opened up through the adoption of the 2000/78 Framework Employment Directive to combat discrimination in employment (on various grounds, including religion or belief).[70] It is important to underscore that the Directive explicitly encompasses indirect discrimination, and, therefore, could in theory justify claims to exemptions and reasonable accommodation in the employment domain. Even more relevant may be Directive 2000/43 on racial and ethnic discrimination, especially since it goes beyond the employment domain by prohibiting societal discrimination in the enjoyment of services.[71]

[68] On the concept of instrumental language rights to refer to linguistic accommodations whose primary purpose is not to protect the cultural-linguistic identity of individuals but just to impede language from being a liability in the general enjoyment of one's civil, social, and political rights and opportunities in society, see R. Rubio-Marín, 'Language Rights: Exploring Competing Rationales', in W. Kymlicka and A. Patten, *Language Rights and Political Theory* (2003) 63.

[69] See, eg, Arts 1 and 5 of the Convention on the Elimination of Racial Discrimination, which incorporate the obligation of states parties to prohibit and eliminate racial discrimination in the enjoyment of civil, political, economic, social, and cultural rights. In *General Comment No. 20*, the CESCR sets forth that 'States parties may be, and in some cases are, under an obligation to adopt special measures to attenuate or suppress conditions that perpetuate discrimination' (para. 9), these conditions not being limited to those directly created by the state, but also possibly stemming from the conduct of private actors.

[70] Council Directive 2000/78/EC of 27 November 2000, OJ 2000 L 303/16, establishing a general framework for equal treatment in employment and occupation.

[71] Council Directive 2000/43/EC of 29 June 2000, OJ 2000 L 180/22, implementing the principle of equal treatment between persons irrespective of racial or ethnic origin. See the recent

Finally, one can find signs in human rights law of the recognition of the importance of 'cultural facilitation', or the overcoming of 'cultural barriers', as an essential element to guarantee the effective enjoyment of human rights. Guarantees of linguistic access have been spelled out in general human rights treaties, but mostly concerning detention and fair trial guarantees.[72] Broader references to linguistic facilitation can be found in migrant-specific instruments. For instance, Article 33 ICRMW mentions migrant workers' right to information with regard to their employment conditions, their rights and obligations according to the laws and practice of the host state, and the rights they are entitled to, specifying that this information 'shall be provided upon request to migrant workers and members of their families, *free of charge*, and, as far as possible, *in a language they are able to understand*' (emphasis added). Worth mentioning in the health domain is the Report to the UN General Assembly by the UN Special Rapporteur on the Human Rights of Migrants, highlighting the importance of a state's health policy to be sensitive to both culture and gender, as well as conducive to reducing linguistic, communication, and cultural barriers.[73] Also, the UN Committee on Economic, Social and Cultural Rights has developed the concept of cultural adequacy, which refers to the idea that every human right (for example, the right to housing or to health) has a cultural component that public policies should respect. Moreover, the UN Committee on the Protection of the Rights of All Migrant Workers and Members of their Families, the supervisory body of the ICRMW, has duly underlined the detrimental effect of language barriers in the effective enjoyment of rights by migrants in its first *General Comment No. 1 on Migrant Domestic Workers*, of 2011, encouraging state parties

interesting development by the Court of Justice of the EU (CJEU) in Case C-394/11, *Valeri Hariev Belov*, judgment of 20 September 2012, not yet published, concerning the placing of electricity meters at unreachable places in areas considered as being Roma neighbourhoods. In her Opinion, Advocate-General Kokott allowed the Bulgarian Commission for Protection against Discrimination, a quasi-judicial equality body, to refer the case to the CJEU for a preliminary ruling, in a bold step towards broadening legal standing rules. However, in its judgment of 31 January 2013, the Court rejected this position and denied *locus standi* to the Bulgarian equality body, thus missing the opportunity to decide on a case of indirect discrimination based on ethnic origin and the possibilities for justification of such discrimination.

[72] See, for instance, Art. 3 ICCPR, recognizing that everyone shall be entitled to be informed promptly and in detail in a language which he understands of the nature and cause of the charge against him; Art. 16(5) ICRMW recognizing that migrant workers and members of their families who are arrested shall be informed at the time of arrest as far as possible in a language they understand of the reasons for their arrest; Art 5(2) ECHR, similarly recognizing to everyone who is arrested a right to be informed in a language that he understands about the reasons for his arrest—a guarantee interpreted by the ECtHR as not requiring information in the mother tongue, but in a language which ensures that the person understands the information (see *Egmez v. Cyprus*, ECHR (2000) Appl. No. 30873/96, judgment of 21 December 2000)—and Art. 6(3) recognizing that everyone charged with a criminal offence has the right to be informed promptly in a language which he understands of the nature and cause of the accusation against him, and adding the right to have free assistance of an interpreter if the person cannot understand or speak the language used in court (see *Kamasinski v. Austria*, ECHR (1989) Series A, No. 168).

[73] UN Special Rapporteur on the Human Rights of Migrants, Jorge Bustamante, Enjoyment of the rights to health and adequate housing by migrants, Annual Report to the Human Rights Council, UN Doc A/HRC/14/30, 16 April 2010, para. 78.

sending migrant workers 'to develop more specific pre-departure training and awareness raising programmes'—including, where appropriate, the provision of 'basic language preparation'.[74]

Because of its relevance to successful integration, linguistic facilitation in the educational domain deserves particular mention. Article 14 of the European Migrant Workers' Convention recognizes that 'in order to promote access to general and vocational schools and to vocational training centres, the receiving State shall facilitate *the teaching of its language* or if there are several, one of its languages to migrant workers and their families'. Although special measures to facilitate the learning of the language of the host society may be called for, one could also defend the need for transitional bilingualism based on similar instrumental reasons, if sufficient evidence were to back the hypothesis that this may be best for migrant children's cognitive development. In short, when one looks at the question of obstacles of linguistic access through the lens of substantive equality, it is easy to understand that the main approach to language learning must be that of rights-based entitlements once more. This is an approach which integration tests making the consolidation of status and enjoyment of rights conditional on the proof of a certain linguistic capacity certainly do not convey.

IV. Immigrant Integration and the Possibility of Complex Identities in Human Rights Law

So far, we have seen that human rights law indirectly constrains national immigrant integration policies in several ways. Firstly, by recognizing venues for cultural affirmation of migrants, setting limits to nationalist agendas which strive for cultural assimilation. Secondly, by affirming equality and non-discrimination in the enjoyment of rights as a tool for integration, and as grounding claims for assistance in overcoming the barriers of societal discrimination and cultural obstacles to access. There are, however, also a few scattered human rights norms and doctrinal evolutions which directly concern themselves with the question of migrants' integration in both sending and receiving societies. Embedded in such provisions seems to be the idea that receiving states are generally under the obligation to both facilitate immigrants' integration in the receiving society *and* respect their ties with their cultures of origin.

It should come as no surprise that the need to ensure that immigrants can preserve their cultural ties with the societies which they left is explicitly recognized in human rights treaties crafted at a time when many countries thought, and fully expected, migration to be a temporary phenomenon. In fact, the 1977 European Migrant Workers' Convention candidly acknowledges that 'the Contracting Parties . . . shall take actions by common accord to arrange, so far as practicable, for the

[74] CMW, *General Comment No. 1 on Migrant Domestic Workers*, CMW/C/GC/1, 23 February 2011, paras 27(b), 29, and 30(a); see also paras 7, 11, and 40.

migrant worker's children, special courses for the teaching of the migrant worker's mother tongue, to facilitate, inter alia, their return to their State of origin' (Article 15). It also includes a provision indicating that states shall, as far as possible, take appropriate *measures* to assist migrant workers and their families on the occasion of the *final return* to their state of origin (Article 30), including travel facilitation (Article 7), adding however that 'the provision of financial assistance shall be left to the discretion of each Contracting Party' (Article 30(1)).[75] Later instruments would more clearly recognize that, in this, a non-instrumental rationale, the respect owed to migrants' cultural identity, is also at stake. In particular, the 1990 ICRMW, otherwise rightly criticized for being particularly silent on integration matters,[76] indicates that state parties 'shall ensure respect for the cultural identity of migrant workers and members of their families and shall not prevent them from maintaining their cultural links with their State of origin' (Article 31(1)); and that they '*may* take appropriate measures to assist and encourage efforts in this respect' (Article 31(2), emphasis added). While these provisions can be seen as duly acknowledging the importance of immigrants not being discouraged from developing rich and complex cultural identities, the Convention also recognizes the instrumental dimension linked to the possibility of reintegrating in the country of origin, indicating under Article 67(2) that 'States Parties concerned shall co-operate as appropriate, on terms agreed upon by those States, with a view to promoting adequate economic conditions for their resettlement and to facilitating their durable *social and cultural reintegration* in the State of origin' (emphasis added). The view that conditions for self-respect may require both respect for one's culture of origin, as well as respect for other cultures, including that of the country of residence, is maybe most clearly articulated in the UN Convention on the Rights of the Child. The latter sets forth in Article 29(c) that 'the education of the child shall be directed to . . . the development of respect for the child's parents, his or her own cultural identity, language and values, for the national values of the country in which the child is living, the country from which he or she may originate, and for civilizations different from his or her own'.

The preservation of ties with the originating societies is not to be seen as legitimizing the creation of migrant ghettos in receiving countries, nor the perception of migrants as commodities which can be disposed of when no longer needed. Rather, the view seems to be one of accepting a path that combines the possibility of preserving features of one's cultural identity and the ties with the country of origin, or of one's ancestors, while at the same time integrating in the receiving society. This becomes clear from, for instance, Article 45(2) and (3) ICRMW, which specifically indicate that 'States of employment shall pursue a policy, where

[75] In fact, the Convention sets forth a certain duty of coordination signalling that states shall take steps to enable migrant workers to know, before they set out on their return journey, the conditions on which they will be able to *resettle in their state of origin,* communicating such conditions to the receiving state (this includes, inter alia, information on employment conditions in the state of origin, the possibility of financial aid, or the possibility to maintain the social security scheme acquired abroad, etc). See, eg, Arts 7, 30(1), and 30(2).

[76] De Guchteneire and Pécoud (n 1), at 20.

appropriate in collaboration with the States of origin, aimed at facilitating the integration of children of migrant workers in the local school system, particularly in respect of teaching them the local language', while acknowledging that 'States of employment shall endeavour to facilitate for the children of migrant workers the teaching of their mother tongue and culture and, in this regard, States of origin shall collaborate whenever appropriate'.[77] The result can therefore only be integration without assimilation. Only the European Framework Convention on National Minorities fully recognizes this when, in Article 5(2), it states that 'without prejudice to measures taken in pursuance of their general integration policy, the Parties shall refrain from policies or practices aimed at assimilation of persons belonging to national minorities against their will and shall protect these persons from any action aimed at such assimilation'.

While the expectation that migration would simply be a temporary feature was gradually being abandoned in all European countries, the economic crisis, and consequently higher unemployment rates, the undermining of the welfare state, and rising nationalism and xenophobia all became part of the political landscape in many European societies. This reality fuels a perception of migrants and the labour potential they offer as disposable goods, shedding a new and unexpected light on the importance of migrants retaining ties with the originating societies. On account of this, we must not only recall the existence of human rights provisions banning collective expulsions,[78] but also celebrate jurisprudential inroads, such as those of the European Court of Human Rights, pointing out the fact that when migrants have become integrated in receiving societies (on an emotional, social, and cultural level), deportation orders, which fail to duly take into account this integration, may amount to a violation of migrants' family and private life under Article 8 ECHR. This jurisprudence sets limits to the commodification of non-citizens' presence in the receiving countries.[79]

Indeed, over the last decades, in spite of the sovereign discretion traditionally recognized as a right of states under international law on immigration affairs in general, and regarding substantive grounds for deportation of non-citizens in particular, the ECtHR has come to accept that it may be a violation of their human rights to private and family life under Article 8 ECHR to deport non-citizens who are fully integrated into the society of residence, especially if they have not maintained (or never had) meaningful ties with their nation of a social, familial, or linguistic kind. Relevant factors in making this decision will be where migrants have been born and/or raised, been educated, spent most of their lives, developed

[77] Education in mother-tongue provisions had originally been introduced in view of re-migration to the countries of origin, but have since expanded beyond that particular intention. See A. Kondo, 'Comparison of Citizenship and Aliens' Rights', in A. Kondo (ed.), *Citizenship in a Global World: Comparing Citizenship Rights for Aliens* (2001) 236. The Revised European Social Charter (ESC) has added two new provisions, which are both concerned with language teaching. The first is aimed at the integration of migrant workers and their families in the host society through the teaching of the host country's national language(s) (Art. 19(11) ESC) whereas the second concerns the need to ensure that the children of migrant workers are able to learn the mother tongue of their parents (Art. 19(12) ESC).

[78] See Art. 4 Protocol No. 4 to the ECHR and Art. 19(1) EUCFR.

[79] See Chapter 3, this book.

family ties, and acquired linguistic skills.[80] In other words, immigrants' integration in receiving societies has become an object of protection under human rights law, setting limits to the almost unfettered discretion that states have traditionally enjoyed in deciding both on the residence of non-citizens in their territory, and on the definition of who qualifies as a citizen. Whether this jurisprudential line will survive the pressures of a context which is increasingly focused on security concerns remains to be seen.[81] Human rights law is at a crossroads. Even if it does survive, it will be interesting to watch this case law evolve. Because in some of its decisions the European Court has placed a lot of emphasis on the extent to which migrants have cut, or never had, meaningful ties with their countries of nationality, it is not clear whether the Court will endorse the belief that a migrant can have multiple meaningful, non-exclusive, and non-contradictory ties and identities, and that the ability to preserve them may be essential to their well-being. The evolution in international law, if not towards positive embracing, at least towards increasing tolerance of dual nationality, coupled with the fact that—at least in Europe, and especially in the EU—this evolution has come about partly as a result of a concern with the integration through naturalization of immigrants, seems to be a hesitant, but promising, sign of the gradual acceptance of complex and fluid identities in immigrant societies.[82]

[80] See, for instance, *Dalia v. France,* ECHR (1998) Appl. No. 26102/95, where the Court assessed these relevant factors but ultimately concluded that there had not been a violation of Art. 8, something which was opposed by the Dissenting Opinion of three judges. In this judgment, the Court observed that the applicant had *real ties* in France, but it also considered that she had *important links with Algeria.* In considering knowledge of the country of origin as a relevant factor, the Court noted that the applicant, having lived in Algeria until the age of seventeen or eighteen, for two years without her parents, had maintained certain family relations, spoke the *local language*, and had established *social and school relationships*. In those circumstances, the ECtHR deemed her Algerian nationality not to be *merely a legal fact*, but instead to reflect certain *social and emotional links* (para. 53). In *Slivenko et al. v. Latvia*, ECHR (2003) Appl. No. 48321/99 (GC) and *Maslov v. Austria*, ECHR (2008) Appl. No. 1638/03 (GC), though, the Court concluded that there had been a violation of Art. 8. In *Maslov*, for instance, the Court gave weight to the applicant speaking German and having received his entire schooling in Austria, concluding that he had his principal *social, cultural, and family ties* in Austria. As to the applicant's ties with his country of origin, the Court noted that he convincingly explained that he *did not speak Bulgarian* at the time of his expulsion as his family belonged to the Turkish minority in Bulgaria (paras 96 and 97).

[81] In this respect, it is useful to compare *Maslov v. Austria* with the more recent *Trabelsi v. Germany*, ECHR (2011), Appl. No. 41548/06, judgment of 13 October 2011, upholding the expulsion of a man of Tunisian origin from Germany. The applicant was born in Germany and his parents of Tunisian nationality and his three sisters of German nationality all lived in Germany. He had all his schooling there. Thus, due to birth, his links to Germany were arguably stronger than those of Maslov to Austria. In *Trabelsi,* the applicant argued that he did not know Arabic or French, and that the language spoken at home was only the German language, which his parents had learned before settling in Germany (para. 38). The expulsion order, taken on the basis of his commission of criminal actions as a minor and young adult, was harsher than in *Maslov,* as in *Trabelsi* the German authorities had ordered his 'indefinite expulsion'. The Court acknowledged that the applicant of Tunisian origin had undoubtedly strong ties with Germany, including language ties. However, it ultimately stressed—based on very weak evidence—that it could not be 'pretended either' that the applicant no longer had any link with the country of origin or that he had *no notion of* Arabic (paras 62–64, see also para. 42), thereby setting an extremely low threshold of relevant connections to the country of nationality.

[82] See European Parliament, 'Dual citizenship: Policy trends and political participation in EU member states', Directorate-General Internal Policies, Policy Department C, Citizens' Rights and

V. Human Rights and Citizenship Virtues in Pluralistic Societies

So far, I have shown that human rights law provides relevant normative parameters to assess the limits, contents, and underlying philosophy of integration policies in immigrant societies. I have also identified where the law stands at relevant crossroads which will determine its evolution towards either universalism or nationalism, hinting at how this evolutionary trend may further constrain the range of legitimate integration policies. However, fighting against the general retrenchment of rights, or for the equal recognition of rights to immigrants—including their right to complex identities—may not be enough to exhaust the challenge of keeping increasingly culturally diverse and fluid societies cohesive, especially if these societies are keen on preserving a commitment to redistributive justice, even under adverse conditions. Broader questions need to be tackled, including ways to ensure that the proper set of dispositions and civic virtues are promoted to sustain the health of democratic institutions.

Insisting on the need to abide by the law, as integration tests sometimes do, can be as symbolically reassuring for those setting the tests as it is alienating to those having to pass them. Also, the recognition of rights obviously requires the acceptance of duties as a natural corollary. But the real question confronting democracies in general, and immigrant societies in particular, goes deeper: can the mere recognition of rights, placing an emphasis on the state–citizen relationship, be enough to generate the preconditions of empathy, mutual recognition, respect, and tolerance, but also prudence, and self-containment, in the exercise of rights? And are some of these virtues not required for the long-term sustainability of our egalitarian democratic institutions? This is not a conversation that can, or should, be 'externalized' by placing the debate primarily under the 'immigrant integration' canopy. Instead, it is a discussion which must be held on a continuous basis, from a self-critical perspective, and refer to the entire population. It is a dialogue about the generation of public goods, from which all can benefit, and to which all should contribute.

Some human rights instruments have incorporated clauses to guide state action in furthering precisely the types of virtues and dispositions that might be needed, including some which can be formulated as duties. Knowledge of, and respect for, the 'other' is expected in Article 34 ICRMW, which recognizes that 'nothing in the present part of the Convention shall have the effect of relieving migrant workers and the members of their families . . . from the obligation to respect the cultural identity of the inhabitants of [states of employment]'.[83] Also, Article 14(3) of the European Framework Convention on National Minorities clarifies that the

Constitutional Affairs, PE 408.299, April 2008, at 5. See also T. Faist, and J. Gerdes, 'Dual Citizenship in an Age of Mobility', Migration Policy Institute (2008), 5 and 7.

[83] Art. 4 of the 1985 UN Declaration on the human rights of individuals who are not nationals of the country in which they live already indicated that 'Aliens shall observe the laws of the State in which they reside or are present and regard with respect the customs and traditions of the people of that State'.

'learning of the official language or in the official language can be expected'. Indeed, there is nothing a priori problematic about expecting migrants joining a community to learn the basics, in terms of its language, culture, history, and political institutions. After all, national citizens too, when subject to mandatory schooling, are expected to learn skills which will not only ensure their self-sufficiency and maximize their opportunities, but also their capacity to function as members of a collectivity committed to democracy and human rights.[84] There may consequently be good reasons to argue that the right/duty of education should be reassessed in immigrant societies where adults join the community without having been brought up in the national educational system. This may legitimize reception policies that expect new members to acquire knowledge important for them, but also for ensuring societal cohesion. A problem only appears in the event that this educational agenda is set in narrow terms, and selectively advanced through repressive means.

In no European democracy are literacy tests required as a condition for the enjoyment of social or political rights, even though in most cases there exists an obligation to learn the majority, or official, state language. However, this is in fact expected from migrants if they are required to pass integration tests requiring such knowledge as a condition to consolidating a certain membership status (for example, permanent residence or citizenship), and such a status is then made a precondition for the enjoyment of rights, which are arguably essential to both their well-being and societal integration. As for selectivity, the worrying concern is that an overemphasis is placed on the kinds of things that migrants must learn or know, separate from considerations of what citizens in general must learn and know; and, more importantly, about the kind of experience that the educational environment should provide *for all* in increasingly multi-ethnic and multi-religious societies. If part of the justifying rationale underlying the mandatory nature of education is to prepare persons to be citizens, the right and duty to education in immigrant societies should increasingly be read as requiring education in pluralism, and the reality of increasingly segregated school environments be seen as troublesome from a human rights perspective.[85] Human rights law stands at a crossroads.

It is worth recalling that human rights instruments have articulated state obligations to generate the proper set of dispositions in a way that involves both citizens

[84] See Art. 17 of the Revised ESC, including a state obligation to take appropriate and necessary measures 'to provide to children and young persons a free primary and secondary education as well as to encourage regular attendance at schools'; and with more decisive language, Art. 14 EUCFR specifies that the right of 'everyone' to education 'includes the possibility to receive free *compulsory* education' (emphasis added); and Art. 13 ICESCR setting forth that 'primary education shall be *compulsory* and available free to all' and that other forms of education (secondary—including technical or vocational—as well as higher education) shall be made 'accessible to all . . . by every appropriate means' (Art. 13(2) (a), (b), and (c), emphasis added). The rationale underlying education and mandatory schooling is to allow for the full flourishing of human dignity, the promotion of human rights and fundamental freedoms, as well as *tolerance and friendship* among all nations and *all racial, ethnic, or religious groups* (Art. 13(1) ICESCR, emphasis added).

[85] R. Rubio-Marín and L. Alvarez-Alvarez, 'Education, Crucifixes and Headscarves: Appropriation of Meanings and Content of Rights in Divided Societies', in A. Schwartz and C. Harvey (eds), *Rights in Divided Societies* (2012) 221.

and non-citizens. For instance, the 1992 UN Declaration on Rights of Persons belonging to national or ethnic, religious, and linguistic minorities addresses the precondition of knowledge of the 'other', which seems essential in the fight against bias, prejudice, and stereotype, by recognizing that 'States should, where appropriate, take measures in the field of education, in order to encourage knowledge of the history, traditions, language and culture of the minorities existing within their territory', and that 'persons belonging to minorities should have adequate opportunities to gain knowledge of the society as a whole' (Article 4(4)). Similarly, Article 12 of the European Framework Convention on National Minorities states the need for states 'to take measures in the fields of education and research to foster knowledge of the culture, history, language and religion of their national minorities and of the majority'. Even more to the point, Article 6(1) recognizes that 'the Parties shall encourage a spirit of tolerance and intercultural dialogue and take effective measures to promote mutual respect and understanding and co-operation among all persons living on their territory, irrespective of those persons' ethnic, cultural, linguistic or religious identity, in particular in the fields of education, culture and the media'. Finally, Article 9(4) acknowledges the need for state parties to 'adopt adequate measures in order to facilitate access to the media for persons belonging to national minorities and in order to promote tolerance and permit cultural pluralism'.

VI. Conclusion

In this chapter, I have explored the different angles that a human rights law perspective offers to the integration debate in immigrant societies. First, I have explored the ways in which human rights could open up channels for (but also set limits to) the cultural affirmation of migrants, thereby constraining the possibility of culturally assimilationist agendas. I have then considered the contours of the right to equality under human rights law, as applied to non-citizens and as expressive of the integration philosophy embedded in the human rights order, paying particular attention to the obligations that fall to the state in fighting against societal forces of discrimination, and removing culturally rooted access obstacles. I have subsequently analysed the norms that explicitly address the question of immigrants' integration, and shown that they provide the basis for a vision of integration which does not require migrants to dissolve the ties with their countries of origin, yet allows them to escape an isolated existence as part of, but distinct from, the receiving societies. Finally, I have traced signs in human rights law which recognize the limits of a rights-centred debate when discussing integration, bringing into the discussion civic virtues that are necessary to sustain well-functioning democratic institutions in increasingly pluralistic societies. This discussion, I have claimed, can neither be migrant-exclusive, nor migration-focused, if it is not to defeat its purpose. I have tried to show that, in all of these domains, human rights law currently stands at an important crossroads: it could advance in either the direction of affirming universalism or a nationalist agenda. Its chosen course will affect the kinds of integration policies that are seen to be compatible (or incompatible) with human rights law.

In 2004, the Council of the European Union approved the Common Basic Principles for Immigrant Integration Policy.[86] These principles advanced a perception of integration as a 'dynamic, two-way process of mutual accommodation' by all immigrants and residents of member states in a spirit of mutual understanding, 'resting on clear expectations of all residents—new and old'. The Basic Principles reiterated that the failure of an individual member state to develop and implement a successful integration policy can undermine the respect for human rights, mentioning that the practice of diverse cultures and religions is guaranteed under the Charter of Fundamental Rights, and must be safeguarded, unless practices conflict with other inviolable European rights or with national law. The Principles underscored the importance of immigrants' inclusion through employment opportunities and participation in the democratic process, especially in the formulation of integration policies, and at the local level. They highlighted that knowledge of the host society's language, history, and institutions is indispensable to integration, drawing the conclusion that 'enabling immigrants to acquire this basic knowledge was essential to successful integration', in particular emphasizing efforts in 'education as critical to preparing immigrants, and particularly their descendants, to be more successful and more active participants in society'. Value was furthermore attached to guaranteeing 'immigrants' access to institutions, as well as to public and private goods and services' on a non-discriminatory basis. Generating the conditions for successful integration, the Principles acknowledged, required 'frequent interaction' between immigrants and member-state citizens through 'shared forums, inter-cultural dialogue, education about immigrants and immigrant cultures, and stimulating living conditions in urban environments'.

Read as a whole, and in the light of what I described above, these integration guidelines reflect the integration philosophy embedded in human rights law, its shortcomings included. However, instead of trying to go beyond this baseline—or even insisting on its implementation by underscoring the importance of acknowledging rights, accommodating cultures, removing obstacles, fighting discrimination, encouraging participation, and furthering citizenship virtues among all—an increasing number of states in Europe are choosing to place emphasis on 'integration through testing', including, as of recently, by testing migrants' 'integration skills' or 'dispositions' even before they enter the territory. This trend may serve governments' electoral purposes, especially since it is seen as an attempt to convey the 'security of closure' or, at least, a sense of retained 'sovereignty' and 'control', which will ensure the economic, cultural, and political survival of the host nation. Both are understandable tendencies in a climate of competition for scarce jobs and resources, a diminishing role for welfare, and increasingly culturally mixed societies, in which the immigration debate has focused on security concerns, partly because

[86] 14615/04 (Presse 321)17, 19 November 2004.

of the presence of Muslim migrants, and their assumed illiberal, if not terrorist, dispositions.

However, as we have seen, even when genuinely intended to serve integration purposes, the shifts in framing, from 'citizenship' to 'immigration', and from 'recognizing and enabling' to 'expecting and testing', are not deprived of important, negative implications. Firstly, these shifts may serve to legitimize another shift, namely that from rights and enabling conditions to selectively imposed duties and obligations, which could result in migrants bearing all, or most of, the costs, something which can only further entrench the extractive features of a system that only wants to derive net gains from immigration. Secondly, by making membership status and rights enjoyment conditional on the fulfilment of tests of knowledge and dispositions, states are in fact delaying rights, and possibilities for the meaningful exercise of rights, in ways which are likely to undermine, rather than encourage, integration. These ways include access to full political participation, even though such participation would allow migrant views and voices to play a central role in deciding what integration actually means and requires. Thirdly, a framing of integration as an 'immigration' rather than a 'citizenship' concern naturally and unduly narrows the debate about the civic virtues necessary to sustain democratic institutions in pluralistic societies, a debate which should encompass the entire population, and not just migrants. In fact, in symbolic terms, the single most important effect of the dominant framing of the 'integration through testing' approach may be its contribution to the 'othering' of migrants, many of whom are becoming, and will remain, permanent members of society, by expressing essentialist, negative, and stereotypical views about them in ways which can be counterproductive to securing due recognition for immigrants' worth and society's overall integration. In human rights terms, the regulatory transfer of integration policies away from policies to ensure equal rights, accommodate cultural differences, and remove obstacles in order to ensure social inclusion and participation, entails an expansion of state sovereignty that defeats the lexical order embedded in the human rights system, and the notion of societal integration around which this order is inherently built.

3

Residence as De Facto Citizenship? Protection of Long-term Residence under Article 8 ECHR

Daniel Thym

I. Introduction

Economic interdependence and societal transnationalism sustain a growing number of cross-border movements which reflect wider 'globalization' processes.[1] As a consequence, migration has become a major policy issue in countries around the world. There are abundant legal disputes both in domestic and international legal forums based on formidable questions which both the courts and academics struggle to disentangle. At the same time, legal disputes exposed by migratory movements are not limited to problems of dogmatic interpretation and adjudication. International migration raises profound questions about the theoretical underpinning of legal regimes in question. Conferring (human) rights on transnational migrants poses a direct challenge to sovereign statehood upon which the state's prerogative to regulate the entry and stay of foreigners was traditionally founded.[2] Within this overall context, this chapter considers the expansion of the European Convention on Human Rights (ECHR) and explores theoretical implications.

When it comes to the protection of human rights of foreigners, the European Court of Human Rights (ECtHR) in Strasbourg has long assumed a pioneering role. It was the first international court to extend the human rights of foreigners beyond the sphere of forced migration, which has been subject to international law guarantees since the 1950s,[3] to voluntary migration on the basis of Article 8 ECHR. In 1991, the Court first qualified the deportation of a foreigner as a violation of his right to family life.[4] Ten years later, judges in Strasbourg obliged

[1] Cf. S. Castles and M. J. Miller, *The Age of Migration: International Population Movements in the Modern World* (2009), chapters 5–7.

[2] See D. Martin, 'The Authority and Responsibility of States', in T. A. Aleinikoff and V. Chetail (eds), *Migration and International Legal Norms* (2003) 31.

[3] Cf. the 1951 Refugee Convention and the humanitarian activities of UNHCR.

[4] See *Moustaquim v. Belgium*, ECHR (1991) Appl. No. 12313/86, judgment of 18 February 1991.

a contracting state to grant foreigners the option of cross-border family reunion in its territory with family members living abroad.[5] In recent years, the Grand Chamber has further extended the protective reach of Article 8 ECHR to cover long-term residence status, including a potential right to regularize illegal stay.[6] This protection of long-term residence status is the subject of this chapter, since it accentuates the loss of 'sovereign' state control over the entry and stay of foreigners. Is the traditional distinction between foreigners without a secure residence status and national citizens obsolete?

This contribution begins with an examination of the ECtHR's standpoint from a legal-doctrinal angle. Despite radical judgments, the Court has always been careful not to overstretch its case law by leaving some leeway for the contracting parties under the margin of appreciation doctrine, and when it comes to the protection of long-term residence status (part II). On this basis, the remainder of this chapter explores conceptual implications of Strasbourg's case law. Almost twenty years ago, the ECtHR's judicial innovations were first identified as the manifestation of an emergent post-national society with an incipient form of transnational membership, which supersedes national citizenship.[7] Notwithstanding the originality and relevance of the judicial approach, this chapter supports a differentiated evaluation. Article 8 ECHR gives voice to migrants' perspectives by protecting long-term residence. This rejects the assertion of unfettered state control, but does not necessarily lead towards de facto citizenship. Protecting the human rights of all non-citizens is in itself an important cosmopolitan achievement (part III).

II. Doctrinal Foundations

The application of the ECHR to the entry and stay of foreigners was not a foregone conclusion. Article 8 states in rather general terms, 'Everyone has the right to respect for his private and family life, his home and his correspondence'. Although this provision was not originally considered to cover migration, it was its imprecision which facilitated dynamic interpretation by the ECtHR. The concept of 'private life', in particular, is so vague that it can potentially be extended to different domains, as the Court's case law illustrates. Article 8 ECHR has been employed by the judges to push the Convention beyond its original scope into new domains, such as environmental issues, the decriminalization of homosexuality,

[5] *Şen v. the Netherlands*, ECHR (2001) Appl. No. 31465/96, judgment of 21 December 2001.

[6] See *Slivenko et al. v. Latvia*, ECHR (2003) Appl. No. 48321/99, judgment of 9 October 2003 (GC) and ECtHR, *Sisojeva v. Latvia*, ECHR (2007) Appl. No. 60654/00, judgment of 15 January 2007 (GC).

[7] For a pioneering study, see Y. N. Soysal, *Limits of Citizenship: Migrants and Postnational Membership in Europe* (1994), chapters 8 and 9.

data protection.[8] The following sections explore the methodological foundations of the case law (A); the protection of long-term residence status (B), including the potential right to regularize illegal stay (C); countervailing public policy considerations (D); and recent innovations within the EU framework (E).

It is not the purpose of this contribution to provide an extensive overview of the case law.[9] Instead, our focus shall be the protection of long-term residence status and conceptual implications. Notwithstanding their practical relevance, associated social and economic rights of migrants, such as access to the labour market, education, or welfare services[10] as well as cultural or religious rights[11] of those residing (il)legally within a country will not be considered. Similarly, this study does not consider universal human rights instruments, which generally provide a lesser degree of protection than the ECHR.[12] Our focus on Strasbourg's protection of residence *ipso jure* illustrates the emergence of a human right to residence security in a country where one does not possess nationality. Such guarantee directly challenges state control over the entry and stay of non-citizens.

A. The ECHR and immigration cases

As the starting point, the ECtHR maintains that the contracting states enjoy 'as a matter of well-established international law and subject to their treaty obligations [the right] to control the entry, residence and expulsion of aliens'.[13] This assertion reflects wider methodological uncertainties about the application of human rights to immigration cases, since human rights have traditionally been conceived as guarantees *within* existing states without assurances for transnational movement. Certainly, the ECHR was always meant to confer rights upon non-citizens.[14] Yet migration has been deliberately left outside the scope of the Convention.[15] It is not surprising, therefore, that the Strasbourg institutions

[8] For an overview of non-immigration case law, see R. C. A. White and C. Ovey, *Jacobs, White and Ovey: the European Convention on Human Rights* (2010), chapter 16.

[9] For a well-written overview of the ECtHR's case law on Art. 8 ECHR in immigration cases, see P. Boeles and M. den Heijer, *European Migration Law* (2009), at 144–70.

[10] See the comparative study by D. Weissbrodt, *The Human Rights of Non-Citizens* (2008), and Chapter 5 in this volume.

[11] Cf. W. Kälin, 'Human Rights and the Integration of Migrants', in Aleinikoff and Chetail (n 2) 271.

[12] For the ICCPR, see V. Chetail, 'Freedom of Movement and Transnational Migrations: A Human Rights Perspective', in Aleinikoff and Chetail (n 2) at 47–60; E. Decaux, *Le Pacte international relatif aux droits civils et politiques* (2010), Art. 12 section IV, and S. Joseph, J. Schultz, and M. Castan, *The International Covenant on Civil and Political Rights: Cases, Materials, and Commentary* (2004), sections 12.27–12.37.

[13] This standard formula was first used in *Moustaquim* (n 4) para. 43.

[14] As is evident from Art. 1 ECHR, which secures the rights of 'everyone' (not just citizens or nationals of the High Contracting Parties only) within the jurisdiction of states.

[15] The *travaux préparatoires* show that the issue of asylum was discussed, but left outside the ECHR framework, also with a view to ongoing discussion on the 1951 Refugee Convention; cf. H.-J. Uibopuu, 'Der Schutz des Flüchtlings im Rahmen des Europarats', 21 *Archiv des Völkerrechts* (1983) 60, at 61–4, while legal migration was considered to fall within the *domaine réservée* of state

remained largely silent on matters of migration in the first thirty years of their existence. The extension of human rights to migration conflicts with the Court's assertion of sovereign state control over the entry and residence of foreigners 'as a matter of well-established international law'. The Court responded to this tension by giving the contracting parties principled discretion (subsection 1 below) and by distinguishing different situations in which migrants may invoke ECHR guarantees (subsection 2 below).

1. Methodological starting-point

Interpreting international human rights has never been a straightforward exercise in discovering the contents of a pre-existing norm. The ordinary meaning and purpose of provisions such as Article 8 ECHR are far too vague to guide the adjudication of individual cases.[16] In its case law, the ECtHR has developed generalized principles guiding the interpretation of the Convention. Many of these principles appear regularly in immigration cases and try to rationalize the Court's findings. Two sets of interpretative principles can be distinguished: those supporting the dynamic extension of the Convention in favour of migrants, and others reflecting concerns of the high contracting parties about the limits of judicial innovation.

On the one hand, the Court has always viewed the Convention as a 'living instrument', thereby facilitating the proactive recognition of social developments which were originally not meant to be covered and to which the Court nonetheless extends the ECHR by means of dynamic interpretation.[17] Dynamic interpretation is solidified by the Court's assertion that the Convention's purpose of protecting human beings implies that 'its provisions be interpreted and applied so as to make its safeguards practical and effective',[18] as well as the sporadic invocation of the Convention's character 'as a constitutional instrument of European public order (*ordre public*)'[19] which both serve as additional bases for the quantitative and qualitative extension of migrant rights.[20]

On the other hand, Strasbourg is careful not to appear biased. As mentioned previously, most judgments on migration start with a principled assertion of

sovereignty, which only carefully drafted international norms—such as Arts 2 and 4 of Additional Protocol No. 4 to the ECHR—would selectively limit, while maintaining the principle of state discretion in immigration matters at large.

[16] Wording (meaning) as well as object and purpose remain the starting point for the interpretation of international (human rights) treaties in accordance with Art. 31(1) VCLT.

[17] See White and Ovey (n 8) chapter 3; critics obviously argue that dynamic interpretation sidesteps the original will of the high contracting parties and the mechanisms for amendment of the Convention; for a powerful critique, see K. Hailbronner, 'Art. 3 EMRK—ein neues europäisches Konzept der Schutzgewährung?' 52 *Die Öffentliche Verwaltung* (1999) 617.

[18] *Soering v. the United Kingdom*, ECHR (1989) Appl. No. 14038/88, judgment of 7 July 1989, para. 87.

[19] *Loizidou v. Turkey*, ECHR (1995) Appl. No. 15318/89, judgment of 23 March 1995 (GC), para. 75.

[20] Cf. the general survey by A. Mowbray, 'The Creativity of the European Court of Human Rights', 5 *Human Rights Law Review* (2005) 57, at 72–9 and related arguments for international refugee law in J. C. Hathaway, *The Rights of Refugees under International Law* (2005) at 48–74.

sovereign state control over the entry and stay of foreigners 'as a matter of well-established international law'.[21] Moreover, Strasbourg acknowledges that the reach of states' obligations under Article 8 ECHR in immigration cases 'do not lend themselves to precise definition' and that, therefore, 'the State enjoys a *certain* margin of appreciation'.[22] The margin of appreciation is complemented by the institutional assumption that Strasbourg should yield to decisions at national level, since 'the machinery for the protection of fundamental rights established by the Convention is subsidiary to the national systems safeguarding human rights'.[23]

Academic commentators have rightly criticized the lack of a solid foundation in legal theory for the Court's methods of interpretation.[24] As a result, it is easy to criticize the Court's findings as either overly restrictive or too extensive. Some academics argue that the margin of appreciation, in particular, misses the priority which the judges should give to the interests of the migrant,[25] while other commentators stress, to the contrary, the primacy of national democratic choices,[26] reflecting the traditional dichotomy between (constitutional) courts and the majority will of the legislator in democratic societies.[27] As an international human rights court, the ECtHR cannot avoid these intricacies and pitfalls which are inherent in human rights adjudication in democratic societies and which are, in the case of migration, further complicated by legal and theoretical uncertainties about the moral-philosophical legitimacy of transnational migration and its limits.

Moreover, the interpretative principles outlined earlier in this chapter remain rather vague on a practical level: where does the 'effectiveness' of private life of individual migrants command priority over the high contracting parties' margin of appreciation which the Court acknowledges to a 'certain' extent? Such statements are far too abstract and lack internal prioritization when deciding which consideration should prevail under which circumstances; they do not provide guidance for the adjudication of individual cases. Both restrictive and permissive positions can easily be defended on their basis. Instead of providing guidance, the core

[21] Again, *Moustaquim* (n 4) para. 43.

[22] *Gül v. Switzerland*, ECHR (1996) Appl. No. 23218/94, judgment of 19 February 1996, para. 38 (emphasis added) indirectly limits the assertion of a '*wide* margin of appreciation' in *Abdulaziz, Cabakes & Balkandali v. the United Kingdom*, ECHR (1985) Appl. Nos. 9214/80, 9473/81 and 9474/81 judgment of 28 May 1985, para. 67.

[23] *Sisojeva* (n 6) para. 90 and, for further reflection, former President of the ECtHR Wildhaber, 'A Constitutional Future for the European Court of Human Rights?', 23 *Human Rights Law Journal* (2002) 161, at 162; similarly, from a dogmatic perspective, P. Mahoney, 'Marvellous Richness of Diversity or Invidious Cultural Relativism?', 19 *Human Rights Law Journal* (1998) 1, at 3–4.

[24] Cf. the prominent critique by S. Greer, *The European Convention on Human Rights: Achievements, Problems and Prospects* (2006), chapter 4.

[25] A general argument for the 'liberal' interpretation of the ECHR is presented by G. Letsas, *A Theory of Interpretation of the European Convention on Human Rights* (2007), whereas S. Saroléa, *Droits de l'homme et migrations: De la protection du migrant aux droits de la personne migrante* (2006), at 317 et seq. and A. Farahat, 'The Exclusiveness of Inclusion: On the Boundaries of Human Rights in Protecting Transnational and Second Generation Migrants', 11 *European Journal of Migration and Law* (2009) 253, at 262–4, criticize the approach to migration cases more specifically.

[26] Consult the contributions to T. Campbell, K. D. Ewing, and A. Tomkins (eds), *The Legal Protection of Human Rights: Sceptical Essays* (2011).

[27] Cf. the references to classic constitutional theory by Greer (n 24) chapter 3.

achievement of the interpretative principles seems to be more pragmatic. They allow the Court to rationalize its judicial conclusions. They guide the argumentative juxtaposition of opposing arguments, which may ideally support the Court to achieve a 'fair balance that has to be struck between the competing interests of the individual and of the community as a whole'.[28] The aspiration to strike a 'fair balance' between countervailing interests may not have much theoretical grounding, but arguably this is what the Court does regularly.

2. *Different immigration configurations*

International migration does not follow a uniform pattern. Some migrants invoke human rights at the point of entry, when state authorities reject their claim for admission; others rely on the ECHR against expulsion measures after having lived (il)legally in the country concerned. At an abstract level, we may distinguish two situations: first, Article 3 ECHR serves as the central guarantee against mistreatment in the country of origin which the (European) host state is asked to provide shelter from; second, Article 8 ECHR is activated by migrants against (European) countries, in which they live, without primary consideration to the situation in their country of origin. In short, refugees are protected against *refoulement* under Article 3 ECHR, whereas Article 8 ECHR is based upon legitimate ties which migrants have developed in their European host state. Against this background, three configurations may be differentiated which are complemented by the protection of long-term residence status (discussed later in this chapter).

(a) *Non-refoulement* under Article 3 ECHR

There is a broad consensus among political theorists and international lawyers that states should not return refugees to their countries of origin or transit where their life or essential well-being is at risk.[29] For this purpose, the 1951 Refugee Convention was set up to which the ECHR was originally meant to concede protection against *refoulement*.[30] In the early 1990s, the ECtHR started nonetheless to activate Article 3 ECHR as an additional instrument for refugee protection, which has since been expanded beyond the reach of the Refugee Convention. It not only protects individuals against political prosecution in the country of origin, but covers threats by non-state actors and also extends to severe violations of basic human rights. Even threats to life as a result of indiscriminate violence in situations of armed conflict or the total absence of medical treatment may be covered by Article 3 ECHR.[31] Recently, the ECtHR has stretched the Convention even

[28] *Gül* (n 22) para. 38.

[29] See, among many, C. Brown, 'The Only Thinkable Figure? Ethical and Normative Approaches to Refugees in International Relations', in A. Betts and G. Loescher (eds), *Refugees in International Relations* (2010) 151, at 152–9.

[30] See the text in n 15.

[31] For an overview see Boeles and Den Heijer (n 9) at 291–314; and M. Bossuyt, *Strasbourg et les demandeurs d'asile: des juges sur un terrain glissant* (2010) at 7–48; for the extension of Art. 3 ECHR to

further: although the prohibition of *refoulement* has traditionally been applied to foreigners present in the territory only, the ECtHR emphasized the extraterritorial reach of Article 3 ECHR, including a potential associated right to entry into the national territory.[32] In short, Article 3 ECHR has been turned into an instrument for refugee protection also in situations which are not covered by the Refugee Convention.

(b) Expulsion of family members

For the first three decades of its existence, the ECtHR maintained that the ECHR does not regulate the entry and stay of foreigners.[33] It took until 1988 for the expulsion of an alien who had been residing legally in the Netherlands for several years to be declared incompatible with Article 8 ECHR, since the expulsion threatened the continuation of family life with his young daughter.[34] Since then the ECtHR has played a crucial role in providing a human rights safety net against the expulsion of migrants who had, in many cases, spent their whole life in the territory of the high contracting parties as the children of 'guest workers' who moved to Europe after the Second World War.[35] Although security of residence was a driving force behind the case law from the beginning, it was dogmatically constructed as a means for the protection of family life (that is, ties to parents and siblings, not residence in the host country as such). The protection of long-term residence status as an end in itself under the heading of 'private life' surfaced only at a later point and will be analysed later (see section B.3).

(c) Admission for purposes of family reunion

Protection against expulsion concerns foreigners living in the host country. In such cases, the Court may rely on the classic doctrinal classification of human rights as a shield against (negative) state interference. One step further, the doctrine of positive obligations may be relied upon to request state action which (positively) supports the realization of individual interests.[36] More specifically, Article 8 ECHR may

'a situation of extreme material poverty' see *M.S.S. v. Belgium & Greece*, ECHR (2011) Appl. No. 30696/09, judgment of 21 January 2011 (GC), paras 235–264.

[32] Cf. *Hirsi Jamaa et al. v. Italy*, ECHR (2012) Appl. No. 27765/09, judgment of 23 February 2012 (GC), paras 70–82 concerning border control activities on the High Seas in the Mediterranean (it should be noted that a right to entry exists only when the 'jurisdiction' test described in the judgment is met, eg, when border guards control the movement of ships carrying refugees), and Chapter 6 in this book.

[33] Early indications that Art. 8 ECHR might be applied to immigration cases can be found in decisions of the European Commission of Human Rights (the historic antechamber of the ECtHR) although the relevant claims were ultimately dismissed as manifestly ill-founded; cf. *X. & Y. v. Germany* (1977) Appl. No. 7816/77, DR 9, 57, decision of 19 May 1977, and *X. & Y. v. Liechtenstein* (1977) Appl. Nos. 7289 and 7349/75, DR 9, 219, decision of 14 July 1977.

[34] See *Berrehab v. the Netherlands*, ECHR (1988) Appl. No. 10730/84, judgment of 21 June 1988, where the Court emphasizes in para. 29 that the case did not concern first admission to the territory.

[35] For an overview, see, again, Boeles and Den Heijer (n 9) at 144–70.

[36] Cf. A. R. Mowbray, *The Development of Positive Obligations under the European Convention on Human Rights by the European Court of Human Rights* (2004) at 171–6; it should be noted that in immigration cases, in particular, the ECtHR is not always consistent in distinguishing between negative interference and positive obligations; cf. Boeles and Den Heijer (n 9) at 144–5.

oblige states to grant permission for cross-border family reunions on their territory, including family members living abroad. In contrast to expulsion, the entry of the family member concerned has not been authorized by the host state on an earlier occasion. It is therefore convincing that the Court has been reluctant to deduce admission rights from Article 8 ECHR. Most claims in the category were dismissed in Strasbourg, since the Convention 'cannot be considered as extending to a general obligation . . . to respect the choice by married couples of the country of their matrimonial residence'.[37] To date, only two applications claiming admission for purposes of family reunion, which had not been resolved domestically,[38] have been successful.[39] Protection against expulsion therefore remains the backbone of the ECtHR's immigration case law.

B. Protecting long-term residence status

The ECHR has always defended a wide understanding of family life. It focuses on the existence of substantive family life in real terms, not in abstract legal criteria.[40] It also extended the substantive reach of Article 8 ECHR to 'ties between near relatives, for instance those between grandparents and grandchildren'.[41] Against this background, it did not come as a great surprise when the Court started examining expulsion measures against foreigners in light of Article 8 ECHR, whenever the expulsion entailed separation from family members. Given the wide meaning of family life, the ECtHR not only examined the effects on the joint life of spouses and children, but extended its reasoning to the relationships of the applicant with (grand)parents and siblings.[42] Since the Court does not perform an intensive analysis of the depth and quality of the family bond with the relatives in most cases,[43] family life has become a generalized concept claimed by many migrants. Most foreigners have one or more relatives living in the country of

[37] *Abdulaziz et al.* (n 22) para. 68 and, more recently, *Rodrigues da Silva & Hoogkamer v. the Netherlands*, ECHR (2006) Appl. No. 50435/99, judgment of 31 January 2006, para. 39.

[38] Most claims for family reunion with reasonable grounds for success will never reach the ECtHR, since most national immigration laws provide statutory family reunification rights in accordance with Art. 3 of the EU Council Directive 2003/86/EC, OJ 2003 L 251/12, on the right to family reunification.

[39] See *Şen v. the Netherlands*, ECHR (2000) Appl. No. 31465/96, judgment of 21 December 2000, and *Tuquabo-Tekle et al v. Netherlands*, ECHR (2005) Appl. No. 60665/00, judgment of 1 December 2005.

[40] Thereby leading the legal push for the equal treatment of 'illegitimate' children and the recognition of non-married couples; for details see White and Ovey (n 8) chapter 15, and J. A. Frowein and W. Peukert, *Europäische Menschenrechtskonvention: EMRK-Kommentar* (2009), Art. 8 EMRK, paras 17–41.

[41] *Marckx v. Belgium*, ECHR (1979) Appl. No. 6833/74, judgment of 13 June 1979, para. 45.

[42] The wide understanding of family life in an expulsion case was first applied to the deportation of a deaf and dumb adult delinquent without a family (spouse or children) of his own in *Nasri v. France*, ECHR (1995) Appl. No. 19465/92, judgment of 13 July 1995, para. 34.

[43] It did however reject the invocation of Art. 8 ECHR by an aunt who had looked after nieces and nephews before their full age due to the lack of 'further elements of dependency involving more than the normal emotional ties' in *Javeed v. the Netherlands*, ECHR (2001) Appl. No. 47390/99, decision of 3 July 2001.

residence, so they can build their claim against expulsion decisions upon these relations.[44]

Academic observers soon identified a 'hidden agenda' of the Court to protect the long-term residence status of second-generation immigrants, who had often been born in the Western European reception states or joined their migrant parents at a young age.[45] In cases involving adult foreigners most judgments referred not only to family life, but also highlighted the length of stay in the reception country.[46] The Court, however, never renounced the link to family life, despite recurring calls by judges in separate opinions to grant autonomous protection to personal bonds within the receiving country regardless of family life.[47] The protection of the social environment as such was only accepted by the Court in the mid-2000s in a series of cases concerning the ethnic Russian minority in the Baltic States who had settled there during the period of the Soviet Union and later often became stateless when the Soviet Union disintegrated (subsection 1 below). Protection of residence *ipso jure* under the heading of 'private life' concentrates on the human rights protection of residence in a country where one does not possess that nationality (subsection 2 below).

1. Distinguishing private and family life

The crucial innovation of the Court's new approach concerns the reconceptualization of family and private life: the Court restricted its formerly wide understanding of 'family life' by concentrating on the nuclear family of spouses and minor children below the age of eighteen, while at the same time broadening the protective reach of Article 8 ECHR to the network of personal, social, and economic relations that make up the 'private life' of every human being. The central passage on the

[44] The ideas in this section build upon my earlier article: D. Thym, 'Respect for Private and Family Life under Art. 8 ECHR in Immigration Cases: A Human Right to Regularize Illegal Stay?', 57 *ICLQ* (2008) 87, at 89–95.

[45] Cf. R. Cholewinski, 'Strasbourg's "Hidden Agenda"?: The Protection of Second-Generation Migrants from Expulsion under Art. 8 of the European Convention on Human Rights', 12 *Netherlands Quarterly of Human Rights* (1994) 287 and S. Hobe, 'Aufenthaltsbeendende Maßnahmen und Menschenrechte (Art. 8 EMRK und andere Verträge)', in K. Hailbronner and E. Klein (eds), *Einwanderungskontrolle und Menschenrechte—Immigration Control and Human Rights* (1999) 197, at 200.

[46] See, eg, *El Boujlifa v. France*, ECHR (1997) Appl. No. 25404/94, judgment of 21 October 1997, para. 36: interference with 'private *and* family life' (emphasis added); for an overview, see former Judge P. Van Dijk, 'Protection of "Integrated" Aliens Against Expulsion under the European Convention on Human Rights', 1 *European Journal of Migration and Law* (1999) 293, at 298–301 and J. Vedsted-Hansen, 'Migration and the Right to Family and Private Life', in V. Chetail (ed.), *Mondialisation, migration et droits de l'homme: un nouveau paradigme pour la recherche et la citoyenneté*, vol. II (2007) 689, at 695–7.

[47] See, in particular, the concurring and separate opinions of Judges Martens and De Meyer in *Beldjoudi v. France*, ECHR (1992) Appl. No. 12083/86, judgment of 26 March 1992, and the concurring and partly dissenting opinions of judges Wildhaber, Morenilla, and De Meyer in *Nasri v. France* (n 42). Similarly in the UK, Sedley LJ held in *B v. SSHD* [2000] Imm AR 478 that the network of everyday contacts was protected as private life under Art. 8 ECHR.

redefinition of family life with a new focus on spouses and minor children (the 'core family' in the terminology of the ECtHR) reads:

> [T]he existence of 'family life' could not be relied on by the applicants in relation to the first applicant's elderly parents, *adults who did not belong to the core family* and who have not been shown to have been dependent members of the applicants' family, the applicants' arguments in this respect not having been sufficiently substantiated.[48]

It should be highlighted that the restrictive reading of family life does not translate into a diminution of human rights protection, since it is complemented by the autonomous protection of wider social relations that constitute the foreigners' private life, which had not been explicitly recognized by the Court previously:

> They were thus removed from the country where they had developed, uninterruptedly since birth, the *network of personal, social and economic relations that make up the private life of every human being*... In these circumstances, the Court cannot but find that the applicants' removal from Latvia constituted an interference with their 'private life' and their 'home within the meaning of Article 8 § 1 of the Convention.[49]

As a result, long-term-residence status now enjoys autonomous human rights protection independent of the family situation. This is remarkable. Residence in itself is now covered by Article 8 ECHR. Non-citizens cannot be automatically expelled from a country for the sole reason that they have lived there for an extended period of time during which they have developed a 'network of personal, social and economic relations that make up the private life of every human being'. This is a crucial extension of human rights protection to include long-term residency in countries of which one does not possess the nationality. Unfortunately, the reversal of prior case law was not spelt out in clear terms, but hidden behind superficial references to earlier judgments.[50] The structure of Article 8 ECHR, which constitutes a single human right with one set of justificatory requirements for state interference with 'private' or 'family life' alike, allowed the Court to avoid being more explicit about its change of direction. Yet, a change of direction there certainly was.

2. *A systematic delineation of private and family life*

The distinction between the protection of the nuclear family and the private life of wider social relations should be welcomed. It takes into account social changes, which have in recent years reinforced the importance of the immediate family in European societies to the detriment of wider family relations. Of course, the narrow reading of 'family life' draws criticism for ignoring social traditions of immigrants

[48] *Slivenko et al.* (n 6) para. 97 (emphasis added); more recently confirmed, eg, in *A.W. Khan v. the United Kingdom*, ECHR (2010) App. No. 47486/06, judgment of 12 January 2010, paras 31–33.

[49] *Slivenko et al.* (n 6) para. 96 (emphasis added). In casu, the Court held that the expulsion was disproportionate; for more details on the judgment see Thym (n 44) at 91–2 and A. Mowbray, *Cases, Materials, and Commentary on the European Convention on Human Rights* (2012) 514–18.

[50] This is shown persuasively in the partially concurring and partially dissenting opinion of Judge Kovler, *Slivenko et al.* (n 6) para. 1; on the prior wide understanding of family life see n 41 and n 42.

from African societies in particular, where the individual is often still firmly embedded in the network of extended family bonds.[51] Yet, special circumstances may dictate the occasional return to the traditional, wide understanding of family life in individual cases, whenever the applicant substantiates a special degree of personal dependence on relatives beyond the nuclear family which amounts to de facto family ties.[52] The Court has repeatedly emphasized that the distinction between family and private life will, ultimately, depend on the circumstances of the particular case.[53] Protection of family life beyond immediate relatives should however be limited to exceptional situations. The heading of 'private life' is the adequate standard to take into account wider social relations.

Generally speaking, the differentiation between the 'family life' and 'private life' in cases involving the entry and stay of foreigners reflects different needs for protection. The nuclear family is protected by Article 8 ECHR *ratione materiae* independent of the length of its existence—while private life becomes pertinent after the lapse of a time period and gains importance the longer a person has lived in a country and the more he or she has established societal, identificatory, and economic links. From a purely linguistic perspective, the Court's protection of the wider social environment under the heading of 'private life' is not intuitively convincing. Linguistically, 'private life' could easily be construed as the inner circle of human feelings, relations, and activities which define a person's character and which is much narrower than the Court's wide definition of 'the network of personal, social and economic relations that make up the private life of every human being'.[54] Ultimately, these objections must be rejected, since the broad reading of private life reflects the Court's methodological approach to dynamic interpretation of the Convention as a living instrument,[55] mirrors well-established ECtHR case law on other matters,[56] and corresponds to cultural-sociological findings about socially embedded personal identities.[57] In the words of the

[51] For the contextual debate on conflicting cultural traditions and human rights protection see H. J. Steiner, P. Alston, and R. Goodman, *International Human Rights in Context: Law, Politics, Morals* (2008).

[52] Cf. *Slivenko et al.* (n 6) para. 97; for a recent example, see *Mallah v. France*, ECHR (2011) Appl. No. 29681/08, judgment of 10 November 2011, in which the Court finds that 'family life' may encompass, depending on the circumstances of the case, ties between a father-in-law and his daughter's husband; another example are disabled persons depending on continued support from relatives.

[53] See, eg, *Maslov v. Austria*, ECHR (2008) Appl. No. 1638/03, judgment of 23 June 2008 (GC), para. 63 and, more recently, *A.A. v. the United Kingdom*, ECHR (2011) Appl. No. 8000/08, judgment of 20 September 2011, paras 46–50; *Trabelsi v. Germany*, ECHR (2011) Appl. No. 41548/06, judgment of 13 October 2011, paras 46–50 and *Balogun v. the United Kingdom*, ECHR (2012) Appl. No. 60286/09, judgment of 10 April 2012, para. 47.

[54] See, again, *Slivenko et al.* (n 6) para. 96; note also that Art. 8 ECHR similarly protects the 'home' and 'correspondence'.

[55] See II.A(1), this chapter.

[56] For environmental protection under Art. 8 ECHR, see n 8, or, on the protection of professional offices under the heading of 'private (!) life', *Niemitz v. Germany*, ECHR (1996) Appl. No. 13710/88, judgment of 16 December 1996; the parallelism between the judgments shows the internal consistency of the Court's case law only and does not, in itself, provide a justification for the wide interpretation.

[57] For a similar argument see R. Rubio-Marín and M. O'Connell, 'The European Convention and the Relative Rights of Resident Aliens', 5 *ELJ* (1999) 4, at 7–9; M. Nettesheim and O. Diggelmann, 'Grundrechtsschutz der Privatheit', 70 *Veröffentlichungen der Vereinigung Deutscher Staatsrechtslehrer*

Court, 'Article 8 also protects the right to establish and develop relationships with other human beings and the outside world and can sometimes embrace aspects of an individual's social identity'.[58]

What follows from the case law for the purposes of our analysis? Through the prism of 'private life', residence in a 'foreign' country is protected by Article 8 ECHR as an end in itself. The Court's decidedly general definition of private life as 'the network of personal, social and economic relations that make up the private life of *every* human being'[59] suggests that the judges will not embark upon the substantive analysis of the quantity of personal relations of individual claimants. It will also not qualitatively assess the merits of different social relations, since it must, instead, 'be accepted that the *totality* of social ties between settled migrants such as the applicants and the community in which they are living constitutes part of the concept of "private life" within the meaning of Article 8'.[60] Against the background of such a general definition, it is not surprising that the Court considers irregular residence status to also be covered by the notion of private life.[61] Qualitative criteria, such as education, employment, non-reliance on social assistance, language skills, and legality of the residence status or criminal offences, will play an important role, however, when the judges consider the justification of state interference in individual cases.[62]

C. A human right to regularize illegal stay

Human rights of illegally resident foreigners pose a direct challenge to the concept of state sovereignty. Exceptions to this rule are recognized internationally for refugees, including on the basis of Article 3 ECHR.[63] For the purposes of our analysis, it should be highlighted that foreigners who do not face the risk of ill-treatment upon return to their home country are not covered by these rules. States retain the authority to deport them under international human rights law. This applies to illegal migrants in particular who had not been authorized to enter the state territory in the first place. It is a considerable expansion of human rights law to protect their long-term residence in itself.[64] If their deportation interferes with Article 8 ECHR (subsection 1 below), state sovereignty is restricted.

(2011) 50, at 65–70 shows that the ECHR follows a much broader vision of privacy than US constitutional law, possibly a reflection of the less individualistic visions about the individual's place in society within Europe.

58 *A.W. Khan* (n 48) para. 31.

59 *Slivenko et al.* (n 6) para. 96 (emphasis added).

60 *A.W. Khan* (n 48) para. 31 (emphasis added).

61 For details, see section C this chapter; it does not convince me that some German authors question the *potential* of Art. 8 ECHR to cover illegal residence (see eg, F. Fritzsch, *Der Schutz sozialer Bindungen von Ausländern: Eine Untersuchung zu Artikel 8 EMRK* (2009)), although it is certainly correct that Art. 8 ECHR will only apply after an extended residence period for years/decades (as described in n 73 and accompanying text).

62 On countervailing public policy considerations see II.D(2) this chapter.

63 See II.A(2)(a), this chapter.

64 Other human rights, such as access to healthcare, education, etc., are of great practical importance (cf. n 10), but do not directly limit state discretion to control the entry and stay of foreigners, since they presuppose—but do not regularly guarantee—presence on the state territory.

Precisely that happened in Strasbourg: respect for each individual's 'private life' may, in certain circumstances, entail a human right to regularize illegal stay (subsection 2 below).

1. Protecting illegal residence status

It should be remembered that the Court moved towards the protection of illegal residence status by distinguishing between the 'family life' among members of the nuclear family and the wider network of personal, social, and economic relations that make up the 'private life' of every human being.[65] Against the background of such a general definition of the concept of 'private life', it was not surprising that the Court also considered irregular residence status to be covered by Article 8 ECHR. This became evident in the judgment of the Grand Chamber in *Sisojeva et al. v. Latvia* which concerned an ethnic Russian family who had been living in Latvia for twenty years and whose residence status was not recognized by the Latvian authorities after the break-up of the Soviet Union.[66] The Grand Chamber confirmed that Article 8 ECHR extends to illegal residence, but nevertheless rejected the applicants' claim, since it concluded that the regularization offered by the Latvian authorities (which the applicants had rejected) satisfied human rights requirements.

> Where the domestic legislation provides for several different types [of residence permits], the Court must analyse the legal and practical implications of issuing a particular permit. If it allows the holder to reside within the territory of the host country and to exercise freely there the right to respect for his or her private and family life, the granting of such a permit represents in principle a sufficient measure to meet the requirements of that provision.[67]

In casu, the complaint failed because the Latvian authorities had undertaken the necessary steps to regularize the illegal stay of the applicants (even though they did so only after the ECtHR's positive decision on the admissibility of the complaint). If Latvia had continued not to grant a residence permit to the applicants, the Grand Chamber would have concluded that the denial of regularization amounted to a violation of Article 8 ECHR, mirroring the earlier finding of the Court's first section in the same case.

> [W]hile the chief object of Article 8 . . . is to protect the individual against arbitrary interference by the public authorities, it does not merely compel the State to abstain from such interference: in addition to this negative undertaking, there may be positive obligations inherent in effective respect for private or family life. In other words, it is not enough for the host State to refrain from deporting the person concerned; it must also, by means of positive measures if necessary, afford him or her opportunity to exercise the rights in question without interference.[68]

[65] See II.B, this chapter. [66] See *Sisojeva* (n 6) and, for more detail, Thym (n 44) at 98–9.

[67] *Sisojeva* (n 6) para. 91.

[68] *Sisojeva v. Latvia*, ECHR (2005) Appl. No. 60654/00, judgment of 16 June 2005 (first section, not final), para. 104; the first section went on to find that Art. 8 ECHR moreover comprised a right to a permanent residence permit (para. 105)—a conclusion which the Grand Chamber did not agree

More recent cases, discussed later in this chapter,[69] confirm that the ECtHR protects illegal residence status under the heading of 'private life' and that Article 8 ECHR may oblige the high contracting parties to regularize illegal stay. De facto residence in a country comes within the protective reach of international human rights law, irrespective of relationships with family members and the absence of state permission to enter the territory. Put differently, the European Convention embraces the right to regularize illegal stay.

Beyond this general conclusion much uncertainty persists. To date, the Court has failed to indicate general criteria under which irregular migrants may rely upon their 'private life' within the meaning of Article 8 ECHR (one reason being that few cases reach the Strasbourg court, since most national immigration laws provide routes for regularization for migrants who could reasonably make claims under Article 8 ECHR).[70] Its general definition indicates that qualitative criteria, such as education, are not a decisive measure for an evaluation of whether the 'private life' of an applicant is affected.[71] All cases decided so far have concerned extended periods of residence over many years, if not decades.[72] As a matter of principle, however, a more generous reading remains possible, since the definition of 'private life' is wide enough to apply after shorter periods of residence, whenever migrants have integrated themselves into the social environment of their country of residence. However, ECtHR case law does not point in this direction. Illegal migrants who have lived in a country for a few months or years only are usually not considered to have developed sufficient 'private life' in order to invoke Article 8 ECHR.[73] In short: while the Court is primarily concerned with long-term residence, the criteria guiding the assessment of individual cases remain notoriously vague.

2. (Limited) relevance of migration control

In a couple of judgments, the ECtHR has fine-tuned the potential of Article 8 ECHR for the regularization of illegal stay. The underlying argument is simple: as a

with, while acknowledging that the applicants' insecurity ended when the Latvian authorities made the regularization offer; cf. the judgment of the Grand Chamber in *Sisojeva* (n 6) para. 94.

[69] See the next subsection.

[70] See comments on long-term residence status in EU law in II.E, this chapter.

[71] Cf. II.B(2), this chapter; qualitative criteria do matter, however, when the justification of state interferences is evaluated under the proportionality test.

[72] *Üner v. the Netherlands*, ECHR (2006) Appl. No. 46410/99, judgment of 18 October 2006 (GC), para. 59 and *Maslov* (n 53) para. 75 emphasized that 'settled migrants' who have 'spent most, if not all, their childhood in the host country, were brought up there and received their education there' (*Üner*, para. 58) deserve—and require—special protection insofar as their private life is concerned.

[73] In *Nnyanzi v. the United Kingdom*, ECHR (2008) Appl. No. 21878/06, judgment of 8 April 2008, paras 76–77 the Court did not decide whether 10 years of residence before/after the rejection of an asylum claim amount to 'private life' within the meaning of Art. 8 ECHR, since the deportation would have been justified even if the situation was covered by Art. 8 ECHR; *Nada v. Switzerland*, ECHR (2012) Appl. No. 10593/08, judgment of 12 September 2012 (GC), considered the prohibition to leave the small Italian enclave of Campione (inside Switzerland) for more than six years sufficient to find interference with the applicant's private life.

starting point, the judges accept that those without leave to remain may nonetheless invoke Article 8 ECHR insofar as their expulsion would interfere with private or family life (the distinction does, as discussed earlier, depend on the circumstances of the case). One step further, these human rights concerns must be balanced with countervailing public policy objectives which include 'factors of immigration control (e.g. history of breaches of immigration law)'.[74] In so doing, the Court accepts that illegal entry and residence status do not hinder the application of Article 8 ECHR. In other words: the legitimate interests of the migrant are the starting point for the analysis of coercive measures against illegal immigrants. Migration control is only one, albeit important, element in the proportionality test and requires balancing with other factors arguing in favour of illegal residents,[75] a conclusion which the ECtHR has recently reaffirmed with reference to the UN Convention on the Rights of the Child.[76]

Balancing migration control against human rights is a clear limitation of state discretion over the entry and stay of foreigners: even if state authorities have at no point taken a deliberate decision to authorize entry or stay, it is be expected that illegal immigrants remain in the country, if the weighing exercise under Article 8 ECHR comes down in their favour. This outcome is no foregone conclusion and depends, ultimately, on the relative weight of countervailing considerations in the proportionality test. Indeed, the ECHR does not bring about a general right to regularization. The Court maintains that 'persons who, without complying with the regulations in force, confront the authorities of a Contracting State with their presence in the country as a *fait accompli*' (that is, irregular migrants) cannot usually expect to benefit from Article 8 ECHR.[77] Indeed, Strasbourg found in only two cases that the deportation of illegal residents would violate Article 8 ECHR, and both these cases involved either minor children of an illegally resident mother or two siblings whose illegal entry and stay was primarily a decision of their parents.[78] In most other situations, the Court rejected the complaints.[79] In the words of the Court: in cases involving private and/or family life of those who entered or stay illegally, 'the removal of the applicants would be incompatible with Article 8 only in exceptional circumstances'.

[74] This formulation was first used by *Ajayi et al. v. the United Kingdom*, ECHR (1999) Appl. No. 27663/95, decision of 22 June 1999, and *Solomon v. the Netherlands*, ECHR (2000) Appl. No. 44328/98, decision of 5 September 2000, and has been taken up in general terms by the judgments mentioned subsequently in this chapter.

[75] For more detail, see the next section.

[76] See *Nunez v. Norway*, ECHR (2011) Appl. No. 55597/09, judgment of 28 June 2011, in particular para. 84 together with the joint dissenting opition by Judges Mijvic and Gaetano.

[77] *Rodrigues Da Silva & Hoogkamer* (n 37) paras 39 and 43.

[78] See *Rodrigues Da Silva & Hoogkamer* (n 37) paras 39 and 43, and my earlier comments on the case: Thym (n 44) at 100–2 and *Butt v. Norway*, ECHR (2012) Appl. No. 47017/09, judgment of 4 December 2012.

[79] By way of example, see the two decisions in n 74 and *Antwi et al. v. Norway*, ECHR (2012) Appl. No. 26940/10, judgment of 14 February 2012.

D. Public policy considerations

For a while, one may have assumed that the ECHR was moving towards a general prohibition of the deportation of foreigners who have lived in European states for an extended period of time. Yet, the enhanced protection of long-term residence should not divert our attention from the continued relevance of public policy considerations which limit the human right to remain a resident of a country where one does not possess the nationality. Notwithstanding the caveats it established, the ECtHR has stated unambiguously that 'Article 8 provides *no absolute* protection against expulsion for any category of aliens'.[80] By way of example, one can look at the judicial conclusions that a father of young children living in Norway, a man who had lived in the United Kingdom since the age of three and a thirty-year old who had been born in Germany may all be deported.[81] In 2012, there was a surprisingly great number of cases in which the Court rejected complaints against expulsion measures by immigrants who had been residing in a country for years, if not decades.[82] Some of the applicants invoked both private and family life and expected to be separated from their children or spouses if the ECtHR rejected their claim.[83] For those who had expected the Court to extend the human rights of (illegal) immigrants ever further, this apparent hardening of the judicial standpoint must come as a disappointment (some tight votes and dissenting opinions show that these verdicts were not reached without controversy).[84]

Although it is highly unlikely that the Court took a deliberate decision to send a signal of toughness, a number of contextual factors may have favoured the rejection of a series of complaints based on Article 8 ECHR. First, immigration ranks high on the list of complaints of the Conservative British government, which undertook steps to restrain the influence of the Court on the occasion of the 'Brighton Conference' on the future of the Court in 2012; Strasbourg was certainly aware of the political pressure. Second, the backlog of cases keeps on rising; in subject areas with a potential for thousands of applications, such as immigration, the Court must be careful not to be swamped by ever more applications; instead it focuses on guidance for national courts, which will be discussed later in this chapter. Third, national immigration laws may be better than their reputation; arguably, most hardship cases are nowadays resolved domestically. Fourth, the Court accepts that there are limits to Article 8 ECHR; if settled migrants want absolute protection

[80] See *Maslov* (n 53) para. 74 (emphasis added) and, two years earlier, *Üner* (n 72) paras 55–56; for a divergent view, see the dissenting opinions referred to in n 47.

[81] Cf. the facts of *Omoregie v. Norway*, ECHR (2008) Appl. No. 265/07, judgment of 31 July 2008; *Balogun* (n 53); and *Trabelsi* (n 53).

[82] See *Shala v. Switzerland*, ECHR (2012) Appl. No. 52873/09, judgment of 15 November 2012; *Samsonnikov v. Estonia*, ECHR (2012) Appl. No. 52178/10, judgment of 3 July 2012; and *Balogun* (n 53).

[83] *Nacic et al. v. Sweden*, ECHR (2012) Appl. No. 16567/10, judgment of 15 May 2012; *Bajsultanov v. Austria*, ECHR (2012), Appl. No. 54131/10, judgment of 12 June 2012, and *Kissiwa Koffi v. Switzerland*, ECHR (2012) Appl. No. 38005/07, judgment of 15 November 2012; in the first two cases the Grand Chamber rejected the applicants' appeals.

[84] See, among the judgments above, *Kissiwa Koffi*, *Shala*, *Samsonnikov*, *Balogun*, and *Antwi*.

against expulsion, they should apply for naturalization, which many European states offer nowadays.[85] As a result, it seems that we are left with the abstract criteria established by the Court. Instead of prohibiting deportation of long-term residents outright, the ECtHR obliges the high contracting parties to pay respect to migrants' legitimate interests (subsection 1 below) and identifies general criteria guiding the proportionality test (subsection 2 below).

1. Orientation at the individual case

In its case law, the Court follows a steady dogmatic line reflecting the wording and structure of Article 8 ECHR. It evaluates individual cases along a four-pronged test: first, judges ascertain whether states have interfered with family and/or private life in the meaning of Article 8 ECHR; second, they proceed by verifying that public authorities have acted in accordance with the law; third, they must have pursued one of the legitimate aims listed in Article 8(2) ECHR, such as the economic well-being of the country or the prevention of disorder or crime; fourth, the judges assess the necessity of the interference in a democratic society, having recourse to the proportionality test.[86] One may criticize this four-pronged test for its lack of theoretical underpinning.[87] The outcome of the proportionality assessment, in particular, is characteristically dependent on the individual case and is, therefore, difficult to predict.[88] It nonetheless provides a coherent and stable foundation for the argumentative juxtaposition of countervailing arguments with a view to achieving a 'fair balance that has to be struck between the competing interests of the individual and of the community as a whole'.[89] This evaluation defines ECtHR judgments.

Studying the ECtHR's immigration judgments, three considerations stand out. Firstly, the Court has made a noticeable effort not to overstretch its case law. As an international human rights court, it should work towards the effective domestic application of its jurisprudence and must take note of the diversity of national immigration laws. From a doctrinal point of view, the margin of appreciation and the principle of subsidiarity serve as methodological tools to recognize a certain leeway of national decision-making.[90] In its *Sisojeva* judgment on the regularization of illegal stay, the Grand Chamber prominently reaffirmed the corresponding prerogatives of the national authorities to integrate Strasbourg's case law into the specific context of their national legal systems.

> The Court further reiterates that the machinery for the protection of fundamental rights established by the Convention is subsidiary to the national systems safeguarding human rights . . . The choice as to the most appropriate means of achieving this is in principle a matter for the domestic authorities, who are in continuous contact with the vital forces of

[85] See following, III.D. [86] See, by way of example, *Maslov* (n 53) paras 61–101.
[87] See, generally, II.A(1)(b), this chapter, and, on Art. 8 ECHR, Greer (n 24) at 257–73.
[88] See Vedsted-Hansen (n 46) at 700. [89] *Gül* (n 22) para. 38.
[90] For further comments, see Thym (n 44) at 105–6, and II.A(1), this chapter.

their countries and are better placed to assess the possibilities and resources afforded by their respective domestic legal systems.[91]

Secondly, the effective domestic application of the Convention ideally allows the ECtHR to focus on hardship cases. While national and EU immigration law resolve most disputes domestically,[92] the Strasbourg court may concentrate on situations of failure of national bodies by correcting intolerable outcomes in individual cases. A closer look at the court's case law does indeed show a collection of cases where the individual circumstances of the applicant explain the judicial conclusion.[93] These cases illustrate the importance of the proportionality test as a key measure.

Thirdly, the familiarization of the individual circumstances does not preclude the Court from developing a coherent and predictable set of criteria for the interpretation and application of Article 8 ECHR—reflecting its hybrid function between the binding force of its judgments *inter partes* and its quest for a pan-European human rights superstructure with constitutional characteristics.[94] Such generalized criteria guarantee the comparability of the judicial conclusions and guide national authorities and courts in the autonomous interpretation and application of Article 8 ECHR in immigration cases.

2. *Criteria for the proportionality assessment*

Although each case is different, the biographies of migrants follow similar patterns. The Court may therefore rationalize the application of Article 8 ECHR in immigration cases—both by national courts and the ECtHR itself—by distinguishing different categories for the justification of state interference with private and family life.[95] Indeed, the Court started developing such generalized criteria in response to repeated criticism that its case law lacked a coherent approach.[96] Of course, these standards cannot (and should not) prejudge the outcome of individual cases. The balancing of conflicting private and state interests under the proportionality test remains inherently dependent on the circumstances of each individual case. Guidance should remain abstract and concentrate on the criteria which are to be fed into this balancing act. In its case law on Article 8 ECHR, the Court tends towards an abstract evaluation of private and state interests without

[91] *Sisojeva* (n 6) para. 90. [92] See also this chapter, II.E.

[93] For more detail, see Thym (n 44) at 106–8.

[94] Compare the binding character *inter partes* in accordance with Art. 46(1) ECHR and the quest for 'constitutional' standards for the effective and consistent domestic application of the ECHR.

[95] Reflecting the differences between migration configurations (*non-refoulement*, deportation of family members, admission for purposes of family reunion, protection of long-term residence status) discussed in II.A(2) and II.B, this chapter.

[96] This criticism became prominent in the late 1990s; cf. M.-B. Dembour, 'Human Rights Law and National Sovereignty in Collusion: the Plight of Quasi-Nationals at Strasbourg', 21 *Netherlands Quarterly of Human Rights* (2003) 63, at 66: 'judicial lottery'; and M. Caroni, *Privat- und Familienleben zwischen Menschenrecht und Migration: Eine Untersuchung zu Bedeutung, Rechtsprechung und Möglichkeiten von Art. 8 EMRK im Ausländerrecht* (1999).

synchronizing them with the list of public policy grounds which are mentioned in Article 8(2) ECHR.[97]

(a) The '*Boultif* criteria' after criminal convictions

Most immigration cases decided by the Strasbourg court concern the expulsion of foreigners who had been authorized to live in the host country at some point but have lost their right of residence after a criminal conviction.[98] To date, the deportation of foreigners after criminal convictions remains a core concern for many immigration authorities and causes plenty of practical disputes, including in Germany[99] and the United Kingdom,[100] where ECtHR case law has considerable practical impact. In expulsion cases after criminal convictions, both regular interference with family life (when the migrant concerned lives with members of the nuclear family) and novel claims under the heading of private life (concerning long-term residence and the protection of the corresponding social environment) can be considered. It depends on the circumstances of the individual case as to whether family and/or private life serves as the key yardstick.[101]

In order to rationalize the application of Article 8 ECHR in such circumstances, the Court developed the eight '*Boultif* criteria', which essentially require a balance to be struck between the preservation of family unity and/or private life, and the maintenance of public order. More specifically, these criteria concern: the nature and seriousness of the criminal offence; the length of the stay in the host country; the nationalities of the various persons concerned; the solidity of social, cultural, and family ties with the host country and with the country of destination; the time elapsed since the offence was committed and the conduct during that period; the applicant's family situation and the solidity of the family ties; whether the spouse knew about the offence when they entered into the relationship; the age, best interests and well-being of children; and any difficulties which the spouse is likely to

[97] It tends to treat the balancing act as an abstract exercise (similar to Art. 52(1) of the EU Charter of Fundamental Rights, OJ 2007 C 303/1); nonetheless, all arguments discussed below can be associated more or less directly with one or different justification criteria mentioned in Art. 8(2) ECHR (in particular the economic well-being of the country and prevention of crime or disorder); moreover, it should be noted that the general prerogatives of the high contracting parties to control the entry and stay of aliens under public international law supports, in itself, a certain leeway irrespective of the precise wording of Art. 8(2) ECHR; cf. Thym (n 44) at 103–4.

[98] The circumstances vary in national immigration laws, but the underlying pattern is similar: legal residence comes to an end as a reaction to a criminal offence.

[99] For the judicial revision of statutory automatic expulsion in Germany after serious criminal convictions, in which the ECtHR case law played a crucial role, see D. Thym, 'Abschied von Ist- und Regelausweisung bei Verwurzelung: zugleich ein Beitrag zur Vielfalt europäischer Grundrechtsordnungen', 21 *Deutsches Verwaltungsblatt* (2008) 1346.

[100] Cf. the political debate/complaint about 'lengthy' deportation proceedings, which are regularly delayed by court cases after the invocation of Art. 8 ECHR, see House of Commons, Home Affairs Committee: Work of the UK Border Agency (August–December 2011), 21st Report of Session 2010–12, paras 44–51.

[101] Cf. II.B(2), this chapter.

encounter in the country of origin.[102] If a foreigner was born in the host country or moved there in his young childhood, the Court limits its assessment to the first three criteria, thereby effectively extending the degree of protection.[103]

(b) Special requirements for private-life cases

The Court's balancing act on the basis of the '*Boultif* criteria' is often complex and has important implications for the foreigner involved, but from a doctrinal point of view the two sides are relatively easy to identify (family unity versus sanction for criminal behaviour).[104] After an extended period of residence, the protection of family life may be complemented by the protection of wider social relations under the heading of private life. In such cases involving the protection of 'private life', the judges have to broaden their analysis to the integration of the applicant into the host society. This is the logical consequence of the wide understanding of every person's private life, which is not limited to cohabitation with family members but characterized by 'the network of personal, social and economic relations that make up the private life of every human being'.[105] In such situations, the living conditions, employment situation and education possibilities serve as additional sub-criteria which have to be taken into account in the evaluation process.[106] Similarly, states may take linguistic integration into account in expulsion proceedings.[107] In private life cases, all these factors have to be fed into the juxtaposition of countervailing private and public interests.

The resulting proportionality test is much more complex than in 'simple' family life cases after a criminal conviction. It covers criteria which do not always interact straightforwardly in a complex balancing exercise, covering wider social integration and involving migration control. However, this complexity arising from the proportionality test concerns the conclusion. From a dogmatic point of view, there is no need to depart from the '*Boultif* criteria' in private life cases, since considerations of social integration can easily be construed as sub-criteria of the aforementioned

[102] Established case law since *Boultif v. Switzerland*, ECHR (2001) Appl. No. 54273/00, judgment of 2 August 2001, para. 48; at a later stage *Üner* (n 72) paras 57–58; and *Nunez* (n 76) para. 84 specify the best interests and the well-being of the children in line with the 1990 UN Convention on the Rights of the Child and the solidity of the family ties as sub-criteria; *Maslov* (n 53) para. 71 added the solidity of social, cultural, and family ties with the host country and with the country of destination.

[103] See *Benhebba v. France*, ECHR (2003) Appl. No. 53441/99, judgment of 10 July 2003, para. 33 and *Maslov* (n 53) para. 71.

[104] For an overview of different cases, see Boeles and Den Heijer (n 9) at 144–70 and E. Néraudau-D'Unienville, *Ordre public et droit des étrangers en Europe: la notion d'ordre public en droit des étrangers à l'aune de la construction européenne* (2006) at 453–75.

[105] See II.B, this chapter.

[106] See, among others, for education and labour market participation: *Sisojeva* (n 6) paras 91 and 95; *Slivenko et al.* (n 6) paras 122–124; *Kaya v. Germany*, ECHR (2007) Appl. No. 31753/02, judgment of 28 June 2007, para. 64; *A.H. Khan v. the United Kingdom*, ECHR (2010) Appl. No. 6222/10, judgment of 20 December 2011, para. 41; and *Bajsultanov* (n 83) para. 85.

[107] Language was considered part of the '*Boultif* package' from the beginning (including the absence of knowledge of the language spoken in the home country), but gained new prominence with the private-life cases, including *Slivenko et al.* (n 6) para. 123; *Maslov* (n 53) paras 96–97; *Dalia v. France*, ECHR (1998) Appl. No. 26102/95, judgment of 19 February 1998, para. 63; *Trabelsi* (n 53) paras 62–64; *Antwi* (n 79) para. 94; and *Kissiwa Koffi* (n 83) para. 66.

Boultif benchmark.[108] Also, the different criteria have no internal hierarchy; the relative importance of individual factors varies from case to case; if individual factors are irrelevant (for example, if a foreigner does not have children or is expelled for reasons other than a criminal offence), they are ignored.[109] The assessment of individual cases under the proportionality test was never supposed to resemble a mathematical formula. Both national courts and the ECtHR have to make their own value judgments in light of the specific circumstances of each individual case.

For the purposes of our study, it should be highlighted that considerations of effective migration control may justify restrictive state policies, especially in cases of illegal migration—reflecting state control over the entry and stay of foreigners under public international law, which the Court rightly mentions as the starting point of its jurisprudence and which represents a legitimate public policy ground on the basis of Article 8(2) ECHR.[110] The protection of illegal residence under Article 8 ECHR in recent judgments limits the discretion of the high contracting parties, but does not form an unconditional right to regularize illegal stay, since migration control remains a legitimate public policy objective which may justify interference on the basis of Article 8(2) ECHR.[111] In short, immigration control is one factor among many which has to be fed into the proportionality assessment. Article 8 ECHR does not bring about an unconditional right to regularize illegal stay. It rather obliges the high contracting parties to justify their restrictive control measures. The European Convention gives migrants a voice with legal sway, also in cases of illegal migration.

E. Novelties within the EU framework

The plurality of immigration laws in Europe is coming to an end. In recent years, the European Union has adopted numerous legislative instruments creating an 'area of freedom, security and justice'.[112] For the purposes of this contribution, Directive 2003/109/EC concerning the status of third-country nationals who are long-term residents and Directive 2003/86/EC on the right to family reunification deserve particular attention.[113] In its judgments, the Court does not mention either EU

[108] In particular, the length of the stay in the host country and the solidity of social, cultural and family ties with the host country and with the country of destination.

[109] For a criticism of the inherent relativity of this somewhat arbitrary approach of the ECtHR, see C. Steinorth, '*Üner v. the Netherlands*: Expulsion of Long-term Immigrants and the Right to Respect for Private and Family Life', 8 *Human Rights Law Review* (2008) 185, at 192–4.

[110] See, again, II.C(2), this chapter.

[111] See, on the legitimacy of migration control measures, in particular, *Omoregie* (n 81) paras 60, 61, and 63; *Kamaliyevy v. Russia*, ECHR (2010) Appl. No. 52812/07, judgment of 3 June 2010, para. 63; *Mallah* (n 52) para. 40; *Nunez* (n 76) paras 70–76; *Antwi* (n 79) paras 89, 90, and 104; and *Butt* (n 78) paras 77–85; see n 97 for how migration control relates to Art. 8(2) ECHR. For a proposal to distinguish different categories of illegal migration, see the President of the Federal (German) Administrative Court, Eckertz-Höfer, 'Neuere Entwicklungen in Gesetzgebung und Rechtsprechung zum Schutz des Privatlebens', 28 *Zeitschrift für Ausländerrecht und Ausländerpolitik* (2008) 41, at 44–5.

[112] See the overview by S. Peers, *EU Justice and Home Affairs Law* (2011).

[113] Cf. Council Directive 2003/109/EC, OJ 2004 L 16/44, 25 November 2003, concerning the status of third-country nationals who are long-term residents and Council Directive 2003/86/EC, OJ 2003 L 251/12, 22 September 2003, on the right to family reunification.

Directive, which is convincing insofar as the Court has no jurisdiction over EU law until after EU accession to the ECHR.[114] While the United Kingdom, Ireland, and Denmark are not bound by said directives on the basis of their respective opt-outs, the Strasbourg jurisprudence does still apply to them. It would nonetheless not come as a great surprise if EU harmonization measures had an indirect influence on the reasoning of the Strasbourg judges. Their interpretation of Article 8 ECHR in immigration cases occurs in the awareness that the case law will impact upon the EU. Three considerations deserve our attention in this respect.

Firstly, the ECtHR interprets the Convention aware that the Court of Justice of the European Union (CJEU) in Luxembourg refers to the ECHR and the Strasbourg case law as the principal source of its human rights jurisprudence. The Charter of Fundamental Rights, which became legally binding with the entry into force of the Lisbon Treaty,[115] reinforces this trend. Article 52(3) states unambiguously: '[i]n so far as this Charter contains rights which correspond to rights guaranteed by the [ECHR], the meaning and scope of those rights shall be the same as those laid down by the said Convention'.[116] So far as Article 8 ECHR is concerned, the CJEU recognized quickly that 'Article 7 of the Charter must therefore be given the same meaning and the same scope as Article 8(1) of the ECHR, as interpreted by the case law of the ECtHR'.[117] Hence, all judgments analysed above directly affect the interpretation and adjudication of EU law by the CJEU and national courts.

Secondly, Article 52(3) of the EU Charter recognizes that '[t]his provision shall not prevent Union law providing more extensive protection'. Indeed, one Charter provision in particular may have an impact on immigration cases. Article 24 of the Charter mandates public authorities to treat the child's best interests as a primary consideration and support the maintenance, on a regular basis, of a personal relationship and direct contact with both parents. This provision could considerably reinforce the human rights protection of migrant parents, whenever the deportation of a foreigner (or even cases of first admission) has a direct impact on the well-being of a child. In a similar vein, the ECtHR and the UK Supreme Court have recently started to reinforce the relevance of children's interests within the context of immigration cases and Article 8 ECHR.[118]

[114] Cf. *Bosphorus Airways v. Ireland*, ECHR (2005) Appl. No. 45036/98, judgment of 30 June 2005 (GC), and the call for the EU's future accession in Art. 6(2) TEU.

[115] Charter of Fundamental Rights of the European Union, OJ 2007 C 303/1, which became legally binding with the entry into force of Art. 6(1) TEU-Lisbon.

[116] It should be noted that it remained unclear *which* Charter articles correspond to ECHR provisions within the meaning of Art. 52(3) ECHR.

[117] Case C-400/10 PPU, *J. McB. v L.E.*, [2010] ECR I-08965, Rec. 53; cf. Case C-105/03, *Pupino*, [2005] ECR I-5285, Rec. 60.

[118] Cf. *Nunez* (n 76) para. 84, with reference to the 1990 UN Convention on the Rights of the Child—and not the EU Charter; and UK Supreme Court, judgment of 1 February 2011, *ZH (Tanzania) v Secretary of State for the Home Department* [2011] UKSC 4; see also T. Spijkerboer, 'Structural Instability: Strasbourg Case Law on Children's Family Reunion', 11 *European Journal of Migration and Law* (2009) 271.

Thirdly, EU law may extend the protection of long-term residence status and family unity beyond the reach of Article 8 ECHR. In its first judgment on the Family Reunification Directive 2003/86/EC, the CJEU refers extensively to the ECtHR's case law and concludes that the Directive complies with the ECHR in principle (although it may require consistent interpretation in conformity with Strasbourg case law in cases of conflict).[119] Yet, EU directives are not limited to specifying human rights requirements. On the contrary: as legislative instruments, directives may lay down rights and privileges for foreigners that are more generous than Article 8 ECHR. They may, for example, recognize an individual, statutory right to family reunion also in cases where Article 8 ECHR would ultimately fail.[120] The ECtHR should be careful not to confuse such legislative rules, which are the outcome of political decisions and may be amended in accordance with the legislative procedure, with human rights guarantees which benefit from constitutional status and trump the legislator's will in most jurisdictions.[121]

In a similar vein to the Family Reunion Directive, the Long-Term Residence Directive 2003/109/EC must also be interpreted in the light of the Strasbourg case law on Article 8 ECHR. More specifically, the '*Boultif* criteria' on the justification of expulsion measures, discussed earlier, may guide the interpretation of the Directive's public order provision.[122] Yet again, the Long-Term Residence Directive is not limited to specifying human rights guarantees but establishes statutory guarantees for long-term residents including in situations where the ECHR would not offer protection. The existence of such an extended legislative safety net may be one crucial reason why the Court has found fewer violations of Article 8 ECHR in recent years.[123] For EU member states which are bound by the Directive, its rules have become the first point of reference. Long-term residents, who obtain stable residence permits on the basis of the Directive, do not have to invoke Article 8 ECHR. This does not, however, undo the relevance of the ECHR as a last resort for other jurisdictions or whenever the application of EU rules leads to intolerable outcomes.

[119] See Case C-540/03, *Parliament v. Council*, [2006] ECR I-5769, paras. 104–106; for consistent interpretation in light of the EU Charter, see, more recently and explicitly, Case C-403/09, *Detiček*, [2009] ECR I-12193, Rec. 53–55.

[120] Cf. Art. 4(1) Directive 2003/86/EC (n 113) and Case C-540/03, *Parliament v. Council*, Rec. 59–60.

[121] More specifically, it should *not* enhance human rights protection under Art. 8 ECHR with the argument that EU legislation offers more generous protection; this would limit the prerogatives of the EU legislator and national parliaments to the detriment of national courts; for a similar argument with a view to ECtHR, *M.S.S. v. Belgium & Greece* (n 31) para. 263, which could possibly be seen as a step in this direction within the context of Art. 3 ECHR, see D. Thym, 'Menschenrechtliche Feinjustierung des Dublin-Systems zur Asylzuständigkeitsabgrenzung—Zu den Folgewirkungen des Straßburger M.S.S.-Urteils', *Zeitschrift für Ausländerrecht and Ausländerpolitik* (2011) 368, at 370.

[122] Cf. Art. 12 Directive 2003/109/EC (n 113), the wording of which takes up ECtHR case law.

[123] As put forward by Y. Ronen, 'The Ties that Bind: Family and Private Life as Bars to the Deportation of Immigrants', 8 *International Journal of Law in Context* (2012) 283, at 289.

F. Conclusion

Human rights law holds the potential to reverse immigration law's traditional orientation towards the public interest and redirect it towards the individual, even including situations of illegal migration, which poses a direct challenge to the traditional notion of unfettered state control over the entry, stay, and departure of aliens. Against this background, the originality of the ECtHR case law stands out: migrants without regular residence status may, under certain circumstances, invoke Article 8 ECHR in order to regularize their illegal stay. Their interests are not subject to discretion in the legislative process, but must be respected as a matter of international law. The ECtHR obliges national authorities to justify restrictive laws and practices; Article 8 ECHR gives the migrant perspective a voice with legal authority. Unfettered state sovereignty over the entry, stay, and departure of foreigners has come to an end. Refugee protection in situations of forced migration is complemented by human rights guarantees for 'voluntary' migrants, including in situations of irregular residence.

Step by step, the ECtHR has moved towards the protection of long-term residence as an end in itself under the heading of 'private life', irrespective of relationships with family members, which are equally protected by Article 8 ECHR. This extension of international human rights law to long-term residence status provides immigration lawyers, interest groups, and national courts with a legal tool to redesign national immigration law. Abstract national rules which imply negative outcomes to individual cases can be challenged through Article 8 ECHR. International human rights serve as a mechanism to feed individual interests into domestic decision-making and adjudication, also in situations in which national immigration law does not recognize nuanced solutions. Notwithstanding the efforts of the ECtHR to define criteria guiding the proportionality assessment, the case law continues to lack clarity and guidance for national courts on how to resolve individual cases. The weighing of interests under the proportionality test is inherently dependent on the circumstances of the individual case and opens the law up to considerations of equity.

It is not surprising that the protection of long-term residents became an issue for the ECtHR in the early 1990s when it became evident that the 'guest workers' and other migrants in the industrialized societies of Western Europe had turned into de facto immigrants who would remain in the host state indefinitely. In many cases, the second generation of children had been born in Europe, rarely visiting their parents' home country. Article 8 ECHR was an adequate tool to protect the legitimate interests of these migrants. In so doing, it became evident that the protection of family life was not always the appropriate yardstick. Most applicants relied on the legitimacy of wider social relations independent of links with the nuclear family. This was recognized by the Court in the 2000s, when it extended the protective reach of Article 8 ECHR to 'the network of personal, social and economic relations that make up the private life of every human being'. As a result, long-term residence status is protected *ipso jure*; even illegal residents obtain a potential right to regularize their stay. In most cases, the decision is taken in the proportionality assessment, when qualitative factors, including linguistic and professional integration, are taken into consideration.

The ECtHR's readiness to point at the specific situation of each applicant under the proportionality test should not, however, be misread as a judicial call for legal revolution. Strasbourg forces the high contracting parties to take the migrant perspective into account, but it does not reject the capacity of the high contracting parties to control the entry and stay of foreigners. Migration control does not justify the deportation of any migrant, but represents a legitimate public policy objective in the proportionality assessment. Recent judgments indicate that the ECtHR gives states some leeway. Article 8 ECHR gives the migrant perspective a voice with legal sway and limits state discretion, but it neither mandates open borders nor does it remove the capacity of states to pursue countervailing public policy objectives in a proportionate manner. This solution not only presents a pragmatic compromise between individual human rights and public policy objectives, but also reflects deeper theoretical considerations about the legitimacy of public control over immigration law.

III. Towards De Facto Citizenship?

Conventional definitions of state sovereignty include the control over the entry and stay of foreigners. With the exception of international refugee law, this prerogative has persisted until the modern day. States are generally considered to hold a largely unfettered power to control the entry, residence, and departure of non-citizens[124]—a principle which the ECtHR holds 'as a matter of well-established international law'.[125] Against this background, the conceptual relevance of the ECtHR case law on Article 8 ECHR is clear. By extending the protective reach of the Convention to long-term residence status, including a potential right to regularize illegal stay, the Strasbourg court restricts the traditional concept of sovereign state control. Non-citizens may invoke international human rights to protest against expulsion or regularize illegal stay. Stated differently, the ECHR may, under certain conditions, include a human right to be a resident of a country where one does not possess nationality—a right which under classic international law has been reserved for nationals.

The protection of human rights of migrants by the ECtHR has wide implications for our understanding of the state control of migratory flows. While states

124 See Martin (n 2); R. Jennings and A. Watts, *Oppenheim's International Law*, Volume II (2008), chapter 6 and 9, and K. Hailbronner and J. Gogolin, 'Aliens', in R. Wolfrum (ed.), *The Max Planck Encyclopedia of Public International Law;* online edition available at: <http://www.mpepil.com>, accessed June 2012, paras 14–22.

125 This standard formula was first used in *Moustaquim* (n 4) para. 43.

have never enjoyed absolute freedom in the treatment of foreigners,[126] international rules limiting state discretion have been, on the whole, insignificant. That is not to say that foreigners were necessarily treated badly under domestic law (the United States, for example, has for a long time supported immigration from Europe by facilitating the acquisition of property by settlers). Unfettered state discretion meant that states were not constrained by international legal standards. From an international legal perspective, nothing fundamental had changed in terms of state control over voluntary (although not forced) migration since Lord Chief Justice Jeffreys' confirmation of the trading monopoly of the East India Company under English law in 1684: 'I conceive the King had an absolute power to forbid foreigners, whether merchants or others, from coming within his dominions, both in times of war and in times of peace, according to his royal will and pleasure'.[127] In today's Europe, that conclusion cannot be maintained. Article 8 ECHR gives the migrant perspective a voice with legal sway.

After having mapped the evolution and foundations of the ECtHR case law on Article 8 ECHR in the previous sections, part III presents the conceptual implications. It concentrates on the question as to whether the protection of long-term residence *ipso jure* renders the traditional distinction between foreigners and national citizens obsolete insofar as residence rights are concerned. From a descriptive point of view, it is certainly correct to highlight the similarities between the protection of long-term residence and classic state citizenship (A). This finding does not necessarily mean, however, that a new legal category of long-term residence status as *de jure* citizenship has emerged on the basis of Article 8 ECHR. As a human right, the protection of private and/or family life defies the stable distinction between in- and outsiders (B). That is not to say that changing legal norms and social realities do not require normative rearrangement of the citizenship concept towards a more inclusive and nuanced understanding of membership. Yet, there is little evidence in ECtHR judgments supporting such undertaking (C). Strasbourg instead follows a conventional approach by emphasizing the need for gradual integration of migrants into the domestic community and favouring naturalization (D).

A. De facto citizenship as a descriptive category

State sovereignty gave rise to the principled distinction between nationals and foreigners. In the same way as classic international law divided the planet into sovereign states, human beings were categorized as nationals of different states (or stateless persons). Only nationals/citizens had a right to live within the borders of

[126] On the customary rules of the international law of aliens see Jennings and Watts (n 124) and K. Hailbronner and M. Kau, 'Der Staat und der Einzelne als Völkerrechtssubjekte', in W. Graf Vitzthum (ed.), *Völkerrecht*, (2010) paras 267–292.

[127] *The East India Company v. Sandys* [1684] 10 ST 371 at 530–1, George Jeffreys, J.C., cited after Lord Bingham of Cornhill for the House of Lords, judgment of 9 December 2004, *ex parte European Roma Rights Centre et al.* [2004] UKHL 55, para. 11.

'their' states.[128] Notwithstanding the distinct experience of federal states,[129] state sovereignty served as the dividing line between nationals/citizens and foreigners. Distinct migration regimes applied to both groups: citizens benefited from a right to abode, while foreigners had to apply for leave to remain. The corresponding distinction between 'nationals/citizens' and 'foreigners' will be the basis of the following reflection. It will be based on simplified legal terminology which equates 'citizenship' with 'nationality',[130] as opposed to 'foreigners' or 'aliens' who possess the nationality of another state or are stateless. Does the protection of long-term residence status render this categorization obsolete?

By protecting long-term residents against expulsion, the ECtHR transcends the neat dividing line between insiders and outsiders. Non-nationals obtain a right which usually only would benefit citizens. Reading the judgments, one recognizes that the judges in Strasbourg are less occupied with the formal status of the applicants (their nationality), but focus more on living conditions in the real world. Second-generation immigrants may still possess the nationality of their state of origin. Yet, the absence of the formal bond of nationality with the host state does not call into question the relevance of their links:

> They received their education, established most of their social contacts and hence developed their personal identity there. They were born or relocated in the host country as a consequence of the emigration of their parents and usually maintain their principal family relations there. Some of these immigrants have conserved with the country of their nationality nothing else than the sole link of nationality.[131]

The ECtHR recognizes that second-generation immigrants live in comparable circumstances to nationals and protects their residence status.

What are the theoretical implications of the case law? Unquestionably, it signifies an important restriction of state sovereignty. This is most tangible in situations of illegal migration, in which a state had never authorized the entry of migrants into its territory in the first place and may, nonetheless, be obliged to accept the future presence of certain foreigners.[132] Residence is protected on the basis of real social links, not formal status or state authorization. Human rights, which by definition belong to every person, serve as the legal ground for residence rights.

[128] Even if there is no consensus about a customary international rule on the right not to be deported from and to return to your home in accordance with Art. 13(2) UDHR 1948 and Art. 12(4) ICCPR 1966.

[129] Which have always had more nuanced legal concepts of nationality/citizenship; for a comparative study of the USA, Germany, Switzerland, and the European Union, see C. Schönberger, *Unionsbürger: Europas föderales Bürgerrecht in vergleichender Sicht* (2005).

[130] The meaning of 'citizenship' is notoriously vague, especially from an interdisciplinary perspective, cf. R. Bellamy, *Citizenship: A Very Short Introduction* (2008) and T. Kostakopoulou, *The Future Governance of Citizenship* (2008), chapters 1–3. Most lawyers use the term 'nationality' with reference to formal status or *frame*, while citizenship is either used interchangeably or with a wider connotation hinting at the *contents* under domestic (constitutional) law, including political rights; see also S. Kadelbach, 'Union Citizenship', in A. von Bogdandy and J. Bast (eds), *Principles of European Constitutional Law* (2009) 443.

[131] *Benhebba* (n 103) para. 33 (only available in French; own translation).

[132] For the evolution and contents of the case law see II.C, this chapter.

This approximation of human rights guarantees to citizenship rights deserved—and obtained—academic attention, since Article 8 ECHR calls the distinction between citizens/nationals and foreigners into question.[133] Does the factual convergence of human rights and citizenship imply a post-national society in which universal personhood replaces distinctions based on status?

B. Long-term residence as de jure citizenship?

In the early years of ECtHR case law, it seemed that Strasbourg was moving towards a general prohibition of expulsion of long-term residents on the basis of Article 8 ECHR. In the 1990s, the core impetus for the dynamic interpretation of the European Convention was the expulsion of second-generation children of former 'guest workers', who had often been born in their host states or moved there in their early childhood. Most cases decided in Strasbourg concerned this category of long-term residents with regard to which dissenting opinions explicitly called for a general prohibition of expulsions.[134] Furthermore, academic commentators pointed to the impending legitimacy gap of international human rights regimes from a normative standpoint if the distinction between nationals and foreigners was accepted as the starting point of human rights interpretation, thereby ignoring the contents of the rules on access to membership.[135] Moreover, political momentum was building up at the time to protect second-generation immigrations against expulsion.[136] Against this background, it appeared as a possible way forward to establish long-term residence as a legal status with far-fetched rights—a sort of 'citizenship light'.

1. Long-term residence status under EU law

Indeed, long-term residence was established as a formal status for most EU member states with the adoption of the Long-Term Residence Directive 2003/109/EC.[137]

[133] For a pioneer study see, again, Soysal (n 7) and, from a legal perspective, Saroléa (n 25).

[134] See the dissenting opinions referred to in n 47.

[135] Cf. Rubio-Marín and O'Connell (n 57) at 5–9 and for a related argument supporting a right to membership (in terms of naturalization) S. Benhabib, *The Rights of Others: Aliens, Residents, and Citizens* (2004) at 134–43.

[136] In a non-binding recommendation, the Parliamentary Assembly of the Council of Europe: Non-expulsion of long-term immigrants, Recommendation 1504 (2001) of 14 March 2001 explicitly called for a general protection against expulsion, while the Committee of Ministers wanted to maintain expulsion as a measure of last resort, in Recommendation Rec(2000)15 of 13 September 2000, which the Court notes, inter alia, in *Mutlag v. Germany*, ECHR (2010) Appl. No. 40601/05, judgment of 25 March 2010, para. 37; see also the political commitment of equal rights for long-term residents in parallel to EU citizens of the European Council (of the EU) in Tampere of 15/16 October 1999, Presidency Conclusions, para. 21; for further references see K. Groenendijk, 'Long-term Immigrants and the Council of Europe', in E. Guild and P. Minderhoud (eds), *Security of Residence and Expulsion: Protection of Aliens in Europe* (2001) 7.

[137] See II.E, this chapter; the Directive mirrors similar statuses of permanent residence for settled migrants in national immigration laws of many European countries.

Its rules guarantee that third-country nationals who have resided legally and continuously in EU member states for a five-year period and have stable and sufficient resources shall be recognized as long-term residents with an extended set of rights to equal treatment, enhanced protection against expulsion and intra-EU migration.[138] Although the new status undoubtedly solves many of the social concerns pro-migrant NGOs had highlighted in their lobbying work, it does not cover all migrants.[139] In particular, those residing illegally in European states are not covered by the Long-Term Residence Directive (which need not be a disadvantage, since it is a legitimate policy objective to constrain illegal migration);[140] similar limitations apply to migrants with temporary or humanitarian residence permits.[141] These people may certainly obtain security of residence on other grounds, including national regularization measures which many states adopt regularly.[142] But not everyone is covered by these measures. De jure long-term residence status under Directive 2003/109/EC or national law remains a privilege of some. It does not cover all migrants.

2. *Universal application of Article 8 ECHR*

For the purposes of our analysis it should be emphasized that the moral and political concerns which underpin the case law on Article 8 ECHR (that is, residence security for long-term residents, including second-generation immigrants) was similarly a driving force behind the adoption of the Long-Term Residence Directive. Many migrants covered by the Directive would also qualify for leave to remain under Article 8 ECHR, which, conversely, may still be invoked by those migrants who are not covered by the Directive.[143] On this basis, the continued and independent relevance of Article 8 ECHR stands out. Strasbourg does not limit the use of Article 8 ECHR to a designated group of long-term

[138] Cf. Arts 4–5, 11–12 and 14 Directive 2003/109/EC (n 113) and, for further detail, Peers (n 112) chapter 6.7 and D. Acosta Arcarazo, *The Long-Term Residence Status as a Subsidiary Form of EU Citizenship: An Analysis of Directive 2003/109* (2011), chapters 4–10.

[139] Ronen (n 123) at 293 contends that the extension of formal protection status to some foreigners diminishes the incentives to strive for protection for all.

[140] For the legitimacy of 'enhanced measures to combat illegal immigration' (Art. 79(1) TFEU) from a human rights perspective see II.D(2)(b), this chapter.

[141] Directive 2003/109/EC (n 113) was extended to beneficiaries of international protection, including refugees and those with subsidiary protection, by Directive 2011/51/EU, OJ 2011 L 32/1; still, numerous forms of 'complementary' protection below the threshold of the EU Asylum Qualification Directive persist in national immigration laws; for a comparative study, see J. Schieber, *Komplementärer Schutz* (2013).

[142] See P. de Bruycker, J. Apap, and C. Schmitter, 'Rapport de synthèse sur la comparaison des régularisations d'étrangers illégaux dans l'Union européenne', in P. de Bruycker and J. Apap (eds), *Les régularisations des étrangers illégaux dans l'Union européenne* (2000) 23; once residence has been made regular, migrants may qualify for long-term residence status under Directive 2003/109/EC (n 113) (or switch to a residence status covered by the Directive later). Yet, this gradual move towards formal long-term residence status under Directive 2003/109/EC is quite uncertain and does not work for all migrants concerned.

[143] On the distinction between broader (statutory) protection rules in EU directive and (constitutional) human rights guarantees see this chapter, II.E.

residents whose status as quasi-citizens requires enhanced protection. Rather, it upholds Article 8 ECHR as a universal human right which any person may invoke—second-generation immigrants in the same way as illegal immigrants, failed asylum seekers, or people who have lost their nationality; those relying on ties with members of the nuclear family benefit from Article 8 ECHR in the same way as foreigners without relatives. Strasbourg is not concerned with one specific category of people, but rather with upholding the legitimate interests of *all* migrants. It defies the categorization of migrants—an undertaking which would necessarily exclude some. Anyone may invoke Article 8 ECHR, not only selected target groups.[144]

This universality of Strasbourg's approach has important legal implications. If anyone may invoke Article 8 ECHR, the judges must put in place general dogmatic criteria which are capable of addressing the various and divergent living situations of individual migrants. This is precisely what has happened, albeit at the price of a certain level of arbitrariness: there is no clear guidance on what circumstances foreigners may rely upon their private life to object to expulsion or claim regularization.[145] In addition, the criteria for the evaluation of countervailing public policy objectives under the proportionality test remain imprecise and without internal hierarchy.[146] Judicial flexibility is confirmed by the assumption that no category of migrants may claim absolute protection: second-generation immigrants benefit from the strict proportionality assessment and one may argue that those born in a country have an a priori right to stay there indefinitely. But Article 8 ECHR does not bring about absolute protection against expulsion; even second-generation immigrants may be expelled in specific circumstances.[147] The situation of each individual migrant is measured against the same set of criteria. Any foreigner may invoke Article 8 ECHR, which, as a human right, rejects stable differentiations between distinct status groups.

C. Normative reconceptualization of citizenship?

The starting point of our reflection is a straightforward question: does the protection of long-term residence render the distinction between foreigners and citizens obsolete? Evidently, the question is based upon a simple dichotomy which characterized interstate relations in the era of sovereign nation states. One is either a national/citizen or a foreigner/alien.[148] Arguably, this juxtaposition reflects a methodological nationalism with black-and-white paradigms which leave no

[144] For an intelligent study of the underlying conceptual distinction between status and personhood against the background of the US doctrine see L. Bosniak, *The Citizen and the Alien: Dilemmas of Contemporary Membership* (2006) and, for the ECtHR, S. Morano-Foadi and S. Andreadakis, 'The Convergence of the European Legal System in the Treatment of Third Country Nationals in Europe: The ECJ and ECtHR Jurisprudence', 22 *EJIL* (2011) 1071, at 1080–3.

[145] For details see this chapter, II.B(2).

[146] See II.D(2), this chapter.

[147] In contrast to earlier calls to the contrary, mentioned above, the ECtHR's Grand Chamber explicitly recognizes the absence of an *absolute* right against expulsion in *Üner* (n 72) paras 55–56 and *Maslov* (n 53) para. 74 (while recognizing that the proportionality test must be applied strictly).

[148] See III.A, this chapter.

room for intermediate solutions or compromises recognizing the relativity of statehood in today's world.[149] Both at the macro level of interstate relations and at the micro level of immigration law, social and legal realities of today's world differ from the interstate paradigm. States have lost the prerogative to regulate the entry and stay of foreigners at will: the Long-Term Residence Directive, free movement of EU citizens, temporary and permanent residence statuses established in national laws, and the guarantees enshrined in Article 8 ECHR are only four categories which illustrate the transformative disaggregation of residence rights which traditionally have been reserved to people holding the nationality of a state.[150] In today's world, nationality no longer serves as the only gateway to residence security. Non-citizens may invoke legal guarantees limiting state discretion and protecting their domestic residence status.

If rights which have traditionally been associated with citizenship are increasingly conferred upon foreigners, the time has arguably come to reconceptualize the meaning of citizenship. That is precisely what different authors are considering, bearing in mind that 'citizenship' (in contrast to 'nationality') has never been a purely legal concept designating the dividing line between nationals and foreigners. Citizenship has always had wider connotations, calling for the inclusion of social groups which did not originally achieve equal treatment.[151] One prominent group of authors propagates the emergence of a novel form of stakeholder citizenship where the formal link of state-based nationality is replaced by residence-based locality as the demarcation line between outsiders and insiders participating in the formation and evolution of communities.[152] Is residence security under Article 8 ECHR an expression of such de-nationalized de facto citizenship based on residence as a social pact? Three arguments support my conclusion that ECtHR case law lends only limited support to such reading of Article 8 ECHR as a building block for residence-based citizenship concepts.

Firstly, the cross-border movement of people remains a diverse social phenomenon with numerous reasons and multiple individual circumstances. To regard all these cases in the same way would inevitably not offer the proper respect for the complexity of social realities.[153] That is not to say that migration law should not

[149] Cf. U. Beck, *Cosmopolitan Vision* (2006), at 24–32; J. Halfmann, 'World Society and Migrations: Challenges to Theoretical Concepts of Political Sociology', in M. Bommes and E. Morawska (eds), *International Migration Research: Constructions, Omissions and the Promises of Interdisciplinarity* (2005) 129, at 137–45; and S. Sassen, *Territory, Authority, Rights: From Medieval to Global Assemblages* (2006), chapter 6.

[150] For more detailed analyses of disaggregation processes see Soysal (n 7) chapters 8 and 9; Benhabib (n 135); and A. Graser, *Gemeinschaften ohne Grenzen? Zur Dekonzentration der rechtlichen Zugehörigkeiten zu politischen Gemeinschaften* (2008), chapters 6–8.

[151] Cf. on the inclusiveness of citizenship A. Honneth, *Kampf um Anerkennung* (1992) and, in the US context, J. N. Shklar, *American Citizenship: The Quest for Inclusion* (1991).

[152] See the (different) arguments put forward by Kostakopoulou (n 130) chapter 6; R. Bauböck, 'Global Justice, Freedom of Movement and Democratic Citizenship', 50 *European Journal of Sociology* (2009) 1; J. Shaw, 'Citizenship of the Union: Towards a Post-National Membership?', VI-1 *Collected Courses of the Academy of European Law* (1998) 237; and Rubio-Marín and O'Connell (n 57).

[153] See also J.-Y. Carlier, 'L'Europe et les étrangers', in Caloz-Tschopp and Dasen *Mondialisation, migration et droits de l'homme: un nouveau paradigme pour la recherche et la citoyenneté*, vol II (2007) 239, at 271–8.

strive for categorizations (like the long-term resident status established by the EU legislator and other migration categories for diverse purposes such as family reunion, seasonal work, students, etc.). However, to do so is not the function of human rights law. As universal guarantees, human rights should—unlike citizenship[154]—apply to all categories of people.[155] Hence, the approach of the ECtHR to reject firm categorizations in the application of Article 8 ECHR should be welcomed.[156] Human rights strive for universality—not for a distinction between insiders and outsiders.

Secondly, the protection of residence status remains one-sided. While physical presence is certainly important, residence alone does not constitute citizenship (slaves also had a right/obligation to reside within a designated territory). Notwithstanding the diversity of citizenship concepts, there is agreement that 'citizenship' implies a certain degree of participation in community affairs.[157] Residence is a necessary condition for citizenship but does not suffice to establish citizenship in itself.[158] Without political participation, residence security degenerates into depoliticized 'denizenship'.[159] Political participation of foreigners, however, is not guaranteed by the ECtHR.[160] Strasbourg's case law cannot, therefore, establish meaningful citizenship. Additional steps are necessary to do so.[161]

Thirdly, we should be careful not to fall back into the black-and-white paradigm of classic international law. Our discussion is not about either full citizenship with equal rights or alienage without legal protection. In today's world, there is room for

[154] In contrast to human rights, 'citizenship', no matter how liberally or inclusively defined, presupposes a certain degree of distinction; cf. C. Harvey, 'Promoting Insecurity: Public Order, Expulsion and the European Convention on Human Rights', in Guild and Minderhoud (n 136) at 41 and J. H. H. Weiler, 'To Be a European Citizen: Eros and Civilization', in J. H. H. Weiler, *The Constitution of Europe: 'Do the New Clothes Have an Emperor?' and Other Essays on European Integration* (1999) 324, at 332–5.

[155] Since not everyone staying one night in a city can be defined as 'citizen', institutional arrangements for residence-based stakeholder citizenship would require dividing lines (mirroring, eg, the Long-Term Residence Directive), thereby excluding others—whereas human rights strive for universality.

[156] See III.B; of course, there are multiple interactions between Art. 8 ECHR and institutionalized forms of long-term residence status: if, for example, Art. 8 ECHR mandates regularization (cf. II.C), illegal residents obtain a preliminary residence permit, which, in the medium term, will be upgraded to long-term residence status.

[157] Cf. Bellamy (n 130) and, in addition to transnational residence rights, Rubio-Marín and O'Connell (n 57) at 14–19; Graser (n 150) chapters 9 and 10; and J. Shaw, 'Citizenship: Contrasting Dynamics a the Interface of Integration and Constitutionalism', in P. Craig and G. de Búrca (eds), *The Evolution of EU Law* (2011) 575, at 576–7 and 597–608.

[158] Although the Long-Term Residence Directive 2003/109/EC (n 113) mandates equal treatment, including trade union membership, it does not guarantee political participation.

[159] Cf. N. Walker, 'Denizenship and Deterritorialisation in the European Union', in H. Lindahl (ed.), *A Right to Inclusion and Exclusion? Normative Fault Lines of the EU's Area of Freedom, Security and Justice* (2009) 261, and T. Hammar, *Democracy and the Nation State: Aliens, Denizens, and Citizens in a World of International Migration* (1990), at 12 et seq.

[160] Art. 16 ECHR does, on the contrary, authorize states to restrict political activities of foreigners, mirroring classic notions of non-interference in the domestic affairs of other states by not allowing their nationals (eg, Iranians living in the EU) to pursue expatriate propaganda against their home state; cf. C. Tomuschat, *Zur politischen Betätigung des Ausländers in der Bundesrepublik Deutschland* (1968), at 12–39.

[161] See the next subsection.

intermediate solutions. It is not a trivial assertion to say that the ECtHR protects long-term presence, including illegal residence, under the heading of private life, even if this protection does not bring about citizenship.[162] Many countries around the world do not give the perspective of illegal migrants similar legal weight.[163] Rejecting the classification of Article 8 ECHR as de facto *citizenship* does not deny its legal and theoretical relevance: it constitutes a first layer of concentric circles of protection, a first step towards citizenship. But even without later consolidation, respect for human rights of non-citizens is in itself a cosmopolitan achievement. Non-citizens are not necessarily aliens without rights.

D. Support for integration into domestic communities

In its case law, the ECtHR concentrates on the protection of residence security, whenever deportation has negative repercussions upon private and/or family life. More extensive rights are beyond the reach of Article 8 ECHR. That is not to say, however, that migrants should not hold other rights. On the contrary, there are convincing normative arguments supporting the gradual integration of foreigners on the basis of a conditional right to membership for long-term residents.[164] Without convergence of the de facto resident population with de jure citizenship, a legitimacy gap would form.[165] Although international law does, to date, not oblige states to support the gradual extension of citizenship rights to long-term residents, this analysis is based upon the normative assumption that such a legitimacy gap should be prevented. In principle, this objective can be achieved in two alternative ways: either by granting long-term residents similar rights as citizens (mirroring the status of EU citizens) or by supporting their naturalization.[166] Although the ECtHR has no official position on this question, recent judgments hint at judicial preference for the second solution (subsection 1 below)—reflecting a growing consensus in Europe that long-term residents

[162] See also Bosniak (n 144) chapter 6.

[163] In the US, for example, illegal immigrants may have, under certain conditions, access to education and healthcare, but residence as such does not benefit from human rights protection.

[164] See, among many, S. Benhabib (n 135) at 134–43; A. Shachar, *The Birthright Lottery: Citizenship and Global Inequality* (2009), chapter 6; and C. Chwaszcza, 'The Unity of the People, and Immigration in Liberal Theory', 13 *Citizenship Studies* (2009) 451, at 466–8; it should be noted that such (conditional) right to membership implies that some foreigners are *not* naturalized (those who do not meet the criteria for membership).

[165] Cf. the (controversial) judgment of the German constitutional court (*Bundesverfassungsgericht*), which rejected voting rights for foreigners in municipal elections, while acknowledging that the legislator may/should react to discrepancies between citizenship and the resident population through changes in nationality law; see BVerfG, judgments of 31 October 1991, 2 BvF 2/89 & 3/89, BVerfGE 83, 37, and 60, available at: <http://www.servat.unibe.ch/dfr> (in German).

[166] Among the numerous academic articles discussing both alternatives, see S. Besson and A. Utzinger, 'Introduction: Future Challenges of European Citizenship—Facing a Wide-Open Pandora's Box', 13 *ELJ* (2007) 573, at 580–2; R. Hansen, 'A European Citizenship or a Europe of Citizens? Third Country Nationals in the EU', 24 *Journal of Ethnic and Migration Studies* (1998) 751, and D. Kostakopoulou, 'European Union Citizenship: Writing the Future', 13 *ELJ* (2007) 623, at 643–5.

should have an option to become full and equal members of European societies through naturalization (subsection 2 below).

1. The ECtHR's novel emphasis on social integration

The first indication in favour of naturalization is the Court's implicit decision to focus its analysis on residence security. The concept of 'private life', which the Court defines as the network of personal, social, and economic relations that make up the private life of every human being,[167] is broad enough to embrace other aspects outside of residence security. Why should the high contracting parties' positive obligations under Article 8 ECHR not cover a duty to prevent exclusion from the labour market or a right to vote? Conceptually, such claims could easily be integrated into private life reasoning. Yet, that position is not shared by the ECtHR which focuses on residence security instead. The private life of foreigners shields them against expulsion—no more, no less.[168] Other human rights enshrined in the European Convention and additional protocols have broader repercussions on the position of migrants.[169] Such impacts do not concern immigration statuses however. When it comes to categories of immigration, the ECtHR is primarily concerned with residence security, not wider social integration.[170]

Moreover, the Court's appraisal of countervailing public policy objectives under the proportionality test in expulsion cases has demonstrated a turn towards qualitative reasoning in recent years. As illustrated earlier, Article 8 ECHR shields migrants against state interference with long-term residence, but this is not to say that other factors than de facto presence on the domestic territory are irrelevant. On the contrary, the proportionality of state interferences depends upon the weighing of countervailing public policy objectives.[171] Under the proportionality test the individual circumstances of long-term residence are assessed, thereby supporting qualitative differentiations. By way of example, we may refer to Mr Bajsultanov, whose expulsion from Austria after almost nine years of residence the ECtHR considered to comply with human rights although he would be separated from his family: '[h]e does not seem to have mastered the German language. He has also never worked in Austria and did not develop any significant social or cultural ties there'.[172] Such statements are an important indication of the ECtHR's vision of social integration. They indicate how, in the eyes of the ECtHR, long-term residents should behave in their host society in order to benefit from residence

[167] See II.B(2), this chapter.

[168] See II.C(1), this chapter, and Thym (n 44) at 99 on *Sisojeva* (n 6) para. 91, where the Grand Chamber rejects the argument that a regularization offer by the Latvian authorities did not meet the requirements of Art. 8 ECHR as long as it guaranteed residence security.

[169] Freedom of religion is guaranteed by Art. 9 ECHR and Art. 14 ECHR can be invoked to object to discrimination, but immigration and nationality laws are, by and large, immune from other influences.

[170] Ie, Art. 8 ECHR confers a positive obligation upon states to respect residence security—not labour market integration, etc., which are considered, however, as opposing public policy objectives justifying state interference with long-term residence status.

[171] See, generally, II.D, this chapter.

[172] *Bajsultanov* (n 83) para. 85.

security. Indeed, social integration has turned into a core factor of the Strasbourg case law on Article 8 ECHR in recent years.

In the *Üner* judgment, the Grand Chamber made a noteworthy effort to refine earlier criteria guiding the proportionality assessment.[173] In principle, there was nothing unusual about the case, which concerned a thirty-five-year-old Turkish national who had lived in the Netherlands since the age of twelve and was expelled after a series of crimes which culminated in manslaughter. Not very differently from most other cases decided in Strasbourg before, the applicant maintained that expulsion would interfere with his family and private life. Nonetheless, the Grand Chamber seized the opportunity for a change of direction. Before turning to the evaluation of the case, the ECtHR specified its general reading of Article 8 ECHR in abstract terms. It emphasized that residence security is linked to wider social integration.

> The Court would wish to make explicit two criteria which may already be implicit in those identified in the *Boultif* judgment [and which it takes into account in the proportionality assessment]: the best interests and well-being of the children . . . ; and the *solidity of social, cultural and family ties with the host country* and with the country of destination.[174]

That is a bold statement. It has been demonstrated before that the judges embark upon an analysis of the integration of the applicant into the host society. The proportionality assessment which defines the outcome of most cases extends to qualitative criteria such as the employment situation, education, or linguistic integration.[175] The behaviour of some migrants is categorized as not good enough (expulsion remains possible), while the individual living situation of others commands respect (expulsion would violate Article 8 ECHR).

2. *Towards full membership through naturalization*

In order to fully grasp the bearing of the novel focus on social integration, we should consider the political context. During the past decade, many European states and the EU institutions were discussing policies to support the social, economic and political integration of foreigners into European societies, as the EU's Common Basic Principles for immigrant integration policy illustrate.[176] They recognize the relevance of education and labour market participation and stress the significance of linguistic and civic integration.[177] Moreover, European states are invited to support naturalization, which the European Union cannot dictate due to

[173] See Steinorth (n 109) at 192–4 and C. Murphy, 'The Concept of Integration in the Jurisprudence of the European Court of Human Rights', 12 *European Journal of Migration and Law* (2010) 23, at 27–9.

[174] *Üner* (n 72) para. 58 (emphasis added); see also *Maslov* (n 53) para. 71 which highlights the relevance of the latter criterion in cases of long-term residence, such as for second-generation immigrants, where the ECtHR requires a particularly strict proportionality assessment, which comprises the solidity of social, cultural and family ties with the host country.

[175] See II.D(2)(b), this chapter.

[176] See Common Basic Principles (CBP) for Immigrant Integration Policy in the European Union, Council doc. 14615/04 of 19 November 2004.

[177] Cf. Common Basic Principles (n 176) paras 3 (labour market), 5 (education), and 4 (civic and linguistic integration).

a lack of competence in this area, but does nonetheless advocate through soft-law instruments.[178] Indeed, many European states have amended their nationality laws in recent years with a view to establishing an option for naturalization;[179] the traditional criticism of ethnic-exclusionary *ius sanguinis* regimes no longer holds[180] (and accumulated numbers of naturalizations during the past decade are impressive in some countries, as the following table illustrates). At the same time, the self-perception of European societies is undergoing profound change; cultural, or even ethnic, definitions of national identity are gradually being supplanted by the acceptance of cultural diversity and non-discrimination,[181] sometimes with active support from Strasbourg.[182] In short, European societies accommodate migratory movements, including a conditional option for naturalization.

	Naturalizations	**Third-country nationals**
	accumulated numbers 1998–2009	incl. short-term residence in 2010
	(% of resident population)	(% of resident population)[183]
EU-27	**8,139,700 (1.6%)**	**20,157,200 (4.0%)**
Germany	1,584,700 (2.0%)	4,584,700 (5.6%)
France	1,698,100 (2.6%)	2,451,400 (3.8%)
United Kingdom	1,492,900 (2.4%)	2,445,100 (3.9%)
Italy	309,100 (0.5%)	2,993,700 (5.0%)
Spain	489,900 (1.0%)	3,335,700 (7.3%)
Poland	19,900 (0.1%)	30,700 (0.1%)
Estonia	55,200 (4.1%)	201,700 (15.1%)
Netherlands	464,600 (2.8%)	341,300 (2.1%)
Sweden	448,500 (4.7%)	324,700 (3.5%)
Slovakia	25,400 (0.5%)	24,200 (0.4%)

[178] See the (deliberately weak) formulation, Common Basic Principles (n 176) paras 6 and 9, and J. Shaw, *The Transformation of Citizenship in the European Union: Electoral Rights and the Restructuring of Political Space* (2007), at 209–37.

[179] Naturalization depends upon a number of criteria and not all states accept dual nationality—nonetheless the figures are impressive: many third-country nationals are naturalized; see the comparative study by I. Kalnina, 'Justice as a Common Denominator of EU Member State Citizenship Policies', in D. Thym and F. G. Snyder (eds), *Europe—A Continent of Immigration? Legal Challenges in the Construction of European Migration Policy* (2011), at 325–46 or the overview by C. Joppke, *Citizenship and Immigration* (2010), chapter 2.

[180] Current debates focus on dual nationality and integration requirements as preconditions for naturalization—not on the option of naturalization per se; *cf.* the contributions to E. Guild, K. Groenendijk, and S. Carrera (eds), *Illiberal Liberal States: Immigration, Citizenship and Integration in the EU* (2009).

[181] This process is not free from irritation and controversies, but a trend towards cultural diversity is tangible; by way of example in the EU's CBP (n 176) paras 1, 7, and 8.

[182] Eg ECtHR judgments on religious diversity or freedom of speech.

[183] Source: Eurostat, Statistics in focus 34/2011, Population and social Conditions, at 2; available at: <http://epp.eurostat.ec.europa.eu/cache/ITY_OFFPUB/KS-SF-11-034/EN/KS-SF-11-034-EN.PDF>.

Against this background, the relevance of the novel emphasis on social integration stands out. By highlighting the 'solidity of social, cultural and family ties with the host country' (and with the country of origin),[184] the ECtHR indicated that its vision about respectful long-term residence is not based upon de facto presence on the domestic territory only. Instead, qualitative criteria matter when assessing the proportionality of state interferences. Integration efforts, achievements, and failures of individual migrants are relevant factors as to whether the Court finds a violation of Article 8 ECHR. In recent judgments, judges have indeed started discussing considerations of labour market participation, education, and linguistic integration, even if it must be concluded that the ECtHR lacks a clear vision of how to assess the solidity of social integration in individual cases. One sub-criterion features regularly in recent judgments: language skills.[185] Other factors, such as labour market participation or education, are considered, albeit on a more or less random basis only.[186] I am also unaware of any judgment which would elaborate upon 'cultural ties' with the host society (a criterion which the *Üner* judgment mentions explicitly).[187] But this hesitation on the part of the Court to apply its own criteria in individual cases does not discount the conceptual relevance of the novel emphasis on the solidity of social integration.

None of this presents an irrefutable argument that the ECtHR perceives naturalization to be the ultimate objective of the successful integration of foreigners. Yet, there are indications that naturalization matters. First, the ECtHR's rejection of absolute protection against expulsion on the basis of Article 8 ECHR[188] maintains a (deliberate) distance between long-term residents within the meaning of the provision and naturalized immigrants, who benefit from absolute protection against expulsion in accordance with Article 3(1) of Additional Protocol No. 4 to the European Convention. Second, the introduction of qualitative integration criteria (that is, the solidity of social, cultural and family ties with the host country) shows that the judicial interpretation of Article 8 ECHR does not pursue an overly individualistic vision of society. Residence security is not solely a matter of the length of stay, but depends upon the interaction with society at large. Naturalization sanctions this process and in a couple of judgments, the ECtHR did indeed confront the applicant with the failure to apply for naturalization although the application might have been successful; absence of naturalization plays a role in the

[184] In its judgments, the ECtHR combines both criteria, since the judges evaluate the specific impact of potential deportation for each applicant (the effect of deportation would be return to the home country); conceptually, it would be more convincing, however, if both aspects were not to be mixed and integration into the host country was judged independently (on negative effects for transnational migrants who maintain links with their home country, see Farahat (n 25) at 260–1).

[185] For detail see the references in n 107.

[186] See II.D(2)(b), this chapter, and Murphy (n 173) at 34–8.

[187] It remains dubious what the Court means by 'culture' in this context: in light of Art. 9 ECHR certainly not religion, but what else: knowledge of Goethe and Shakespeare? Acceptance of 'cultural' norms such as equality of men and women or non-discrimination of homosexuals? Marriage to a partner from your host/home society (as indicated *en passant* in *A.H. Khan* (n 106) para. 41 and discussed by B. de Hart, 'Love Thy Neighbour: Family Reunification and the Rights of Insiders', 11 *European Journal of Migration and Law* (2009) 235)?

[188] See II.D, this chapter.

proportionality assessment.[189] To put it otherwise, migrants can prove affiliation with the host society by becoming part of it. Naturalization is the formal legal confirmation of this undertaking, which, in qualitative terms, the Court also considers beforehand when assessing the proportionality of expulsion measures in individual cases.

IV. Conclusion

Immigration law has long been characterized by its orientation towards the public interest. The concept of state sovereignty is the ultimate legal-doctrinal justification for the freedom of states to control the entry and stay of aliens. Conversely, human rights pose a direct challenge to state sovereignty with their orientation towards the individual. Against this background, the originality of the ECtHR case law stands out: if long-term residence is protected as an end in itself under the heading of 'private life', refugee protection ceases to be the only area in which unfettered state control over the entry and stay of foreigners is abandoned. Residence security is protected as an end in itself. Even migrants without regular residence status may, under certain circumstances, invoke Article 8 ECHR in order to regularize illegal stay. That is the ultimate achievement of ECtHR: it obliges national authorities to take legitimate interests of individual migrants into account. States are under an obligation to justify restrictive laws and practices. Article 8 ECHR gives the migrant perspective a voice with legal authority.

At the same time, Strasbourg is careful to accommodate countervailing public policy objectives. It forces states to take the migrant perspective into account, but it does not renounce their capacity to control the entry and stay of foreigners altogether. Migration control does not justify the deportation of any illegal migrant, but represents a legitimate public policy objective which plays an important part in the proportionality assessment. Article 8 ECHR has limits. Migrants can be expelled and deported, even after extended periods of residence. Countervailing public policy objectives, including migration control, matter. Unfortunately, it remains difficult to predict the outcome of individual cases, since the set of criteria which the ECtHR has developed for the proportionality assessment remains vague and lacks internal hierarchy. This conclusion holds for 'private life' cases, in particular, since the network of personal, social, and economic relations that make up the private life of every human being is notoriously difficult to define. Notwithstanding the difficulty to predict the outcome of individual cases, we may identify a shift towards qualitative criteria of social integration. The Court takes seriously 'the solidity of social, cultural and family ties' with the host country and considers issues such as labour market participation, education or linguistic integration in the proportionality assessment.

[189] See *Boughanemi v. France*, ECHR (1996) Appl. No. 22070/93, judgment of 24 April 1996, para. 39; *Baghli v. France*, ECHR (1999) Appl. No. 34374/97, judgment of 30 November 1999, para. 48; and *Kaya* (n 106) para. 64.

From a descriptive point of view, it is certainly correct to portray the protection of long-term residence status under the heading of 'private life' as a move towards de facto citizenship, since migrants do, under certain circumstances, obtain a right which traditionally only citizens would have: not to be expelled from their country of residence. Without diminishing the achievements of the case law, we should be careful, however, not to overstretch its similarities with the conventional concept of citizenship. Citizenship, no matter how broadly and inclusively defined, is not limited to residence security, but encompasses wider social engagement and political participation. On this basis, one may possibly design a special status of de facto citizenship with extended rights for certain categories of long-term residents (such as those covered by the Long-Term Residence Directive of the European Union). However, that is not the path followed by the ECtHR. Strasbourg concentrates on residence security only, thereby underlining the predisposition of Article 8 ECHR as a universal human right. It protects everyone (not only de facto citizens) and rejects attempts to categorize migrants. Anyone may invoke Article 8 ECHR, not just de facto citizens.

It is not a trivial assertion to say that the ECtHR protects foreigners, including in situations of illegal residence, under the heading of private life, even if this protection does not bring about de facto citizenship. It would be a false dichotomy to classify human beings either as citizens (with full rights) or aliens (without protection of the law). Such juxtaposition reflects the paradigm of sovereign statehood in which intermediate solutions between citizenship and alienage are unknown. Rejecting an academic reconstruction of Strasbourg's case law as de facto citizenship does not strip migrants of legal protection. On the contrary; by recognizing and assessing the solidity of social, cultural, and family ties of each individual migrant with the host country as relevant criteria in the proportionality assessment, Strasbourg recognizes that residence security is a necessary but not sufficient condition for citizenship. Further advances the ECtHR cannot dictate. Article 8 ECHR should therefore be conceived of as a first layer of protection, which paves the way towards social integration and naturalization. Despite this conceptual caveat, the protection of long-term residence status under Article 8 ECHR is, in itself, a noteworthy cosmopolitan achievement. In Europe, non-citizens enjoy human rights-based residence rights.

4

Migration, Gender, and the Limits of Rights

Siobhán Mullally

The significance of gender in the context of migration has attracted increasing attention in recent years. The 'feminization of migration', noted in many policy documents and academic commentaries, points to the increasing numbers of women now migrating independently to seek work and the diverse geographical regions within which women are migrating.[1] Reflecting this phenomenon, significant developments have taken place in international human rights law specifically addressing migrant women.[2] As many commentators have noted, however, there are costs to inclusion in the register of human rights discourse.[3] This is particularly true for migrant women who do not fit easily into the inherited structures of human rights law. The terms of inclusion may reinforce gendered and racialized stereotypes of the 'abject' third-world woman or lead to alliances with conservative agendas that further limit migration possibilities. 'Border norms' do not stop at the border.[4] They follow migrants within the territorial borders of states and entrench distinctions not just between citizens and non-citizens, but also between categories of migrants. Gender plays a key role in determining the precariousness and vulnerability experienced by migrants, in shaping the migration routes that are taken, and in determining the terms of belonging imposed by states. Migrant women crossing borders pose significant challenges to the inherited structures and frameworks of international human rights law raising questions as to its transformative potential.

This chapter examines the significance of gender in three areas of law relating to migration: human trafficking, migrant domestic workers, and gender-related asylum law. It starts from the premise that human rights norms, properly interpreted, may challenge the exclusion, exploitation, and abuses experienced by many migrant women. It argues that human rights norms have the potential to address and respond to overlapping axes of discrimination and disadvantage, including 'race', ethnicity,

[1] N. Piper, 'Feminisation of Migration and the Social Dimensions of Development: the Asian case', 29 *Third World Quarterly* (2008) 1287.

[2] See, eg, UN Committee on the Elimination of All Forms of Discrimination Against Women, *General Recommendation no. 26 on Women Migrant Workers* (2009) UN Doc CEDAW/C/2009/WP.1/R.

[3] D. Otto, 'Exile of Inclusion: Reflections on Gender Issues in International Law over the Last Decade, The Feature: Reflections on a Decade of International Law' 10 *Melbourne Journal of International Law* (2009) 11.

[4] L. Bosniak, *The Citizen and the Alien: Dilemmas of Contemporary Membership* (2006).

migration status, and gender. It recognizes, however, that the permeability of human rights law is not without limits, particularly in the context of migration where sovereign prerogatives continue to resist human rights claims. It also matters who is promoting the gender equality agenda and to what end.[5] In the context of migration, migrant women's rights claims have been instrumentalized by states so as to legitimize the expansion of criminal laws (in the context of human trafficking and irregular migration) and to restrict pathways to safe and secure migration.[6] Migrant women are frequently positioned by law as vulnerable to abuse and in need of protection. This constructed vulnerability, in turn, is presumed to justify the coercive interventions of the state. As we shall see, the normative re-emergence of protective categories does little to enhance women's autonomy, agency, or equality, as the 'sexed subject' of human rights law continues to position migrant women at its limits. To the extent that women's autonomy is recognized, such autonomy is viewed as threatening, potentially destabilizing to the certainties required for neoliberal models of migration management, and further evidence that the protections afforded by law may be unnecessary (or undeserved).[7] This duality is reflected in the law's responses to migrant women. The resulting tensions, as we shall see, limit the transformative potential of human rights norms and projects of law reform, both domestically and internationally.

I. Human Trafficking: Rights, Vulnerabilities, and Reform

Attempts to add the harms endured by trafficked persons into the framework of international human rights law have met with many obstacles, revealing the reluctance of states to yield traditional sovereign prerogatives on immigration even in the face of egregious harms.[8] The protective stereotypes of migrant women persist, as trafficked women are positioned as victims but denied the resources and supports most needed to move to a secure and safe migration status. For women who are victims of human trafficking, access to legal protections, effective remedies, and to secure migration status, remains difficult. The trafficked person, although a victim of an egregious harm, is also an irregular migrant in the eyes of the state. An irregular migrant with a possible claim to international protection poses a significant challenge to a state's claim to control its borders and to manage migration. Her potential claim to 'be here' and to remain is one that has been resisted as states have proven reluctant to remedy the fundamental irregularity of her presence. As Gallagher has argued, the trafficked woman is de facto stateless, unlikely to receive effective protection from her country of origin and denied the very form of protection most likely to vindicate her human rights claims to secure residence and access to safe migration pathways.[9]

[5] See V. Munro, 'Of Rights and Rhetoric: Discourses of Degradation and Exploitation in the Context of Sex Trafficking', 25 *Journal of Law & Society* (2008) 240.

[6] V. Munro, 'Stopping Traffic: A Comparative Study of Responses to the Trafficking in Women for Prostitution', 46 *British Journal of Criminology* (2006) 318.

[7] Munro (n 6).

[8] A. Gallagher, *The International Law of Human Trafficking* (2010).

[9] Gallagher (n 8).

Recent years have witnessed the adoption of a growing body of anti-trafficking laws and policies at domestic and international levels. To borrow Agamben's evocative term, we have seen an explosion of laws[10] on human trafficking and in the context of trafficking for purposes of sexual exploitation, a continuing circulation of sexual panic. Many feminist commentators have responded with concern to this proliferation of laws and to the accompanying expansion of sovereign power to regulate migration.[11] The unintended consequences of anti-trafficking measures have included an expansion of state power to regulate border crossings and a further closing off of regular migration pathways for migrant women. This crisis response has negative consequences for migrant women and for longer-term analysis of the substantive impact of anti-trafficking law on gender equality. The preoccupation with criminalization of trafficking and related activities has narrowed the space for responses that foreground the human rights of trafficked persons. As a crisis governance response takes hold, reform proposals that recognize the intersecting axes of discrimination and power linked to gender, 'race', and migration status are marginalized.

This ideological capture is not complete, however. In the practice of human rights law, there is potential for law to move beyond the binary divides that have characterized the crisis governance response to human trafficking to date. In recent years, we have seen a growing resistance to the expansion of criminal law and greater recognition of the requirements of due process in anti-trafficking reforms. There is some, albeit limited, resistance increasingly visible in the incremental changes occurring in relation to residence claims, recovery periods, and restrictions on return of trafficked persons, as well as recognition of states' positive duties to prevent human trafficking and to provide effective remedies to victims. These incremental changes reflect the need to move beyond stereotypical portrayals of the 'victim subject' of human trafficking that have marginalized the agency of the trafficked person and limited the transformative potential of human rights.

A. Standard-setting: problems of definition and competing narratives

As noted in the introduction, who 'sponsors' feminist goals matters a great deal, as becomes very clear when one examines the genealogy and contemporary practice of anti-trafficking measures. The adoption of the Protocol to Prevent, Suppress and Punish Trafficking in Persons, especially Women and Children (Palermo Protocol) in 2000 marked a significant moment in the development of international legal standards on human trafficking.[12] The inclusion of an anti-trafficking instrument in the panoply of international legal instruments, through a Protocol to the Convention on Transnational Organized Crime was also significant, reflecting

[10] G. Agamben, *Means Without End: Notes on Politics* (2000).

[11] See Munro, n 6, and A. T. Gallagher, *Recommended Principles and Guidelines on Human Rights and Human Trafficking: Commentary* (2010); available at: <http://works.bepress.com/anne_gallagher/15>; accessed 20 March 2012.

[12] Protocol to Prevent, Suppress and Punish Trafficking in Persons Especially Women and Children, supplementing the United Nations Convention against Transnational Organized Crime (2000).

the international community's preoccupation with organized crime and irregular movements across borders. The failure to ensure stronger protections for trafficked persons in the Protocol reflects the reluctance of states to recognize the rights claims that arise in the context of irregular migration and the continuing dominance of security and sovereignty concerns.

A key issue in defining the crime of human trafficking is the question of whether consent may be raised as a defence. This issue is a particularly complex one in the context of allegations of trafficking for the purposes of sexual exploitation, where conflicting positions on the appropriate domestic legal responses to sex work muddy the process of reform. The difficult negotiating history of the Palermo Protocol, the delays in securing agreement on the legal definition of trafficking, and the ensuing divisions that arose between human rights activists during the drafting process reflect broader disagreements on the regulation of sex work. The question of how or whether to allow for possible defences of consent to be raised was the subject of protracted negotiation and often acrimonious debate.[13] Familiar disagreements came to the fore in these negotiations. For those pursuing an abolitionist position on prostitution, the possibility of a woman consenting to engage in the commercial sex industry as a sex worker could not be countenanced as a defensible legal position.[14] The move to disallow possible defences of consent being raised follows from this abolitionist position.

The possible consequences of such a position for diverse national systems of criminal law including those that do not criminalize the purchase of sexual services, and the potential for conflict with fair trial rights, led to a compromise in the final text of the Protocol. The possibility of a defence of consent being raised where the victim in question was a child is denied, in recognition of the child's inherent vulnerability.[15] Outside of the context of child trafficking, where any of the aggravating factors of exploitation were found to exist, including the use of force

[13] See Gallagher (n 8).

[14] See C. MacKinnon, 'Prostitution and Civil Rights', 1 *Michigan Journal of Gender and Law* (1993) 13.

[15] Art. 3 of the Protocol provides:

For the purposes of this Protocol:

(a) 'Trafficking in persons' shall mean the recruitment, transportation, transfer, harbouring or receipt of persons, by means of the threat or use of force or other forms of coercion, of abduction, of fraud, of deception, of the abuse of power, or of a position of vulnerability or of the giving or receiving of payments or benefits to achieve the consent of a person having control over another person, for the purpose of exploitation. Exploitation shall include, at a minimum, the exploitation of the prostitution of others or other forms of sexual exploitation, forced labour or services, slavery or practices similar to slavery, servitude, or the removal of organs;

(b) The consent of a victim of trafficking in persons to the intended exploitation set forth in subparagraph (a) of this article shall be irrelevant where any of the means set forth in subparagraph (a) have been used;

(c) The recruitment, transportation, transfer, harbouring, or receipt of a child for the purpose of exploitation shall be considered 'trafficking in persons' even if this does not involve any of the means set forth in subparagraph (a) of this article;

(d) 'Child' shall mean any person under eighteen years of age.

or coercion, consent was deemed to be irrelevant.[16] The compromise adopted leaves open the possibility that women may have chosen to engage in sex work and as such could not be presumed to be victims of violence per se. This position was subsequently followed in the later 2005 Council of Europe Convention on Action Against Trafficking in Human Beings[17] and is also reflected in the position taken by the drafters of the UN Convention on the Elimination of All Forms of Discrimination Against Women (CEDAW).[18]

The compromises adopted in the Palermo Protocol and other international legal instruments fall short of the more radical position taken by Barry et al., who argue that sex work (or the preferred term, prostitution) is inherently exploitative.[19] A 'wrongful use' view of sexual exploitation sees harm as essential to prostitution itself. In this view, regardless of whether a decision to engage in sex work was rational or preferential given the 'pre-transaction baseline' and terms of engagement, exploitation is presumed to occur.[20]

Divisions between regulatory and abolitionist positions on sex work continue to manifest themselves in the context of proposals to criminalize the purchase of sexual services, including the services of a trafficked person.[21] States' positive obligations to prevent human trafficking are increasingly linked to these debates. On the question of combating demand for the services of trafficked persons, the Palermo Protocol requires states to adopt legislative or other measures to discourage the demand that leads to trafficking.[22] While the regulation of prostitution is left to states, it is argued by some that there is a positive obligation on states to combat demand for exploitative commercial sexual services, which encourages human trafficking and ultimately engages states' obligations of deterrence and prevention.[23] The call to criminalize the purchase of sexual services seeks to tackle the apparently 'insatiable demand for cheap labour' that fuels the commercial sex industry and creates a buoyant market for traffickers.[24]

The UN CEDAW Committee has not pursued an abolitionist model, preferring to focus on the substantive impact of regulatory or abolitionist responses to sex work on women, including, in particular, women migrants. In its Concluding Observations on both the Dutch and Swedish reports, the Committee has questioned the impact of differing responses—regulatory and abolitionist—adopted at domestic level and sought concrete data and analysis on the impact of differing

[16] See Art. 3(b). [17] Arts 4(a) and (b).

[18] Convention on the Elimination of All Forms of Discrimination Against Women (1979), 1249 UNTS 13. See Art. 6.

[19] K. Barry, *The Prostitution of Sexuality* (1996); MacKinnon (n 14); C. A. MacKinnon, *Are Women Human? And Other International Dialogues* (2006).

[20] Munro (n 5) at 260–1.

[21] See, eg, recent legal reforms in the UK, Policing and Crime Act 2009 (ss. 14–15). These proposals draw, in particular, on developments in Sweden following the adoption of the Act Prohibiting the Purchase of Sexual Services (1999).

[22] See Art. 9.

[23] Statement of Ms Sigma Huda, Special Rapporteur on Trafficking in Persons, at CSW- Beijing + 10 Review, 7 March 2005; available at: <http://www.un.org/webcast/csw2005/statements/050307traffickinginpersons-e.pdf>.

[24] Munro (n 5) at 242.

regimes on the health, well-being, and rights of sex workers.[25] The 2005 Council of Europe Trafficking Convention adopts a similar compromise, leaving it open to states to consider the introduction of criminal sanctions, but requiring all states at a minimum to address the problem of demand in the context of a growing market for the services of trafficked persons.[26] The 2011 EU Directive on preventing and combating trafficking in human beings and protecting its victims[27] addresses the question of demand for the services of trafficked persons in general, but limits the imposition of positive obligations to prevent human trafficking to programmatic measures relating to education, training, and raising of awareness.[28] States are required only to 'consider' the introduction of offences to criminalize the purchase of the services of a trafficked person with the knowledge that the person is a victim.[29] An earlier European Commission proposal to require states to criminalize the use of such services was not adopted, reflecting disagreements on the regulation of sex work at member state level. The specific reference in the 2011 Directive to use of the services of trafficked persons with knowledge that the person is the victim of an offence, would seem to allow states to move beyond the binary divisions of abolition or regulation of sex work and instead to target specifically the phenomenon of human trafficking. For proponents of an abolitionist response, this position is not enough as the commercialization and sale of sex is, in itself, presumed to be exploitative and to fuel the human trafficking industry.[30]

In *Rantsev v. Cyprus and Russia*,[31] the European Court of Human Rights, while not directly addressing the links between demand for commercial sex services and human trafficking per se, did read Article 4 of the European Convention on Human Rights (ECHR) as imposing positive obligations on states to prevent trafficking for the purposes of sexual exploitation. Specifically, the Court noted that Article 4 requires member states to put in place adequate measures to regulate businesses frequently used as a cover for human trafficking and to ensure that domestic legislation provides 'practical and effective protection of the rights of victims and potential victims of trafficking'.[32] The links between a failure to regulate the sex industry and heightened risks of trafficking on this reading may engage the responsibility of the State. In *Rantsev,* the inconsistencies in the Cypriot government position became evident. The government had earlier introduced a range of anti-trafficking measures including a national action plan to combat trafficking, while at the same time maintaining a widely criticized '*cabaret artiste*'

[25] *Concluding comments of the Committee on the Elimination of Discrimination against Women: Netherlands*, UN Doc CEDAW/C/NLD/CO/4, 2 February 2007, paras 20–22; *Concluding observations of the Committee on the Elimination of Discrimination against Women: Sweden*, 8 April 2008, UN Doc CEDAW/C/SWE/CO/7, para. 33.

[26] Council of Europe Convention on Action against Trafficking in Human Beings, Warsaw, 16 May 2005, Art. 6: Measures to discourage the demand.

[27] Directive 2011/36/EU of the European Parliament and of the Council, OJ 2011 L 101/1, 5 April 2011, on preventing and combating trafficking in human beings and protecting its victims, and replacing Council Framework Decision 2002/629/JHA.

[28] See Art. 18. [29] Art. 18(4). [30] Barry (n 19).

[31] ECHR (2010) Appl. No. 25965/04, judgment of 7 January 2010.

[32] ECHR (2010), n 31, judgment of 7 January 2010, para. 284.

visa scheme.[33] The Court commented that it had 'no doubt' that the Cypriot authorities were aware that the visa scheme was being used by traffickers for the purposes of sexual exploitation.[34]

Ultimately, the Court concluded that the Cypriot government had failed to meet its positive obligations under the Convention by failing to regulate employment in the '*cabaret artiste*' industry, maintaining a visa regime for cabaret artists that did not provide effective protection against trafficking, and failing to carry out an effective investigation into the death of Oxana Rantsev.[35] Audrey Macklin has written elsewhere on similar inconsistencies in Canadian immigration policy, arising from the operation of the so-called 'exotic-dancer' visa scheme.[36] Destination states, she points out, may be complicit in human trafficking by continuing to operate immigration schemes that significantly increase the vulnerability of migrant women.[37] It was this complicity that was recognized in the *Rantsev* judgment. In a far-reaching statement, the Court found that Article 4 requires States to:

> put in place adequate measures regulating businesses often used as a cover for human trafficking. Furthermore, a State's immigration rules must address relevant concerns relating to encouragement, facilitation or tolerance of trafficking. (para. 284)

The next step of opening up safer migration routes is not one that is usually taken, however, reflecting a wider reluctance on the part of states to recognize the links between access to safe migration routes, application of human rights norms to immigration law and policy, and the potential to reduce migrant women's vulnerability to trafficking.

B. The rights of trafficked persons: recognizing the nexus

The Palermo Protocol makes only limited reference to states' obligations to provide support and services to trafficked persons. In contrast, significant attention is given to states' duties of law enforcement and prevention. While states are required to take various steps to criminalize trafficking and to ensure more effective investigation and prosecution of trafficking crimes, the provisions on victim support and services are more cautious. States parties are required only to 'consider'

[33] The position of the Cypriot government had been subject to detailed criticism by the Council of Europe Commissioner for Human Rights. See Report by Thomas Hammarberg, Commissioner for Human Rights of the Council of Europe, following his visit to the Republic of Cyprus on 7–10 July 2008, Strasbourg, 12 December 2008, CommDH(2008) 36, paras 32–53.

[34] ECHR (2010) (n 31) para. 294.

[35] Concerning Cyprus, the Court found it had violated its procedural obligations under Art. 2 ECHR, 'because of the failure to conduct an effective investigation into Ms Rantseva's death' (paras 241–242). The Court, in a novel interpretation of the Convention, found that the corollary of the duty to secure evidence from other relevant countries during an investigation had as a corollary that such countries should, within their means and competence, render such assistance if requested. The procedural obligations under Art. 2 included therefore a duty of transnational cooperation and investigation.

[36] A. Macklin, 'Dancing across Borders: "Exotic Dancers," Trafficking, and Canadian Immigration Policy', 37 *International Migration Review* (2003) 464.

[37] Macklin (n 36) 495.

implementing measures to provide for the physical, psychological, and social recovery of victims, in 'appropriate cases'.[38] On the status of trafficked persons, states are again required only to 'consider' adopting measures in 'appropriate cases' to allow for the issuing of temporary or permanent residence permissions.[39]

The question of status for trafficked persons is one that goes to the heart of states' wider reluctance to recognize rights to be within their borders, particularly in the context of irregular migration. If we are to take trafficking seriously as a human rights violation and if we admit the contributory role played by receiving countries, the provision of secure immigration status would be viewed as a human rights remedy and not merely as 'munificence' on the part of the host country or as 'a contingent benefit conditional upon cooperation with legal authorities'.[40] As yet, a positive obligation to provide secure residence and safe migration pathways as human rights remedies has not been accepted by states. Cautious steps have been taken towards challenging this refusal in an attempt to highlight the complicity of states that limit access to safe migration routes or fail to exercise due diligence in preventing human trafficking. The Council of Europe Convention Against Trafficking goes further than the Palermo Protocol in recognizing the rights claims of trafficked persons. States parties are required to provide for recovery and reflection periods of at least thirty days[41] and for renewable residence permits where such permits are considered necessary either because of the personal situation of the victim or to facilitate cooperation in criminal proceedings.[42] These provisions are in contrast to the conditionality attached to the issuing of residence permits in EU law for trafficked persons.

The 2004 EU Directive on short-term residence permits for victims of trafficking specifically conditions the issuing of residence permits on the trafficked person's cooperation in criminal proceedings.[43] Despite widespread criticism, the Directive remains in force.[44] The 2011 Directive was adopted specifically to enhance support for victims. The motivation behind this reform was not entirely or even primarily a humanitarian one. It was recognized that enhanced victim protections, in particular concerning residence and recovery periods, could strengthen the likelihood of effective trafficking investigations and prosecutions. Following the adoption of the 2011 Directive, member states are now required to ensure that support provided to trafficked persons is not made conditional on cooperation with criminal investigations, prosecution, or trial proceedings. This requirement, however, is 'without prejudice' to the provisions of the 2004 Directive or 'similar national rules',[45] with the result that the issuing of short-term residence permits

[38] See Art. 6. [39] Art. 7. [40] See Macklin, n 36, at 495.

[41] Council of Europe Convention on Action against Trafficking in Human Beings (n 26) Art. 13.

[42] Council of Europe Convention on Action against Trafficking in Human Beings (n 26) Art. 14.

[43] Council Directive 2004/81/EC, OJ 2004 L 261, 29 April 2004 on the residence permit issued to third-country nationals who are victims of trafficking in human beings or who have been the subject of an action to facilitate illegal immigration, who cooperate with the competent authorities.

[44] S. Egan, 'Protecting the Victims of Trafficking: Problems and Prospects', 1 *European Human Rights Law Review* (2008) 106.

[45] Directive 2011/36/EU of the European Parliament and of the Council (n 27) Art. 11(3).

to trafficked persons may continue to be conditional on cooperation with a criminal process. The possibility of continuing conditionality, given the importance of secure residence for trafficked persons and associated risks of re-trafficking, reflects the continuing tensions between member states' interests in migration control and recognition of the rights claims of trafficked persons.

These tensions are evident also in the jurisprudence of the European Court of Human Rights. In *Siliadin v. France*, the Court recognized for the first time that Article 4 ECHR could give rise to positive obligations for states.[46] It failed, however, to recognize that such obligations could extend to regularization of a victim's migration status and positive obligations of rehabilitation.[47] The Court's focus on the need for more effective criminal justice responses to problems of servitude fits within the predominantly prosecutorial model that has shaped international legal developments on human trafficking. It falls short, however, of a response that would support recognition of the complex rights claims of trafficked persons, particularly of children. In *Rantsev,* as already discussed, the Court acknowledged the links between safe migration routes, effective monitoring of immigration regimes, and vulnerability to human trafficking. However, it did not take the additional step of recommending that states expand access to safe migration routes.

In the recent case of *Osman v. Denmark,*[48] the Court was required to distinguish between caring work provided by a minor in a family context and the boundaries of human trafficking. The case concerned a young Somali national who had lived from the age of seven in Denmark. When she was fifteen, her father brought her to Kenya (with her mother's permission), for what was presumed to be a short family visit. She was subsequently left by her father at the Hagadera refugee camp to provide ongoing 24-hour care to her ailing paternal grandmother. After two years, she left the camp and sought to return to Denmark to join her mother and siblings. The Danish authorities refused to reinstate her residence status, however. The Court found that this refusal constituted an interference with her rights to both private and family life and that it was not proportionate to the aim pursued.[49] The AIRE Centre, representing the applicant, had sought to argue that Osman had been subject to intra-familial human trafficking and that the state had failed in its obligation to investigate and prosecute the offence of trafficking.[50] The Danish

[46] ECHR 2005, Appl. No. 73316/01, judgment of 26 July 2005. Further cases on Art. 4 are now pending before the Court, and also involve alleged violations of Art. 4 in the context of domestic service. See *Kawogo v. United Kingdom*, Appl. No. 56921/09; *Milanova and Others v. Italy and Bulgaria*, Appl. No. 40020/03; *C. N. v. United Kingdom*, Appl. No. 4239/08; *O.G.O. v. United Kingdom*, Appl. No. 13950/12, lodged 8 March 2012.

[47] For a detailed analysis of the case, including the Court's finding that the state had breached its positive obligation to provide specific and effective protection against violations of the European Convention on Human Rights, see H. Cullen 'Siliadin v. France: Positive Obligations Under Article 4 of the European Convention on Human Rights', 6 *Human Rights Law Review* (2006) 585.

[48] *Osman v. Denmark*, ECHR (2011) Appl. No. 38058/09, judgment of 14 June 2011.

[49] *Osman v. Denmark*, (n 48), in particular at paras 51–77.

[50] *Osman v. Denmark*, (n 48) at paras 46 and 62.

authorities had a duty, they argued, to look beyond the exercise of parental authority in order to protect the child's best interest.[51] The Court rejected this argument, noting that the applicant had not at any time complained of trafficking to the Danish authorities. The Court also, however, sought to distinguish the work done as part of everyday family life, from the exploitation that constitutes an element of human trafficking offences. Specifically, it noted that 'the exercise of parental rights constitutes a fundamental element of family life, and that the care and upbringing of children normally and necessarily require that the parents . . . impose, or authorise others to impose, various restrictions on the child's liberty'.[52] Interestingly, in finding against Denmark for refusing to reinstate the applicant's residence permit, the Court noted that 'in respecting parental rights, the authorities cannot ignore the child's interest including its own right to respect for private and family life'.[53] The assertion of the child's interests in the context of the alleged intra-familial trafficking did not trump the Court's deference to parental authority, however.

The case is a difficult one, taking place as it does against a background of increasing scrutiny by many European states of the normativity of migrant family life. This scrutiny has been accompanied by an expansion of the human trafficking framework, with all the attendant problems of potential over-reach of the criminal law. The response to the Court's judgment has been mixed, with some welcoming the decision not to pursue the question of human trafficking, while others have pointed to the need to address the problem of intra-familial trafficking particularly for the purposes of forced domestic labour. Given the wider policy context of increasing criminalization of migration, the space for reasoned dialogue on exploitative practices in the context of migration is limited.

The link between safe migration procedures and fulfilment of states' human rights obligations is explicitly recognized in CEDAW's *General Recommendation No. 26 on women migrant workers* (2009).[54] The CEDAW Committee notes that states are entitled to control their borders and regulate migration but must do so in compliance with their obligations to 'respect, protect and fulfil the human rights of women throughout the migration cycle'.[55] The rights claims arising when determining claims to remain within a host state are not yet fully recognized by this emerging international law of migration. Recommendation No. 26 does not address the issue of human trafficking directly. However, it does note its relevance to situations where women migrants may have been victims of trafficking. The Committee also notes that women migrant workers may become victims of trafficking due to varying degrees of vulnerability, arising from their migration status and/or the precariousness of their positions as workers. It is careful to avoid general presumptions of vulnerability, however, and specifically limits the scope of the Recommendation to low-income precarious work.

[51] *Osman v. Denmark* (n 48) at para. 63.
[52] *Osman v. Denmark* (n 48) at para. 64.
[53] *Osman v. Denmark* (n 48) at para. 73.
[54] See *General Recommendation No. 26 on women migrant workers*, UN Doc CEDAW/C/2009/WP.1/R.
[55] *General Recommendation No. 26 on women migrant workers* (n 54) para. 3.

Limitations on the power of states to remove trafficked persons are recognized through the safe and 'preferably voluntary' return standard set out in the Palermo Protocol and replicated in regional and domestic legal instruments.[56] Access to asylum or complementary forms of protection may also herald the possibility of a more durable long-term solution recognizing a right of trafficked persons to remain in a destination state. States are required to ensure that trafficked persons are informed of asylum procedures and possibilities of complementary protection, where available. The Palermo Protocol itself makes reference to rights, obligations, and responsibilities arising under international refugee law.[57] The Council of Europe Anti-Trafficking Convention specifically refers to the right to seek and to enjoy asylum, and to the requirement that all states parties ensure that victims of trafficking have access to appropriate and fair asylum procedures.[58] The 2011 EU Directive requires states to ensure that victims have access to information about recovery and reflection periods and to information on the possibility of accessing international protection.[59] In 2006, the UNHCR published its guidelines on the application of the 1951 Convention Relating to the Status of Refugees to victims of trafficking and persons at risk of being trafficked.[60] The Guidelines explicitly recognize that not all trafficked persons may be entitled to a grant of asylum and note that all elements of the refugee definition must be satisfied in order to secure asylum. Herein lies the difficulty as problems of 'fit' frequently arise for claims of gender-related persecution. In the context of human trafficking, the difficulty of establishing the required nexus with a Convention ground may be compounded by the need to establish a failure of state protection and continuing risks.

The difficulties of securing access to asylum are well documented, as the categories of refugee law and other forms of complementary protection continue to limit the recognition of protection needs.[61] Problems of establishing credibility arise, in particular, for victims of sex trafficking who may find themselves in a double bind, their claims encountering the suspicions that attach to claims of sexual violence linked to the commercial sex industry on the one hand, and by generalized hostilities towards irregular migrants, on the other hand.

[56] See Art. 8(2).

[57] See Art. 14(1). There is now a substantial body of case law recognizing trafficked persons as coming within the scope of the refugee definition. See *Secretary of State for the Home Department v. Dzhygun* (2000) Immigration Appeal Tribunal Decision 00 TH 00728 (the group being women from Ukraine forced into prostitution against their will); *Miss AB v. Secretary of State for the Home Department* (2003) Immigration Appellate Authority decision CC/64057/2002 (the group consisting of girls trafficked from West Africa); *Appellant v. Secretary of State for the Home Department* (2003) UKIAT 00023 (the group consisting of women from the north-east of Albania); *Petition of Olga Shimkova*, Outer House, Court of Session, 23 December 2003 (the group consisting of women trafficked from Ukraine).

[58] Council of Europe Convention on Action against Trafficking in Human Beings (n 26) at Art. 14.

[59] Directive 2011/36/EU of the European Parliament and of the Council, n 27, Art. 11(6).

[60] See UN High Commissioner for Refugees, The Application of Article 1.A(2) of the 1951 Convention and/or the 1967 Protocol Relating to the Status of Refugees to Victims of Trafficking and Persons at Risk of Being Trafficked (2006), UN Doc HCR/GIP/06/07.

[61] See S. Mullally, 'Domestic Violence Asylum Claims and Recent Developments in International Human Rights Law: a Progress Narrative?' 60 *ICLQ* (2011) 459.

Part II of this chapter examines the challenges faced by refugee women seeking to 'fit' into the inherited categories of refugee law and questions the transformative potential of the expanding body of gender asylum law.

II. Gender Asylum Law: Providing Transformative Remedies?

Writing more than a decade ago, Deborah Anker pointed to the potential of expanding human rights standards to transform the practice of refugee law.[62] Grounding the interpretation of refugee law in a human rights paradigm, she argued, has the potential to internationalize refugee law practice. In the context of the evolving practice of gender asylum law, human rights activism on women's human rights, gender, and sexuality law has been crucial in securing recognition of gender-related persecution. Such recognition has been uneven, however. Landmark cases including *Shah and Islam*,[63] *HJ and HT*,[64] *Khawar*,[65] *Kasinga*,[66] and *Fornah*[67] have pushed the boundaries and extended the limits of refugee law. Empirical research suggests that positive decisions recognizing gender-related claims increased following these cases, at least in some jurisdictions.[68] The UNHCR has revised its gender guidelines, its guidelines on sexual orientation and on particular social group asylum claims, drawing on the practice of diverse jurisdictions to reassert the relevance and transformative potential of refugee law.[69] It continues to assert that gendered violations of human rights fall within the scope of the refugee definition and the protections of the 1951 Convention. As the 2002 UNHCR gender guidelines note, the analysis of sex and gender in the context of refugee law has been expanded through the practice of states, the case law of domestic courts, and academic literature.[70] This expansion has occurred in parallel to, and has been assisted by, developments in international human rights law and through the

62 D. Anker, 'Refugee Law, Gender, and the Human Rights Paradigm', 15 *Harvard Human Rights Journal* (2002) 133.

63 *Islam (A.P.) v. Secretary of State for the Home Department, Regina v. Immigration Appeal Tribunal and Another Ex Parte Shah (A.P.)* (Conjoined Appeals), [1999] 2 AC 629, [1999] 2 All ER 545.

64 *HJ (Iran) v. Secretary of State for the Home Department (Rev 1)*, [2010] Imm AR 729, [2011] 1 AC 596, [2010] 3 WLR 386, [2010] UKSC 31.

65 *Minister for Immigration & Multicultural Affairs v. Khawar* [2000] FCA 1130, per Lindgren J, para. 160.

66 *In re Kasinga*, Interim Dec. 3278 (B.I.A. 1996).

67 *SSHD v. K* and *Fornah v. SSHD*, [2006] UKHL 46, [2007] 1 AC 412, [2007] 1 All ER 671, [2006] 3 WLR 733.

68 C. Dauvergne and J. Millbank, 'Forced Marriage as a Harm in Domestic and International Law' 73 *Modern Law Review* (2010) 57.

69 See UNHCR, Guidelines on International Protection No. 2: 'Membership of a Particular Social Group' Within the Context of Art. 1A(2) of the 1951 Convention and/or its 1967 Protocol Relating to the Status of Refugees, UN Doc HCR/GIP/02/02, adopted 7 May 2002; UNHCR Guidance Note on Refugee Claims Relating to Sexual Orientation and Gender Identity, 21 November 2008; available at: <http://www.unhcr.org/refworld/docid/48abd5660.html>.

70 Guidelines on International Protection No. 1: Gender-Related Persecution within the context of Art. 1A(2) of the 1951 Convention and/or its 1967 Protocol relating to the Status of Refugees, UN Doc HCR/GIP/02/01.

jurisprudence of the ad hoc international criminal tribunals and the Rome Statute of the International Criminal Court. It is UNHCR's position that the refugee definition, 'properly interpreted', includes gender-related claims and that further amendment is not necessary in order to recognize the gender dimension of persecution.[71] Yet, as the UNHCR Guidelines also note, women continue to face difficulty in bringing gender-related claims within the scope of refugee law.

A. Recognizing persecution: the continuing significance of public/private divides

Gender-related asylum claims unsettle the boundaries and categories of refugee law and other forms of complementary protection. Fitting into the institutional frameworks and policy agendas of refugee law is not easy. Fauziya Kasinga or Rodi Alvarado were not in the minds of the drafters of the 1951 Convention. The sexed subject of refugee law was the paradigmatic political dissident fleeing the imposition of restrictions on freedoms of assembly, expression, or religion. Persecution occurred in the public sphere and political activity was defined by engagement with the traditional structures of state authority. Although Eleanor Roosevelt commented that human rights begin in 'small places' close to home, international refugee law was not intended to capture those harms that occur in such small places at the hands of non-state actors. Expanding the boundaries of refugee law has required transforming ambiguous legal categories such as that of the particular social group, drawing on developments in international human rights law that have belatedly recognized the responsibility of states for systemic gender-related harms and demonstrating the relevance to refugee law of states' failures to protect against such harms.

In 2009, the Special Rapporteur on Violence against Women recognized that 'work remains to be done to establish gender as independent grounds for claiming asylum as a refugee'.[72] The Council of Europe Convention on Preventing and Combating Violence against Women and Domestic Violence requires parties to take the necessary legislative or other measures to ensure that gender-based violence against women may be recognized as a form of persecution within the meaning of the 1951 Convention and as a form of serious harm that may support a claim to subsidiary protection.[73] This provision builds on incremental developments within EU asylum law, which have included some recognition of gender-related persecution. The 2004 EU Qualification Directive provided that acts of persecution can, inter alia, take the form of acts of a gender-specific nature.[74] It also recognized that

[71] Guidelines on International Protection No. 1 (n 70) at 3, para. 6.

[72] Y. Ertűrk, *15 years of the United Nations Special Rapporteur On Violence Against Women, Its Causes and Consequences* (2009).

[73] Council of Europe Convention on Preventing and Combating Violence against Women and Domestic Violence, Art. 60(1).

[74] European Council Directive 2004/83/EC, OJ 2004 L 304, 29 April 2004, on minimum standards for the qualification and status of third country nationals or stateless persons as refugees or as persons who otherwise need international protection and the content of the protection granted, Art. 9(2)(f).

non-state actors may constitute actors of persecution, where there is a failure of state protection. No further guidance on gender-related claims was given by the Directive, and so the practice of states has varied considerably. As is discussed later in this chapter, demonstrating a failure of state protection may be difficult, however. Where human rights violations occur in the private, domestic sphere, the evidence required to support an asylum claim may not be easily attained. The recast Qualification Directive does little to improve the gender dimension of asylum determination processes,[75] despite extensive advocacy campaigns from the European Women's Lobby, ILGA-Europe, and other NGOs,[76] and detailed recommendations on gender-related amendments from the LIBE Committee.[77] Inconsistencies in the interpretation and application of the Directive at domestic level are likely, therefore, to persist.

A recent study of asylum claims in Europe highlighted the difficulties that persist in securing recognition of gender-related harms as persecution. Combined with the problem of identifying the requisite nexus with a Convention ground, the problems faced in bringing gender claims within the scope of the refugee definition have meant that seeking subsidiary protection may be a more productive avenue to protection. The UNHCR gender guidelines note that female asylum applicants may face forms of persecution specific to their sex, including forms of sexual violence, dowry-related violence, female genital mutilation (FGM), domestic violence, and trafficking. At domestic level, such gender-related harms are not always recognized as persecution, however. In France, for example, asylum claims related to FGM are more likely to lead to a grant of subsidiary protection. Past experience of FGM may not always be recognized as persecution in and of itself, and future risks may be assessed differently depending on age or existence of other 'exotic' elements to the claim such as forced marriage. Similarly, domestic violence is often more likely to be defined as serious harm rather than as persecution for the purposes of a grant of asylum.[78] Fitting into the inherited categories of refugee law presents hurdles to gender-related claims that do not surface in the same way in the more porous concept of subsidiary protection.

As Edwards has noted, violence against women is 'exceptionalised' in international human rights law, as are the remedies for the harms caused.[79] Given the absence of explicit prohibitions of violence against women in core international human rights treaties, additional tests to identify the cause of the violent act are applied so as to trigger the application of sex discrimination or torture

[75] See Asylum Aid, *Gender-Related Asylum Claims in Europe* (2012).

[76] Asylum Aid (n 75) 40.

[77] Council of the European Union, Proposal for a Directive on minimum standards for the qualification and status of third country nationals or stateless persons as beneficiaries of international protection and the content of the protection granted (recast)—Examination of draft compromise text, 12337/1/11 REV 1; available at: <http://www.statewatch.org/news/2011/jul/eu-council-qualification-tcn-12337-rev1-11.pdf>.

[78] See, eg, in France CNDA, *BA*, no. 09 023 070, 17 November 2010, cited in Asylum Aid (n 75) at 46.

[79] A. Edwards, 'Violence against Women as Sex Discrimination: Judging the Jurisprudence of the United Nations Human Rights Treaty Bodies', 18 *Texas Journal of Women and the Law* (2008) 101.

prohibitions.[80] This step of building the cause of the act into the definition of the prohibited act is not one that is required in other areas of international human rights law.[81] It is a step that reflects the continuing reluctance to recognize violence against women as a human rights violation, in and of itself.[82] These additional hurdles that are found in the practice of human rights law recur in the everyday practice of refugee law. Although significant progress has been made in naming gender-related harms as persecutory, in practice, beyond the leading cases of selected jurisdictions, studies on gender asylum claims reveal continuing difficulties in securing a grant of asylum. The moment of crisis, of rupture, that continues to shape our understanding of human rights violations may not be present in a gender-based asylum claim. The 'continuum of violence' that often defines the experiences of refugee women does not fit easily in refugee law's tests for persecutory harms and failures of state protection. This continuum stretches from the 'gender violence of everyday life, through the structural violence of economic systems that sustain inequalities and the repressive policing of dictatorial regimes, to the armed conflict of open warfare'.[83] At the same time, while such a continuum may be part of the structure of a refugee woman's life, violence may also be experienced as a 'shattering experience of discontinuity',[84] regardless of the inequities of the everyday. Refugee law is not well equipped to capture the complexities of such experiences or the multi-dimensional nature of suffering endured.

B. Definitional problems and the requirements of 'fit'

Overcoming such exclusions and marginalization in the application of the refugee definition poses many hurdles. A gendered lens has long shaped both definitions of persecution and acknowledgment of the nexus with Convention grounds. Recognizing the links requires a questioning of the gender of refugee law concepts, and of the limits of accepted definitions of the political. Both the *Shah and Islam*[85] and the *Matter of R-A-*[86] cases highlight the difficulties of establishing a nexus with Convention grounds. In *Shah and Islam,* the claim of persecution on grounds of political opinion was dismissed as being 'unsustainable'[87] despite the Court's finding that discrimination against women in Pakistan was institutionalized in

[80] See generally, C. A. MacKinnon, 'Equality Remade: Violence Against Women', in MacKinnon (n 19) at 105.

[81] Edwards (n 79). [82] Edwards (n 79).

[83] W. Giles and J. Hyndman, 'Introduction', in W. Giles and J. Hyndman (eds), *Sites of Violence: Gender and Conflict Zones* (2004) 3, at 19.

[84] M. Walker, 'Gender and Violence in Focus: A Background for Gender Justice in Reparations', in R. Rubio-Marín (ed.), *The Gender of Reparations: Unsettling Sexual Hierarchies While Redressing Human Rights Violations* (2009) 29.

[85] *Islam (A.P.) v. Secretary of State for the Home Department, Regina v. Immigration Appeal Tribunal and Another Ex Parte Shah (A.P.),* n 63.

[86] *Matter of R-A-*, 22 I&N Dec. 906 (BIA 1999), vacated, 22 I&N Dec. 906 (A.G. 2001), remanded, 23 I&N Dec. 694 (A.G. 2005), remanded, 24 I&N Dec. 629 (A.G. 2008). See K. Musalso, 'Matter of R-A-: An Analysis of the Decision and its Implications', 76 *Interpreter Releases* (1999) 1177.

[87] *Islam (A.P.) v. Secretary of State for the Home Department, Regina v. Immigration Appeal Tribunal and Another Ex Parte Shah (A.P.),* n 63, per Lord Steyn.

the law and practice of the state itself. This finding reveals again the difficulties of capturing women's human rights claims within the Convention's political opinion ground. Lord Hoffman acknowledged the threat of violence to the claimants from their husbands, but described this as 'a personal affair, directed against them as individuals'.[88] It was only through the additional recognition of the absence of state protection that 'the otherwise private violence' was defined as coming within the meaning of the 1951 Convention.

Having dismissed political opinion as a possible nexus, much of the debate before the House of Lords turned on how to define the particular social group. Ultimately, the court found by a majority (Lord Millet dissenting), that 'women of Pakistan' or 'women who had offended against social mores or against whom there were imputations of sexual misconduct', could form a particular social group within the meaning of the Convention.[89] A systematic failure of state protection was identified recognizing that the state's failure to meet its obligations of due diligence to prevent intimate violence can represent, in Macklin's words, 'an uncoordinated yet highly efficient matrix of inertia, consolidated at all loci of the criminal justice system'.[90]

Defining a particular social group was also to prove problematic in the *Matter of R-A-* proceedings. In that case, the Board of Immigration Appeals found that the respondent had not shown that 'Guatemalan women who have been involved intimately with Guatemalan male companions, who believe that women are to live under male domination' is a group that is recognized and understood to be a societal faction, or is otherwise a recognized segment of the population within Guatemala.[91] The size of the potential social group, and the concomitant consequences of rising numbers of asylum applicants was clearly to the fore in the Board's decision. As the UNHCR and others noted, however, other Convention grounds are not restricted in this way, and jurisprudential authorities did not support such a finding.[92] The UNHCR, in its advisory opinion on the case, had argued that Ms Alvarado could be identified as a member of a particular social group because of her sex, her marital status and her position in a society that condones discrimination against women.[93] Having sought the protection of the state and having complained of her abuse, she could be identified as a woman who had 'transgressed social mores' in a society where women were 'expected to accept their fate'. This view was not heeded, however.

88 *Islam (A.P.) v. Secretary of State for the Home Department, Regina v. Immigration Appeal Tribunal and Another Ex Parte Shah (A.P.)*, n 63, per Lord Hoffman.

89 *Islam (A.P.) v. Secretary of State for the Home Department, Regina v. Immigration Appeal Tribunal and Another Ex Parte Shah (A.P.)*, n 63 at 645, 655, 658–9.

90 A. Macklin, 'Refugee Women and the Imperative of Categories', 17 *Human Rights Quarterly* (1995) 213, at 234.

91 *In the Matter of R-A-*, n 86, at 918.

92 See UNHCR, Re: Matter of Rodi Alvarado Peña (A73-753-922), Advisory Opinion on International Norms: Gender-Related Persecution and Relevance to 'Membership of a Particular Social Group' and 'Political Opinion', 9 January 2004, at 3; available at: <http://cgrs.uchastings.edu/campaigns/alvarado.php#advocacy>.

93 UNHCR, Re: Matter of Rodi Alvarado Peña (n 92) at 9.

Difficulties were also encountered in identifying a nexus with the political opinion ground. In a majority decision, the Board found that Rodi Alvarado had not succeeded in establishing that the violence she had endured was the result of her political opinion, or imputed political opinion, as to her gender role and status as a spouse. As was noted in subsequent submissions on the case, and in the dissenting opinion, the Board's rejection of the political opinion ground seemed to contradict its own statements on the nature of the abuse suffered in the case, and the repeated links made by Ms Alvarado's spouse to her status and role as a woman.[94] The political context within which domestic violence occurs with impunity was highlighted by the dissent in the *R-A-* case.[95] It was precisely this context of domestic violence that was set aside by the majority opinion of the Board, however.

In the *Fornah* case,[96] the House of Lords addressed the applicability of the social group ground to gender asylum cases, this time in the context of female genital mutilation. Situating the case within the broader context of gender discrimination, Lord Bingham distinguished the particularity of the relevant group, either 'women of Sierra Leone' or 'intact or uninitiated women and girls who are in tribes in Sierra Leone which practise FGM'.[97] He concluded that the distinguishing feature of the group in this case was not the persecution complained of, but rather the 'position of social inferiority as compared with men'[98] within which women in Sierra Leone found themselves. As the *Fornah* case illustrates, the process of 'fitting' an asylum claim into the refugee definition may also bring with it the risk of essentializing the position of all women in a particular society. It is a risk that is particularly evident when women's claims are constrained within the parameters of the particular social group ground. The asylum adjudication process is sometimes criticized as positing a 'victim subject', denied of agency and defined by patriarchal forces of religion and culture,[99] with limited attention paid to the historical, socio-economic, and cultural specificities that shape experiences of gender discrimination, and that fragment the categories of gender and women. The categories of refugee law reinforce such tendencies. More nuanced presentations of gendered persecution risk falling victim to the all-encompassing requirements to demonstrate a failure of state protection, the absence of an internal protection alternative, or the requirement to identify a social group. And so 'women of Pakistan' or 'women of Sierra Leone' become a social group in the quest to make an asylum claim 'fit' with refugee law's categories.[100] As a result of these legal gymnastics, refugee women often find themselves in a

[94] See Harvard Immigration and Refugee Project, Brief of Amici Curiae in Support of Affirmance of Decision of the Immigration Judge in Re R-A- A73-753-922, at 42.

[95] *Matter of R-A*, n 86, at 925.

[96] *SSHD v. K* and *Fornah v. SSHD*, [2006] UKHL 46, [2007] 1 AC 412, [2007] 1 All ER 671, [2006] 3 WLR 733.

[97] *SSHD v. K* and *Fornah v. SSHD* (n 96) per Lord Bingham of Cornhill, [2006] UKHL 46, para. 31.

[98] *SSHD v. K* and *Fornah v. SSHD* (n 96), per Lord Bingham of Cornhill, [2006] UKHL 46, para. 31.

[99] R. Kapur, 'The Tragedy of Victimization Rhetoric: Resurrecting the "Native" Subject in International/Post-Colonial Feminist Legal Politics', 15 *Harvard Human Rights Journal* (2002) 1.

[100] See *Secretary of State for the Home Department v. ZH (Women as Particular Social Group) Iran*, CG [2003] UKIAT 00207, in which women in Iran were found not to constitute a social group.

double bind.[101] In presenting a claim for protection, it becomes necessary to position the asylum applicant as an abject victim, powerless in the face of the coercive powers of state or non-state actors. The gendered stereotypes of third-world women are thereby reinforced.[102]

The racial 'othering' of the asylum applicant raises further difficulties in securing recognition of the asylum claim, as presumptions concerning the extent of gendered harms in a country or region of origin reinforce the view that to recognize a claim for asylum would potentially open the floodgates to such claims.[103] Asylum adjudicators as 'internationalist gatekeepers' are keenly aware of migration control imperatives and not immune to the 'migration panics' that so frequently circulate in the global north. Against this background, despite the expansion of concepts of due diligence, persecution, and social groups, gender-related asylum claims continue to face procedural and substantive hurdles to making their arguments heard.

C. On persecutory harms and 'being discreet'

The recent decisions of the High Court of Australia and the UK Supreme Court in the *S395*[104]and *HJ and HT*[105] cases, rejecting the application of the discretion test to sexual-orientation asylum claims reveal how troubled the fixed categories of refugee law are by the appearance of gender and sexuality. The *HJ and HT* case involved two gay men, HJ, an Iranian national, and HT, a Cameroonian national. Both men, the Supreme Court noted, were 'practising homosexuals'. At issue was the test to be applied when considering an application for asylum based on sexual orientation and membership of a particular social group. As with other gender- and sexuality-related asylum claims, the difficulties highlighted in this case link directly to the ambiguities surrounding the particular social group ground, its 'catch-all' potential, and its ad hoc deployment to remedy the gaps in the 1951 Convention definition. The specific question before the Supreme Court was whether the so-called 'discretion test', stated by Maurice Kay LJ in *J v. Secretary of State for the Home Department*,[106] and applied in this case to the claims of HJ and HT, was correct. Specifically, the test required assessment of whether

> 'discretion' is something that the appellant can reasonably be expected to tolerate, not only in the context of random sexual activity but in relation to 'matters following from, and relevant to, sexual identity' in the wider sense.[107]

[101] See Macklin, n 90, at 263–4.

[102] See A. Sinha, 'Domestic Violence and U.S. Asylum Law: Eliminating the "Cultural Hook" for Claims Involving Gender-related Persecution', 76 *NYU Law Review* (2001) 1562.

[103] See Dauverne and Millbank (n 68).

[104] *Appellant S395/2002 v. Minister for Immigration & Multicultural Affairs (S395)* [2003] 216 CLR 473.

[105] *HJ (Iran) v. Secretary of State for the Home Department (Rev 1)* (n 64).

[106] [2007] Imm AR 73.

[107] [2007] Imm AR 73, n 106, per Maurice Kay LJ, para. 11.

Rejecting the test applied by Maurice Kay LJ, Lord Hope described the term 'discretion' as 'euphemistic'. It failed, he said, to tell the whole truth of what was required by the test—not discretion but concealment.[108] Requiring such concealment, the Court found, established a form of 'secondary persecution'[109] in response to the primary persecution and failed to recognize the right of an applicant to live 'openly and freely'[110] as a gay man or a lesbian woman. Ultimately, the 'discretion test' was found by the Supreme Court to be 'wrong in principle, unworkable and inconsistent with Article 1(A)2 of the Convention'.[111] To require an asylum applicant to live 'discreetly' was, Lord Roger held, 'unacceptable'. It involved requiring the applicant to deny or hide 'precisely the innate characteristic which forms the basis of his claim for persecution'.[112] The Supreme Court distinguished between those individuals who choose to live discreetly to avoid 'social pressures' from those who were required to live discreetly because of the 'material fact' of a risk of persecutory harm.[113] Previous decisions applying the discretion test, including that of the Court of Appeal in this case, were found to be based on a misunderstanding of the Australian High Court's findings in *S395*.

S395 was a case before the Australian High Court, involving two gay men from Bangladesh, who claimed to be at serious risk of persecution because of their sexual orientation. Rejecting their applications for asylum, the Refugee Review Tribunal found that the men had lived together for four years at various places in Bangladesh and had not encountered anything more than minor problems. The shunning, gossip, and taunts that they had experienced from family members and neighbours were not viewed as constituting serious harm. The men had 'conducted themselves in a discreet manner', and there was no reason to believe that they would not do so again if returned home now.[114] The High Court found that the Refugee Review Tribunal, in rejecting the applicants' asylum claims, had erred in law by 'impliedly dividing homosexual men into two particular social groups—discreet and non-discreet homosexual men'. The Court also found that the Tribunal had erred by failing to consider whether a requirement of 'being discreet' in order to avoid serious harm, in itself, constituted persecution.[115]

In a series of cases involving persecution claims linked to sexual orientation, the courts had decided that the capacity of an asylum applicant to avoid persecutory harm was relevant to the assessment of risk being faced. This approach to risk assessment had been rejected in the context of asylum claims linked to political opinion.[116] It had persisted, however, in sexual-orientation-related claims,

[108] *HJ (Iran) v. Secretary of State for the Home Department (Rev 1)* (n 64).

[109] *HJ (Iran) v. Secretary of State for the Home Department (Rev 1)* (n 64) para. 75 per Lord Roger.

[110] *HJ (Iran) v. Secretary of State for the Home Department (Rev 1)* (n 64) para. 78 per Lord Roger.

[111] *HJ (Iran) v. Secretary of State for the Home Department (Rev 1)* (n 64) para. 81 per Lord Roger.

[112] *HJ (Iran) v. Secretary of State for the Home Department (Rev 1)* (n 64), per Lord Roger, at paras 75–76.

[113] *HJ (Iran) v. Secretary of State for the Home Department (Rev 1)* (n 64). paras 61–62.

[114] *Appellant S395/2002 v. Minister for Immigration & Multicultural Affairs (S395)*, n 104, para. 30 per McHugh and Kirby JJ.

[115] *Appellant S395/2002 v. Minister for Immigration & Multicultural Affairs (S395)*, n 104, para. 18.

[116] *Win v. Minister for Immigration and Multicultural Affairs* [2001] FCA 132.

suggesting a failure to recognize sexuality and sexual orientation as integral to human personhood. There is also a suggestion of 'burden-sharing' implicit in the imposition of the discretion test—that is, that the asylum applicant should take some responsibility for ensuring that she or he avoids persecution by 'being discreet'. By not 'being discreet', the implication here is that the asylum seeker may have provoked the persecutory harm complained of, and therefore bears some culpability. Choosing to reject this gendered line of reasoning, the Court concluded that the use of the terms 'discretion' and 'being discreet' may obscure more than they illuminate. A test requiring a gay or lesbian asylum seeker to 'take reasonable steps to avoid persecutory harm' was, they said, 'wrong in principle and should not be followed'.[117]

Already, the ripples of these decisions have been felt across many jurisdictions and in leading commentaries on refugee law. Hathaway and Pojboy, in a wide-ranging critique of the decisions, challenge the courts' failures to 'draw lines' to distinguish between integral and peripheral activities linked to gender identity, or between exogenous and endogenous harms.[118] Their critique, however, overlooks the difficulties in making such distinctions and, perhaps more seriously, ignores the very real risk of exogenous harms occurring regardless of an individual's way of life, activities, or the existence or otherwise of 'precipitating behaviour'. Control over such risks of persecution is rare. That it has taken so long for the discretion test to be finally rejected in sexual orientation asylum claims and that this rejection has led to such anxiety from leading refugee law scholars tells us much about the slow pace of reform in the practice of asylum law. It also highlights the many and varied hurdles that must be surmounted when seeking to add asylum claims 'in'. Hathaway and Pojboy criticize the judgments in these cases for what they describe as a 'fundamental distancing' from the framework of non-discrimination for analysing persecution, and an abandonment of the nexus requirement.[119] Distinguishing between identity and behaviour, between core and peripheral activities, is a process that is fraught with tensions, however, and allows multiple points at which the biases, misperceptions, and cross-cultural misunderstandings of asylum adjudicators are likely to close off persecution claims. As Millbank notes, the more marginal a group is, in legal or social terms, the more likely that what is experienced as core by members of that group, will be *deemed* marginal by adjudicators.[120]

Accepting that 'being discreet' could potentially avoid persecutory harms, and thereby resolve the state of its 'duty of hospitality' in the asylum context, allowed the status quo to go unchallenged. That the discretion test, or requirement of 'being discreet' could have persisted until very recently in asylum jurisprudence reveals just

[117] *Appellant S395/2002 v. Minister for Immigration & Multicultural Affairs (S395)*, n 104, para. 50, per McHugh and Kirby JJ.

[118] J. Hathaway and J. Pobjoy, 'Queer Cases Make Bad Law', 44 *NYU Journal of International Law & Politics* (2012) 315, at 388.

[119] Hathaway and Pobjoy (n 118).

[120] J. Millbank, 'The Right of Lesbians and Gay Men to Live Freely, Openly, and on Equal Terms Is Not Bad Law: A Reply to Hathaway and Pobjoy', 44 *NYU Journal of International Law & Politics* (2012) 497.

how slow the process of law reform can be, particularly when relying on adjudicative processes. In practice, the discretion test ensured that the promise of protection held out by asylum law did not typically apply to everyone, but rather to 'everyone the same'.[121] Unfamiliar claims, from gay men or lesbian women, who did not fit the refugee norm, faced many additional hurdles in securing recognition. This is what MacKinnon has called the equality of the Enlightenment, where recognition and survival depends on meeting the dominant standard and 'keeping your head low keeps you alive'.[122] The refusal to acknowledge that forced adherence to heteronormativity—in one's way of life and intimate relationships—may constitute persecution in itself, highlights the underlying gender of asylum law in practice.

D. The asylum process: the 'wrong' kind of victim?

Many of the challenges that are now faced by asylum applicants lie beneath the surface, less likely to raise the grand conceptual debates that for so long preoccupied asylum adjudicators. Instead, it is now the lower-level preoccupations with credibility, availability of state protection, and internal relocation alternatives that function as the primary gatekeepers in asylum adjudication. Procedural and evidentiary hurdles present significant barriers to gender asylum claims. The expanding use of accelerated determination procedures in particular raises further difficulties in accessing regular asylum processes. Refugee women face particular difficulties in establishing credibility, despite more than a decade of gender guidelines on international protection standards and procedures. As Munro has argued, improved practices within the criminal justice system relating to gender-related violence have not yet been transferred to asylum services or to the asylum adjudication process.[123] The disparities in practice as between criminal justice and the asylum system are evident, for example, in how late disclosure of domestic violence allegations is received.[124] In the asylum system, late disclosure can bring into question the reliability of the evidence submitted and the credibility of the applicant. Narrative inconsistencies, calm demeanour, or late disclosure of evidence are often viewed negatively in assessing the credibility of the asylum applicant.[125] Findings of lack of credibility persist, even in the face of reliable expert evidence.[126]

[121] See I. M. Young, 'Polity and Group Difference: A Critique of the Ideal of Universal Citizenship', in R. Beiner (ed.), *Theorizing Citizenship* (1995).

[122] MacKinnon (n 19) at 106.

[123] See Asylum Aid, *The rights of women seeking asylum: a charter/Explanatory notes* (2009); available at: <http://www.asylumaid.org.uk/pages/charterbackground.html>.

[124] See H. Baillot, S. Cowan, and V. Munro, 'Seen but Not Heard? Parallels and Dissonances in the Treatment of Rape Narratives across the Asylum and Criminal Justice Contexts', 36 *Journal of Law and Society* (2009) 195. Baillot et al. discuss a range of measures designed to facilitate and support disclosure of rape within the criminal justice process, at 207.

[125] *AS (Pakistan) v. Secretary of State for the Home Department* [2007] EWCA Civ 703, 21 June 2007, involving a domestic violence claim, in which it was found that inconsistencies in the applicant's testimony can lead to a finding of lack of credibility.

[126] See *VH (Malawi) v. Secretary of State for the Home Department* [2009] EWCA Civ 645, 2 July 2009.

Negative findings on credibility can lead to asylum claims being diverted through accelerated procedures, with reduced time limits and rights of appeal, an outcome that stands in marked contrast to the reforms that have been made in the operation of criminal justice systems in addressing crimes of gender-related violence. The opportunities for women to recount their own narratives, an important step in disclosing intimate harms, are seriously constrained by the limits and forms imposed by the asylum process and the constant return to the categories of refugee law. Assumptions as to appropriate victim behaviour may also hinder credibility assessments or a willingness to acknowledge the severity of the risk faced. Such assumptions can be particularly problematic in the context of intimate partner violence, where a woman's previous conduct in remaining within an abusive relationship or seeking to limit the sanctions imposed by law enforcement bodies may not fit well with the expectations of 'discontinuity' and rupture that attend asylum claims.[127]

Disclosure and reporting of gender-related harms, particularly sexual violence, requires a 'leap of faith' on the part of the asylum applicant. It requires a safe, non-judgmental environment, in which there is a possibility of trust and the potential of refuge.[128] Such trust can be difficult to secure in the asylum context, where adjudicators may be preoccupied with factual details concerning country of origin information, travel routes, or alternative protections sought by the applicant. Access to the regular asylum procedure will depend on overcoming initial checklists concerning routes of travel, documentation of identity and status, and 'fit' with complex legal categories. As transitional justice scholars have told us, responses to mass atrocities including sexual and other forms of intimate violence may include silence and repression of the trauma endured. The choice of silence may reflect an exercise of agency, not simply a failure to speak on the part of an abject victim. Such choices are not available, however, in the asylum context where the applicant's testimony may be the primary or only evidence of the harm endured. Given that gender-related persecution may touch deeply on the affective realm, the obstacles to disclosure and to consistent and coherent narratives are many.

III. Migrant Domestic Workers: The Significance of Place

Domestic work, the provision of caring work in the intimate, domestic sphere, is work that is predominantly undertaken by women and increasingly by women migrant workers.[129] The expected reduction in demand for paid domestic workers in Europe and elsewhere has not materialized, leading some to ask whether the

[127] Baillot et al. (n 124). [128] Baillot et al. (n 124) at 207.

[129] Art. 1 of the International Labour Organization (ILO) Domestic Workers Convention defines domestic work as 'work performed in or for a household or households' and a domestic worker as 'any person engaged in domestic work within an employment relationship', excluding those who perform domestic work 'only occasionally or sporadically and not on an occupational basis'. Art. 1, Convention Concerning Decent Work for Domestic Workers, International Labour Organization, adopted at the 100th session of the International Labour Conference, Geneva, 2011.

emergence of 'global care chains' should be assessed as a major defeat for the feminist movement or as 'unfinished business'.[130] Combined with the increased involvement of women in paid employment, the retreat from welfare state supports in Europe and elsewhere has produced care sectors of economies that are increasingly reliant on the outsourcing of intimate, reproductive labour.[131] Reproductive activities (that is, labour activities needed to sustain the productive labour force, including cleaning, care taking of the elderly, children, and other dependants) have become increasingly commodified,[132] resulting in the employment of paid domestic workers in many households.[133] A range of factors have contributed to the demand for domestic labour in the European context, including population ageing, changing household structures, increasing female participation in the labour market, difficulties in reconciling work and family responsibilities, and the availability of a flexible, low-cost, female (and mainly migrant) work force.[134]

Global capitalist relations between north and south are directly implicated in the inequalities and abuses experienced by migrant domestic workers. The structured inequalities built on these relations frequently mirror the relations between colonizer and the colonized, but are not limited either geographically or politically to these sets of relations. The abuse and enslavement of migrant domestic workers in the Arabian Gulf region, as well as in many parts of the global south, is evidence of the wider scope of such human rights abuses. As many parts of the global south have not developed welfare-state supports or have not been permitted to because of the conditions imposed by international financial institutions, reliance on paid domestic work continues as limited resources are made available to support the care of dependants.

For migrants the significance of place is always present. For migrant domestic workers, employed in domestic households, the significance of place is not only linked to the position of living in exile, it extends also to everyday questions of working conditions, security, and status. The significance of place, of the household as a realm within which different tests of justice (or none) apply, is not new. In the field of international law, it is an argument that has frequently delayed the expansion of human rights standards to the gendered domain of the private domestic sphere. The gendered divisions between the public and the private that continue to shape women's legal subjectivity are directly implicated in the precarious position of domestic workers. Exclusions and exemptions that operate in employment laws, in laws and policies on access to social security, in immigration and

[130] H. Lutz, 'Gender in the Migratory Process', 36 *Journal of Ethnic and Migration Studies* (2010) 1647, at 1652.

[131] Lutz (n 130) at 1654; B. Anderson, *Doing the Dirty Work? The Global Politics of Domestic Labour* (2000).

[132] S. Parrenas, 'Migrant Filipina Domestic Workers and the International Division of Reproductive Labour', 14 *Gender & Society* (2000) 560.

[133] H. Lutz, 'At your Service Madam! The Globalization of Domestic Service' 70 *Feminist Review* (2002) 89. See also M. Galotti, The *Gender Dimension of Domestic Work in Western Europe* (2009), in particular at 9–13.

[134] Galotti, (n 133), in particular at 9–13.

citizenship laws and in the scope of diplomatic immunity protections, reinforce the invisibility and constructed vulnerability of domestic workers. These exclusions take the form and shape of de-juridifications that seek to limit the application of transformative norms to domestic work.

A. Human rights standards: remedying the decent work deficit?

The 'decent work deficit' that has characterized domestic work includes low wages, volatile and unpredictable working hours, limited access to social security, and an ambiguous employment status.[135] More extreme types of exploitation and abuse to which domestic workers may be subjected include forced labour or trafficking. Migrant domestic workers, particularly those in an irregular situation, are particularly vulnerable to such risks. The UN Special Rapporteur on Contemporary Forms of Slavery, in her 2010 report to the Human Rights Council, identified a 'net of dependency factors' that prevent domestic workers from leaving situations of exploitation, many of which include constructed vulnerabilities linked to migration status.[136] The exploitation of migrant domestic workers is often presented by states as the action of an aberrant and abusive individual employer. The role played by migration law in creating the conditions within which such exploitation occurs and often goes unchecked, is not acknowledged. Not only does migration law reinforce the unequal power relations between migrant domestic workers and their employers, it also provides unscrupulous employers with mechanisms of control that they might not otherwise have.[137]

In the angst and anxieties played out in feminist commentary on domestic work and advocacy for decent work standards, questions remain as to whether domestic work can move beyond its legacies of slavery, exploitation, and abuse. Is the search for decent work standards misguided? Can law reform initiatives and expanding human rights norms produce transformative remedies? To some commentators the movement to establish decent work standards for domestic work is misguided, given the historical legacy of low status, low pay, and abuse. Legal reforms and standards may not fully account for the wider 'realm of indignities' experienced by domestic workers, or the dynamics of power played out on 'concrete historicized bodies' that are racialized, gendered, or classed.[138] Blackett and others, however, have argued that the notion of decent work, despite recognized limitations, continues to hold out potential to improve the lives of many domestic workers and

[135] M. Tomei, 'Decent Work for Domestic Workers: Reflections on Recent Approaches to Tackle Informality' 23 *Canadian Journal of Women & Law* (2011) 186, at 187. See also A. D'Souza, *Moving Towards Decent Work for Domestic Workers: An Overview of the ILO's Work* (2010), 19.

[136] Report of the Special Rapporteur on contemporary forms of slavery, including its causes and consequences, Gulnara Shahinia, UN Doc A/HRC/15/20, (18 January 2010), para. 47.

[137] B. Anderson, 'Migration, Immigration Controls and the Fashioning of Precarious Workers', 24 *Work, Employment & Society* (2010) 300, 312.

[138] A. Blackett, 'Introduction: Regulating Decent Work for Domestic Workers', 23 *Canadian Journal of Women & Law* (2011) 1, at 43, citing E. Gutiérrez-Rodriguez, *Migration, Domestic Work and Affect: A Decolonial Approach on Value and the Feminization of Labor* (2010) 6.

more generally to provide 'an important corrective to abstract articulations (and applications) of rights'.[139]

Human rights law has somewhat belatedly begun to address the structured inequalities and exclusions that structure the domain of domestic work. As in other areas of international law, it is primarily the moments of crisis—incidents of human trafficking, slavery, or forced labour—that have captured the attention of human rights law. The 'everyday' of workplace exploitation, exclusion from the protections of employment protections, social security, and precarious migration status, have attracted less attention. Recent standard-setting initiatives have attempted to address this gap and have included the adoption of the landmark 2011 ILO Convention Concerning Decent Work for Domestic Workers,[140] a General Recommendation from the UN Committee on the Elimination of All Forms of Discrimination Against Women (CEDAW) on Women Migrant Workers,[141] and a General Comment from the UN Committee on Migrant Workers and their Families on Migrant Domestic Workers.[142] Against the background of this 'justice cascade',[143] however, migration laws continue to limit the cosmopolitan promise of human rights law. Migration status adds yet another axis of discrimination and constructed vulnerability to the status of domestic workers as domestic work is increasingly carried out by migrant women. States remain reluctant, however, to recognize this role or to acknowledge the 'dissensus' that arises between 'border norms' and human rights law.[144]

B. The migration nexus

The UN Committee on Migrant Workers in its General Comment on migrant domestic workers outlines the specific role that immigration law plays in the production of vulnerability.[145] Overly restrictive immigration laws, the Committee notes, lead to higher numbers of migrant domestic workers who are undocumented or in an irregular situation, and thus particularly vulnerable to human rights

[139] Blackett (n 138) at 44, citing Blackett, 'Situated Reflections on International Labour Law, Capabilities, and Decent Work: The Case of Centre Maraîcher Eugène Guinois', (Hors-série) *Revue québécoise de droit international* (2007) 223, at 242.

[140] Convention Concerning Decent Work for Domestic Workers, International Labour Organization, adopted at the 100th session of the International Labour Conference, Geneva, 2011.

[141] Committee for the Elimination of All Forms of Discrimination Against Women, *General Recommendation No. 26 on Women Migrant Workers*, UN Doc CEDAW/C/2009/WP.1/R (2008), 5 December 2008.

[142] Committee on the Protection of the Rights of All Migrant Workers and Members of Their Families, *General Comment No. 1 on Migrant Domestic Workers*, UN Doc CMW/C/GC/1 (2011), 23 February 2011.

[143] This term is borrowed from K. Sikkink, *The Justice Cascade: How Human Rights Prosecutions Are Changing World Politics* (2011).

[144] Bosniak (n 4).

[145] Committee on the Protection of the Rights of All Migrant Workers and Members of Their Families, *General Comment No. 1 on Migrant Domestic Workers* (n 142) at paras 21, 22, and 27 in particular.

violations.[146] Similar vulnerabilities arise where migration laws tie a worker's migration status to the continued sponsorship of a particular employer, with the result that domestic workers may risk deportation if they leave an abusive employment relationship.[147] Migration status and immigration laws may also limit access to remedies and the effective exercise of human rights, including rights to family reunification. Where visa or work permit permissions impose limits on access to public funds, rights to education, healthcare, and housing remain illusory.[148] The difficulties that arise in accessing legal remedies, even where available, is specifically highlighted by the CEDAW Committee, which has noted that migrant domestic workers are 'scarcely ever out of sight of their employers' and so may face difficulties even registering with their embassies or filing complaints.[149] The role played by migration law in limiting access to rights protections is not of course unique to the sphere of domestic work.[150] The difficulties encountered by domestic workers are exacerbated, however, by their positioning at the intersections of many overlapping axes of discrimination and the constructed invisibility and isolation of their work.[151]

The obstacles to claiming rights are many, particularly for migrant domestic workers whose status may be tied to that of their employer, their presence within the territory of the state dependent on the goodwill of an unscrupulous employer, or perhaps irregular/illegal. The isolated and privatized nature of domestic work also limits the emergence of 'contact zones' within which alternative legalities may be presented. Migration laws create further barriers, given the absence of a firewall between the punitive and disciplinary functions of immigration controls and the operation of employment, social security, or wider human rights protections.

The links between limited opportunities for legal migration for domestic workers and the high level of irregularity in the sector have been emphasized by the EU Fundamental Rights Agency, among others.[152] Irregularity, as it notes, leads to high levels of insecurity, producing susceptibility to exploitation and difficulties in accessing rights protections.[153] The nexus between access to safe migration routes, obligations of due diligence, and compliance with human rights standards is rarely acknowledged by states, however. Neither are the wider policy challenges of opening borders and increasing migration opportunities. In response to concerns of abuse and exploitation of migrant domestic workers, it is open to states to

[146] Committee on the Protection of the Rights of All Migrant Workers and Members of Their Families, *General Comment No. 1 on Migrant Domestic Workers* (n 142) at para. 21.

[147] Committee on the Protection of the Rights of All Migrant Workers and Members of Their Families, *General Comment No. 1 on Migrant Domestic Workers* (n 142) at para. 21.

[148] See, generally, S. Spencer and J. Pobjoy, *The Relationship between Immigration Status and Rights in the UK: Exploring the Rationale* (2011).

[149] Committee for the Elimination of All Forms of Discrimination Against Women, *General Recommendation No. 26 on Women Migrant Workers* (n 141) at para. 21.

[150] Anderson (n 137) at 303.

[151] See written comments submitted by Interights to the European Court of Human Rights (pursuant to leave granted by the President of the Chamber in accordance with Rule 44§2 of the Rules of Court) in *Kawogo v. UK* (Appl. No. 56921/09) at para. 18.

[152] EU Fundamental Rights Agency, *Migrants in an irregular situation employed in domestic work: Fundamental rights challenges for the European Union and its Member States* (2011).

[153] EU Fundamental Rights Agency (n 152) at 19.

respond by expanding immigration controls. As Dauvergne notes, '[o]nce an argument is shifted to the terrain of rights, the right of the nation to shut its borders tends to overshadow the rights claims of individuals'.[154] The 'deportability' of the alien persists as a constant threat to the claiming and enjoyment of rights. Retreat to sovereign territorial prerogatives to justify the imposition of migration restrictions, is frequently accompanied by the normative reemergence of protective measures particularly concerning migrant women (often grouped together with children as a vulnerable group). The protective impulse is deployed by states to support the imposition of immigration restrictions. It does not typically extend, however, to challenging the continuum of exploitation that defines the everyday sphere of domestic work or the closing of migration pathways which, in turn, increases the *precarité* of migrant domestic workers.

C. Positive obligations, due diligence: expanding the scope of human rights protections

In *Siliadin v. France*, the European Court of Human Rights recognized that Article 4 ECHR could give rise to positive obligations for states.[155] The case, and particularly the proceedings at domestic level, highlight the difficulties that courts encounter in demarcating exploitative work in the domestic sphere. The applicant, a Togolese domestic worker, Siwa-Akofa Siliadin, complained that French criminal law 'did not afford her sufficient and effective protection against the "servitude" in which she had been held, or at the very least against the "forced and compulsory" labour which she had been required to perform'.[156] The Court concluded that Siliadin, who was fifteen years old when she was brought to France on a tourist visa, had been held in servitude within the meaning of Article 4 of the ECHR and that she had also been subjected to forced labour.[157]

A key question that had arisen in the *Siliadin* case in the domestic legal proceedings was the question of how to demarcate the boundaries of everyday intimate labour in the domestic sphere from working conditions that constituted treatment contrary to Article 4. In domestic legal proceedings, the French Civil Court of Appeal, in concluding that exploitation had taken place, was anxious to clarify that Siliadin was not a member of the family and was not treated as such. The public tests of rights compliance could, therefore, begin to be applied. In contrast (or perhaps not), the European Court of Human Rights found that Siliadin had not been subject to working conditions that were 'incompatible with human dignity', these conditions 'being the lot of many mothers'.[158] The presumption that the usual standards of human dignity could not apply served to distinguish domestic work as 'work like no other'.

[154] C. Dauvergne, *Making People Illegal: What Globalization Means for Migration and Law* (2008) 27.
[155] [2006] 43 EHRR 16. [156] [2006] 43 EHRR 16 at para. 3.
[157] [2006] 43 EHRR 16 at paras 121, 122, and 129. [158] [2006] 43 EHRR 16 at para. 44.

The isolation and belief that one's situation cannot be changed was identified as critical to the definition of servitude in *C.N. and V. v. France*, a case involving two sisters, originally from Burundi, who were living with relatives in Paris following the death of their parents in Burundi's bloody civil war.[159] The impugned legal framework remained the same as that addressed by the Court in *Siliadin* and the Court again found France to have failed to meet its positive obligations under Article 4. In *C.N. and V.*, both sisters were required to undertake extensive domestic work and the older sister, C.N., was also required to undertake care work for the disabled son of her relatives, including working at night. The Court found France to have violated its positive obligations under Article 4 with respect to the elder sister. The younger sister V. was allowed to attend school, developing social networks that were ultimately central to the Court's finding that no violation of the Convention had occurred with respect to her situation. The Court's reasoning in this case, as in *Osman*, shows limited evidence of engaging with the intersections of age, gender, and 'race' that are pertinent to the treatment endured by both girls in this case and that are particularly relevant to the issue of intra-familial abuses, including violations of Article 4.

Differing assessments of credibility and of the significance of the harms endured by migrant domestic workers can be seen in the case of *C.N. v. United Kingdom*.[160] The Court's judgment on the meaning of servitude is an important one. It recognizes 'domestic servitude' as a specific offence, distinct from trafficking and exploitation, 'which involves a complex set of dynamics, involving both overt and more subtle forms of coercion, to force compliance'.[161] Drawing on *Ranstev*, the Court noted that a duty to investigate was triggered wherever a 'credible suspicion' existed that rights protected by Article 4 had been violated. In this case, the Court was particularly critical of the failure to interview key actors, including a private recruitment agent. The case illustrates the challenges that face migrants in engaging with law enforcement bodies, and the role that assessments of credibility can play in limiting migrants' access to a legal remedy. Problems of establishing credibility arise, in particular, for migrant women who may find themselves in a double bind, their claims encountering the suspicions that frequently attach to gendered subjects of law on the one hand, and generalized hostilities towards irregular or temporary migrants, on the other hand.

The obligations of effective deterrence that arise from forced labour and trafficking prohibitions are enshrined in several international and regional instruments, including CEDAW,[162] the International Covenant on Civil and Political Rights,[163] the Palermo Protocol,[164] and the Council of Europe Convention on Action Against Trafficking.[165] The European Court of Human Rights has

[159] (2012) ECHR, Appl. No. 67724/09, judgment of 11 October 2012.

[160] (2012) ECHR, Appl. No. 4239/08, judgment 13 November 2012.

[161] See (2012) ECHR (n 160) at para. 80.

[162] See n 18.

[163] International Covenant on Civil and Political Rights (1966), 999 UNTS 171.

[164] Protocol to Prevent, Suppress and Punish Trafficking in Persons, Especially Women and Children, supplementing the United Nations Convention against Transnational Organized Crime (2000).

[165] Council of Europe Convention on Action against Trafficking in Human Beings (2005), 197 CETS.

repeatedly recognized that a state's positive obligations under the Convention go beyond the imposition of criminal sanctions and include policing and operative measures. Such obligations have been recognized, in particular, in the context of domestic violence. Human rights law's engagement with domestic violence shares key features with its late arrival to the everyday exploitation experienced by domestic workers. In common is a reluctance to intervene in family relationships or 'family-like' relationships. It is moments of crisis only—most likely of extreme physical abuse—that are likely to trigger the application of human rights norms. Fitting states' positive obligations to prevent domestic violence into human rights law has been a slow and painful process, but one that has gained some momentum in recent times.

In *Opuz v. Turkey*, the European Court of Human Rights, for the first time in Strasbourg case law, linked states' obligations to combat domestic violence to Article 14 ECHR non-discrimination requirements.[166] The *Jessica Lenahan* case before the Inter-American Commission on Human Rights,[167] the *Campo Algondero* case[168] before the Inter-American Court of Human Rights, and others, similarly point to the non-discrimination nexus. Given that the majority of domestic workers are women and many are immigrants, a similar nexus between migration law, positive obligations, and non-discrimination norms arises. Making the discrimination claim, within the limits of current anti-discrimination law frameworks, is not an easy one, however, and faces many obstacles, particularly when the requirement to identify an appropriate comparator arises.

D. Intersectionality: 'race', gender, and migration status

As Crenshaw has noted, 'the intersections of racism and sexism . . . cannot be captured wholly by looking at the race or gender dimensions separately'.[169] Addressing the intersections of both expands the possibilities of human rights law's potential to address discrimination. Migration status, however, is often excluded from the scope of race discrimination prohibitions and is frequently ignored in analyses of discrimination that adopt a 'nationally insular approach'.[170] Notably, the reluctance to extend non-discrimination norms to the migration context is evident even in the Migrant Workers Convention, which does not include migration status in the list of non-discrimination prohibitions. In the practice of UN human rights treaty bodies, including the Migrant Workers Committee, however, the significance of migration status as relevant to questions of racial and gender discrimination is increasingly probed, despite apparent textual

[166] Appl. No. 33401/02, judgment of 9 June 2009.

[167] *Jessica Lenahan (Gonzales) et al. v. United States*, IAComHR (2011), Case 12.826, Report No. 80/11, 21 July 2011.

[168] *González et al. ('Cotton Field') v. Mexico*, IACtHR (2009) Series C, No. 205, Judgment of 16 November 2009.

[169] K. Crenshaw, 'Mapping the Margins: Intersectionality, Identity Politics, and Violence Against Women of Color', 43 *Stanford Law Review* (1991) 1241, at 1241.

[170] Bosniak (n 4) at 144, n 23.

exclusions from the treaty standards themselves.[171] As Bosniak notes, the category of immigration status is appearing with more frequency in various 'catalogues of subordination axes'.[172] In the ECHR context, the potential of Article 14 to address the intersections of gender and race discrimination remains to be realized. The gradual expansion of indirect discrimination prohibitions suggests possible strategies for such challenges.[173]

The Inter-American Court of Human Rights advisory opinion on *Undocumented Migrants*[174] highlights the potential—and the limits—of pursuing an equality/non-discrimination argument. The Court rejected the distinction between documented and undocumented workers as a legitimate one, for the purposes of justifying differential treatment. The difficulties of advancing this position can be seen, however, in the reluctance of states to ratify the UN Convention on the Rights of Migrant Workers and their Families. Particularly, migrant-receiving countries of the global north have signed and ratified the Convention in very small numbers. The Convention itself retains distinctions between the rights afforded to regular and irregular migrant workers, ultimately providing lesser safeguards than in general human rights treaties. Against this background of state resistance, progressing equality and non-discrimination arguments is challenging.

IV. Concluding Remarks

Given the normative basis of international human rights law, it is fitting that its application to non-citizens is now explicitly acknowledged. Arendt's categorization of citizenship as 'the right to have rights', if we presume a narrative of progress, would no longer seem to hold true as human rights bodies, from the CEDAW and CERD Committees to various UN special procedures, affirm the applicability of human rights standards to non-citizens. The inclusion of those who are strangers to the state in the panoply of human rights obligations disrupts the settled boundaries and imaginaries of state sovereignty, bringing to the fore the promised universalism of human rights norms and their transformative potential. As with any totalizing movement, however, there is always a remainder which is not addressed. Gender continues to play a significant role in determining who is included and who remains at the limits of such human rights protections. State laws, whether applying to the trafficked person's claims to be here and to remain, or assessing the validity of an asylum claim, impact upon gendered and sexed subjects of law. The precariousness of one's claim and migration status is shaped by many intersecting axes—of gender, sexuality, ethnicity, nationality, and socio-economic status. The transformation and expansion of human rights norms are belatedly addressing the limits of asylum

[171] Committee for the Elimination of All Forms of Racial Discrimination, *General Recommendation No. 30 on Discrimination against Non-Citizens*, 10 January 2004.

[172] Bosniak (n 4) at 11.

[173] *D.H. and Others v. the Czech Republic*, ECHR (2006) Appl. No. 57325/00, 7 February 2006.

[174] *Juridical Condition and Rights of Undocumented Migrants, Advisory Opinion OC-18 of September 17, 2003*, IACtHR (2003) Series A, No. 18.

and migration laws. Egregious human rights violations such as human trafficking, domestic violence, and sexual-orientation-related persecution, have until recently been unable to fit the structures and forms of inherited doctrines of human rights law. It is important to question why this is so and whether the process of adding in gender has been or can be a transformative one. As the earlier discussion on laws relating to human trafficking reveals, there are limits to the reform processes that have taken place to date.

Human rights advocates seek to mobilize law to prevent and to respond to the egregious human rights violations that occur in the context of human trafficking. It is important to reflect also, however, on the potential for law to be complicit in reinforcing gender inequalities and in limiting migrant women's agency. This potential is particularly relevant in the context of human trafficking measures, where the tendency to slide into protective measures is ever present and frequently works against the empowerment of trafficked women as full subjects of human rights law.[175] The concern to respond to women's apparent vulnerability continues to be a core motivating impulse in the anti-trafficking movement, both at national and international levels. The normative re-emergence of this protective impulse may limit the trafficked woman's agency and mobility and may also lend support to the creeping expansion of the criminal law and of immigration control agendas.

As in other areas of the law, the responses of states to egregious human rights violations remain preoccupied with prosecution and the expansion of criminal justice responses. Anti-trafficking policy and legislative reforms are replete with commitments to tackle the root causes of human trafficking. However, limited access to safe migration routes, a key factor in vulnerability to human trafficking, is rarely addressed in such reforms. States remain reluctant to acknowledge the link between precarious immigration status and vulnerability to human trafficking. Where it is acknowledged, it is more likely to provoke a protectionist response from states rather than an expansion of migration options. Access to secure immigration status would mitigate one of the significant causes of vulnerability of the trafficked person. That it would not resolve it completely 'speaks to the multiple sources of the disempowerment that generate the migrant woman's vulnerability, including sex, nationality, class and race/ethnicity'.[176]

Presuming, however, as I have argued, that the ideological capture of feminist agendas is not complete, the question that requires constant scrutiny is whether human rights norms are successfully pushing back, opening up possibilities for an emancipatory politics of gender equality in the context of migration. The potential for transformative steps can be seen in the *Rantsev* judgment, in the continuing push to recognize the rights claims of trafficked persons. States remain reluctant to remedy the fundamental irregularity of the trafficked person's presence; this expansion of the human rights remedies available would further challenge the links between sovereignty, territory, and presence. This reluctance is evident also in

[175] See D. Otto, 'Lost in Translation: Re-scripting the Sexed Subjects of International Human Rights Law', in A. Orford (ed.), *International Law and its Others* (2006) 318.
[176] See Macklin (n 36) at 495.

the expansion of gender asylum law. Yet, despite the continuing resistance of states, and despite the myriad hurdles that have to be overcome to fit the structures of asylum law, significant changes have occurred in practice. Transforming migration and asylum law requires more, however, than a process of 'adding in' or a gradual expansion of existing categories of law. It will require moving international and state law beyond a crisis governance response and shifting instead to a concern with everyday harms. Recognizing the migration nexus will also require acknowledging that remedying those harms entails acceptance of claims to be here and to remain.

5

The Labour and Social Rights of Migrants in International Law

Bernard Ryan and Virginia Mantouvalou

I. Introduction

Questions as to the personal scope of internationally recognized civil rights have largely been resolved today. Because civil rights are linked to basic humanity, it is generally accepted that everyone is entitled to them, simply by virtue of being human.[1] In contrast, the personal scope of labour and social rights is far from settled, as these are often thought to be connected to an individual's position as a worker, or to the status of citizenship, rather than to basic humanity. The content and practical achievement of these rights are themselves deeply controversial amongst activists, academic scholars, lawyers, and judges alike.[2] When it comes to the position of migrants, a further complication is the presumed interconnection between immigration policy and labour and social rights protection, as destination countries often limit the rights of non-nationals in the belief that this will deter migration to their territory.[3]

This chapter is concerned with the evolution of international standards on the labour and social rights of migrants. Part II will summarize the pre-1945 approach, when the position of foreign nationals was considered to be an aspect of the relationship between the state of nationality and that in which the individual was present. In contrast, the decades since 1945 have seen the growing acceptance in international law of the equal treatment of migrants in labour and social matters, irrespective of their state of nationality. The acceptance of equal treatment has been seen in instruments specifically concerning migrants, at both the global and

[1] For a theoretical analysis of the normative core of human rights, see J. Tasioulas, 'On the Nature of Human Rights', in G. Ernst and J.-C. Heilinger (eds), *The Philosophy of Human Rights: Contemporary Controversies* (2012) 17.

[2] For the general debate on social rights, see C. Gearty and V. Mantouvalou, *Debating Social Rights* (2011).

[3] See S. Da Lomba, 'Fundamental Social Rights for Irregular Migrants: The Right to Health Care in France and England', in B. Bogusz et al. (eds), *Irregular Migration and Human Rights: Theoretical, European and International Perspectives* (2004) 363 and R. Cholewinski, *Irregular Migrants: Access to Minimum Social Rights* (2005) at 18.

European levels (see parts III and IV, respectively). It has also been reflected in the increasing role of general human rights instruments in the protection of foreign nationals in economic and social matters, at both the global and regional levels (Parts V and VI, respectively).

The chapter as a whole will show that, today, the main question is no longer whether foreign nationals should be eligible for equal treatment in the labour and social fields. Rather, the questions are whether, and to what extent, such rights may be denied or limited in the case of persons who are not lawfully resident ('irregular migrants'). The general answer is that, while the exclusion of migrants from basic labour and social rights protection is now considered to be incompatible with international human rights law, some differences of treatment may still be acceptable in the case of irregular migrants.

The chapter will also show how general human rights instruments have come to the fore within international law provision for the labour and social rights of foreign nationals. We will see that there are various limitations to migrant-specific instruments, including that that they apply to only a limited number of states, and that they are carefully drafted to deny rights to certain migrant groups. In contrast, general human rights instruments typically have a wider reach and do not have specific exceptions for migrant categories. As a result, general instruments are more likely to lead to the development of international standards in the contemporary context of international migration, within which irregular migration is a significant element.

Before proceeding to the chapter's substantive analysis, it is necessary to outline our understanding of the categories of 'labour' and 'social' rights. We take the category of 'labour' rights to refer to rights concerning access to employed activity or the terms on which that activity is undertaken. In the discussion here, we cover the right to work and the prohibition on forced labour under the first of these headings, and the freedom of association in trade unions and the right to fair terms and conditions of employment under the second. We take the category of 'social' rights to refer to rights concerning the basic needs of individuals in a given society.[4] In this chapter, we focus on access to four important social rights: education, health, housing, and social security.

II. Pre-1945 Developments

In the early twentieth century, the treatment of foreign nationals in other countries remained subject to the overriding principle that only states were the subjects of international law. In Richard Lillich's summary:

[4] On the concept of 'social' rights, see V. Mantouvalou, 'In Support of Legalisation', in C. Gearty and V. Mantouvalou, *Debating Social Rights* (2011) 85, at 90–1. Further literature on social and labour rights includes M. Langford (ed.), *Social Rights Jurisprudence: Emerging Trends in International and Comparative Law* (2008), D. Barak-Erez and A. M. Gross (eds), *Exploring Social Rights: Between Theory and Practice* (2007), and P. Alston (ed.), *Labour Rights as Human Rights* (2005).

If a State committed a wrong against an individual who was an alien, then that wrong, if unaddressed, was translated into a wrong against the alien's State of nationality. . . . [The] alien himself had no right which was cognisable by traditional international law against the host State.[5]

Within this approach, states were generally taken to be bound by a minimum international standard of fair treatment, which covered injuries to a foreigner's person and the expropriation of their property.[6] The traditional principle was therefore concerned neither with equal treatment nor with the labour and social rights at issue in this chapter. Latin American states in particular sought to promote a national standard, based upon the principle of equal treatment. But even when that approach was elaborated after 1945, it applied only to fundamental civil rights, and not to labour and social matters.[7]

As industrialized states came to assume greater responsibility for the economic welfare of their populations from the early twentieth century onwards, international arrangements began to address the treatment of foreign workers in labour and social matters. Initially, the extension of labour and social rights to foreign nationals depended upon bilateral agreements between the states in question. Probably the first example was a 1904 agreement between France and Italy, which provided for the retention of each state's social insurance benefits by the nationals of the other if they ceased to be resident, and for equal treatment in each country's laws on compensation for industrial accidents.[8] That precedent was followed by France in labour recruitment agreements with Poland, Italy (both 1919), and Czechoslovakia (1920), in the period of reconstruction immediately after the First World War.[9] These agreements provided that immigrant workers should be paid equally with nationals, and that they should benefit from the same statutory protection as them.[10]

A second phase in the protection of the labour and social rights of foreign nationals was the emergence of multilateral treaties, applicable on a reciprocal basis between contracting parties. Several conventions of this type were adopted in the interwar years under the aegis of the International Labour Organization (ILO). The Unemployment Convention of 1919 provided for equality in unemployment benefits for foreign nationals once a bilateral agreement had been

[5] R. B. Lillich, *The Human Rights of Aliens in Contemporary International Law* (1984), at 1.

[6] On the minimum standard, see M. McDougal, H. Lasswell, and L. Chen, 'The Protection of Aliens from Discrimination and World Public Order: Responsibility of States Conjoined with Human Rights' 70 *American Journal of International Law* (1976) 432, at 450–1.

[7] For the leading statement of the equal treatment approach, see International Law Commission, *International Responsibility: Second Report by F.V. García Amador, Special Rapporteur*, UN Doc. A/CN.4/96, 15 February 1957.

[8] Convention entre la France et l'Italie, en vue d'assurer des garanties à la personne du travailleur, *Journal Officiel*, 12 October 1904. See Arthur Fontaine, 'Exposé de la convention franco-italienne relative au travail et à la prévoyance sociale' (undated); available at: <http://www.gallica.bnf.fr/ark:/12148/bpt6k6124596v>.

[9] Conventions between France and Poland (3 September 1919, 1 LNTS 337), Italy (30 September 1919, 5 LNTS 280) and Czechoslovakia (20 March 1920, 3 LNTS 139).

[10] Arts 2 and 3 in each case.

entered into by the two states concerned.[11] The Equality of Treatment (Accident Compensation) Convention (1925) provided for the equal treatment of foreign workers in workers' compensation schemes, on a reciprocal basis between contracting states.[12] The same approach was taken in the Maintenance of Migrants' Pension Rights Convention (1935), which provided for the protection of benefits within social insurance schemes when migrants moved between participating states.[13] The Migration for Employment Convention of 1939 (not implemented) sought to apply the principle of equal treatment more generally, to state provisions on 'conditions of work and . . . remuneration', 'the right to be a member of a trade union' and 'legal proceedings relating to contracts of employment'.[14] These provisions of the 1939 Convention were, however, subject to a requirement of reciprocity, and so would have applied only to nationals of contracting states or of third states to which the Convention was expressly extended.[15]

While innovative, these interwar instruments concerning migrant workers remained within a logic of reciprocity. For that reason, League of Nations instruments which give recognition to the labour and social rights of refugees are of particular interest.[16] The first of these was the recommendation in the 1928 Arrangement Relating to the Legal Status of Russian and Armenian Refugees that 'restrictive regulations concerning foreign labour . . . not be rigorously applied to . . . refugees in their country of residence'.[17] The 1933 Convention on the International Status of Refugees—which applied to Russian and Armenian refugees, and others 'assimilated' to them—went somewhat further.[18] In addition to providing that labour market restrictions should 'not be applied in all their severity to refugees domiciled or regularly resident in the country', it added that those restrictions should not be applied to refugees with at least three years' residence, refugees married to a person with the nationality of the country of residence or with a child with that nationality, and refugees who had been combatants in the First World War.[19] The 1933 Convention also went beyond previous instruments in its

[11] ILO Convention No. 2, Art. 3. This Convention remains in force, with fifty-four parties at the time of writing.

[12] ILO Convention No. 19, Art. 1(1). This Convention remains in force, with 121 parties at the time of writing.

[13] ILO Convention No. 48. This Convention was ratified by twelve states. The ILO website describes it as a 'shelved Convention'; available at: <http://www.ilo.org/dyn/normlex/en/f?p=NORMLEXPUB:12100:0:NO:12100:P12100_ILO_CODE:C048>.

[14] ILO Convention No. 66. This Convention was not ratified by any state, and was withdrawn by a decision of the International Labour Conference on 15 June 2000; available at: <http://www.ilo.org/public/english/standards/relm/ilc/ilc88/pdf/pr-6-2.pdf>.

[15] ILO Convention No. 66, Art. 6(2).

[16] For a detailed discussion, see J. C. Hathaway, *The Rights of Refugees under International Law* (2005) 83–91.

[17] 30 June 2008, 89 LNTS 53, para. 6.

[18] 159 LNTS 199. The 1933 Convention was ratified by eight states (Belgium, Bulgaria, Czechoslovakia, Denmark, Egypt, France, Italy, and Norway). The category of 'assimilated refugees' covered stateless Assyrian, Assyro-Chaldean, Syrian, Kurdish, and Turkish persons, as defined in the Arrangement Concerning the Extension to Other Categories of Certain Measures Taken in Favour of Russian and Armenian Refugees of 30 June 1928, 89 LNTS 63.

[19] Convention on the International Status of Refugees, Art. 7.

provision for social rights. In the case of benefits arising out of industrial accidents, 'relief and assistance' and social insurance, it required that resident refugees should benefit from 'the most favourable treatment ... accord[ed] to the nationals of a foreign country'.[20] Education in 'schools, courses, faculties and universities' was subject to a requirement that treatment be at least as favourable as for 'other foreigners in general'.[21] Subsequently, a convention of 1938 would extend essentially the same labour and social rights to refugees from Germany.[22]

These interwar instruments concerning refugees had important limitations. They applied only to specific groups, only covered a limited range of labour and social rights, and aimed at equality of treatment with other foreign nationals in the given state, rather than equality with that state's nationals. Their significance lies in the fact that, for the first time, the treatment of foreigners within international law was separated from any link to a state of nationality. As Hathaway has put it, '[t]he consequential decisions to waive reciprocity, and to guarantee basic ... rights in law, served as a direct precedent for a variety of international human rights projects, including the modern refugee rights regime'.[23] We will see in the rest of this chapter the many ways in which that break with a state-based approach has been elaborated in post-1945 international law.

III. Global Instruments on Migrants' Rights

The period after the end of the Second World War is generally accepted as the moment when respect for human rights came to be recognized within international law. It has been said that the Second World War gave rise to a 'spreading conviction that how human beings are treated anywhere concerns everyone, everywhere', one result of which was 'agreement ... that individual human rights are of "international concern", and a proper subject for diplomacy, international institutions and international law'.[24] While the original impetus to internationalization was primarily to ensure respect for civil and political rights, it has been clear since the 1948 Universal Declaration of Human Rights (UDHR) that labour and social rights were also covered.[25] That shift would prove decisive for the position of migrants.

[20] Convention on the International Status of Refugees, Arts 8, 9, and 10.

[21] Convention on the International Status of Refugees, Art. 12.

[22] Convention concerning the Status of Refugees coming from Germany (1938), 192 LNTS 59, Arts 9–11 and 14. Only Belgium, France and the United Kingdom ratified the 1938 Convention. Note that Art. 9 made no reference to the right to work of former combatants in the First World War.

[23] Hathaway (n 16) at 91.

[24] L. Henkin, *The Age of Rights* (1990) 16–17.

[25] See Arts 22–26 of the Universal Declaration on Human Rights. Note in particular the statement in Art. 22 that 'Everyone ... is entitled to realization ... of the economic, social and cultural rights indispensable for his dignity and the free development of his personality'.

A. Refugees and stateless persons

The early post-1945 period saw particular attention paid to the international provision for refugees and the related category of stateless persons. In relation to refugees, the Convention on the Status of Refugees (Refugee Convention), adopted in 1951, broke with the pre-war approach, which had focused on particular nationalities, by laying down standards which were potentially applicable to all refugees.[26] Initially, the Refugee Convention applied only to persons who were refugees as a result of events prior to 1 January 1951, and contracting states were permitted to confine their obligations to refugees from Europe. Further expansion came with the 1967 New York Protocol, which removed the 1951 cut-off date altogether, while only allowing obligations to be limited to Europe where a contracting state had done so under the 1951 Convention.[27] In practice, few states have retained a European limit, with the result that the economic and social rights set out in the Refugee Convention are now guaranteed to *all* refugees in contracting states.[28]

The substantive provisions of the Refugee Convention are limited in several respects. Refugees are entitled to access to employment after three years' residence, or if they have a spouse or children with the nationality of the country of residence.[29] They are also entitled to full equal treatment with nationals in labour legislation, elementary education, 'public relief and assistance' and social security.[30] But the Refugee Convention falls short of full equal treatment in applying the 'most favourable treatment of foreign nationals' standard to access to employment in the first three years, and to freedom of association.[31] Self-employment, recognition of professional qualifications, access to housing, and post-elementary education are meanwhile governed by an even lower standard: 'treatment as favourable as possible and, in any event, not less favourable than that accorded to aliens generally in the same circumstances'.[32]

Moreover, most of the labour and social rights provisions of the Refugee Convention are subject to limitations concerning the individual's status in the country of residence. The provisions on the right to work, labour law, freedom of association, recognition of professional qualifications, housing, public relief and social security apply only to refugees 'lawfully staying' in the state in question.[33] On any interpretation, this excludes applicants for refugee status who are in a state with an effective procedure for determining such applications.[34] One exception is the

[26] Convention on the Status of Refugees, 189 UNTS 150.

[27] Protocol relating to the Status of Refugees, 606 UNTS 267.

[28] At the time of writing, the Congo and Turkey are the only parties to the Protocol to have continued to limit their obligations to refugees from Europe.

[29] Convention on the Status of Refugees, Art. 17(2).

[30] Convention on the Status of Refugees, Arts 22(1), 23, and 24.

[31] Convention on the Status of Refugees, Arts 15 and 17.

[32] Convention on the Status of Refugees, Arts 18, 19, 21, and 22(2).

[33] For this phrase, see Arts 15, 17, 19, 21, 23, and 24.

[34] On the interpretation of 'lawfully staying', see Hathaway (n 16) at 189 and G. S. Goodwin-Gill and J. McAdam, *The Refugee in International Law* (2007) at 525–6.

right to engage in self-employment, which is stated to apply to those 'lawfully in' the territory of the state in question.[35] A second exception is access to public education, which is stated to apply to 'refugees', without any qualification.[36]

Broadly similar provision was made for the labour and social rights of stateless persons, by virtue of the 1954 Convention on the Status of Stateless Persons.[37] Stateless persons too benefit from the principle of equal treatment with nationals in relation to elementary education, public relief, and labour legislation and social security.[38] One difference from the Refugee Convention is that there is no right of access to employment after three years. In addition, there is no 'most favoured nation' rule for freedom of association or for employment in the first three years, which are instead governed by a requirement of treatment 'as favourable as possible . . . not less favourable than that accorded to aliens generally'.[39] Meanwhile, the provisions concerning the degree of connection to the state in question—'lawfully staying', 'lawfully in' and silence—are identical to those in the equivalent provisions of the Refugee Convention.

B. ILO instruments concerning migrant workers

In the post-1945 era, the ILO was again a pioneer in the development of the labour and social rights of migrants. In 1949, it adopted the Migration for Employment Convention (Revised) 1949 (No. 97), to which it later added the Migrant Workers (Supplementary Provisions) Convention 1975 (No. 143). These two conventions are potentially applicable to everyone who is a 'migrant for employment'.[40] That term is defined to mean a person who 'migrates from one country to another with a view to being employed otherwise than on his own account'. It follows that these conventions do not distinguish between permanent and temporary migrants. For our purposes, it is significant that neither of the conventions is based on reciprocity—that is, contracting states undertake obligations in respect of all migrant workers, irrespective of nationality.

At the time that the 1949 Convention and a related Recommendation (No. 86) were adopted, the ILO's aim was to 'facilitate the international distribution of manpower and in particular the movement of manpower from countries which have a surplus of manpower to countries that have a deficiency'.[41] Accordingly, Convention No. 97 contains standards in relation to both recruitment and working conditions. The full protection of the Convention is limited to 'immigrants lawfully within its territory', who alone are guaranteed treatment equal to the country's nationals with respect to issues such as remuneration, hours of work, pay for overtime, union membership, social security, and access to justice.[42]

[35] Refugee Convention, Art. 18. [36] Refugee Convention, Art. 22.

[37] Convention on the Status of Stateless Persons, 360 UNTS 117.

[38] Convention on the Status of Stateless Persons, 360 UNTS 117, Arts 22(1), 23, and 24.

[39] Convention on the Status of Stateless Persons, 360 UNTS 117, Arts 15, 17, 18, 19, 21, and 22(2).

[40] See Art. 11 in each case. Note that in Convention No. 143, this definition covers only Part II of the Convention, which concerns rights of equal treatment.

[41] ILO Recommendation No. 86 (1949), para. 4(1). [42] ILO Convention No. 97, Art. 6.

When the 1975 Convention and the related Recommendation (No. 151) were adopted, the rationale and approach had changed significantly, as the key concern was now to control migration, rather than to facilitate it. As an ILO study put it: 'Convention No 143 and Recommendation No 151 resulted from the first multilateral attempt to deal with migrant workers in irregular status and to call for sanctions against traffickers'.[43] Because of that background, the personal scope of Convention No. 143 is different to that of Convention No. 97. Firstly, Article 1 of Convention No. 143 covers both regular and irregular migrants, and states that member states have a duty to respect the 'basic human rights' of *all* workers. The ILO Committee of Experts (CEACR) has subsequently given that term a broad interpretation, as referring to the International Bill of Rights (that is, the Universal Declaration on Human Rights, the International Covenant on Civil and Political Rights (ICCPR) and the International Covenant on Economic, Social and Cultural Rights (ICESCR)), the UN Migrant Workers Convention, and the ILO Declaration on Fundamental Principles and Rights at Work.[44] Secondly, Convention No. 143 provides that irregular migrants have rights to remuneration, social security, and other benefits stemming from past employment.[45] That said, lawful migrants are in a stronger position, as they continue to enjoy equal treatment and equality of opportunity, in a manner similar to Convention No. 97.[46] In the case of migrant workers in a lawful position, the Convention also permits states to make the free choice of employment conditional upon a two-year period of residence for the purposes of employment, or, in cases of fixed-term contracts of less than two years, conditional upon the completion of the first work contract.[47]

The ILO has also developed provisions on the social security rights of migrant workers. According to a recent ILO study, 'it is of particular importance for migrant workers (1) to have the same access to coverage and entitlement to benefits as native workers, (2) to maintain acquired rights when leaving the destination country, including the right to export the benefits they have earned, and (3) to benefit from the accumulation of rights acquired in different countries'.[48] The Equality of Treatment (Social Security) Convention 1962 (No. 118), and the Maintenance of Social Security Rights Convention 1982 (No. 157) each provide for equal treatment of migrant workers and the country's nationals, on the basis of reciprocity. Convention No. 118 covers nine areas of social security: medical care, sickness benefit, maternity benefit, invalidity benefit, survivors' benefit, employment injury benefit, unemployment benefit, old-age benefit, and family benefit. Convention No. 157 provides for a system that guarantees that workers who change their residence from one country to another keep acquired social security benefits. Benefits acquired abroad should be maintained when migrants return to

[43] ILO, *International Labour Migration: A Rights-Based Approach* (2010) at 129.

[44] P. A. Taran and E. Geronimi, *Globalization, Labour and Migration: Protection is Paramount* (2003) at 13.

[45] ILO Convention No. 143, Art. 9.

[46] ILO Convention No. 143, Art. 10.

[47] ILO Convention No. 143, Art. 14.

[48] See n 43, at 125.

their home country. The maintenance of acquired rights applies to all areas where the contracting states have legislation in force.

C. Migrant Workers Convention

More systematic recognition for the labour and social rights of foreign nationals, including irregular migrants in particular, came with the International Convention on the Rights of All Migrant Workers and Members of their Families (Migration Workers Convention or ICRMW), adopted in 1990.[49] The background to this treaty was the perception on the part of some states of origin of migrants that ILO Convention No. 143 had focused too much on combating irregular migration and employment. Because that outcome was thought to be linked to the pre-eminence of 'industrialized' countries within ILO decision-making, the Migrant Workers Convention came to be adopted under the aegis of the United Nations General Assembly.[50]

A key feature of the Migrant Workers Convention is its broad personal scope.[51] This arises in particular from its definition of 'migrant worker' as 'a person who is to be engaged, is engaged or has been engaged in a remunerated activity in a State of which he or she is not a national'.[52] This definition covers all economically active migrants, including both employees and the self-employed. It applies to economically active foreign nationals irrespective of their reasons for migration, or the immigration category (if any) they were admitted under. It is also independent of the lawfulness of the person's presence or their economic activity. Because the Convention also covers immediate family members,[53] its breadth means that it is close to being an instrument concerning migrants *as such*.

The rights recognized in the Migrant Workers Convention are differentiated by immigration status. Part III of the Convention recognizes various human rights for all migrant workers and their family members, irrespective of immigration status. Part IV of the Convention then limits certain rights to migrant workers and their family members whose stay complies with immigration laws. This division within the Convention is open to the criticism that it implies that some rights do not apply to persons in an irregular position.[54] Nevertheless, the Convention as a whole

[49] International Convention on the Protection of the Rights of All Migrant Workers and Members of their Families, 2220 UNTS 3.

[50] See R. Böhning, 'The ILO and the New UN Convention on Migrant Workers: The Past and Future', 25 *International Migration Review* (1991) 698.

[51] Art. 3 ICRMW lists several exceptions, including persons sent by international organizations and foreign states, refugees and stateless persons (who are covered by the separate regime discussed earlier in this chapter), and students and trainees.

[52] Art. 2 ICRMW. See R. Cholewinski, *Migrant Workers in International Human Rights Law: Their Protection in Countries of Employment* (1997) 149–52.

[53] Art. 3 ICRMW gives a definition of family members which includes the spouses of migrant workers, persons 'having with them a relationship that, according to applicable law, produces effects equivalent to marriage', and their dependent children.

[54] See L. Bosniak, 'Human Rights, State Sovereignty and the Protection of Undocumented Migrants Under The International Migrant Workers Convention', 25 *International Migration Review* (1991) 737, at 759.

appears to be an improvement for irregular migrants, precisely because it is explicit as to the rights that *do* apply to them.[55] In addition, the supervisory work of the Committee on Migrant Workers (CMW) has shown the particular relevance of the Convention to those in an irregular position.[56]

The provisions of the Migrant Workers Convention concerning the right to work, set out in its Part IV, are limited to migrants in a lawful position. Article 52 provides for the free choice of employment after a maximum of five years. (This is less generous than the two-year maximum set out in Article 14 of ILO Convention No. 143, discussed earlier in this chapter).[57] Article 54 includes provision for equal treatment with nationals in access to public work schemes and—subject to Article 52—to alternative employment in the event of loss of work. Article 55 recognizes the right of migrant workers to equal treatment with nationals in the exercise of remunerated activity for which they have permission.

Other labour and social rights set out in the Convention are of benefit to all migrants, including those in an irregular position. Take first the Convention's provisions concerning the employment relationship. The one provision in that area which applies to legal migrant workers alone is Article 54, which guarantees a right to equal treatment in respect of protection against dismissal. The norm under the Convention, however, is that labour laws apply to all workers, irrespective of the legality of their stay or their employment. In particular, Article 25 recognizes the right of all migrant workers to equal treatment with nationals in remuneration and in other terms and conditions of employment. It specifically provides that migrant workers should not be deprived of the right to equal treatment 'by reason of any irregularity in their stay or employment', and that 'employers shall not be relieved of any legal or contractual obligations, nor shall their obligations be limited in any manner by reason of such irregularity' (Article 25(3)). The CMW has also focused attention on whether national labour laws protect migrants, irrespective of the legality of their stay.[58] It has called for the inclusion of migrant domestic workers within the scope of labour law, and for labour law protections to be made effective for migrant domestic workers and for migrant workers in agriculture.[59] The CMW has also made specific recommendations concerning access by irregular

[55] See I. Slinckx, 'Migrants' Rights in UN Human Rights Conventions' in R. Cholewinski, P. de Guchteneire, and A. Pécoud (eds), *Migration and Human Rights: The United Nations Convention on Migrant Workers' Rights* (2009) 122, at 146–7.

[56] The CMW was established on 1 January 2004. Its main role is the consideration of state reports on the implementation of the Convention. It has also adopted a *General Comment on Migrant Domestic Workers* (2010). The discussion of its work here draws upon material in B. Ryan, 'In Defence of the Migrant Workers Convention: Standard Setting for Contemporary Migration', in S. S. Juss (ed.), *The Ashgate Research Companion to Migration Law, Theory and Policy* (2013) 491.

[57] For a discussion, see Cholewinski (n 52) at 163.

[58] The CMW observations on labour law have not always been expressly based upon Art. 25. It has also relied upon the requirement for an effective remedy for violations of the Convention (Art. 83 ICRMW) or the principle of equal protection under the law (not stated expressly in the Convention). For a fuller discussion, see Ryan (n 56).

[59] In relation to scope, see CMW observations on Egypt (2007), paras 38–39 and in *General Comment No. 1* (2010), para. 38. In relation to effectiveness, see for example CMW observations on Mexico (2006), paras 33–34 and 37–38, and *General Comment No. 1* (2010), para. 41.

migrant workers to labour law protections, through the possibility of initiating legal proceedings and relying upon other complaint mechanisms.[60]

Trade union rights provide a second illustration. These are provided for in two places in the Convention. Article 26 sets out three rights concerning trade unions, which apply to all migrant workers: 'to join freely', 'to seek . . . aid and assistance', and 'to take part in meetings and activities'. Article 40 of the Convention then adds the right 'to form . . . trade unions' for migrants in a lawful position alone. The implication that those in an irregular position cannot *establish* trade unions is at odds with the position under more general international instruments (ILO Convention No. 87, Article 8 ICESCR, and Article 22 ICCPR, discussed below).[61] In practice too, the Committee on Migrant Workers has focused upon Article 40, even though Article 26 might have been applicable—for example, when contracting states fail to fully recognize foreign nationals' trade union rights, and when contracting states exclude foreign nationals from official positions within trade unions.[62] Nevertheless, Article 26 covers the trade union rights that irregular migrants are most likely to need in practice, and has been relied upon by the CMW to criticize provisions which specifically deny workers in an irregular position the right to join trade unions.[63]

A third example concerns social rights. Part III of the Convention contains three provisions in this area of benefit to all migrant workers and their family members. Article 27 provides that they should be treated equally with nationals in relation to social security. Article 28 provides for equal treatment with nationals in respect of medical care that is 'urgently required for the preservation of . . . life or the avoidance of irreparable harm to . . . health', and expressly states that 'shall not be refused . . . by reason of any irregularity with regard to stay or employment'. Article 30 sets out the right of a migrant worker's child to equal access to education, and specifically states that access to pre-school education and schools should not be refused because of irregularity in the position of the child or of either parent. These Articles are supplemented by Article 43(1), which provides for the equal treatment of migrants in a lawful position inter alia in education, vocational guidance and training, housing, and 'social and health services'. While the rights of irregular migrants are therefore incomplete, the extensive recognition given to them is highly significant. It has in particular permitted the CMW to criticize failures to make provision for irregular migrants in relation to each of social security, medical care, and education in social provision for irregular migrants.[64]

[60] CMW observations on Mexico (2006), paras 25–26, Syria (2008), paras 25–26, and Algeria (2010), paras 16–17.

[61] For a discussion, see Cholewinski (n 52) at 164–5.

[62] In relation to trade union rights in general, see the CMW observations on the Philippines (2009), paras 33–34, Sri Lanka (2009), paras 25–26 and 31–32 and Algeria (2010), paras 28–29. In relation to official positions, see the CMW observations on Mexico (2006), para. 36 and (2011), para. 46, Ecuador (2007), para. 42 and (2010), para. 42, El Salvador (2009), para. 32, and Senegal (2010), para. 16.

[63] CMW observations on Albania (2010), paras 29–30, Algeria (2010), para. 19 and Guatelama (2011), para. 31.

[64] CMW observations on Ecuador (2007), paras 39–40 (medical care), Egypt (2007), paras 36–37 (education), Azerbaijan (2009), paras 30–31 (medical care and education), and Algeria (2010), para. 19 (social security and medical care).

IV. European Instruments on Migration

The only migration-specific instruments at a regional level to have addressed labour and social rights have been adopted in Europe. The discussion here firstly considers Council of Europe instruments, which have made extensive provision for migrants' rights, but which are limited by reciprocity rules. This part goes on to consider the contribution of European Union law, and in particular, of directives in the field of immigration and asylum law. These show the opposite pattern: fewer labour and social rights, for defined categories, but without a reciprocity condition.

A. Council of Europe

To date, the Council of Europe has adopted four instruments on the labour and social rights of foreign nationals. The first to be adopted was the 1953 European Convention on Social and Medical Assistance (ECSMA).[65] It establishes a principle of equal treatment in social and medical assistance between foreign nationals of contracting states who are lawfully present, and who have insufficient resources, and the nationals of the state in question.[66] The Convention also provides that a person cannot be repatriated simply because they are in need of such assistance.[67] There are however some exceptions to that principle: a person may be returned to their home country if they have not been continuously resident in the Contracting Party for at least five years if they entered before the age of fifty-five, or for ten years if they entered after that age. In order for repatriation to be compatible with the Convention, the person also needs to be fit to travel and to have no close ties with the country of residence. In addition, the Convention provides that the contracting parties 'agree not to have recourse to repatriation except in the greatest moderation', and only when 'there is no objection on humanitarian grounds'.[68]

Secondly, the 1955 European Convention on Establishment includes a number of provisions on the labour and social rights of nationals of other contracting states.[69] Its Article 10 recognizes the right of those persons to engage in gainful occupation in another state on an equal footing with that state's own nationals, unless there are 'cogent economic or social reasons for withholding this authorization'. Article 12 provides for a foreign national's right to engage in gainful occupation equally with another state's nationals, provided (a) they have lawfully engaged in that occupation in that state's territory for a continuous period of five years, (b) they have lawfully resided in that state for a continuous period of ten years, or (c) they are permanently resident in that state. Equal treatment with respect to wages and working conditions is guaranteed by Article 17, without any express requirement of lawfulness of stay. Finally, Article 20 provides for equal

[65] European Convention on Social and Medical Assistance, CETS No. 14.
[66] European Convention on Social and Medical Assistance, Art. 1.
[67] European Convention on Social and Medical Assistance, Art. 6(a).
[68] Art. 7.
[69] European Convention on Establishment, CETS No. 19.

treatment in access to state education for lawfully resident foreign nationals of school age, but leaves scholarships to the discretion of individual states.

Thirdly, the 1972 European Convention on Social Security deals with issues such as unemployment benefits, invalidity benefits and old-age benefits.[70] In these fields, it establishes a principle of equal treatment between nationals of contracting parties and the state's own nationals. Exceptions may however be made for non-contributory benefits whose amount does not depend on an individual's length of residence. For those benefits, a qualifying period of residence is possible, subject to the following limitations: in the case of maternity and unemployment benefits, a period of not more than six months before a claim; for invalidity and survivors' benefits, a period of not more than five consecutive years before a claim; and, for old-age benefits, not more than ten years' residence between the age of sixteen and the pensionable age, which may include the five years immediately before a claim.[71] With respect to voluntary insurance which depends on periods of compulsory insurance, the Convention provides that periods completed in another contracting party should be taken into account.[72] As with the earlier conventions, the European Convention on Social Security applies in principle only to the nationals of other contracting parties (see its Article 4). In this case, however, refugees and stateless persons are also included among the beneficiaries.

The fourth instrument is the 1977 European Convention on the Legal Status of Migrant Workers (ECLSMW), which elaborates the principle of equal treatment in labour and social rights.[73] The ECLSMW provides, for instance, that migrant workers and their families have equal rights to housing, to education and vocational training, and to access to higher education institutions.[74] Migrant workers should also enjoy working conditions equal to national workers, as provided by law, administrative action, collective agreements, or custom, and derogation by contract from this provision is explicitly prohibited.[75] Similarly, migrant workers enjoy equal rights to national workers with respect to social security, industrial accidents and occupational diseases, as well as equal entitlements concerning labour inspections.[76] As with the earlier instruments, this Convention applies only to nationals of other contracting parties who are in a lawful position. Indeed, Article 1 goes further, and provides that 'the term "migrant worker" shall mean a national of a Contracting Party who has been authorised by another Contracting Party to reside in its territory in order to take up paid employment'. The implication is that nationals of other parties who were authorized to reside for *other* reasons are not covered by the Convention.

It can be seen therefore that the Council of Europe treaties concerning the status of foreign nationals are based on reciprocity, and generally require that a foreign

[70] European Convention on Social Security, CETS No. 78, Art. 2.
[71] European Convention on Social Security, Art. 8.
[72] European Convention on Social Security, Art. 10.
[73] European Convention on the Legal Status of Migrant Workers, 24 November 1977, CETS No. 93.
[74] European Convention on the Legal Status of Migrant Workers, Arts 13 and 14.
[75] European Convention on the Legal Status of Migrant Workers, Art. 16.
[76] European Convention on the Legal Status of Migrant Workers, Arts 18, 20, and 21.

national be lawfully resident. Faced with these limitations, the political organs of the Council of Europe have sought to provide for the position of migrants in an irregular situation through non-binding measures. In 2000, the Committee of Ministers adopted a Recommendation on the Right to the Satisfaction of Basic Material Needs of All Persons in a Situation of Extreme Hardship.[77] According to the Recommendation, member states should recognize a right of persons who are destitute to the satisfaction of 'basic material needs', which right should at least include provision for food, clothing, shelter, and basic medical care. Principle 4 of the Recommendation makes clear that this right is applicable to everyone, irrespective of nationality or legal status. In addition, in 2006, the Council of Europe's Parliamentary Assembly adopted a Resolution specifically on the Human Rights of Irregular Migrants,[78] which urged member states to protect at least a 'core minimum' of rights of irregular migrants. The labour and social rights identified were the following: adequate housing and shelter; emergency healthcare and healthcare for those that have special needs, such as children or the elderly; social protection through social security where that is 'necessary to alleviate poverty and preserve human dignity'; social benefits for those who have made social security contributions; fair wages and working conditions, compensation for accidents, access to justice and trade union rights for all those who work; a right to education for children; and, particular protection for vulnerable groups such as children and the elderly.[79]

B. European Union

The European Union has made several important contributions concerning migrants' labour and social rights. Firstly, its highly developed framework for the free movement of EU citizens and their family members ensures both the right to work in other member states and equal treatment on grounds of nationality in employment conditions and in social provision.[80] Secondly, the European Union's own bilateral agreements with third countries have given extensive recognition to labour and social rights. The most significant of these have been the European Economic Area agreement with Iceland, Liechtenstein and Norway, and an agreement on the free movement of persons with Switzerland, which include those countries' nationals within the framework applicable to EU citizens.[81] Measures

[77] Council of Europe, Committee of Ministers, Recommendation No. R (2000) 3.

[78] Council of Europe, Parliamentary Assembly Resolution 1509 (2006).

[79] Council of Europe, Parliamentary Assembly Resolution 1509, para. 13.

[80] The economic and social rights of EU workers and their families are provided for in Council Regulation 1612/68 of 15 October 1968, OJ 1968 L 257/2, on freedom of movement for workers within the Community, especially Arts 1 and 7–12. The rights of EU citizens and their family members in general are provided for in Directive 2004/38, OJ 2004 L 158/77, on the right of citizens of the Union and their family members to move and reside freely within the territory of the member states, Arts 23 and 24.

[81] Agreement on the European Economic Area, OJ 1994 L 1/3, Annex V, as amended by EEA Joint Committee Decision 158/2007, OJ 2008 L 124/20, and Agreement on the Free Movement of Persons with Switzerland, OJ 2002 L 114/6, Annex I, Art. 9.

adopted under an association agreement with Turkey guarantee equal treatment in working conditions and in social security provision (including non-contributory benefits) to Turkish workers in EU member states.[82] In addition, a series of bilateral agreements guarantee equal treatment either in working conditions and social security, or in working conditions alone, to many other states' nationals who work in the European Union.[83]

More importantly for our purposes, a series of directives on migration since 2003 have addressed the labour and social rights of migrants.[84] Among these, the most extensive provisions are contained in the 2003 Long-term Residents Directive.[85] It applies to non-EU nationals who have been lawfully resident in a member state for five years, and who are not in temporary immigration categories, including—from 20 May 2013—persons who are refugees or beneficiaries of international protection. Those covered by the Directive are eligible for equal treatment across a range of economic and social rights, including access to employment and self-employment, education and vocational training (including study grants), 'core benefits' within social assistance and social protection, housing, and freedom of association.[86]

Extensive provision for labour and social rights has also been made by the Qualification Directives of 2004 and 2011, which concern both refugees and a wider category of humanitarian cases ('subsidiary protection').[87] In the labour field, under the 2011 Directive, both categories are entitled to equal treatment with nationals in access to employment and self-employment, in vocational training, and in 'the law in force' concerning remuneration and other conditions of employment.[88] In the social sphere, both categories benefit from equal treatment with nationals in relation to social security for employed and self-employed persons, the education of minors, and health care.[89] In contrast, a lower standard of equal treatment with 'third country nationals legally resident' applies to the education of

[82] EC–Turkey Association Council Decision 1/80 (unpublished), Art. 10 and EC–Turkey Association Council Decision 3/80, OJ 1983 C 110/60, Art. 3.

[83] For an overview, see S. Peers, *EU Justice and Home Affairs Law* (2011) 424–7.

[84] Britain and Ireland each have a right to choose whether to participate in individual measures. Denmark is excluded automatically from these measures.

[85] Directive 2003/109, OJ 2004 L 16/44, concerning the status of third-country nationals who are long-term residents, as amended by Directive 2011/51, OJ 2011 L 132/1. These Directives do not apply to Britain, Denmark, or Ireland.

[86] Directive 2003/109, Art. 11.

[87] Directive 2004/83, OJ 2004 L 304/12, on minimum standards for the qualification and status of third country nationals or stateless persons as refugees or as persons who otherwise need international protection and the content of the protection granted, and Directive 2011/95, OJ 2011 L 337/9, on standards for the qualification of third-country nationals or stateless persons as beneficiaries of international protection, for a uniform status for refugees or for persons eligible for subsidiary protection, and for the content of the protection granted. The 2011 Directive applies to twenty-four states, Britain and Ireland are bound by the 2004 Directive alone, and Denmark is bound by neither.

[88] Directive 2011/95, Art. 26. Under the 2004 Directive, member states may take 'the situation of the labour market . . . into account' in deciding on access to employment by beneficiaries of subsidiary protection (its Art. 26(3)).

[89] Directive 2011/95, Arts 26(4), 27(1), and 30(1). The rules are the same for social security and the education of minors under the 2004 Directive (its Arts 26(5), 27(1)), but member states may limit equal treatment in health care to 'core benefits' (its Art. 29(2)).

adults and to access to accommodation, for both categories.[90] Finally, refugees alone are entitled to full equal treatment in relation to social assistance, with member states free to limit the equal treatment rights of beneficiaries of subsidiary protection to 'core benefits'.[91] Despite some departures from full equal treatment for refugees, the Qualification Directives have gone beyond the Refugee Convention in giving refugees more extensive rights to employment (equal treatment with nationals in the first three years), to self-employment (equal treatment with nationals), and to education (minors' rights are not limited to elementary education), and an express right to health care. Moreover, in the case of beneficiaries of subsidiary protection, these Directives have been a new departure, as a detailed status had not previously been elaborated for that category at the international level.

More limited recognition is given in EU law to the labour and social rights of foreign nationals who have recently been admitted under immigration law. The Family Reunification Directive of 2003 applies to third-country nationals who hold a residence permit with a period of validity of one year or more, and who have 'reasonable prospects of obtaining the right of permanent residence'. These persons' immediate family members are entitled to be admitted to the member state in question, and are then eligible for employment and self-employed activity after a maximum of twelve months' stay.[92] The Directive does not however provide access to social rights, presumably because self-sufficiency is a condition of admission.

Protection for economic and social rights is also incomplete within the 2009 Directive on Highly Qualified Employment. It provides for equal treatment inter alia in respect of working conditions, freedom of association, access to education and vocational training, and in social security provision.[93] The right to change employer is limited, however: in the first two years, changes are allowed only if the Directive's qualifying conditions continue to be met, and thereafter the right to change employer is confined to highly qualified employment.[94] The Directive also omits provision for equal access to health care, presumably because it is a requirement under the Directive that the person has adequate health insurance.[95]

Finally, what of those who do not have a secure immigration status? One contribution made by EU law concerns the social and economic position of *applicants* for refugee status.[96] The Reception Conditions Directive of 2003

[90] Directive 2011/95, Arts 27(2), and 32(1). The rules are the same under the 2004 Directive (its Arts 27(2) and 31).

[91] Directive 2011/95, Art. 29(2). The same difference between the categories is made by the 2004 Directive (its Art. 28(2)).

[92] Directive 2003/86, OJ 2003 L 251/12, on the right to family reunification, Art. 14. The Directive applies to none of Britain, Denmark, or Ireland.

[93] Directive 2009/50, OJ 2009 L 155/17, on the conditions of entry and residence of third-country nationals for the purposes of highly qualified employment, Art. 14. The Directive applies to none of Britain, Denmark, or Ireland. Note that highly skilled workers may continue to benefit from more generous member state schemes.

[94] Directive 2009/50, Art. 12. [95] Directive 2009/50, Art. 5(1)(e).

[96] Directive 2003/9, OJ 2003 L 31/18, laying down minimum standards for the reception of asylum seekers, Art. 11(2). The Directive applies to Britain, but not Denmark or Ireland. In 2008 and 2011, the European Commission proposed the extension of the Directive to all applicants for refugee status and/or subsidiary protection, and substantive amendments concerning economic and social

requires member states to grant asylum applicants 'access to the labour market' if, through no fault of the applicant's, they have not had an initial determination of their asylum claim within one year.[97] Minors who are applicants for refugee status, or their children, are eligible to full access to the state education system.[98] More generally, asylum applicants and their families are entitled to material provision 'to ensure a standard of living adequate for the health of applicants and capable of ensuring their subsistence'.[99] While these standards are low, the Directive does go further than the Refugee Convention (discussed above) in unequivocally laying down binding standards as to the economic and social position of applicants for international protection.

Reference may also be made to the Employer Sanctions Directive of 2009.[100] Its main purpose is to ensure that member states penalize employers for hiring workers whose stay in a member state is unlawful. In line with the overall purpose of discouraging irregular work by migrants, the Directive also requires that employers be liable for remuneration owed to irregularly staying workers.[101] In support of that requirement, it specifically provides for the pursuit of legal action by workers after having been removed from the state in question.[102] While these guarantees do not recognize the right of irregular migrant workers to the full protection of labour law, they are in line with the acceptance of that principle elsewhere at the international level.

The labour and social rights provided for in the EU's migration directives are therefore highly differentiated by migration category. That said, the EU measures have the advantage over Council of Europe instruments that they are universally applicable, benefitting all non-EU citizens, without the need for agreement with particular countries. They are therefore similar in spirit to international conventions on migration adopted in other fora, while stronger in their effects, as they are covered by the EU law principles of direct effect and supremacy in the legal orders of the member states.

V. General Global Instruments

The discussion of migration-specific instruments in Parts II and III showed the gradual expansion, in the post-1945 era, of the recognition given within international law to the labour and social rights of migrants. In the first place—with the exception of the Council of Europe Conventions up to 1977—reciprocity has generally come to be rejected as a requirement. Secondly, there has been gradual

rights: see COM(2008)360, revised by COM(2011)320. These proposals had not led to legislation at the time of writing.

[97] Directive 2003/9, Art. 11(2). [98] Directive 2003/9, Art. 10(1).

[99] Directive 2003/9, Art. 13(2).

[100] Directive 2009/52 of 18 June 2009, OJ 2009 L 168/24, providing for minimum standards on sanctions and measures against employers of illegally staying third-country nationals.

[101] Directive 2009/52 of 18 June 2009, Art. 6(1)(a).

[102] Directive 2009/52 of 18 June 2009, Art. 6(2)(a).

acceptance that equal treatment with the nationals of the country of residence, rather than with other foreign nationals, is the appropriate standard of treatment. To that, the main exception is that 'foreign national' comparators apply within the Refugee and Stateless Persons Conventions.

Nevertheless, there remain large gaps in the coverage of the migration-specific instruments. Among these instruments, the treaties concerning refugees and stateless persons have had the most extensive participation. At the time of writing (early 2013), of the 193 member states of the United Nations, 146 states are parties to the 1967 Protocol to the Refugee Convention, and seventy-six are parties to the Convention on the Status of Stateless Persons. By contrast there has been far less endorsement of other international standards. At the time of writing, the employment-oriented ILO Conventions 97 and 143 have forty-nine and twenty-three parties, respectively, with fifty-five states having ratified one or both. Meanwhile, the broader Migrant Workers Convention has forty-six parties. Among the Council of Europe instruments, at the time of writing, the ECSMA has been ratified by eighteen of the forty-seven Council of Europe members, the European Convention on Establishment by twelve, the European Convention on Social Security by eight, and the ECLSMW by eleven.[103] The EU migration directives listed above are of greater significance, as they bind between twenty-four and twenty-six EU member states.

Because of these limitations to the coverage of the migration-specific instruments, it is necessary to consider the potential contribution of general human rights standards. As before, the discussion first considers global instruments adopted within the ILO or United Nations (this part), and then those adopted at the regional level—in this case, in Europe and the Americas (part VI).[104]

A. ILO Conventions

In addition to the ILO instruments concerning migrant workers (discussed earlier in this chapter), general ILO Conventions, which apply to everyone, may be of particular importance for migrant workers. This can be illustrated by an examination of three principles which the ILO's 1998 Declaration of Fundamental Principles and Rights at Work treated as binding on all ILO Member States: freedom of association and the right to collective bargaining, the elimination of forced or compulsory labour, and the elimination of discrimination in employment.[105]

[103] Moreover, these Conventions added little to European Union law, as Turkey was the only non-EEA state which was party to the first three Conventions, while the only non-EEA parties to the ECLSMW were Albania, Moldova, Turkey, and the Ukraine.

[104] There is no discussion of the African regional human rights framework, as we could find no example of its having addressed the economic and social rights of foreign nationals.

[105] The abolition of child labour was a fourth fundamental principle listed in the Declaration, but is not discussed here as it does not appear to be of particular relevance to migrants. For a brief presentation of the Declaration and its follow-up procedure see H. Kellerson, 'The ILO Declaration of 1998 on Fundamental Principles and Rights: A Challenge for the Future', 137 *International Labour Review* (1998) 223.

The principle of freedom of association is elaborated within the ILO by the Freedom of Association and Protection of the Right to Organise Convention, 1948 (No. 87) and the Right to Organise and Collective Bargaining Convention, 1949 (No. 98). At the time of writing, these two conventions have been ratified by 152 and 163 states, respectively. The ILO's Committee on Freedom of Association (CFA) examines complaints on freedom of association and collective bargaining against all ILO members, both those that have ratified these Conventions, and those that have not. It has confirmed that Article 2 of ILO Convention No. 87 applies to *all* workers, irrespective of their immigration status. Accordingly, in 2002, the CFA ruled that it was incompatible with Convention No. 87 for Spanish legislation to exclude irregular migrants from the scope of the freedom of association.[106] In 2003, in a complaint against the United States, it found that the failure to protect irregular migrant workers against anti-union discrimination by employers was contrary to 'freedom of association principles'.[107] The principle that Convention No. 87 applies to all workers, irrespective of immigration status, was reiterated by the CFA in its 2007 ruling on a complaint against the Republic of Korea over its refusal to register a trade union which represented migrant workers.[108]

Forced labour is a second area where the ILO has adopted conventions that may be particularly pertinent to migrant workers—in this case, the Forced Labour Convention, 1930 (No. 29) and the Abolition of Forced Labour Convention, 1957 (No. 105). These two Conventions have been ratified by 177 and 174 states, respectively. Article 2, paragraph 1 of Convention No. 29 defines 'forced labour' as 'work or service exacted from any person under the menace of any penalty and for which the said person has not offered himself voluntarily'. The ILO Committee of Experts on the Application of Conventions and Recommendations (CEACR) is the body which examines state reports on compliance with ILO instruments as a whole. It has ruled that retention of passports or other legal documents is a situation that indicates the existence of coercion. This practice, combined with further elements such as physical or sexual violence, restriction of the worker's movement, debt bondage, withholding of wages or refusing to pay the worker, and threat of denunciation to the authorities, points towards the existence of forced labour.[109]

[106] *Spain (Case No. 2121)*, 23 March 2001, Report of the Committee on Freedom of Association No. 327 (Vol. LXXXV 2002 Series B, No. 1), paras 561–562.

[107] *United States (Case No. 2227)*, Report of the Committee on Freedom of Association No. 332 (Vol LXXXVI, 2003, Series B, No. 3), para. 613. As the United States has not ratified ILO Conventions Nos. 87 and 98, its government argued that it had no obligation to comply. In response, the CFA emphasized that it has a specific mandate, which stems from the ILO Constitution, to examine state compliance with both ratified and unratified Conventions: *United States (Case No. 2227)*, Report of the Committee on Freedom of Association No. 332, para. 600. This complaint arose out of the *Hoffman* decision of the US Supreme Court in 2002: see further VI, this chapter.

[108] *Republic of Korea (Case No. 2620)*, 18 December 2007, Report of the Committee on Freedom of Association No. 353 (Vol XCII 2009 Series B, No. 1), para. 788.

[109] International Labour Office, *Human Trafficking and Forced Labour Exploitation: Guidance for Legislation and Law Enforcement* (2005) 19–21.

In the field of non-discrimination, the Discrimination (Employment and Occupation) Convention, 1958 (No. 111) has been ratified by 172 states. It prohibits discrimination in employment on the grounds of 'race, colour, sex, religion, political opinion, national extraction or social origin'. It does not therefore make specific reference to nationality or immigration status as prohibited grounds, which means that migrants are not sufficiently protected by this Convention. However, the CEACR has said that migrant workers are covered by Convention No. 111 when they are discriminated against on the basis of one of the enumerated grounds.[110]

Beyond the instruments covered by the 1998 Declaration, there are other ILO Conventions which are particularly relevant to migrant workers.[111] Of special importance is the Convention on Domestic Workers, 2011 (No. 189), which takes a human rights approach to the regulation of domestic work, and has been ratified by four states. The Preamble to the Convention recognizes that domestic workers are often migrants, and its text contains provisions that are specifically addressed to their migration status. One example is Article 8, which provides that migrant domestic workers recruited in another country should be given a written offer of employment or contract containing the terms of the offer, which is enforceable in the country of destination. Importantly, recognizing that domestic workers may fear going to the authorities themselves or that they may not be aware of their rights, the Convention encourages a system of labour inspection (Article 17 (2)). The Convention is to be welcomed for emphasizing the urgency of domestic workers' claims, targeting the particularities of their sector and making them visible.[112]

B. The International Covenant on Economic, Social and Cultural Rights

The International Covenant on Economic, Social and Cultural Rights (ICESCR) is the general global instrument with the greatest significance for the labour and social rights of migrants. This is partly because of its very wide coverage, with 160 states having ratified it at the time of writing. The significance of the ICESCR is also a consequence of the work of the Committee on the Economic, Social and Cultural Rights (CESCR), which makes observations on state reports concerning implementation of the Covenant, and adopts General Comments on the interpretation of its provisions.[113]

[110] See for instance, the individual observation of the CEACR concerning Convention 111, (Australia), International Labour Conference, 89th Session, Geneva, 2001.

[111] Leading examples are the Labour Inspection Convention, 1947 (No. 81) and the Occupational Safety and Health Convention, 1981 (No. 155). For further discussion, see International Labour Office, *International Labour Migration: A Rights Based Approach* (2010), 124 ff.

[112] For analysis of the Convention, see E. Albin and V. Mantouvalou, 'The ILO Convention on Domestic Workers: From the Shadows to the Light', 41(1) *Industrial Law Journal* (2012) 67.

[113] Information concerning CESCR observations on state reports is for the period from 2000, and has been taken from the Universal Human Rights Index; available at: <http://www.universalhumanrightsindex.org/>.

Under Article 2(2) ICESCR, the contracting states guarantee that Covenant rights 'will be exercised without discrimination of any kind as to race, colour, sex, language, religion, political or other opinion, national or social origin, property, birth or other status'.[114] The relevance of the Covenant to migrants flows from the CESCR's interpretation of the concept of 'other status' to include both nationality and immigration status. As it put it, in its *General Comment No. 20 on Non-discrimination in Economic, Social and Cultural Rights* (2009):

> The ground of nationality should not bar access to Covenant rights . . . The Covenant rights apply to everyone including non-nationals, such as refugees, asylum-seekers, stateless persons, migrant workers and victims of international trafficking, regardless of legal status and documentation.[115]

Building upon that reading, the Committee has repeatedly criticized restrictions upon the labour and social rights of migrant workers and refugees. We will see however that it has been somewhat less consistent in its analysis of the position of asylum seekers and of migrants in an irregular position.

The Committee's strongest rejection of *all* discrimination on grounds of nationality or immigration status has been in relation to the right to education (Article 13 ICESCR). In *General Comment No. 13* on the subject (1999), both nationality and lack of legal status were ruled out as reasons to deny education to 'persons of school age residing in the territory of a State party'.[116] Accordingly, the CESCR has criticized states for excluding the children of migrant workers, refugees and asylum seekers from compulsory education, or for discriminating against them in relation to fees.[117] It has criticized inadequacies in the education actually provided to the children of foreign nationals, such as the failure to provide sufficient instruction in the mother tongue or in the state's official language, and the provision of a separate education system for refugee children.[118] The Committee has also taken the view that the children of irregular migrants should benefit fully from the right to education in practice.[119]

[114] Note that Art. 2(3) allows 'developing countries' to limit the *economic* rights—but not the *social* rights—of non-nationals. For a discussion, see E. V. O. Dankwa, 'Working Paper on Article 2(3) of the International Covenant on Economic, Social and Cultural Rights', 9 *Human Rights Quarterly* (1987) 230. His interpretation of the concept of 'economic' rights is similar to that set out in the Introduction: Dankwa, 239–40.

[115] CESCR, *General Comment No. 20: Non-discrimination in Economic, Social and Cultural Rights* (2009), para. 30.

[116] CESCR, *General Comment No. 13: The Right to Education* (1999), para. 34. The Committee has also taken the view that the freedom to set up educational institutions (Art. 13(4) ICESCR) should not be restricted on grounds of nationality: CESCR, *General Comment No. 13*, para. 30.

[117] In relation to migrants, see the CESCR observations on Kuwait (2004), paras 26 and 46, and on China (2005), paras 89, 101, 116, and 126 (concerning Hong Kong and Macao). In relation to refugees, see the observations on Nepal (2001), paras 29 and 54. In relation to asylum seekers, see the observations on Senegal (2001), paras 33 and 54, and Norway (2005), paras 22 and 43.

[118] CESCR observations on Sweden (2001), para. 38, Liechtenstein (2006), paras 20 and 36, and Macedonia (2008), paras 27 and 48.

[119] CESCR observations on Spain (2004), para. 7, welcoming a system that allowed access to schooling where parents registered with a local authority.

The Committee has been somewhat less clear in relation to the right to health (Article 12 ICESCR). In its *General Comment No. 14* on this right (2000), the CESCR stated that parties were obliged to '[refrain] from denying or limiting equal access for all persons, including... asylum seekers and illegal immigrants, to preventive, curative and palliative health services'.[120] The strength of that statement was that it required those lacking an immigration status to have *equal* access to *all* health services, and not only those of an urgent nature (as in the Migrant Workers Convention).[121] That approach has been reflected in recommendations that Italy 'extend the subsidized health-care system to asylum-seekers without discrimination', that Israel extend its health provisions to persons without a permanent resident permit, that Germany ensure 'equal treatment in access to... health care' for asylum seekers, and that Spain 'not limit the access of persons residing in the State... to health services, regardless of their legal situation'.[122] Elsewhere, the Committee has been less categorical, calling instead for access to 'adequate health care facilities, goods and services' for asylum seekers and irregular migrant workers and members of their families.[123] The requirement to make 'adequate' health care available, rather than all health care, presumably implies something less than full equality in health provision.

An emphasis on adequacy is also evident in the CESCR's approach to the housing of non-nationals, probably because Article 11 ICESCR itself refers to 'the right of everyone to an adequate standard of living for himself and his family, including adequate... housing'. The Committee's *General Comment No. 4* on the subject (1991) was silent in relation to non-nationals, stating simply that '[t]he right to adequate housing applies to everyone' and that 'enjoyment of this right must... not be subject to any form of discrimination'.[124] The CESCR's observations on state reports have typically focused on practical considerations—calling upon states to address the sub-standard housing of certain categories of migrant,[125] and to take measures against de facto discrimination against migrant groups in the housing market.[126] It has also complained about states' own failures to make adequate provision for current asylum seekers, for those whose applications have failed, and for irregular migrants and failed asylum seekers who are in detention.[127] It is therefore clear that the Committee considers that all foreign nationals, including irregular migrants, are covered by the right to adequate housing.

[120] CESCR, *General Comment No. 14: The Right to the Highest Attainable Standard of Health* (2000), para. 34.

[121] See V. Chetail and G. Giacca, 'Who Cares? The Right to Health of Migrants', in A. Clapham and M. Robinson (eds), *Realizing the Right to Health* (2009) 224.

[122] CESCR observations on Italy (2000), para. 32, Israel (2011), para. 31, Germany (2011), para. 13, and Spain (2012), para. 19.

[123] CESCR observations on Belgium (2008), para. 35, in relation to irregular migrant workers and their families only, and on France (2008), para. 47, in relation to asylum seekers as well.

[124] CESCR, *General Comment No. 4: The Right to Adequate Housing* (1991), para. 6.

[125] CESCR observations on Costa Rica (2008), para. 26; and Cyprus (2009), para. 21.

[126] CESCR observations on Denmark (2004), paras 21 and 34; Italy (2004), para. 46; Belgium (2008), para. 14; and France (2008), paras 21 and 41.

[127] CESCR observations on Switzerland (2010), para. 18; Norway (2005), paras 19 and 38; and Cyprus (2009), para. 22, respectively.

Under the Covenant, access to social provision is covered both by the right to social security set out in Article 9 ICESCR and by the right to an 'adequate standard of living' in Article 11 ICESCR. The Committee has frequently criticized states for restricting or delaying migrant workers' access to social security schemes.[128] In addition, in *General Comment No. 19 on The Right to Social Security* (2005), the Committee declared that 'non-nationals should be able to access non-contributory schemes for income support', and that 'refugees, stateless persons and asylum-seekers . . . should enjoy equal treatment in access to non-contributory social security schemes'.[129] That statement must however be read in the light of its call for Austria (2006) to ensure 'adequate social support' for this category.[130] The Committee has also contemplated more limited forms of support for failed asylum applicants and irregular migrants.[131] Its position therefore appears to be that all persons, irrespective of status, are entitled to at least a basic form of social support—probably aimed at subsistence—rather than full equal treatment in social assistance and social security.

In the field of labour rights, the most complex questions concern the scope of the right to work (Article 6 ICESCR). In its *General Comment No. 18* on the subject (2005), the CESCR listed protection from forced labour, policies to assist the unemployed, access to work, and non-discrimination in employment opportunities as falling within this right.[132] The Committee's observations on the right to work of foreign nationals have emphasized the need to address comparatively high levels of unemployment among migrants, and discrimination against foreign nationals in the labour market, where these occur.[133] It is evident from these observations that the CESCR considers that long-term resident foreign nationals and recognized refugees benefit fully from Article 6. CESCR observations concerning the United Kingdom (2009) and Germany (2011) have shown that it also considers asylum seekers to be covered by the principle of equal access to work,[134] and we must presume that they are also therefore covered by the other elements of the right to work listed above. In addition, the Committee has criticized state policies which do not give workers whose right to stay is linked to a specific employment

[128] CESCR observations on Australia (2000), para. 32; Jordan (2000), para. 19; Kuwait (2004), paras 20 and 40; China (2005), paras 84, 96, 114, and 124 (in relation to Hong Kong and Macao); Monaco (2006), paras 10 and 18; and San Marino (2008), paras 13 and 25.

[129] CESCR, *General Comment No. 19: The Right to Social Security* (2008), paras 37 and 38.

[130] CESCR observations on Austria (2006), para. 29.

[131] CESCR observations on the United Kingdom (2009), para. 27 (both groups); and Switzerland (2010), para. 12 (irregular migrants).

[132] CESCR, *General Comment No. 18: The Right to Work* (2005), paras 9 and 12.

[133] In relation to unemployment, see CESCR observations on Denmark (2004), paras 15 and 26; Belgium (2008), paras 16 and 30; Sweden (2008), para. 20; Australia (2009), para. 18; and Switzerland (2010), para. 9. In relation to discrimination, see CESCR observations on Sweden (2001), para. 29; and Azerbaijan (2004), para. 15.

[134] In its concluding observations on the United Kingdom (2009), the CESCR 'encourage[d]' it 'to ensure that asylum-seekers are not restricted in their access to the labour market while their claims for asylum are being processed' (para. 27). It has also called on Germany (2011) to 'ensure, in line with international standards, that asylum-seekers enjoy equal treatment in access to . . . [sic] labour market' (para. 13). In addition, in the case of Slovakia (2012), para. 13, the CESCR criticized a waiting period of one year before asylum seekers gained access to the labour market.

sufficient opportunity to find a new employer when the initial employment comes to an end.[135] What is uncertain is the extent to which these workers also benefit from protection against discrimination in hiring decisions, or from policies aimed at reducing unemployment. Finally, the Committee has to date been silent as to the position of irregular migrant workers. While it appears unlikely that they benefit from rights concerning access to employment, nevertheless, they arguably ought to be included within the principle against forced labour, as they have a particular need for that protection.

The principle that 'everyone' has 'the right . . . to the enjoyment of just and favourable conditions of work' (Article 7 ICESCR) has featured prominently in Committee observations concerning foreign workers. It has expressed concern at the concentration of migrants in the informal economy, on the grounds that they are likely to lack security and/or protection against poor terms and conditions.[136] It has also expressed concern at insufficient labour market enforcement activity on the part of state authorities where migrant workers face exploitative treatment—both in general,[137] and in the particular cases of migrant domestic workers[138] and migrant workers in agriculture.[139] In addition, the Committee has criticized gaps in labour law: both the exclusion of foreign workers as a whole, and the specific exclusion of domestic workers, as that is an occupation in which foreign nationals are highly represented.[140] Finally, it has been clear that both the protection of labour law, and related enforcement measures, should cover workers in an irregular position.[141] There therefore appear to be no categories of foreign national which are not fully protected by Article 7 ICESCR.

Article 8 ICECSR provides for freedom of association into trade unions, including 'the right of everyone to form trade unions and join the trade union of his choice', 'the right of trade unions to function freely', and the right to strike. In this area, the CESCR has criticized the exclusion of foreign nationals from the right to join trade unions,[142] their exclusion from holding trade union office,[143] and their being 'denied participation in trade union activities' in practice.[144] In addition—as in the case of Article 6—the Committee has been explicit that trade union rights

[135] CESCR observations on China (2001), para. 15 and (2005), paras 78 and 95; and South Korea (2009), para. 21.

[136] CESCR observations on Russia (2003), paras 17 and 45; Serbia (2005), para. 17; Costa Rica (2008), paras 19 and 38; and Kenya (2008), para. 13.

[137] CESCR observations on Kuwait (2004), para. 16; Cyprus (2009), para. 14; South Korea (2009), paras 18 and 21; and the United Kingdom (2009), para. 22.

[138] CESCR observations on Spain (2004), paras 15 and 32; China (2005), para. 83 (in relation to Hong Kong); Canada (2006), para. 49; and Costa Rica (2008), para. 18.

[139] CESCR observations on Kazakhstan (2010), para. 20.

[140] CESCR observations on Jordan (2000), para. 19 (foreign nationals excluded from minimum wage); and Kuwait (2004), paras 17 and 27 (domestic workers excluded from coverage of labour law).

[141] CESCR observations on the Dominican Republic (2010), para. 18.

[142] CESCR observations on Kuwait (2004), paras 18 and 38; and Peru (2012), para. 12.

[143] CESCR observations on Senegal (2010), paras 22 and 44.

[144] CESCR observations on Jordan (2000), para. 19.

apply to workers in an irregular position.[145] This absence of limits to the trade union rights of foreign nationals may be contrasted with the convoluted position under the Migrant Workers Convention (discussed earlier in the chapter).

C. The International Covenant on Civil and Political Rights

The contribution of the International Covenant on Civil and Political Rights (ICCPR) to the economic and social rights of foreign nationals may be addressed more briefly.[146] The ICCPR is of potential interest because 167 states are parties to it. Moreover, in its *General Comment on The Position of Aliens under the Covenant*, published in 1986, the Human Rights Committee (HRC) set out the general view that, unless otherwise stated in the Covenant, the rights it contained applied 'to everyone, irrespective of reciprocity, and irrespective of his or her nationality or statelessness'.[147]

The ICCPR contains only two provisions which clearly address labour and social rights. The first is the prohibition on forced labour in Article 8(3). Relying upon Article 8, in 2001 the HRC expressed its concern at 'the failure to protect Haitians living or working in the Dominican Republic from serious human rights abuses such as forced labour'.[148] The prohibition on forced labour was also cited in criticism of Thailand in 2005, when the Committee's assessment was that '[t]he deplorable conditions in which migrants are obliged to live and work indicate serious violations of [article 8] of the Covenant'.[149]

The second ICCPR provision of relevance is Article 22, which recognizes the right of association into trade unions. The HRC expressed its concern that in Kuwait (2000) the rights to form trade unions and to take part in their activities were 'restricted *de facto*' for both foreign and domestic workers.[150] Article 22 ICCPR was referred to as one of the rights that should be guaranteed to Haitian workers in the Dominican Republic (2001), in order to address their poor working and living conditions.[151] In the same vein, in the case of South Korea (2006), the HRC noted that 'migrant workers face[d] persistent discriminatory treatment and abuse in the workplace, and [were] not provided with adequate protection and redress', and recommended that the state ensure that migrant workers enjoyed Covenant rights, including the right to form trade unions.[152]

145 CESCR observations on South Korea (2009), para. 21; and the Dominican Republic (2010), para. 18.

146 The discussion here of HRC observations on state reports is for the period from 2000 only, and draws upon the Universal Human Rights Index; available at: <http://www.universalhumanrightsindex.org/>. We are unaware of any examples of individual complaints to the Human Rights Committee that concerned the economic and social rights of foreign nationals.

147 HRC, *General Comment No. 15: The Position of Aliens under the Covenant* (1986), para. 1.

148 HRC observations on the Dominican Republic (2001), para. 17.

149 HRC observations on Thailand (2005), para. 23.

150 HRC observations on Kuwait (2000), para. 22.

151 HRC observations on the Dominican Republic (2001), para. 17.

152 HRC observations on South Korea (2006), para. 12.

In its comments concerning Thailand and South Korea (which have been referred to earlier), the HRC also commented on deficiencies in the remedies available to migrant workers who faced discriminatory or exploitative conditions at work. Here, the Committee relied on the non-discrimination principles contained within the Covenant: Article 2, under which a contracting state 'undertakes to respect and to ensure to all individuals within its territory and subject to its jurisdiction the rights recognized in the present Covenant, without distinction of any kind', and Article 26, which requires states to '[prohibit] any discrimination and guarantee to all persons equal and effective protection against discrimination'.[153] Through this creative use of non-discrimination principles to call for effective remedies, the HRC has given partial recognition under the ICCPR to the right to fair conditions at work, usually taken to be protected under Article 7 ICESCR (discussed earlier).

VI. Regional Human Rights Instruments

We saw in part IV that, with the exception of those adopted at European Union level, regional migration-specific instruments are limited in their provision for the labour and social rights of migrants. The Council of Europe instruments on the subject are constrained by reciprocity rules, and generally do not cater for persons who are not lawfully resident. In other regions, moreover, there are no specific instruments of any kind on the subject.

In this part we will see that general human rights instruments at the regional level have gone some way to redress that deficit, particularly in relation to persons in an irregular position. The Council of Europe has two general human rights documents with implications for the labour and social rights of migrants. Because of the subject matter of this chapter, the European Social Charter (ESC), adopted in 1961, which guarantees labour and social rights, will be considered first, before a consideration of the implications in the socio-economic field of the European Convention on Human Rights (ECHR), adopted in 1950, which primarily concerns civil and political rights. The part will then examine the provision for labour and social rights made within the American regional human rights system.

A. European Social Charter

The ESC protects labour and social rights, and is gradually being replaced by the Revised ESC, which entered into force in 1999. Of the forty-seven Member States of the Council of Europe, forty-three have ratified either the 1961 or the 1996 ESC.[154]

[153] HRC observations on Thailand (2005), para. 23 (Art. 26 only); and South Korea (2006), para. 12 (Arts 2 and 26).

[154] At the time of writing, the 1961 Charter has been ratified by twenty-seven states, and the Revised ESC by thirty-two states. Liechtenstein, Monaco, San Marino, and Switzerland have not ratified either version.

The Charter has a particularity that distinguishes it from other human rights documents, in that it allows contracting parties discretion as to the rights by which they will be bound. There are seven core provisions in the ESC, of which five must be ratified. Some provisions that are applicable to migrants and are discussed below are included in these core provisions.[155] The Revised ESC contains a similar undertaking.[156] The Charter initially contained no complaints procedure, but rather a reporting obligation, with the European Committee of Social Rights (ECSR) assessing state compliance in its conclusions. Today, the ECSR also has jurisdiction over collective complaints, brought by international organizations of employers and employees, national representative organizations of employers and employees, and some international non-governmental organizations, under the Collective Complaints Protocol, which entered into force in 1998.

Article 12 ESC sets out a right to social security, and includes provision for contracting states to 'take steps' to ensure both the equal treatment of foreign nationals and the retention of benefits arising out of periods of employment and insurance in other contracting states (Article 12(4)). The ESC also includes a right to social and medical assistance (Article 13), which is to apply 'on an equal footing... to nationals of other Contracting Parties lawfully within their territories', in accordance with the obligations under the ECSMA 1953 (Article 13(4)). The ECSR has concluded that this paragraph applies to nationals of contracting parties who are lawfully present in another contracting state, even if they do not have a legal right of residence in its territory.[157]

In relation to the right to work, Article 18 of the Charter provides for the right of nationals of contracting states to engage in a gainful occupation in other contracting states. This article provides that existing regulations should be applied in a spirit of liberality, that formalities ought to be simplified, and that regulations on the employment of foreign workers should be liberalized. It also recognizes the right of nationals of contracting states to leave their home country so as to engage in gainful occupation in other member states. The ECSR has examined the question of expulsion following the loss of a job and has stated that 'the threat of being obliged to leave the host country... in fact constitutes an infringement of the freedom of the individual that it cannot be regarded as evidence of "a spirit of liberality" or of liberal regulations'.[158]

Article 19 provides for a right of migrant workers and their families to 'protection and assistance' when 'in the territory of any other Contracting Party'. From as early as its first set of Conclusions, the ECSR said that the provision's aim was to assist

[155] The core provisions are Art. 1 (right to work), Art. 5 (right to organize), Art. 6 (right to bargain collectively), Art. 12 (right to social security), Art. 13 (right to social and medical assistance), Art. 16 (right of the family to social, legal and economic protection), and Art. 19 (right of migrant workers to protection and assistance).

[156] States must sign up to six out of nine core provisions of the Revised ESC, which adds Art. 6 (right of children and young persons to protection), and Art. 20 (the right to equal opportunities and equal treatment in matters of employment and occupation without discrimination on the grounds of sex).

[157] Conclusions XIII-4 (1996) at 60–1.

[158] Conclusions XIII-1 (1995) at 262.

migrant workers and their families.[159] In its view, the challenges that migrants face mean that equal treatment between foreign and national workers may be insufficient, and that positive action towards migrants may be required. Under Article 19 (4), contracting states undertake to secure for 'workers lawfully within their territories' treatment not less favourable than that given to their own nationals in three areas, in so far as these are regulated by law or regulations, or are subject to the control of administrative authorities: 'remuneration and other employment and working conditions'; 'membership of trade unions and enjoyment of the benefits of collective bargaining'; and, accommodation. This provision mirrors Article 6(1)(a) of ILO Convention No. 97 (discussed earlier). In the work of the ECSR, the phrase 'employment and working conditions' has been interpreted to cover vocational training.[160] In relation to union membership, the ECSR has found, for instance, that Turkey did not comply with its obligations because it restricted the union membership of migrant workers.[161] The Committee has also emphasized the importance of accommodation to migrant workers and their families, and has criticized states that make public assistance with housing conditional upon the length of employment.[162]

The express personal scope of the Charter is narrow, in much the same way that the Council of Europe's migration-specific instruments are (see part IV above). In the first place, the benefits of the Charter are limited to nationals of other contracting states. A provision in the Appendix to both the ESC and the Revised ESC on the 'Scope of the Social Charter in Terms of Persons Protected' confines Articles 1 to 17 to 'foreigners only insofar as they are nationals of other Contracting Parties'. The same limitation arises in the text of Articles 18 and 19, as indicated earlier. The Appendix to the Revised European Social Charter sets out exceptions for refugees and stateless persons lawfully staying in the territory of a contracting state. These categories are to be treated as favourably as possible, and in any event no less favourably than is required of the given contracting state under its obligations under the Refugee Convention of 1951, the 1967 Protocol, the Convention on the Status of Stateless Persons 1954, and other international treaties.[163]

Secondly, persons in an irregular position appear to be excluded from the scope of the Charter's substantive Articles other than Articles 18 and 19. This is achieved by a reference in the Appendix to 'nationals of other Contracting Parties lawfully resident or working regularly within the territory of the Contracting Party'. There is however a caveat—the precise implications of which are unclear—that the narrow personal scope of those Articles is 'subject to the understanding that these Articles are to be interpreted in the light of the provisions of Articles 18 and 19'.

Recently, the ECSR has attempted to address the limitations on the personal scope of the ESC in the context of collective complaints. In the case *International Federation of Human Rights Leagues (FIDH) v. France*, the lack of access to healthcare

[159] Conclusions I (1969) at 81. [160] Conclusions VII (1981) at 103.

[161] Conclusions XIII-3 (1995) at 418. [162] Conclusions I (1969) at 215.

[163] The equivalent provision in the 1961 European Social Charter refers only to refugees, and only specifically mentions the 1951 Refugee Convention.

of children of undocumented migrants was held to breach the right of children and young persons to social, legal, and economic protection under Article 17 of the Revised ESC.[164] While that conclusion appeared contrary to the clear wording of the Appendix, the Committee ruled that the exclusion of irregular migrants would be contrary to human dignity, which constitutes one of the document's most fundamental underlying values.[165] This interpretation was confirmed in a subsequent ruling against the Netherlands, which held that the exclusion of children in an irregular position from access to housing was a breach of the specific right to housing in Article 31 of the Revised ESC, and the right of migrants to protection in Article 17.[166]

The decision to interpret the Appendix in a manner apparently opposed to its wording is not uncontroversial. It is difficult to predict with certainty whether the Committee would be prepared to extend the coverage of other Charter Articles to irregular migrants. It may be that it was willing to extend the coverage of the Charter only in cases of those that are most vulnerable, namely migrant children. More fundamentally, it might have been preferable for a re-examination of the personal scope of the ESC to be achieved through a revision of the text, so as to extend key principles of protection to irregular migrants. In that way, the ECSR would not find itself in the invidious situation of feeling compelled to disregard the wording of the documents that it interprets.

B. European Convention on Human Rights

Like the ICCPR, which was discussed earlier, the ECHR protects civil and political rights. Even though the ECHR does not contain social rights, the European Court of Human Rights (ECtHR) stated early on in its case law, in *Airey v. Ireland*, that there is no watertight division between the Convention and the area of socio-economic rights.[167] In recent years, the Court has adopted what has come to be known as an 'integrated approach' to interpretation.[168] In the case of the ECHR, that approach has meant that certain labour and social labour rights are treated as essential elements of what is primarily a civil and political rights document, and protected as such.[169]

[164] *International Federation of Human Rights Leagues (FIDH) v. France*, ECSR (2004) Complaint No. 14/2003, Decision of 8 September 2004.

[165] *International Federation of Human Rights Leagues (FIDH) v. France*, paras 26 ff.

[166] *Defence for Children International (DCI) v. Netherlands*, ECSR (2009) Complaint No. 47/2008, Decision of 20 October 2009.

[167] *Airey v. Ireland*, ECHR (1979) Series A, No. 32, Appl. No. 6289/73, judgment of 9 October 1979.

[168] See M. Scheinin, 'Economic and Social Rights as Legal Rights', in A. Eide, C. Krause, and A. Rosas (eds), *Economic, Social and Cultural Rights: A Textbook* (2001) 32, and V. Mantouvalou, 'Labour Rights in the European Convention on Human Rights: An Intellectual Justification for an Integrated Approach to Interpretation', 13 *Human Rights Law Review* (2013) (forthcoming; available at: <http://doi:10.1093/hrlr/ngt001>).

[169] See *Sidabras and Dziautas v. Lithuania*, ECHR (2004) Appl. Nos. 55480/00 and 59330/00, judgment of 27 July 2004. For analysis, see V. Mantouvalou, 'Work and Private Life: *Sidabras and Dziautas v Lithuania*', 30 *European Law Review* (2005) 573.

Article 3 ECHR, which prohibits torture and inhuman or degrading treatment or punishment, is of particular relevance to migrants. In the case of *M.S.S. v. Belgium and Greece*, the Grand Chamber of the European Court of Human Rights examined whether the extreme poverty in which an asylum seeker lived in Greece, while his asylum application was pending, was compatible with that prohibition.[170] The applicant had found himself homeless with no access to sanitary facilities; had slept in fear that he would be attacked; and had spent days looking for food, receiving some material support only from passers-by and a church. His claim before the Court was that his situation amounted to such vulnerability and deprivation that it breached Article 3. In response, the Greek government argued that the Convention did not contain a right to asylum or a right to housing, which raised budgetary issues. Nevertheless, the Court held that 'the applicant had been the victim of humiliating treatment showing a lack of respect of his dignity and . . . this situation has, without doubt, aroused in him feelings of fear, anguish or inferiority capable of inducing desperation'.[171] As these living conditions were due to the inaction of the authorities, Greece was in breach of Article 3. It is significant that in *M.S.S.* the Court took note of budgetary limitations that Greece faced because of an economic crisis, but ruled that such circumstances could not absolve a contracting state from its duties under Article 3, which contains an absolute prohibition.[172]

Article 4 ECHR, which prohibits slavery, servitude, and forced and compulsory labour, is a second provision from which migrants may benefit. The landmark case of *Siliadin v. France* illustrated the operation of an integrated approach to interpretation.[173] It involved a migrant domestic worker from Togo who lived and worked in appalling conditions in France. The Court did not classify the situation as 'slavery' because the employers did not exercise a right of legal ownership over the applicant, but did find that the situation amounted to 'servitude, forced and compulsory labour'. The applicant's immigration status was viewed as a factor that made her particularly prone to exploitation. The Court placed special emphasis on the fact that she had been promised by her employers that her status would be regularized—something that never occurred—and on her fear that she would be arrested, which as the Court stressed, the employers further nurtured.[174] In relation to France, the Court held that the lack of legislation criminalizing these extremely harsh working conditions amounted to a breach of Article 4. In support of the imposition of positive obligations on the state, the Court made reference to the ILO Forced Labour Convention, 1929 (No. 30), which contains a special provision on the horizontal application of the prohibition on private individuals.

[170] *M.S.S. v. Belgium and Greece*, ECHR (2011), Appl. No. 30696/09, judgment of 21 January 2011 (GC). For analysis see G. Clayton, 'Asylum Seekers in Europe: *M.S.S. v Belgium and Greece*', 11 *Human Rights Law Review* (2011) 758.

[171] *M.S.S.* (n 170), para. 263.

[172] *M.S.S.* (n 170), para. 223.

[173] *Siliadin v. France*, ECHR (2005) Appl. No. 73316/01, judgment of 26 July 2005. For analysis, see V. Mantouvalou, 'Servitude and Forced Labour in the 21st Century: The Human Rights of Domestic Workers', 35 *Industrial Law Journal* (2006) 135. On the social rights of domestic workers, see also V. Mantouvalou, 'Human Rights for Precarious Workers: The Legislative Precariousness of Domestic Labor', 34 *Comparative Labor Law and Policy Journal* (2012) 133.

[174] See, for example, paras 118 and 126.

The situation of migrant domestic workers was again examined in the case of *C.N. v. United Kingdom.*[175] The applicant had entered the United Kingdom unlawfully, and worked as a live-in domestic worker for an elderly couple, with only one afternoon off per month. During her employment, her wages were withheld in order to pay off a debt of which she was unaware, her passport was withheld, and she was threatened with denunciation to the authorities. When she did contact the authorities, the police investigation unit specializing in human trafficking concluded that there was no evidence of that offence. At the time (2007–2009) there was no legislation in the United Kingdom criminalizing slavery, servitude, or forced or compulsory labour. The absence of such legislation was incompatible with the Convention, as *Siliadin* had already shown. In addition, the Court ruled that the authorities had not had an adequate basis to investigate the offence of 'domestic servitude', which was the aspect of Article 4 at issue in the case. This ineffective investigation on the part of the authorities, due to the lack of criminal legislation, was also ruled to have breached Article 4 of the Convention.

The Convention contains a non-discrimination provision (Article 14), which is not a free-standing equality right; instead, it prohibits discrimination in the enjoyment of the rest of the Convention rights. It also contains a right of everyone to the peaceful enjoyment of their possessions (Article 1 of Additional Protocol 1). These two provisions were examined in the case of *Gaygusuz v. Austria*, which concerned the social security benefits of foreign nationals.[176] The applicant was a Turkish national lawfully resident and working in Austria, who had paid contributions to an unemployment insurance fund in the same way as Austrian nationals. The authorities refused to pay an advance on his pension as an emergency payment under Austrian legislation for the sole reason that he did not have Austrian nationality. Reading social rights into the right to property and in this way adopting an integrated approach to the interpretation of the Convention, the ECtHR held that the benefit that Mr Gaygusuz claimed could be classified as 'possessions', so that his claim was within the ambit of Article 1 of Additional Protocol 1. Turning to Article 14, the Court considered whether the difference of treatment between the applicant and Austrian nationals was justified, and ruled that it was not based on an 'objective and reasonable justification'. There was therefore a violation of the prohibition of discrimination in conjunction with the right to property. A similar finding was later made in the case *Koua Poirrez v. France*, where the authorities refused a non-contributory disability benefit to the applicant, who was a lawful resident in France.[177] The refusal of the authorities was again ruled to breach Article 14, in conjunction with Article 1 of Protocol 1.

This case law shows that the ECtHR recognizes an overlap between civil, political, economic, and social rights.[178] The coverage of the ECHR, as developed

[175] *CN v. UK*, ECHR (2012) Appl. No. 4239/08, judgment of 13 November 2012.

[176] *Gaygusuz v. Austria*, ECHR (1996) Appl. No. 17371/90, judgment of 16 September 1996.

[177] *Koua Poirrez v. France*, ECHR (2003) Appl. No. 40892/98, judgment of 30 September 2003.

[178] Cf. *N v. UK*, ECHR (2008) Appl. No. 26565/05, judgment of 27 May 2008 (GC). For criticism of *N v. UK*, see V. Mantouvalou, '*N v UK*: No Duty to Rescue the Nearby Needy?', 72 *Modern Law Review* (2009) 815.

through the case law of the Court, appears to address some of the shortcomings of the ESC with its narrow personal scope. The ECtHR does not hesitate to extend the scope of protection to irregular migrants when faced with grave hardship in circumstances that can fall within the scope of the ECHR, and is willing to find that the discriminatory treatment of migrant workers is incompatible with the Convention.

C. The Organization of American States

The key regional organization in the Americas is the Organization of American States (OAS), which has thirty-five member states. It has adopted three significant texts in the field of human rights. The first was the American Declaration of the Rights and Duties of Man (1948). It mainly covers civil and political rights, but also includes three labour and social rights: the right to health (Article XI), the right to education (Article XII) and the right to work (Article XIV). The second is the American Convention on Human Rights (ACHR) (1978).[179] It focuses on civil and political rights, and its only provision concerning labour and social rights is a general, vague provision for the 'progressive implementation' of those rights (Article 26). The third is the Additional Protocol in the Area of Economic, Social and Cultural Rights (the San Salvador Protocol), which was adopted in 1988 and entered into force in 1999. Labour and social rights included in the San Salvador Protocol are the right to work, which makes reference to states' duty to promote full employment (Article 6), the right to just conditions of work, including a right to decent remuneration, rest, and leisure (Article 7), trade union rights (Article 8), the right to social security (Article 9) and the right to health (Article 10).

The ACHR protects the rights of everyone within the contracting states' jurisdiction, irrespective of national origin (Article 1). The San Salvador Protocol contains a similar obligation (Article 3), which is also emphasized in its Preamble, which states: 'the essential rights of man are not derived from one's being a national of a certain State, but are based upon attributes of the human person, for which reason they merit international protection in the form of a convention reinforcing or complementing the protection provided by the domestic law of the American States'.

The American Convention on Human Rights is monitored by the Inter-American Court of Human Rights (IACtHR), where individuals can lodge an application for an alleged violation of rights under the Convention. An integrated approach to interpretation, which reads certain labour and social rights in a civil and political rights document, has appeared in the case law under the ACHR as well.[180] Two

[179] For a discussion of the relationship between the Declaration and the Convention, see M. Craven, 'The Protection of Economic, Social and Cultural Rights under the Inter-American System of Human Rights', in D. Harris and S. Livingstone (eds), *The Inter-American System of Human Rights* (1998) 292.

[180] See the discussion in T. Melish, 'Rethinking the "Less as More" Thesis: Supranational Litigation of Economic, Social and Cultural Rights in the Americas', 39 *NYU Journal of International Law and Politics* (2006–2007) 171, at 193 ff.

landmark cases under the ACHR illustrate the expansive approach that the IACtHR has taken to the question of the social rights of migrants.

The first of these is the IACtHR's much-discussed advisory opinion on the rights of undocumented migrants.[181] This opinion was adopted in response to a question brought by the government of Mexico, as to whether it was lawful to exclude undocumented migrants from access to labour rights. While that question did not refer to a particular state, it was understood to relate to the decision of the US Supreme Court in *Hoffman Plastic Compounds v. NLRB*,[182] in which undocumented migrant workers were denied back-pay for lost wages, after their dismissal for attempts to organize a trade union. The IACtHR ruled that the exclusion of undocumented migrants from labour rights breached international principles of equality before the law and non-discrimination, which it recognized as norms of *jus cogens*. The Court accepted that it would be compatible with human rights law to deny employment to undocumented migrants, but emphasized that it would not be lawful to deny labour rights once someone is already employed. In its words:

> Labor rights necessarily arise from the circumstance of being a worker, understood in the broadest sense. A person who is to be engaged, is engaged or has been engaged in a remunerated activity, immediately becomes a worker and, consequently, acquires the rights inherent in that condition . . . [T]he migratory status of a person can never be a justification for depriving him of the enjoyment and exercise of his human rights, including those related to employment.[183]

The Court's advisory opinion suggests that, while the state has no duty to provide employment to undocumented migrants, once they are employed, they are protected equally with other workers.[184]

The second case is *Yean and Bosico Children v. the Dominican Republic*, which involved stateless children.[185] The applicants were two girls born and raised in the Dominican Republic, but who were of Haitian ancestry. Against a background of prejudice and discrimination against individuals of Haitian descent, when their parents applied for their birth certificate in order for the girls to attend school, the authorities refused it to them. The reason for the refusal was that they were not recognized as nationals of the Dominican Republic. The IACtHR held that that was discriminatory and breached the ACHR. It rendered the children stateless, and therefore unable to have access to several rights, including the right to education. It ruled that '[t]he State should comply with its obligation to guarantee access to free primary education for all children, irrespective of their origin or parentage, which arises from the special protection that must be provided to children'.[186]

181 *Juridical Condition and Rights of the Undocumented Migrants*, IACtHR (2003) Series A No. 18, Advisory Opinion OC-18/03, 17 September 2003.

182 535 US 137 (2002).

183 Paras 133–134.

184 For a case note, see S. Cleveland, 'Legal Status and Rights of Undocumented Workers', 99 *American Journal of International Law* (2005) 460.

185 *Yean and Bosico Children v the Dominican Republic*, IACtHR (2005) Series C, No. 130, 8 September 2005.

186 Para. 244.

These two decisions show that there is scope for the effective protection of the labour and social rights of irregular migrants within the Inter-American human rights system. In both cases, migrants who had lived and worked without legal documentation in a country, have been protected by the Court, which has focused on foundational values of human rights law—values such as dignity—rather than nationality and lawful residence.

VII. Conclusion

The initial aim of this chapter was to document the ways in which contemporary international law addresses the labour and social rights of migrants. It has shown that these questions are now covered in international texts specifically concerned with migration adopted within the ILO, United Nations, Council of Europe and European Union. It has also given evidence of a particular emphasis upon migrants' labour and social rights on the part of supervisory bodies, including the Committee on Migrant Workers, the CESCR, the ILO Committee on Freedom of Association, the European Committee of Social Rights, the European Court of Human Rights and the Inter-American Court of Human Rights. On the evidence of this chapter, these committees and courts are far freer to accept that *all* persons are eligible for key labour and social rights than the political actors who negotiate migration-specific texts.

The widespread interest in the labour market and social position of migrants within international law is presumably linked to the growth in international migration, and to the rise in political controversy concerning it, in developed countries and elsewhere. This chapter suggests that it also has another source: a fundamental evolution in the international law approach to the treatment of foreign nationals. The traditional view—that the treatment of foreigners is an aspect of the relationship between the two states in question—characterized pre-1945 international law. It was also evident in the reciprocity limit to the Council of Europe conventions concerning migrants adopted between 1953 and 1977. The first departures from that approach came with the provision for refugees and stateless persons and ILO Conventions on migrant workers. The move beyond reciprocity has become clearer over the past twenty-five years, as is evidenced by the Migrant Workers Convention of 1990, the European Union norms adopted since 2003, and the supervisory body activity already discussed. The presumption today in international law is that all migrants are entitled to equal treatment in the labour market and in social provision.

The main controversies in the contemporary context concern the position of irregular migrants. There is now clear support for the right of irregular migrant workers to the full protection of labour law, both in international texts and in the work of supervisory bodies. Similarly, there is clear support for the equal treatment of irregular migrants in respect of schooling. In the case of other social rights, meanwhile, the emerging consensus is for equal access to a basic level of social support and a basic level of health care, but not necessarily more than that.

It may perhaps be objected that a focus on international standards is too abstract, as states continue to limit the labour and social rights of migrants with short periods of residence, asylum seekers, and those without status. Our response to any such objection is that international norms, and related supervisory activity, define the limits of acceptable policies in a perennially controversial field. The emerging international consensus concerning labour and social rights is of potential relevance within national level debates, even in those states that are not fully bound by the international standards examined here.

6

Human Rights and Immigration at Sea

Tullio Scovazzi

I. Introduction: The Asymmetrical Right to Emigrate

Immigration at sea is a subject matter that needs to be understood in a broad perspective. This chapter will first address a number of questions of the international law of the sea, relating to the different regimes that apply to immigration in different kinds of maritime waters. It will then deal with the international crime of smuggling migrants by sea and with the rules aiming at ensuring the safety of human life at sea. It will finally consider the human rights that must be granted to migrants in general and to refugees in particular.[1]

A complication is the fact that the legal status of the human beings who are the subjects of this chapter varies according to whether they are to be considered illegal migrants, persons in distress at sea, or refugees. Moreover, in certain cases they could simultaneously satisfy the requirements of two or even three of these qualifications.

A further complication is due to the presence of so-called asymmetrical human rights. Under Article 13(2) of the 1948 Universal Declaration of Human Rights, every individual has the right to leave any country, including his own. The same rule can be found in Article 12(2) of the 1966 International Covenant on Civil and Political Rights. If the human right to emigrate can be considered as generally recognized, it remains an asymmetrical right, since it is not complemented by a corresponding right to immigrate.[2] As a general rule and unless different provisions are applicable under treaties in force, any state has the right to permit or prohibit migrant aliens to enter its territory and to adopt legislation governing and restricting the entry of aliens.

Yet legislation restricting the right to immigrate is in force in many states for different and more or less understandable reasons, such as to preserve the welfare or the cultural identity of a country which receives massive waves of immigration. But, looking at the question from the point of view of the human being, what is the meaning of a right to emigrate without a corresponding right to immigrate? Where

[1] For the relevant documents see United Nations High Commissioner for Refugees, *Rescue at Sea, Stowaways and Maritime Interception: Selected Reference Materials* (2011).

[2] For another asymmetrical right, see III.C, this chapter.

should emigrants be entitled to settle? In the unclaimed sector of Antarctica? On the high seas? On the moon or in outer space?

In fact, there is no human right to mobility. Even in a globalized world, goods and capital can move freely, but not human beings. If they want to escape from poverty or conflict, humans are often driven to cross borders clandestinely and illegally at the cost of great suffering, including risk to life, threats by criminals, and social vulnerability after arriving somewhere and living there irregularly. Just one example of this occurs regularly across the border between Mexico and the United States, which is increasingly open to the free circulation of goods and capital, as a result of the 1982 North American Free Trade Agreement. But today, that same border is virtually a military zone, designed to prevent illegal migration.[3] Some semi-enclosed seas, such as the Mediterranean or the Red Sea, are today the graveyard of too many human beings who are merely trying to find a place where they can live in decent conditions.

II. The International Law of the Sea

A. Immigration at sea in the different marine jurisdictional zones

By definition, a migrant (or immigrant or emigrant, depending on the point of view) is someone who crosses a border to leave the territory of a state and to settle in the territory of another state. Immigration is illegal if the crossing of the border occurs without complying with the legal requirements for entry into the state of destination.

A number of rules of the international law of the sea, as reflected in customary international law and codified in the 1982 United Nations Convention on the Law of the Sea (UNCLOS),[4] are relevant in discussing questions of migration at sea. The classical approach of the international law of the sea is rooted in the question of jurisdiction, in order to determine which state can exercise state powers over ships found in the different areas into which the sea is divided for the purposes of international law.

1. The territorial sea

The territory of a state includes a land portion and, in the case of a coastal state, also a maritime portion. Under Article 2(1) UNCLOS, 'the sovereignty of a coastal State extends, beyond its land territory and internal waters and, in the case of an

[3] See U. Leanza (ed.), *Le migrazioni—Una sfida per il diritto internazionale, comunitario ed interno* (2005); S. Quadri, *Le migrazioni internazionali* (2006). For a challenge to conventional views on the need to control and restrict migration, see A. Pécoud and P. de Guchteneire (eds), *Migration without Borders* (2007).

[4] This treaty entered into force on 16 November 1994 and is today (February 2013) binding on 165 states and one international organization (the European Union). Unless explicitly provided, all further references to treaty articles in this part refer to UNCLOS.

archipelagic State, its archipelagic waters, to an adjacent belt of sea, described as the territorial sea'. The breadth of the territorial sea cannot exceed 12 nautical miles from the baselines from which the territorial sea is measured (Article 3).[5] This means that for the purposes of immigration at sea, the territory of a state goes as far as the breadth it has established for its territorial sea.

An exception to the rule that the territorial sea is fully subject to the sovereignty of the coastal state is the right of innocent passage that is granted to ships flying the flag of any state (Article 17). If a foreign ship transporting migrants merely passes through the territorial sea of a coastal state without engaging in any activity that is prejudicial to the peace, good order, or security of such state (Article 19(1)), no violation to the immigration legislation of the latter occurs.

However, passage cannot be considered as innocent if whilst in the territorial sea the foreign ship engages in any of the activities listed in Article 19(2). Such activities include 'the loading or unloading of any . . . person contrary to the . . . immigration . . . laws and regulations of the coastal State'. Accordingly, the coastal state may adopt laws and regulations, in conformity with the provisions of UNCLOS and other rules of international law, relating to innocent passage through the territorial sea in respect of the prevention of infringement of its immigration laws and regulations (Article 21(1)(h)). Foreign ships exercising the right of innocent passage through the territorial sea must comply with all such laws and regulations (Article 21(4)). The coastal state may also take necessary steps in its territorial sea to prevent passage which is not innocent (Article 25(1)).

If the ship is passing through the territorial sea for the purpose of calling at a port of the coastal state, the latter has the right to close its ports to ships carrying illegal immigrants, except in case of distress. This right is implied in Article 25(2), according to which, in the case of ships proceeding to internal waters or calling at a port facility outside internal waters, the coastal state has the right to take the necessary steps to prevent any breach of the conditions to which admission of ships is subject.[6]

As regards the question of jurisdiction, Article 27(1) provides that 'the criminal jurisdiction of the coastal State should not be exercised on board a foreign ship passing through the territorial sea to arrest any person or to conduct any investigation in connection with any crime committed on board the ship during its passage'.[7] However, this provision allows for four exceptions where the criminal jurisdiction of the coastal state can be exercised. Two exceptions ('if the consequences of the crime extend to the coastal State' and 'if the crime is of a kind to

[5] One nautical mile corresponds to 1852 m. The normal baseline of the territorial sea corresponds to the low-water line (Art. 5 UNCLOS). In particular cases, such as deeply indented coastlines or fringes of islands (Art. 7), mouths of rivers (Art. 9), bays (Art. 10), or archipelagic states (Art. 47), one or more straight baselines can be drawn to join appropriate points on land or islands.

[6] A regime similar to innocent passage applies for transit passage through international straits, a right granted to all ships and aircraft (Art. 38). States bordering international straits may adopt laws and regulations relating to transit passage in respect of, inter alia, the loading or unloading of any person in contravention of their immigration laws and regulations (Art. 42(1)(d)).

[7] The conditional mood ('should not be exercised') does not contribute to the clarity of this provision.

disturb the peace of the country or the good order of the territorial sea') can easily be applied in cases where illegal immigrants are disembarked within the territorial sea.

2. *The contiguous zone*

Under Article 33(1) UNCLOS (contiguous zone):

> In a zone contiguous to its territorial sea, described as the contiguous zone, the coastal State may exercise the control necessary to:
> (a) prevent infringement of its customs, fiscal, immigration or sanitary laws and regulations within its territory or territorial sea;
> (b) punish infringement of the above laws and regulations committed within its territory or territorial sea.

Unlike the territorial sea, the contiguous zone does not exist *ipso iure* as a natural prolongation of the land territory of a state, but must be explicitly proclaimed under the domestic legislation of the coastal state concerned. The contiguous zone may not extend beyond 24 nautical miles from the baselines from which the breadth of the territorial sea is measured (Article 33(2)).

The contiguous zone is not a part of the territory of the coastal state. The critical threshold to determine whether illegal immigration has taken place is the limit between the territorial sea and the contiguous zone, if any, and not the limit between the contiguous zone and the high seas. The control that the state can exercise in such zone is limited to the purpose of preventing or punishing infringements of its immigration laws and regulations that, respectively, are likely to occur or have already occurred within its territory or territorial sea. For instance, the coastal state cannot board a foreign ship that is navigating in its contiguous zone, unless there are clear grounds for believing that the ship is going to infringe the state's immigration rules by disembarking illegal immigrants into its territory or territorial sea or that the ship has already committed such an infringement and is trying to escape from criminal proceedings and sanctions.

3. *The exclusive economic zone*

Rights in the field of immigration are not granted to the coastal state within its exclusive economic zone.[8] This means that, as far as immigration matters are concerned, the regime applying in the exclusive economic zone is not different from that applying on the high seas in general.[9]

[8] For the rights granted, see Art. 56 UNCLOS. Under Art. 57, the exclusive economic zone cannot extend beyond 200 nautical miles from the baselines from which the breadth of the territorial sea is measured.

[9] Under Art. 58(2) UNCLOS, Arts 88–115, relating to the high seas, and other pertinent rules of international law apply to the exclusive economic zone in so far as they are not incompatible with Part V UNCLOS (exclusive economic zone).

4. The high seas

On the high seas, no claims of sovereignty can be validly put forward by any state (see Article 89 UNCLOS). Under Article 92(1), save in exceptional cases expressly provided for in international treaties or in UNCLOS, ships on the high seas are subject to the exclusive jurisdiction of the state that has granted them its nationality (the flag state). A ship which sails under the flags of two or more states, using them according to convenience, may not claim any of the nationalities in question with respect to any other state and may be assimilated to a ship without nationality (Article 92(2)).

The high seas are open to ships of all states, whether coastal or land-locked. Of the freedoms pertaining to the high seas, the main one is freedom of navigation (Article 87(1)(a)).

On the high seas, the boarding of a foreign private ship in order to verify the right to fly its flag (so-called right of visit) can take place only in a limited number of cases specified in Article 110(1):

> Except where acts of interference derive from powers conferred by treaty, a warship which encounters on the high seas a foreign ship, other than a ship entitled to complete immunity in accordance with articles 95 and 96, is not justified in boarding it unless there is reasonable ground for suspecting that:
> (a) the ship is engaged in piracy;
> (b) the ship is engaged in the slave trade;
> (c) the ship is engaged in unauthorized broadcasting and the flag State of the warship has jurisdiction under article 109;
> (d) the ship is without nationality; or
> (e) though flying a foreign flag or refusing to show its flag, the ship is, in reality, of the same nationality as the warship.

As the transportation of migrants is not listed among the activities that would justify a visit, a ship that is suspected of engaging in migrant smuggling cannot be visited by a warship flying a flag that is different from the flag of the ship in question.[10] Nor do ships engaged in migrant smuggling indirectly fall into any of the cases listed in Article 110. The smuggling of migrants is something very different from piracy, as defined in Article 101. Only in exceptional circumstances can smugglers of migrants be considered as slave traders, since migrants travel voluntarily and are not deprived of their freedom.

It follows that on the high seas so-called 'interception at sea'[11] to prevent migrant smuggling can take place only with the consent of the flag state.[12] Nobody is an immigrant without having crossed, or at least attempted to cross, a border.

[10] However, there are agreements allowing a visit and other forms of jurisdiction (see this chapter, II.B and II.C).

[11] See this chapter, III.D and III.E

[12] Interception has been defined 'as encompassing all measures applied by a State, outside its national territory, in order to prevent, interrupt or stop the movement of persons without the required documentation crossing international borders by land, air or sea, and making their way to the country of prospective destination'. United Nations High Commissioner for Refugees, *Interception of Asylum-*

Freedom of navigation and the exclusive jurisdiction of the flag state prevail. This is a matter of fact, although it may be seen as a legal gap that should be filled.

B. The transnational crime of smuggling migrants by sea

A more specific international regime to address the significant increase in the activities of organized criminal groups engaged in the smuggling of migrants has been set up under the 2000 Protocol against the Smuggling of Migrants by Land, Sea and Air,[13] supplementing the 2000 United Nations Convention against Transnational Organized Crime. The Migrants Protocol, which entered into force on 28 January 2004 and is today binding on 138 states, establishes the international crime of smuggling of migrants, defined by Article 3(a), as follows:

> 'smuggling of migrants' shall mean the procurement, in order to obtain, directly or indirectly, a financial or other material benefit, of the illegal entry of a person into a State Party of which the person is not a national or a permanent resident.

This definition confirms that there is a clear distinction between the smuggler and the migrant and that the latter is not the criminal against whom the Migrants Protocol has been negotiated and adopted. An illegal immigrant cannot become the smuggler of himself.[14]

As can be inferred from Article 3, the Migrants Protocol aims at establishing international cooperation for the prevention, investigation, and prosecution of a number of offences, provided that they are transnational in nature[15] and involve an organized criminal group. The states parties are bound to establish as criminal offences the smuggling of migrants and a number of specified other acts which facilitate smuggling (see Article 6(1)). The Migrants Protocol also has the different, but equally important, purpose to ensure 'the protection of the rights of persons who have been the object of such offences'; that is, the illegal migrants who are the victims of the smugglers.[16]

Three provisions of the Migrants Protocol address the special problems posed by the smuggling of migrants by sea. They do not substantively change the approach taken by UNCLOS, based on the principle of freedom of navigation on the high

Seekers and Refugees: the International Framework and Recommendations for a Comprehensive Approach, UN Doc EC/50/SC/CPR.17, 9 June 2000, para. 10.

[13] Hereinafter: Migrants Protocol.

[14] The illegal migrant could become a smuggler if, in order to get a financial or other material benefit, he organizes a trip for himself and for other migrants as well. However, the Migrants Protocol applies where the offences 'involve an organized criminal group' (Art. 4). This is unlikely to happen in the case mentioned above.

[15] Under Art. 3(2) of the United Nations Convention against Transnational Organized Crime, an offence is transnational in nature if '(a) it is committed in more than one State; (b) it is committed in one State but a substantial part of its preparation, planning, direction or control takes place in another State; (c) it is committed in one State but involves an organized criminal group that engages in criminal activities in more than one State; or (d) it is committed in one State but has substantial effects in another State'.

[16] For the provisions of the Migrants Protocol aiming at the protection of the safety and the human rights of migrants see this chapter, II.D.3 and III.A.

seas and in the exclusive economic zone and on the exclusive jurisdiction of the flag state.[17] As regards the question of jurisdiction beyond the territorial sea, according to Article 8(2):

> A State Party that has reasonable grounds to suspect that a vessel exercising freedom of navigation in accordance with international law and flying the flag or displaying the marks of registry of another State Party is engaged in the smuggling of migrants by sea may so notify the flag State, request confirmation of registry and, if confirmed, request authorization from the flag State to take appropriate measures with regard to that vessel. The flag State may authorize the requesting State, inter alia:
> (a) To board the vessel;
> (b) To search the vessel; and
> (c) If evidence is found that the vessel is engaged in the smuggling of migrants by sea, to take appropriate measures with respect to the vessel and persons and cargo on board, as authorized by the flag State.

It is only after having received the authorization by the flag state that the boarding and searching of the suspected foreign ship exercising freedom of navigation can take place. Article 8(2) allows the boarding state also to take 'appropriate measures with respect to the vessel and persons and cargo on board', always with the prior authorization of the flag state. While more precision in the wording would have been desirable, measures such as the seizure of the ship and the arrest of the smugglers to be subsequently surrendered to the authorities of the flag state for criminal prosecution can be envisaged in this regard.

During the negotiations for the Migrants Protocol, a proposal was made by Austria and Italy to include a provision allowing a state to intervene on the high seas if a vessel having no nationality is involved in the trafficking of migrants and 'based on its route, the vessel is undoubtedly bound for its coasts' or if 'the vessel is armed or governed or manned by nationals'.[18] The proposal was not adopted.

As the boarding of a ship, which is something that is normally done in circumstances of urgency, is subject to the condition of request and receipt of authorization by a foreign state, the Migrants Protocol is going to enter into questions of communication. Far from being a banality, as it could at first sight appear, the communication issue becomes the core of the Migrants Protocol. If the official interstate means of communication is used—that is, a note given by the Ministry of Foreign Affairs to the ambassador of the other state, followed by a note of response transmitted by the same ambassador—how long would the accomplishment of such a procedure require?[19] The Migrants Protocol finds a solution to the problem by resorting to the adverb 'expeditiously' and providing for an obligation to 'respond expeditiously'. This can be interpreted in the sense that also informal and quick means of communication, such as telephone calls, facsimile letters, or email can be used:

[17] This chapter, II.A.4.
[18] See UN Doc A/AC.254/4/Add.1, 15 December 1998, Art. F(1)(b).
[19] It is easy to imagine what could be the speed of reaction to requests of authorization addressed to states granting flags of convenience.

A State Party shall respond expeditiously to a request from another State Party to determine whether a vessel that is claiming its registry or flying its flag is entitled to do so and to a request for authorization made in accordance with paragraph 2 of this article (Article 8(4)).

The second practical question of communication is the precise determination of the name, address (possibly, electronic address), or telephone number of the foreign authority bound to respond expeditiously. In this regard Article 8(6) provides as follows:

Each State Party shall designate an authority or, where necessary, authorities to receive and respond to requests for assistance, for confirmation of registry or of the right of a vessel to fly its flag and for authorization to take appropriate measures. Such designation shall be notified through the Secretary-General to all other State Parties within one month of the designation.

Article 8(7) of the Migrants Protocol does not clearly specify what the visiting state can do after having found that a ship engaged in the smuggling of migrants is without nationality:

A State Party that has reasonable grounds to suspect that a vessel is engaged in the smuggling of migrants by sea and is without nationality or may be assimilated to a vessel without nationality may board and search the vessel. If evidence confirming the suspicion is found, that State Party shall take appropriate measures in accordance with relevant domestic and international law.

It is self-evident that here the normal course of action—that is, to request authorization from the flag state—cannot be followed, for the simple reason that there is no flag state. The reference to the right to 'take appropriate measures in accordance with relevant domestic and international law' is of no concrete help, considering that international law does not provide for any specific action which could have some effectiveness[20] and that domestic law can only be in conformity with rules of international law. A possible action that could be envisaged is to ask the state of whom the smugglers are nationals for authorization to arrest them in order to be surrendered to this state later for criminal prosecution, and to ask the state of nationality of the owner of the ship for authorization to seize it. Such a course of action seems logical and would not be prejudicial to the existing international law of the sea. But, if this is the case, why is it not specified in the Migrants Protocol?

The conclusion that can be drawn from this analysis is that the drafters of the Migrants Protocol, probably because they were too concerned with the preservation of the traditional law of the sea, have not been able to give many effective tools to states to help counteract the smuggling of migrants by sea. The improvement in the means and methods of communication between states parties, which seems to be the major innovation of the Protocol, has so far achieved modest results, considering that, despite Article 8(6), only twenty-three out of all the states parties have announced the name of the authority bound to respond expeditiously to the

[20] Just to take note that a ship without nationality engaged in the smuggling of migrants has been found beyond the territorial sea does not seem to be a very effective action.

requests by other states parties.[21] It thus appears that, with or without the Migrants Protocol, the legal framework would not substantively change as far as the international law of the sea is concerned. But this conclusion does not detract from the merits of the Migrants Protocol in another—even more important—respect, which is the clear specification of the rights that must be granted to illegal migrants.[22]

C. Some bilateral agreements against the smuggling of migrants by sea

Both UNCLOS (Article 311(2) and (3)) and the Migrants Protocol (Article 17) allow for special agreements on a regional or bilateral basis.

Even though they are less numerous than the treaties aimed at countering drug trafficking, a number of bilateral agreements against illegal immigration at sea have been concluded by the states concerned. Due to the fact that the flow of migrants normally goes only in one direction, the agreements in question do not have a reciprocal content but provide for different rights and obligations with respect to either party. Some examples are provided here.

A) On 23 September 1981, Haiti and the United States of America concluded in Port-au-Prince an Agreement to Stop Clandestine Migration of Residents of Haiti to the United States.[23] The Agreement aims at establishing 'a cooperative program of interdiction and selective return to Haiti of certain Haitian migrants and vessels involved in illegal transport of persons coming from Haiti' (Preamble). Under the Agreement, Haiti consents to boarding by the United States authorities of private vessels flying the Haitian flag which may be involved in the irregular carriage of passengers outbound from Haiti. As the boarding can take place on the high seas, the Agreement sets forth a derogation to the rule of the exclusive jurisdiction of the flag state. After the boarding, further action can follow.

> Upon boarding a Haitian flag vessel, in accordance with this agreement, the authorities of the United States Government may address inquiries, examine documents and take such measures as are necessary to establish the registry, condition and destination of the vessel and the status of those on board the vessel. When these measures suggest that an offense against United States immigration laws or appropriate Haitian laws has been or is being committed, the Government of the Republic of Haiti consents to the detention on the high seas by the United States Coast Guard of the vessels and persons found on board.

The persons and vessels detained by the United States must be returned to Haiti or surrendered to the Haitian authorities.

[21] According to the data available from the depositary (the Secretary-General of the United Nations). Some states parties (for example, Italy and Panama) have only indicated the name of an authority (the Italian Coast Guard Headquarters and the Maritime Authority of Panama, respectively), without pointing out the postal address, the electronic mail address, and the facsimile or telephone number to contact the said authority. Others (for example, the Netherlands) have only given an ordinary mail address. Is posting a letter in a mail box and waiting for an answer a way to communicate 'expeditiously' nowadays?

[22] See this chapter, III.A and III.C.

[23] 20 *International Legal Materials* (1981) 1198.

The Government of Haiti agrees to permit upon prior notification the return of detained vessels and persons to a Haitian port, or if circumstances permit, the United States Government will release such vessels and migrants on the high seas to representatives of the Government of the Republic of Haiti.

Haiti is under an obligation to prosecute those who are suspected of illegal trafficking and, under certain circumstances, to confiscate the vessels involved in it.

The Government of the Republic of Haiti agrees, to the extent permitted by Haitian law, to prosecute illegal traffickers of Haitian migrants who do not have requisite permission to enter the country of the vessel's destination and to confiscate Haitian vessels or stateless vessels involved in such trafficking.[24]

Haiti is entitled to keep an eye on what the United States is doing in the implementation of the Agreement.

The Government of the United States agree to the presence of a representative of the Navy of the Republic of Haiti as liaison aboard any United States vessel engaged in the implementation of this cooperative program.

The Agreement was followed on 29 September 1981 by a Proclamation by the President of the United States on interdiction of illegal aliens[25] and by Executive Order 12324, applying to ships carrying undocumented aliens and flying the flag of the United States, to ships without nationality and to ships flying the flag of a state with which the United States has arrangements authorizing the stopping and boarding.[26]

B) Under an Exchange of Notes concluded on 25 March 1997,[27] Albania and Italy point out that, due to the massive illegal flow of Albanian migrants to other countries, they had agreed 'to strengthen their collaboration in the legal and humanitarian fields'. Albania accepts that Italy provides 'its collaboration and its assistance in the control and the restraint at sea of illegal expatriations by Albanian nationals'. For an initial and renewable period of thirty days, Albania authorizes Italy, through the Italian Navy, 'to stop in international waters and to divert to Albanian ports ships flying the Albanian flag or in any way referable to the Albanian State, as well as to stop in Albanian territorial waters ships of any flag, which are engaged in the transport of Albania nationals who have escaped the controls carried out by the competent authorities in Albanian territory'.

[24] It is also provided that 'the United States Government likewise agrees, to the extent permitted by United States law, to prosecute traffickers of United States nationality and to confiscate United States vessels engaged in such trafficking'. This and subsequent translations are by the author.

[25] According to the Proclamation, 'the continuing illegal migration by sea of large numbers of undocumented aliens into the southeastern United States' has 'severely strained the law enforcement resources of the Immigration and Naturalization Service' and has 'threatened the welfare and safety of communities in that region'.

[26] The Executive Order does not prejudice the 'strict observance of our international obligations concerning those who genuinely flee persecution in their homeland' (III). It was revoked and replaced by Executive Order 12807 of 24 May 1992 (see this chapter, III.F).

[27] Text, in the Albanian and Italian official versions, in *Gazzetta Ufficiale della Repubblica Italiana*, supplement to No. 163 of 15 July 1997.

However the 'necessary technical procedures to implement this collaboration in Albanian territorial waters and in international waters' were to be established as soon as possible through an ad hoc protocol. This was done under an Implementation Protocol adopted in Rome on 2 April 1997.

The Exchange of Notes sets forth derogations to the rule of the exclusive jurisdiction of the flag state on the high seas and of the exclusive jurisdiction of the coastal state in its territorial sea. Albania is granted no control or supervision over what Italian ships are doing at sea. Here the intercepting party is entitled not to board, but to stop and divert the ships flying the flag of the other party. In fact, a ship can be stopped and diverted even without the need to board it. But this simple consideration would bring about very sinister consequences in the tragic story of one implementation of the Exchange of Notes.[28]

C) On 20 May 2003, the Dominican Republic and the United States concluded an Agreement Concerning Cooperation in Maritime Law Enforcement,[29] based on the need for international cooperation in suppressing the smuggling of migrants, as reflected, inter alia, in the Migrants Protocol,[30] in the principles of international law, such as the sovereign equality of states and 'the principle of the right of freedom of navigation' (Preamble).[31] The parties bind themselves to

> cooperate in combating the unsafe transport of migrants by sea and smuggling of migrants to the fullest extent possible, consistent with international law and available law enforcement resources and priorities related thereto. (Article 2)

Interestingly, the Agreement is not limited to the smuggling of migrants, but covers also their unsafe transport. It consequently applies also to the (albeit unlikely) cases where the migrants are entitled to legally enter the country of destination, but are transported in unsafe conditions. The Agreement establishes 'a combined law enforcement shiprider program' between the law enforcement authorities of the parties (Article 4), where,

> 'shiprider' means a law enforcement official of one Party authorized to embark on a law enforcement vessel or aircraft of the other Party. (Article 1(14))[32]

The Agreement sets forth derogations to the rule of exclusive jurisdiction of the flag state on the high seas and of exclusive jurisdiction in its territorial sea by the coastal state from which the flow of illegal migrants originates. In addition, it provides for the use of shipriders, who can be embarked on the ships of either party, in order to

[28] See this chapter, III.D.4.

[29] USA Department of State, *Treaties and Other International Acts Series*, No. 03-520.

[30] See this chapter, II.B. Even though at the moment of conclusion of the Agreement they were not parties to the Migrants Protocol, both the Dominican Republic and the United States are today parties to it.

[31] Is freedom of navigation a right? Is it a principle? Is it a principle of a right? The latter terminology, used in the Agreement, seems too cumbersome.

[32] The Agreement between the Bahamas and the United States Concerning Cooperation in Maritime Law Enforcement, concluded in Nassau on 29 June 2004, also provides for a shiprider programme.

ensure the most expeditious means of communication between the parties. If a treaty is bilateral, practical problems of addresses, facsimile or telephone numbers[33] can be avoided by embarking an official of the other party. Under the Agreement, shipriders are given quite broad powers.

When a shiprider is embarked on the other Party's law enforcement vessel . . . , any law enforcement measure, including boardings, search or seizure of property, any detention of a person, and any use of force pursuant to this Agreement, whether or not involving weapons, shall be carried out by the shiprider.

a. Crew members of the other Party's vessel may assist in any such action if expressly requested to do so by the shiprider, and only within the limits of such request and in the manner requested. Such request, including any request for the use of force, may only be made, agreed to, and acted upon in accordance with the law and policies of both Parties.

b. Such crew members may use force in self-defense and defense of others in accordance with the applicable laws and policies of their Government. (Article 4(5))

With regard to suspect ships flying the flag of the Dominican Republic, maritime migration law enforcement operations can take place in 'Dominican waters' (Article 5(1)), meaning the internal waters and the territorial sea of the Dominican Republic, as well as 'seaward of any State's territorial sea' (Article 8(1)). In the first case, the Agreement constitutes permission by the Dominican Republic for maritime migration law enforcement operations by the United States if any of three circumstances specified in Article 5(2) occurs, the first being the authorization by an embarked Dominican shiprider to enter into Dominican waters. In the second case, the Dominican Republic authorizes the United States to board, address enquiries, inspect the documents of, and search the suspect vessel and the persons found on board (Article 8(1)). If evidence of unsafe transport of migrants by sea or smuggling of migrants is found, the United States may detain the vessel and the persons on board, pending expeditious disposition of instructions from the Dominican Republic (Article 8(2)).

The right to exercise jurisdiction is primarily granted to the Dominican Republic, but it can be waived in favour of the United States.

In all cases arising in Dominican waters, or concerning Dominican flag vessels seaward of any State's territorial sea the Government of the Dominican Republic shall have the primary right to exercise jurisdiction over a detained vessel, cargo and/or, subject to Article 10 of this Agreement, persons on board (including repatriation, seizure, forfeiture, arrest, and prosecution), provided, however, that the Government of the Dominican Republic may, subject to its Constitution and laws, waiver its primary right to exercise jurisdiction and authorize the enforcement of United States law against the vessel, cargo and/or persons on board. (Article 9(1))

[33] See this chapter, II.B.

D) On 29 December 2007 Italy and Libya concluded in Tripoli a Protocol to Face the Phenomenon of Clandestine Immigration.[34] It aims at implementing the Agreement on Collaboration in the Fight against Terrorism, Organized Crime, Illegal Trafficking of Drugs and Psychotropic Substances and Clandestine Immigration, previously concluded by the two countries in Rome on 13 December 2000.[35] The Protocol acknowledges in the Preamble that Libya faces great problems due to the fact that it is a transit country for migrants and it has to control more than 5000 km of land borders in the desert and more than 2200 km of sea borders.

Under the Protocol, Italy and Libya bind themselves to organize maritime patrolling activities using six ships temporarily ceded by Italy to Libya. While the ships take on board a mixed crew, the Italian police personnel can only engage in activities in the areas of training, formation, technical assistance, and maintenance of the ships. The activities of control, search, and rescue allowed by the Protocol can be undertaken in the localities of departure and transit of ships transporting clandestine migrants, as well as within the Libyan territorial sea[36] and on the high seas, in compliance with international treaties in force and according to the operational modalities to be agreed upon. It is not clear whether the Protocol applies also to ships flying a flag different from those of the two parties.

The Protocol is supplemented by an additional protocol of a technical and operational character, also concluded on 29 December 2007. The additional protocol specifies that the activities to be carried out relate to the 'prevention and countering of illegal migratory flows'. This seems however something different from the activities of 'control, search and rescue' mentioned in the main Protocol. The additional protocol also provides that the command of the ships ceded by Italy to Libya is exercised by Libyan personnel, who are responsible for the actions undertaken. A further Protocol was concluded on 4 February 2009. It provides that the two countries will organize maritime patrols with joint crews, to be conducted in Italian, Libyan, and international waters. They also undertake to repatriate clandestine immigrants and to conclude agreements with the countries of origin in order to limit clandestine immigration.[37]

[34] The Protocol has not been published in the Italian official journal, in violation of the domestic provisions on the publication of treaties; see C. Fioravanti, 'Scatole cinesi. Quale controllo democratico sulla cooperazione italo-libica-europea in materia d'immigrazione?', in G. Brunelli, A. Pugiotto, and P. Veronesi (eds), *Scritti in onore di Lorenza Carlassare* (2009) 539. The Protocol is recalled in Art. 19(1) of the Treaty of Friendship, Partnership and Cooperation by Italy and Libya, signed in Benghazi on 30 August 2008 (*Gazzetta Ufficiale della Repubblica Italiana*, supplement to No. 40 of 18 February 2009). This treaty was concluded to 'definitively close the sad chapter of the past, for which Italy has already . . . expressed its regret for the sufferings caused to the Libyan people as a consequence of Italian colonization' (preamble). See also F. De Vittor, 'Soccorso in mare e rimpatri in Libia: tra diritto del mare e tutela internazionale dei diritti dell'uomo', *Rivista di Diritto Internazionale* 92 (2009) 800.

[35] *Gazzetta Ufficiale della Repubblica Italiana*, supplement to No. 111 of 15 May 2003.

[36] Libya claims the Gulf of Sidra as an extent of historical internal waters. It is uncertain whether the Protocol applies to the waters of this Gulf.

[37] On the operations carried out under the Protocol see this chapter, III.F.

Unlike the three bilateral treaties described above, the instruments agreed upon by Italy and Libya do not establish any derogations to the rules of the international law of the sea on the exercise of jurisdiction on the high seas or in the territorial sea. They merely provide technical assistance by one party to the activities against illegal migration carried out by the other party.

D. The safety of life at sea

The duty to render assistance to persons in danger at sea is provided for in several treaties applicable to various activities taking place at sea.[38] It is at the border between the international law of the sea and international human rights law. In fact, the duty in question can be considered as a manifestation of the principle of protection of human life which has a long-standing tradition in maritime custom. It can be included among the general principles of law, as recalled in Article 38(1)(c) of the Statute of the International Court of Justice. It can also be understood as an aspect of the human right to life set forth in the relevant multilateral treaties, such as Article 2(1) of the Convention for the Protection of Human Rights and Fundamental Freedoms (Rome, 1950; more commonly known as the European Convention on Human Rights)[39] or Article 6(1) of the International Covenant on Civil and Political Rights (New York, 1966).

The beneficiaries of the right to be assisted at sea are all persons who are in distress, irrespective of the nationality of the ship and including those who engage in illegal activities, such as stowaways, migrant smugglers, drug, weapons or slave traffickers, pirates, and terrorists. In the case of migration by sea, the right to be assisted takes on special importance, due to the fact that migrants are often transported in the most hazardous and inhuman conditions in unseaworthy and overcrowded water craft, exposed to the dangers caused by bad weather, starvation, dehydration, and illness. In too many cases, the illegal migrant is at the same time a person in distress at sea.

1. The UNCLOS regime

A duty to render assistance to persons in danger at sea, which takes different forms (from rescuing and taking on board persons in distress to organizing a search and rescue service), is provided for in Article 98 UNCLOS in the following terms:

[38] See T. Scovazzi, 'La tutela della vita umana in mare, con particolare riferimento agli immigrati clandestini diretti verso l'Italia', *Rivista di Diritto Internazionale* (2005), 106; B. Miltner, 'Irregular Maritime Migration: Refugee Protection Issues in Rescue and Interception', *Fordham International Law Journal* (2006) 75; M. Carta, 'Misure di contrasto al traffico di migranti via mare', in G. Palmisano (ed.), *Il contrasto al traffico di migranti* (2008) 81; S. Trevisanut, 'Search and Rescue Operations in the Mediterranean: Factor of Cooperation or Conflict?', *The International Journal of Marine and Coastal Law* (2010) 523; L. Salamone, *La disciplina giuridica dell'immigrazione clandestina via mare, nel diritto italiano, europeo e internazionale* (2011); S. Trevisanut, *Immigrazione irregolare via mare—Diritto internazionale e diritto dell'Unione Europea* (2012).

[39] Hereinafter: ECHR.

1. Every State shall require the master of a ship flying its flag, in so far as he can do so without serious danger to the ship, the crew or the passengers:
(a) to render assistance to any person found at sea in danger of being lost;
(b) to proceed with all possible speed to the rescue of persons in distress, if informed of their need of assistance, in so far as such action may reasonably be expected of him;
(c) after a collision, to render assistance to the other ship, its crew and its passengers and, where possible, to inform the other ship of the name of his own ship, its port of registry and the nearest port at which it will call.
2. Every coastal State shall promote the establishment, operation and maintenance of an adequate and effective search and rescue service regarding safety on and over the sea and, where circumstances so require, by way of mutual regional arrangements cooperate with neighbouring States for this purpose.

Article 98 is included in UNCLOS Part VII (high seas). But the duty to render assistance at sea has a broader scope of application, and covers any kind of marine waters, irrespective of their legal status. For instance, under Article 18(2), foreign ships exercising their right of innocent passage through the territorial state are entitled to stop to render assistance to people in distress.

The general obligation incumbent on every state to assist people in distress at sea goes together with the obligation, primarily incumbent on the flag state, to ensure that ships having its nationality navigate under appropriate safety conditions. Under Article 94(3) UNCLOS:

Every State shall take such measures for ships flying its flag as are necessary to ensure safety at sea with regard, *inter alia*, to:
(a) the construction, equipment and seaworthiness of ships;
(b) the manning of ships, labour conditions and the training of crews, taking into account the applicable international instruments;
(c) the use of signals, the maintenance of communications and the prevention of collisions.

Article 94(4) further specifies what kind of measures, relating to surveys of ships and qualification of masters and crews, are required to ensure safety at sea. Under Article 94(5), the measures in question must comply with generally accepted standards, in particular those resulting from the multilateral treaties adopted within the framework of the competent international organization (the International Maritime Organization).[40] In this way, these instruments indirectly acquire a binding character on all UNCLOS parties.

The obligation of the flag state to ensure the safety of human life at sea can be seen also under another perspective by combining Article 91(1) (nationality of ships) and Article 94(1) (duties of the flag state), which respectively provide as follows:

Every State shall fix the conditions for the grant of its nationality to ships, for the registration of ships in its territory, and for the right to fly its flag. Ships have the nationality of the State whose flag they are entitled to fly. There must exist a genuine link between the State and the ship.

[40] Hereinafter: IMO.

> Every State shall effectively exercise its jurisdiction and control in administrative, technical and social matters over ships flying its flag.

It thus appears that, under the logic of UNCLOS, the obligation to ensure a genuine link between a state and ships flying its flag is also to be understood in the light of the capacity and willingness of this state to exercise effective control in administrative, technical, and social matters relating to the ships. These matters, as Article 94(3) and (4) quoted earlier clearly show, surely include the safety of life on board the ship.

In a paper prepared in 2006 on 'Examination and clarification of the role of the "genuine link" in relation to the duty of flag States to exercise effective control over ships flying their flags, including fishing vessels',[41] the International Labour Office took the view that:

> if the full range of flag State duties in the 1982 Convention are considered, in order to effectively exercise jurisdiction, the ship, the shipowner and the seafarers must be susceptible to jurisdiction of the national legal system of the flag State, including the application of penalties. In this respect, it is noted that article 228 of the 1982 Convention also envisages situations in which the flag State loses its ability to require suspension of legal proceedings against its ships for marine pollution violations outside the territorial sea of another State. Article 228 refers to situations in which the flag State has 'repeatedly disregarded its obligations to enforce effectively the international rules and standards in respect of violations committed by its vessels'. It appears then, that in some circumstances, a flag State claim to primacy with respect to exercise of jurisdiction over its ship may be lost.
>
> It may be that the legal system could be developed to provide that, where there is sufficient evidence of a failure by a flag State to exercise responsibilities with respect to the ships that fly its flags, it could lose its right to be considered the 'flag State' with respect to the right of primary control over the ship, in matters other than marine pollution. While this may not lead to the extreme response of non-recognition of its flag by other States, it may mean that the international legal community could consider mechanisms to take action to enforce international standards. The linkages between ship safety, environmental protection, security and working conditions are increasingly well accepted.[42]

As pointed out by the International Labour Office, it might be helpful to apply by analogy to the safety of human life an UNCLOS provision (Article 228) that has been drafted for the specific objective of the protection of the marine environment. However, it seems that resort to customary international rules is already sufficient against flag states which do not comply with the obligation to ensure the safety of human life on board ships flying their flag, including ships transporting migrants. If a state is responsible for a breach of an international obligation, injured states are entitled to obtain from it full reparation in the form of restitution, compensation, or satisfaction (see Article 34 of the Articles on Responsibility of States for Internationally Wrongful Acts, adopted by the

[41] The paper is reproduced in Appendix I to the Report of the Ad Hoc Consultative Meeting of Senior Representatives of International Organizations on the 'Genuine Link', UN Doc A/61/160, 17 July 2006.

[42] Paras 27–29.

International Law Commission in 2001). The taking of countermeasures is also admissible, subject to certain conditions and restrictions (see Articles 49–54 of the same ILC Articles). It would be disappointing if, in the case of the obligation to ensure a genuine link, the rights of the injured states were to be limited to the very meagre remedy of reporting the facts to the responsible state and waiting for an investigation and other actions that the latter would hopefully take.[43] Such a derogation from the ordinary rules on state responsibility should have been explicitly expressed in UNCLOS. If migrants are transported in conditions that endanger their lives, every state can intervene on the ships in question to rescue and assist the people in peril. This kind of action can be justified under customary international law as an application of the rule on distress.[44] But it is also reasonable to think that lawful countermeasures can be adopted against a state that is persistently responsible for the internationally wrongful act of not ensuring the existence of a genuine link, in particular as regards safety of life at sea.[45] In this case countermeasures might well consist of the non-recognition of the right to fly the flag of the state in question, the refusal of access to ports to the ships flying that flag (except in cases of distress), or other measures proportionate to the wrongful act.

2. The IMO treaties

Several treaties adopted within the IMO framework aim at ensuring safety at sea.[46] They include, *inter alia*, the 1972 Convention on the International Regulations for Preventing Collisions at Sea, the 1974 Convention for the Safety of Life at Sea (amended several times),[47] the 1978 International Convention on Standards of Training, Certification and Watchkeeping for Seafarers, the 1979 International Convention on Maritime Search and Rescue (amended in 1998 and 2004),[48] and the 1989 International Convention on Salvage.

Search and rescue activities are carried out both by dedicated shore-based rescue units and by any ships that happen to navigate in the vicinity of the ship and

[43] Such a disappointing conclusion could be drawn from the reading of Art. 94(6) UNCLOS. It can easily be guessed how effective investigations made by states granting flags of convenience are likely to be.

[44] The wrongfulness of an act of a state not in conformity with an international obligation of that state is precluded if the author of the act in question had no other reasonable way, in a situation of distress, of saving the author's life or the lives of other persons entrusted to the author's care (Art. 24(1) of the Articles on Responsibility of States for Internationally Wrongful Acts). The lives of people in distress at sea are entrusted to the care of the masters of all ships that must intervene to rescue them.

[45] According to Art. 54 of the Articles, under certain circumstances measures can be taken also by states other than the injured state in the interest of the beneficiaries of the obligation breached. The latter, in the case of migration at sea, would be the people whose lives are placed in peril.

[46] In the current terminology 'safety' is different from 'security', the latter referring to the prevention and suppression of human wilful acts.

[47] Hereinafter: SOLAS Convention. See J. Coppens and E. Somers, 'Towards New Rules on Disembarkation of Persons Rescued at Sea?', 25 *The International Journal of Marine and Coastal Law* (2010) 377.

[48] Hereinafter: SAR Convention.

persons in distress. Under Article 10(1) of the International Convention on Salvage:

every master is bound, so far as he can do so without serious danger to his vessel and persons thereof, to render assistance to any person in danger of being lost at sea.

The main obligation set forth by the SAR Convention is that:

Parties shall ensure that assistance is provided to any person in distress at sea. They shall do so regardless of the nationality or status of such a person or the circumstances in which that person is found (Chapter 2.1.10).

The definitions of the terms 'search' and 'rescue' given by the Annex to the SAR Convention show that the obligations incumbent on parties are not limited to the retrieving of persons in distress, but extend also to their delivery to 'a place of safety'.

'Search'. An operation, normally co-ordinated by a rescue co-ordination centre or rescue sub-centre, using available personnel and facilities to locate persons in distress;

'Rescue'. An operation to retrieve persons in distress, provide for their initial medical or other needs, and deliver them to a place of safety. (Chapters 1.3.1 and 1.3.2)

Under the SAR Convention, the Parties are called to establish by agreement search and rescue regions (Chapter 2.1.4), intended as areas 'of defined dimension associated with a rescue co-ordination centre within which search and rescue services are provided' (Chapter 1.2.4).[49] The party accepting the responsibility to provide search and rescue services for a specified area is bound to 'use search and rescue units and other available facilities for providing assistance to a person who is, or appears to be, in distress at sea' (Chapter 2.1.9).[50]

The thorny question arising from the SAR Convention, and from other treaties providing for assistance at sea as well, is how to determine the place of safety to which the rescued persons are to be delivered. In fact, after being taken on board, the rescued people do not dematerialize: they are entitled to be delivered somewhere. The different states that may be involved in the rescue operation, namely the flag state, the state responsible for the search and rescue region, the state in whose exclusive economic zone or territorial sea the search and rescue take place, the states of nationality of the rescued persons, the state from where the rescued ship has sailed and perhaps other states, can have different views in this regard. The presence on board of many people may raise problems of overcrowding, lack of food and water, or spreading of infectious diseases that make the disembarkation of the rescued persons an urgent need. If the operations have been carried out by a private ship, its master, who has already incurred the burden and the expenses of searching and rescuing people in distress, may have an interest in not further delaying the

[49] The delimitation of search and rescue regions is not related and shall not prejudice the delimitation of any boundary between States (Chapter 2.1.7).

[50] However, '[p]arties shall co-ordinate their search and rescue organizations and should, whenever necessary, co-ordinate search and rescue operations with those of neighbouring States' (Chapter 3.1.1).

voyage by landing at an unforeseen port to disembark them. The rescued people may have some reasons to ask not to be disembarked in a certain state.

The SAR Convention, as amended in 2004, addresses the question of the place of safety, without however providing a clear-cut answer to it:

> Each Party should authorize its rescue co-ordination centres: . . .
>
> to make the necessary arrangements in co-operation with other rescue co-ordination centres to identify the most appropriate place(s) for disembarking persons found in distress at sea. (Chapter 3.1.6.4)
>
> Parties shall co-ordinate and co-operate to ensure that masters of ships providing assistance by embarking persons in distress at sea are released from their obligations with minimum further deviation from the ships' intended voyage, provided that releasing the ship from these obligations does not further endanger the safety of life at sea. The Party responsible for the search and rescue region in which such assistance is rendered shall exercise primary responsibility for ensuring such co-ordination and co-operation occurs, so that survivors assisted are disembarked from the assisting ship and delivered to a place of safety, taking into account the particular circumstances of the case and guidelines developed by the Organization. In these cases, the relevant Parties shall arrange for such disembarkation to be effected as soon as reasonably possible. (Chapter 3.1.9)
>
> The rescue co-ordination centre or rescue sub-centre concerned shall initiate the process of identifying the most appropriate place(s) for disembarking persons found in distress at sea. It shall inform the ship or ships and other relevant parties concerned thereof. (Chapter 4.8.5)

From the provisions reproduced above it appears that all parties to the SAR Convention, depending on the circumstances, are called upon to coordinate and cooperate in order that the rescued persons are disembarked from the assisting ship and delivered to a place of safety. The party responsible for the search and rescue region is neither bound to disembark the persons in its own territory nor, at least if the provisions are understood literally, to find another state where they can be disembarked. It must only exercise a 'primary responsibility' to ensure that the expected coordination and cooperation among parties occur in order to deliver the rescued people to a place of safety, taking into account the interest of minimizing any further deviation from the assisting ships' intended voyage. Such convoluted wording can only imply that, at the moment of amending the Annex to the SAR Convention, the Parties were not able to reach a generally agreed solution to the problem.

Yet, as stated by the International Court of Justice in its judgment of 20 February 1969 in the *North Sea Continental Shelf* cases (*Federal Republic of Germany v. Denmark; Federal Republic of Germany v. Netherlands*), an obligation to cooperate implies a duty to act in good faith in order to reach an agreement on matters of common interest or concern.[51] If the states concerned comply with the obligation

[51] 'The parties are under an obligation to enter into negotiations with a view to arriving at an agreement, and not merely to go through a formal process of negotiation . . . ; they are under an obligation so to conduct themselves that the negotiations are meaningful, which will not be the case when either of them insists upon its own position without contemplating any modification of it' (ICJ Reports (1969) at para. 85).

to act in good faith, it is likely that an agreement will be reached. But there is no legal guarantee that such a result will necessarily be achieved.

As regards cases of distress, the SOLAS Convention provides as follows:

> The master of a ship at sea which is in a position to be able to provide assistance, on receiving information from any source that persons are in distress at sea, is bound to proceed with all speed to their assistance, if possible informing them or the search and rescue service that the ship is doing so. This obligation to provide assistance applies regardless of the nationality or status of such persons or the circumstances in which they are found. (Regulation 33-1)
>
> Masters of ships who have embarked persons in distress at sea shall treat them with humanity, within the capabilities and limitations of the ship. (Regulation 33-6)

A notable provision has been included in the 2004 SOLAS amendments to relieve the master from the risk of personal liability.

> The owner, the charterer, the company operating the ship . . . or any other person shall not prevent or restrict the master of the ship from taking or executing any decision which, in the master's professional judgement, is necessary for safety of life at sea and protection of the marine environment. (Regulation 34-1)

On the thorny question of the determination of the place of safety, the SOLAS Convention, as amended in 2004, provides for a regime close to the regime contextually established under the SAR Convention. The remarks on that regime made above can consequently be repeated for the SOLAS Convention.

Taking into account the amendments to the SAR and SOLAS Conventions, in 2004 the Maritime Safety Committee of IMO adopted in Resolution MSC.167 (78) a set of Guidelines on the Treatment of Persons Rescued at Sea, 'realizing the need for clarification of existing procedures to guarantee that persons rescued at sea will be provided a place of safety regardless of their nationality, status or the circumstances in which they are found'. Without having a mandatory character, the Guidelines aim at providing guidance to governments and shipmasters. In fact, the master who rescues people at sea, as he is bound to do, should not be left alone.[52]

> The obligation of the master to render assistance should complement the corresponding obligation of IMO Member Governments to co-ordinate and co-operate in relieving the master of the responsibility to provide follow up care of survivors and to deliver the persons retrieved at sea to a place of safety. . . . (Guideline 1.2)

According to Guideline 2.5, the intent of the 2004 amendments to the SAR and SOLAS Conventions is 'to insure that in every case a place of safety is provided within a reasonable time'. The responsibility to provide such a place or to ensure that it is provided 'falls on the Government responsible for the search and rescue region in which the survivors were recovered'. As each case involves different circumstances, states should be given enough flexibility to address each situation (Guideline 2.6).

[52] For the *Tampa* case, which is relevant in this respect, see this chapter, II.D.4.

The Guidelines describe the behaviour that is expected from the shipmaster and the states concerned. The former should, inter alia:

understand and heed obligations under international law to assist persons in distress at sea (such assistance should always be carried out without regard to the nationality or status of the persons in distress, or to the circumstances in which they are found);

do everything possible, within the capabilities and limitations of the ship, to treat the survivors humanely and to meet their immediate needs; . . .

keep the RCC [rescue coordination centre] informed about conditions, assistance needed, and actions taken or planned for the survivors; . . .

seek to ensure that survivors are not disembarked to a place where their safety would be further jeopardized; and

comply with any relevant requirements of the Government responsible for the SAR [search and rescue] region where the survivors were recovered, or of another responding coastal State, and seek additional guidance from those authorities where difficulties arise in complying with such requirements. (Guideline 5.1)

The state responsible for the search and rescue region is called upon to exercise its primary responsibility.

When the RCC responsible for the SAR region in which assistance is needed is informed about the situation, that RCC should immediately accept responsibility for co-ordinating the rescue efforts, since related responsibilities, including arrangements for a place of safety, fall primarily on the Government responsible for that region. (Guideline 6.7)

All states parties are called to cooperate to achieve two main objectives:

Governments and the responsible RCC should make every effort to minimize the time survivors remain on board the assisting ship. (Guideline 6.8)

Responsible State authorities should make every effort to expedite arrangements to disembark survivors from the ship; however, the master should understand that in some cases necessary co-ordination may result in unavoidable delays. (Guideline 6.9)

The type of information that should be provided by the master to the rescue and coordination centre shows that the concerns of the assisting ship should also be taken into account, as well as the master's views about the development of the situation. But it is clear that it is not for the master of the assisting ship alone to decide where the rescued persons should be disembarked.[53]

The RCC should seek to obtain the following information from the master of the assisting ship:

information about the survivors, including name, age, gender, apparent health and medical condition and any special medical needs;

[53] To leave the choice to the master would follow a certain logic. Considering that he is legally bound to provide assistance to people in distress, the master could be given the choice of where to disembark the rescued people. It could be in the next intended port of call of the voyage, unless exceptional circumstances make another choice more appropriate. States would be bound to accept the master's choice and to cooperate with him. The only limit to the master's discretion would be to respect the human rights of the rescued people (see this chapter, III.B and III.C). But it appears that states are not prepared to accept a procedure which would leave them without control of the situation.

the master's judgment about the continuing safety of the assisting ship;
actions completed or intended to be taken by the master;
assisting ship's current endurance with the additional persons on board;
assisting ship's next intended port of call;
the master's preferred arrangements for disembarking the survivors;
any help that assisting ship may need during or after the recovery operation; and
any special factors (e.g., prevailing weather, time sensitive cargo). (Guideline 6.10)

Potential health and safety concerns aboard a ship that has recovered persons in distress include insufficient lifesaving equipment, water, provisions, medical care, and accommodations for the number of persons on board, and the safety of the crew and passengers if persons on board might become aggressive or violent.... (Guideline 6.11)

The Guidelines explain how the notion of place of safety should be understood. In fact it is an intermediate location between the assisting ship[54] and the final destination of the rescued persons.

A place of safety ... is a location where rescue operations are considered to terminate. It is also a place where the survivors' safety of life is no longer threatened and where their basic human needs (such as food, shelter and medical needs) can be met. Further, it is a place from which transportation arrangements can be made for the survivors' next or final destination. (Guideline 6.12)

A place of safety may be on land, or it may be aboard a rescue unit or other suitable vessel or facility at sea that can serve as a place of safety until the survivors are disembarked to their next destination. (Guideline 6.14)

However, the Guidelines cannot specify what the SAR and SOLAS Conventions were not able to specify; that is, which state is bound to provide a place of safety. The problem should hopefully be solved through international cooperation, taking into account a number of relevant circumstances.

Governments should co-operate with each other with regard to providing suitable places of safety for survivors after considering relevant factors and risks. (Guideline 6.16)

... These circumstances may include factors such as the situation on board the assisting ship, on scene conditions, medical needs, and availability of transportation or other rescue units. Each case is unique, and selection of a place of safety may need to account for a variety of important factors. (Guideline 6.15)

Some of the relevant circumstances are directly related to the particular condition of the rescued people.

The need to avoid disembarkation in territories where the lives and freedoms of those alleging a well-founded fear of persecution would be threatened is a consideration in the case of asylum-seekers and refugees recovered at sea. (Guideline 6.17)

[54] The Guidelines point out that 'an assisting ship should not be considered a place of safety based solely on the fact that the survivors are no longer in immediate danger once aboard the ship. An assisting ship may not have appropriate facilities and equipment to sustain additional persons on board without endangering its own safety or to properly care for the survivors. Even if the ship is capable of safely accommodating the survivors and may serve as a temporary place of safety, it should be relieved of this responsibility as soon as alternative arrangements can be made' (Guideline 6.13).

The conclusion that can be drawn from the developments in the present international law of the sea is that there is an obligation on a number of states to cooperate to deliver the rescued people to a place of safety as soon as possible.[55] It is however impossible to predetermine with precision where the place of safety is located.[56]

3. *Treaties relating to migration by sea*

The obligation to assist people in distress is confirmed by some of the already mentioned treaties which specifically address the subject of migration by sea.[57]

The states parties to the Migrants Protocol declare themselves 'concerned that the smuggling of migrants can endanger the lives or security of the migrants involved' (Preamble). They are bound to adopt legislative measures to establish as an aggravating circumstance to the offence of smuggling of migrants the fact that it takes place in conditions 'that endanger, or are likely to endanger, the lives or safety of the migrants concerned' (Article 6(3)(a)). While the authorization by the flag state is needed for interventions on ships exercising freedom of navigation, measures taken without authorization are allowed if 'necessary to relieve imminent danger to the lives of persons' (Article 7(5)). More generally, under Article 9(1), where measures are taken, states parties must

(a) Ensure the safety and humane treatment of the persons on board;
(b) Take due account of the need not to endanger the security of the vessel or its cargo.[58]

Under the 1997 Exchange of notes between Albania and Italy,[59] the parties agree to strengthen their collaboration also to provide 'immediate humanitarian assistance when the life of those who attempt to leave the country [Albania] is endangered'.

The 2003 Agreement between the Dominican Republic and the United States[60] provides the following definition:

'Unsafe transport of migrants by sea' means the carriage of migrants on board a vessel that is:
a. obviously operating in conditions which violate fundamental principles of safety of life at sea, including but not limited to those of the SOLAS Convention, or
b. not properly manned, equipped or licensed for carrying passengers on international voyages and that thereby constitutes a serious danger for the lives or the health of the

[55] See, in general, *The Treatment of Persons Rescued at Sea: Conclusions and Recommendations from Recent Meetings and Expert Round Tables Convened by the Office of the United Nations High Commissioner for Refugees*, UN Doc A/AC/259/17, 11 April 2008.

[56] The disagreement between Italy and Malta as to whether disembarkation should be in a port of the state of the SAR zone or in the nearest safe port is an example of a situation of persistent lack of clarity on an essential question.

[57] See this chapter, II.B and II.C.

[58] The other safeguard clauses provided for in Art. 9(1) are the following: '(c) Take due account of the need not to prejudice the commercial or legal interests of the flag State or any other interested State; (d) Ensure, within available means, that any measure taken with regard to the vessel is environmentally sound'.

[59] See this chapter, II.C.

[60] See this chapter, II.C.

> persons on board, including the conditions for embarkation and disembarkation. (Article 1(2))

When conducting boarding and search, the law enforcement officials must 'take due account of the need not to endanger the safety of life at sea' (Article 13(2)(d)). Moreover,

> when taking action with regard to a vessel found to be engaging in unsafe transport of migrants by sea or smuggling of migrants, the Party concerned shall also ensure the safety and the humanitarian handling of the persons on board and that any actions taken with regard to the vessel are, within available means, environmentally sound (Article 13(2)(e)).[61]

*4. Some relevant cases (*Kater I Rades, Tampa, Cap Anamour*)*

A few cases illustrate how much the safety of migrants by sea can be endangered. Unfortunately, in certain circumstances, the dangers are posed not only by the criminal behaviour of migrant smugglers, but also by the wrongful action taken by states that are obliged to protect human life at sea.

A) On 28 March 1997, three days after the entry into force of the already mentioned exchange of notes between Albania and Italy,[62] a collision occurred on the high seas, 35 nautical miles off the Italian Adriatic coast, between the ship *Kater I Rades*,[63] overcrowded with illegal Albanian migrants, and the corvette *Sibilla* of the Italian Navy. *Sibilla*, acting on the basis of the rights granted to Italy by the exchange of notes, enjoined *Kater* to change her route, but this instruction was not obeyed. *Sibilla* then manoeuvred in order to divert *Kater*. The final result was a collision between a smaller and a much bigger ship (56 against 1285 tons). The smaller ship sank. Only thirty-four of the migrants could be rescued by *Sibilla* herself and survived. Fifty-eight corpses were subsequently recovered. The total number of the Albanian migrants who died has not been precisely determined and is estimated at more than one hundred. Several among them were women and children.

[61] Subject to certain conditions, 'the Government of the Dominican Republic does not object to the U.S. Coast Guard destroying any vessel subject to the jurisdiction of the Dominican Republic and detained pursuant to this Agreement that the U.S. Coast Guard deems to be unseaworthy and/or a hazard to navigation' (Art. 9(4)).

[62] See this chapter, II.C.

[63] The *Kater I Rades* was a ship cancelled from the registry of the Albanian Navy. It is uncertain whether, at the moment of the accident, she had the Albanian flag or was to be considered as a ship without flag. On the accident see E. Cannizzaro, 'La tutela della sfera territoriale da intrusioni non autorizzate: in margine al caso Sibilla', 80 *Rivista di Diritto Internazionale* (1997) 421; T. Scovazzi, 'Le norme di diritto internazionale sull'immigrazione illegale via mare con particolare riferimento ai rapporti tra Albania e Italia', in A. De Guttry and F. Pagani (eds), *La crisi albanese del 1997* (1999) 239; A. Leogrande, *Il naufragio* (2011).

The judgment rendered in Italy on 19 March 2005 by the Tribunal of Brindisi on the criminal aspects of the case sheds light on appalling elements of fact. First, *Sibilla* tried, without success, to block *Kater*'s propeller by throwing a cable in the water. Second, as *Kater* made an attempt to escape, *Sibilla* tried to divert her from her route, engaging in 'kinematics and interposition manoeuvres' based on the harassment modalities used within the North Atlantic Treaty Organization (NATO) framework.[64]

Even though there was clearly no intention to cause such a massacre, the behaviour of Italy is an instance of grossly negligent action in total violation of the international law obligation to protect human life at sea. A further and unexpected detail is that on 28 March 1997, Italy had no right to divert Albanian ships on the high seas. The exchange of notes, while concluded and entered into force on 25 March 1997, clearly provided that it was conditional, as regards its implementation, on a further agreement on 'necessary technical procedures'. This agreement was concluded only on 2 April 1997,[65] five days after the tragic event. If on 28 March 1997 *Sibilla* was ever entitled to interfere with *Kater*, it was only to offer assistance to people on an unseaworthy ship and not to further endanger their safety.

Looking at the *Kater I Rades* accident from a moral point of view, the most appropriate term to use is not 'unfortunate', but 'shameful': an egregious instance of how the stronger (a ship of the navy) can disregard the most fundamental rights of the weaker (a ship overcrowded with poor people hoping for a decent future). Naval battles deserve to be fought against other enemies.

B) Following a request by Australia on 26 August 2001, *Tampa*, a Norwegian private ship en route from Australia to Singapore, rescued on the high seas and within the Indonesian search and rescue region an Indonesian fishing vessel transporting 433 persons having the nationality of various states (Afghanistan, Pakistan, Iraq, Indonesia, and Sri Lanka).[66] They were trying to reach Australia to request asylum. As the assisted people threatened a mutiny if the ship were to disembark them in Indonesia, the master decided to proceed to the Australian Christmas Island where, however, Australia refused access. *Tampa* stopped in the

[64] The captain of *Sibilla* was sentenced to a three-year term of imprisonment and the Albanian pilot of *Kater* to a four-year term which were reduced by a decision of the Court of Appeal of Lecce of 19 October 2010 to, respectively, two years and four months, and three years and four months. It is not clear how Italian jurisdiction can be exercised against the Albanian pilot, considering that, under Art. 97(1) UNCLOS, 'in the event of a collision or any other incident of navigation concerning a ship on the high seas, involving the penal or disciplinary responsibility of the master or of any other person in the service of the ship, no penal or disciplinary proceedings may be instituted against such person except before the judicial or administrative authorities either of the flag State or of the State of which such person is a national'.

[65] See this chapter, II.C.

[66] See M. Fornari, 'Soccorso di profughi in mare e diritto di asilo: questioni di diritto internazionale sollevate dalla vicenda della nave Tampa', *La Comunità Internazionale* 46 (2002) 61; P. Mathew, 'Australian Refugee Protection in the Wake of the *Tampa*', *American Journal of International Law* 96 (2002) 661.

Australian territorial sea, after having transmitted an emergency signal. She was boarded by Australian troops who took control of the ship. On 3 September, the rescued people were taken on board an Australian warship to be transported to New Zealand and Nauru. This was done after Australia had reached agreements with Nauru and New Zealand which accepted the rescued people on their territory to process their asylum applications.

The *Tampa* case placed emphasis on the need not to place an excessive burden on the rescuing ship and promptly provide migrants or asylum seekers with a place of safety. It led to the already mentioned 2004 amendments to the SAR Convention and the SOLAS Convention.[67]

C) On 20 June 2004, the German private ship *Cap Anamour*, run by a humanitarian association, rescued thirty-seven migrants on the high seas in the Channel of Sicily.[68] The ship subsequently made a brief stop for repairs in Malta without informing the local authorities of the presence of rescued people who stayed on board. Then she sailed for Italy, following the request by the same people to be disembarked there to ask for asylum. However, for over three weeks Italy refused *Cap Anamour* access to its territorial sea. According to Italy, Malta, as country of first arrival, was under an obligation to receive the rescued people and examine their applications for asylum, as provided for by Article 10 of European Union Regulation 343/2003 of 18 February 2003,[69] establishing the criteria and mechanisms for determining the member state responsible for examining an asylum application lodged in one of the member states by a third-country national. Only on 12 July did Italy authorize disembarkation on its territory. All the applications for asylum were processed and rejected, with the exception of one. The captain and the crew of the *Cap Anamour* were arrested under the charge of breach of the Italian immigration legislation, but they were subsequently released and acquitted.

The *Cap Anamour* case showed the need for better coordination among the states concerned, both at the international and at the European Union level. Rescued people cannot be considered as hostages who must wait for the solution of intra-European legal intricacies.

[67] See this chapter, II.D.2.

[68] See S. Trevisanut, 'Le Cap Anamur: Profils de droit international et de droit de la mer', 9 *Annuaire du Droit de la Mer* (2004) 49.

[69] OJ 2003 L 50. See also Regulation 1560/2003, OJ 2003 L 222 of 2 September 2003, laying down detailed rules for the application of Regulation 343/2003. The European Union has established a common policy on asylum. See A. Caligiuri, 'Le operazioni di contrasto dell'immigrazione clandestina alle frontiere marittime dell'Unione europea e la tutela dei richiedenti asilo', in A. Caligiuri, G. Cataldi, and N. Napoletano (eds), *La tutela dei diritti umani in Europa* (2010) 359; P. De Pasquale, 'Respingimenti, rimpatri e asilo: la tutela degli immigrati irregolari nell'UE', *Il Diritto dell'Unione Europea* (2010) 19; V. Moreno Lax, 'Current Legal Developments: European Union. The EU Regime on Interdiction, Search and Rescue, and Disembarkation: The Frontex Guidelines for Intervention at Sea', 25 *The International Journal of Marine and Coastal Law* (2010) 621.

III. Human Rights Law and Refugee Law

The protection of the international law of the sea does not extend beyond the moment when rescued people are disembarked in a place of safety. From the place of safety they are expected to proceed to the place of final destination. If illegal migrants are among the rescued people, as a general rule they should be returned to the state of which they are nationals or permanent residents. Under Article 18(1) of the Migrants Protocol:

> each State Party agrees to facilitate and accept, without undue or unreasonable delay, the return of a person who has been the object of conduct set forth in article 6 of this Protocol and who is its national or who has the right of permanent residence in its territory at the time of return.

However, illegal migrants are entitled to certain rights granted to them by international human rights law,[70] including refugee law, such as the right not to be returned to certain states. A number of general or specific questions need to be addressed in this regard.

A. The human rights specifically granted to migrants

A human right that must be specifically granted to migrants is the right to be humanely treated. The purpose to protect the migrants is clearly stated in the Migrants Protocol.

> The purpose of this Protocol is to prevent and combat the smuggling of migrants as well as to promote cooperation among States Parties to that end, while protecting the rights of the smuggled migrants. (Article 2)

Migrants, in particular the most vulnerable among them, have the right to be treated humanely by immigration officials, and to be protected from violence that may be inflicted on them by others.

> States Parties shall provide or strengthen specialized training for immigration and other relevant officials in preventing the conduct set forth in article 6 of this Protocol and in the humane treatment of migrants who have been the object of such conduct, while respecting their rights as set forth in this Protocol. (Article 14(1))
>
> Each State Party shall take appropriate measures to afford migrants appropriate protection against violence that may be inflicted upon them, whether by individuals or groups, by reason of being the object of conduct set forth in article 6 of this Protocol. (Article 16(2))
>
> In applying the provisions of this article, States Parties shall take into account the special needs of women and children. (Article 16(4))[71]

[70] See in general T. Treves, 'Human Rights and the Law of the Sea', 28 *Berkeley Journal of International Law* (2010) 1.

[71] States parties to the Migrants Protocol are also bound to adopt legislative measures to establish as an aggravating circumstance to the offence of smuggling of migrants the fact that it takes place in

From a moral point of view, the right to be humanely treated can be considered as a sign of the respect due to the overarching dignity of people who try to find the means to earn a living. This right exists even in cases where migrants are not smuggled, but travel by their own means. It is also stated in some of the relevant bilateral treaties:

> Such officials [law enforcement officials] shall also bear in mind the need to observe norms of courtesy, respect, and consideration for the persons on board the suspect vessel (Article 13 (2)(d) of the Agreement between the Dominican Republic and the United States).[72]
>
> All use of force pursuant to this Agreement shall be in strict accordance with the applicable laws and policies of the respective Party and shall in all cases be the minimum reasonably necessary under the circumstances.... (Article 14(1) of the same agreement).

Another human right that is granted to migrants seems to be that of not being treated as criminals because of their attempt to migrate. Even an asymmetrical right, such as the right to emigrate, should have some concrete meaning. While it cannot go so far as to be transformed into a right to be admitted into a foreign country, it should at least have the effect of preventing the criminal liability of those who have attempted to immigrate. Illegal migrants are very different from migrant smugglers. In most cases, the former are the victims of the latter. As rightly declared by Ecuador when ratifying the Migrants Protocol in 2002:

> migrants are the victims of illicit trafficking in persons on the part of criminal organizations whose only goal is unjust and undue enrichment at the expense of persons wishing to perform honest work abroad.

In treaty law the following provisions may be found in this regard:

> migrants shall not be liable to criminal prosecution under this Protocol for the fact of having been the object of conduct set forth in article 6 of this Protocol (Article 5 of the Migrants Protocol).
>
> The United States Government appreciates the assurances which it has received from the Government of the Republic of Haiti that Haitians returned to their country and who are not traffickers will not be subject to prosecution for illegal departure (Agreement between Haiti and the United States).[73]
>
> The Government of the Dominican Republic agrees that Dominicans and third country nationals returned to the Dominican Republic and who are not migrant smugglers will not be subject to prosecution for illegal departure (Article 10(3) of the Agreement between the Dominican Republic and the United States).[74]

The basic remark that illegal migrants are different from criminals who act at sea, such as pirates, or also elsewhere, such as terrorists,[75] or drug or weapons traffickers, is not understood by everyone, perhaps due to ignorance and sentiments of aggressive

conditions 'that entail inhuman or degrading treatment, including for exploitation, of such migrants' (Art. 6(3)(b)).

[72] See this chapter, II.C. [73] See this chapter, II.C. [74] See this chapter, II.C.

[75] On the distinction between migrants and terrorists, see M. R. Saulle and L. Manca (eds), *Migrazione e terrorismo: due fenomeni impropriamente abbinati* (2006).

xenophobia that are growing in some countries of destination. Two instances may be recalled in this regard.

In 2003 a collection of studies, sponsored by two research institutions, on the control of illegal migrant trafficking in the Mediterranean Sea was published in Italy.[76] One of the papers deals with the subject of non-lethal weapons.[77] It starts with the assumption that illegal migrants mingle with potential terrorists and their flankers.[78] In such a situation, the paper suggests the use of non-lethal weapons to counter craft transporting migrants by sea, the most appropriate of which is an 'intelligent torpedo' devised to block propellers. It would be launched by ships or aircraft. The paper devotes great attention to the economic aspects of the proposal, pointing out that the cost of an intelligent torpedo is about €1 million, but that it can be used for about one hundred missions, with a regenerating cost of €150,000. It also suggests that spare torpedoes which the Italian Navy keeps in its depots could be usefully transformed into intelligent torpedoes at low cost. Another non-lethal weapon considered in such an 'intelligent' paper is the vehicle-mounted active denial system. It produces a radiation beam that causes the skin to overheat and also causes shooting pain. The paper is kind enough to explain to the illegal migrants, including the potential terrorists who are surely on board, how to prevent the main harm threatened by such a device, 'permanent eye damage'. They can merely turn their heads to look in the opposite direction.[79] Unworthy of any further consideration, this paper is evidence of a blatant disregard for legal rules and moral principles.

In 1999 the meeting of heads of state and governments of NATO member states adopted a document entitled *The Alliance's Strategic Concept*. It also deals with NATO's military capabilities as well as its ability to contribute to conflict prevention and crisis management through response operations:

> Any armed attack on the territory of the Allies, from whatever direction, would be covered by Articles 5 and 6 of the Washington Treaty [the NATO Treaty]. However, Alliance security must also take account of the global context. Alliance security interests can be affected by other risks of a wider nature, including acts of terrorism, sabotage and organised crime, and by the disruption of the flow of vital resources. The uncontrolled movement of large numbers of people, particularly as a consequence of armed conflicts, can also pose problems for security and stability affecting the Alliance. Arrangements exist within the Alliance for consultation among the Allies under Article 4 of the Washington Treaty and, where appropriate, co-ordination of their efforts including their responses to risks of this kind. (paragraph 24)

Do these unclear , but clearly threatening, sentences mean that the 'uncontrolled movement of large numbers of people' can also be considered an 'armed attack', allowing NATO member states to use military force to 'defend' themselves

[76] Scuola Superiore dell'Economia e delle Finanze and Centro di Studi Geopolitica Economica, *Il controllo dei traffici migratori illeciti nel Mare Mediterraneo* (2003). The research was coordinated by C. Jean and G. M. Piccinelli, and directed by O. Cucuzza.

[77] L. Caglioti and F. Pierantoni, 'Profili tecnologici—Armi non letali' in Jean and Piccinelli (n 76) 421.

[78] Caglioti and Pierantoni (n 77) 424.

[79] Caglioti and Pierantoni (n 77) 437.

against the state from which the people come? Is such a movement a weapon, like a missile, against which military force can be used? Can the movement itself consequently be attacked by NATO member states? An affirmative answer to any of the questions would involve a sense of unbridled aggression and total distortion of the meaning of Article 51 of the Charter of the United Nations (and of Articles 5 and 7 of the NATO Treaty itself).

In this regard it should be remembered that in 1993 the United Nations Security Council, in Resolution 841 (1993), noted with concern the occurrence of a humanitarian crisis in Haiti, 'including mass displacement of population, becoming or aggravating threats to international peace and security'. It adopted a number of measures to establish a trade embargo against Haiti, from where a massive flow of people seeking refuge in neighbouring countries was originating. But it never went as far as considering that situation as an armed attack or an act of aggression by Haiti against other states. Yet there are some cases of states that considered massive flows of people fleeing from other countries as a threat to their territorial integrity. These kinds of movements, however, have a predominant humanitarian character and should never be assimilated to armed attacks.

B. The prohibition of returning an individual to a state where he risks being tortured

Besides the rights specifically granted to them, illegal migrants enjoy all the human rights granted to any individual and arising from customary international law and the treaties in force. Under the Migrants Protocol:

> in implementing this Protocol, each State Party shall take, consistent with its obligations under international law, all appropriate measures, including legislation if necessary, to preserve and protect the rights of persons who have been the object of conduct set forth in article 6 of this Protocol as accorded under applicable international law, in particular the right to life and the right not to be subjected to torture or other cruel, inhuman or degrading treatment or punishment. (Article 16(1))

The most fundamental human right is the right not to be subjected to torture or to inhuman or degrading treatment or punishment, provided for in Article 3 of the ECHR, Article 7 of the 1969 International Covenant on Civil and Political Rights, Article 5 of the American Convention on Human Rights, Article 5 of the 1981 African Charter on Human and Peoples Rights, and specifically regulated by the 1984 Convention against Torture and Other Cruel, Inhuman or Degrading Treatment or Punishment.[80] All these treaties provide that no derogation from this human right can be made.[81] They confirm that to the question as to whether a

[80] Hereinafter: CAT.

[81] According to the International Criminal Tribunal for the Former Yugoslavia, 'the prohibition of torture laid down in human rights treaties enshrines an absolute right, which can never be derogated from, not even in time of emergency (on this ground the prohibition applies to situations of armed conflicts). This is linked to the fact... that the prohibition of torture is a peremptory norm or *jus cogens*' (judgment of 10 December 1998 in the *Furundžija* case (Case IT-95-17/1), para. 144).

human being can be tortured, there is only one very simple answer: no, never. As stated in Article 2(2) CAT:

no exceptional circumstances whatsoever, whether a state of war or a threat of war, internal political instability or any other public emergency, may be invoked as a justification of torture.

The individual is protected against torture also in an indirect way, in the sense that international law prevents states from extraditing, expelling, or returning a person to a state where there are substantial grounds for believing that the person would be in danger of being subjected to torture. This is clearly stated in Article 3 CAT[82] and is constantly repeated in many decisions of international human rights courts.[83]

It also follows that illegal migrants cannot be returned to a state where, given the specific circumstances, they run the risk of being tortured or subjected to cruel, inhuman, or degrading treatment, even if the state in question is their own state or the state of their permanent residence. For the states which are parties to treaties that ban the death penalty, a similar prohibition applies also as regards extradition, expulsion, or return to states where the individuals concerned run the risk of being subjected to capital punishment.

C. Refugee rights

Other human rights relevant for migrants by sea are those linked to the condition of refugee, as provided for in the 1951 Convention Relating to the Status of Refugees (amended by the 1967 Protocol).[84] These rights are explicitly recognized by the Migrants Protocol[85] and by some bilateral treaties applicable to migration by sea,

[82] 'No State Party shall expel, return ('*refouler*') or extradite a person to another State where there are substantial grounds to believe that he would be in danger of being subjected to torture'.

[83] For example, the European Court of Human Rights found in the judgment of 7 July 1989 in *Soering v. United Kingdom*, ECHR (1989), Series A, No. 161, that '[i]t would hardly be compatible with the underlying values of the Convention, that "common heritage of political traditions, ideals, freedom and the rule of law" to which the Preamble refers, were a Contracting State knowingly to surrender a fugitive to another State where there were substantial grounds for believing that he would be in danger of being subjected to torture, however heinous the crime allegedly committed. Extradition in such circumstances, while not explicitly referred to in the brief and general wording of Art. 3, would plainly be contrary to the spirit and intendment of the Article' (at 88). For the judgment in the case *Saadi v. Italy* see n 91, this chapter.

[84] UNTS 189, 137, and UNTS 606, 267; hereinafter: Refugee Convention. 145 states are parties to the Refugee Convention and 146 to the 1967 Protocol. See G. Goodwin-Gill and J. McAdam, *The Refugee in International Law* (2007); S. Kneebone (ed.), *Refugees, Asylum Seekers and the Rule of Law* (2009); F. Lenzerini, *Asilo e diritti umani* (2009); C. Favilli (ed.), *Procedure e garanzie del diritto di asilo* (2011); T. Gammeltoft-Hansen, *Access to Asylum* (2011).

[85] 'Nothing in this Protocol shall affect the other rights, obligations and responsibilities of States and individuals under international law, including international humanitarian law and international human rights law and, in particular, where applicable, the 1951 Convention and the 1967 Protocol relating to the Status of Refugees and the principle of non-refoulement as contained therein' (Art. 22(1)).

such as the Agreement between Haiti and the United States,[86] and the Agreement between the Dominican Republic and the United States.[87]

A refugee is defined by the Refugee Convention as a person who,

> owing to well-founded fear of being persecuted for reasons of race, religion, nationality, membership of a particular social group or political opinion, is outside the country of his nationality and is unable or, owing to such fear, is unwilling to avail himself of the protection of that country; or who, not having a nationality and being outside the country of his former habitual residence, is unable or, owing to such fear, is unwilling to return to it. (Article 1(A)(2))

The status of refugee is a matter of fact and does not depend on an official recognition by any authority. The definition covers people who are persecuted for a number of specified reasons.[88] But it does not include people who, without being persecuted in their countries, are trying to flee conflicts, either international or internal, natural disasters, or poverty.[89]

It is important to note that the Refugee Convention does not provide the refugee with a right to receive asylum in any of its states parties.[90] In this respect, the Refugee Convention does not comply with Article 14(1) of the Universal Declaration of Human Rights ('everyone has the right to seek and to enjoy in other countries asylum from persecution'). Under the Refugee Convention, the refugee is granted only the right not to be returned to a state, including his own, where he would be threatened for a number of specific reasons (right of *non-refoulement*).

> No Contracting State shall expel or return ('refouler') a refugee in any manner whatsoever to the frontiers of territories where his life or freedom would be threatened on account of his race, religion, nationality, membership of a particular social group or political opinion. (Article 33(1))[91]

[86] See this chapter, II.C.'It is understood that under these arrangements the United States Government does not intend to return to Haiti any Haitian migrants whom the United States authorities determine to qualify for refugee status.'

[87] See this chapter, II.C 'Nothing in this Agreement shall . . . restrict the ability of either Party to take whatever steps it deems appropriate with regard to individuals whom its authorities determine may qualify for refugee status or otherwise merit international protection' (Art. 21).

[88] See J. Fishel de Andrade, 'On the Development of the Concept of "Persecution" in International Refugee Law', 3 *Anuário Brasileiro de Direito Internacional* (2008) 114.

[89] Arts 9 and 10 of European Union Council Directive 2004/83 of 29 April 2004, OJ 2004 L 304, provide an interpretation on how the concept of 'persecution' should be understood by member states. For a particular category of refugees see L. Westra, *Environmental Justice and the Rights of Ecological Refugees* (2009).

[90] Such a right might be granted by the domestic legislation of the states concerned. For example, under Art. 10(3) of the Constitution of Italy, enacted in 1947, 'an alien who in his country is prevented from effectively exercising the democratic freedoms guaranteed by the Italian Constitution, has the right of asylum in the territory of the Republic according to the conditions established by the law' (unofficial translation).

[91] The right of not being returned is subject to a condition: 'The benefit of the present provision may not, however, be claimed by a refugee whom there are reasonable grounds for regarding as a danger to the security of the country in which he is or who, having been convicted by a final judgment of a particularly serious crime, constitutes a danger to the community of that country' (Art. 33(2)). In the judgment of 28 February 2008 in *Saadi v. Italy* (Application No. 37201/06), relating to the expulsion to Tunisia of a Tunisian refugee convicted in his country for crimes related to terrorism, the European Court of Human

Here can be found another example of asymmetrical rights. A refugee, who has a right not to be returned to a country where he is threatened, has no right of entry into a given state. He could be rejected and expelled to a state where he is not threatened, but the latter in its turn has no obligation to allow the entry of the refugee. If states, one after the other, reject the refugee, where should he be entitled to settle? In the unclaimed sector of Antarctica? On the high seas? On the moon, or in outer space?

Even though the Refugee Convention is not clear on this crucial question, it seems implied in a treaty that recognizes 'the social and humanitarian nature of the problem of refugees' (Preamble) that a refugee who is outside his country and presents himself to an official of a state party has a right to submit an application for asylum and to have it processed and screened. States cannot play with 'asymmetrical rights' beyond a certain limit and reach the point where the true objective of a treaty is overturned. If the refugee cannot decide whether, where, and when he will be admitted, he should at least be granted a right to present himself to submit an application to a state party to the Refugee Convention; a right to fair and efficient asylum procedures. The right of the refugee to have access to the territory of a state party to seek asylum is indirectly implied in Article 31(1) Refugee Convention.

> The Contracting States shall not impose penalties, on account of their illegal entry or presence, on refugees who, coming directly from a territory where their life or freedom was threatened in the sense of article 1, enter or are present in their territory without authorization, provided they present themselves without delay to the authorities and show good cause for their illegal entry or presence.

As remarked by the United Nations High Commissioner for Refugees,[92] who is in charge of supervising the application of the Refugee Convention:

> As a general rule, in order to give effect to their obligations under the 1951 Convention and/or 1967 Protocol, States will be required to grant individuals seeking international protection access to the territory and to fair and efficient asylum procedures.[93]

Already in 1979, the UNHCR Executive Committee (*Conclusions No. 15 on refugees without an asylum country*) placed emphasis on the need to grant to asylum seekers temporary refuge:

Rights found that Art. 3 ECHR, which prohibits torture or inhumane or degrading treatment, has priority over Art. 33(2) of the Refugee Convention: 'Since protection against the treatment prohibited by Article 3 is absolute, that provision imposes an obligation not to extradite or expel any person who, in the receiving country, would run the real risk of being subjected to such treatment. As the Court has repeatedly held, there can be no derogation from that rule. It must therefore reaffirm the principle . . . that it is not possible to weigh the risk of ill-treatment against the reasons put forward for the expulsion in order to determine whether the responsibility of a State is engaged under Article 3, even where such treatment is inflicted by another State. In that connection, the conduct of the person concerned, however undesirable or dangerous, cannot be taken into account, with the consequence that the protection afforded by Article 3 is broader than that provided for in Articles 32 and 33 of the 1951 United Nations Convention relating to the Status of Refugees' (para. 138).

[92] Hereinafter: UNHCR.

[93] [UNHCR, *Advisory Opinion on the Extraterritorial Application of Non-Refoulement Obligations under the 1951 Convention relating to the Status of Refugees and its 1967 Protocol*, 26 January 2007, para. 8.

In cases of large-scale influx, persons seeking asylum should always receive at least temporary refuge. States which because of their geographical situation, or otherwise, are faced with a large-scale influx should as necessary and at the request of the State concerned receive immediate assistance from other States in accordance with the principle of equitable burden-sharing. Such States should consult with the Office of the United Nations High Commissioner for Refugees as soon as possible to ensure that the persons involved are fully protected, are given emergency assistance, and that durable solutions are sought (paragraph f).

D. Refugees on the high seas

Under Article 1(A)(2) of the Refugee Convention, the status of refugee is attributed to a person who is 'outside the country of his nationality'.[94] This wording can only be interpreted as referring to the national territory of the country in question, including the territorial sea. A person who is on the high seas—that is, beyond the territory of his country, or in the territorial sea of a country different from his own—does qualify as a refugee, provided that also the other relevant conditions are met. It follows that the rights of *non-refoulement* and of seeking asylum apply also to refugees found everywhere at sea, with the exception of the territorial sea of their state.

As pointed out by the UNHCR, there is concern that immigration control measures at sea (so-called interception at sea)[95] do not distinguish between refugees and illegal migrants. In the absence of adequate safeguards, this may result in refugees in need of international protection being turned back, sometimes in situations of danger:

States have a legitimate interest in controlling irregular migration. Unfortunately, existing control tools, such as visa requirements and the imposition of carrier sanctions, as well as interception measures, often do not differentiate between genuine asylum-seekers and economic migrants.[96]

As the identification of asylum seekers and the processing of their applications are activities which normally cannot be carried out on ships, the obligation of the intercepting state is to disembark the refugees in a state where they can exercise the right to fair and efficient asylum procedures, normally the intercepting state itself.

UNHCR's position is that claims for international protection made by intercepted persons are in principle to be processed in procedures within the territory of the intercepting State. This will usually be the most practical means to provide access to reception facilities and to

[94] Nobody can be a refugee in his own country.

[95] Document quoted n 12, this chapter. See also N. Ronzitti, 'Coastal State Jurisdiction over Refugees and Migrants at Sea', in N. Ando, E. McWhinney, and R. Wolfrum (eds), *Liber Amicorum Judge Shigeru Oda* (2002), II, 1271; G. Goodwin-Gill, 'The Right to Seek Asylum: Interception at Sea and the Principle of Non-Refoulement', 23 *International Journal of Refugee Law* (2011) 443.

[96] UNHCR, *Interception of Asylum-Seekers and Refugees: The International Framework and Recommendations for a Comprehensive Approach*, UN Doc EC/50/SC/CPR.17, 9 June 2000, para. 17.

fair and efficient asylum procedures – core components of any protection-sensitive entry system – and to ensure protection of the rights of the individual.[97]

The UNCHR has recently taken the position that, under certain circumstances, also the extraterritorial processing of asylum claims can take place as an acceptable alternative to processing by the intercepting state.

However, under certain circumstances, the processing of international protection claims outside the intercepting State could be an alternative to standard 'incountry' procedures. Notably, this could be the case when extraterritorial processing is used as part of a burden-sharing arrangement to more fairly distribute responsibilities and enhance available protection space.[98]

Arrangements for the temporary reception of refugees for the extraterritorial processing of their asylum claims must address their basic needs 'and provide for a stay consistent with the right to an adequate standard of living'.[99] Prolonged stays in closed reception facilities are not appropriate.[100] People with special needs, such as children, women, trafficked persons, or victims of torture or trauma, require special consideration.[101] States with jurisdiction over extraterritorial reception and processing arrangements, such as the intercepting state and all states involved in the processing, are responsible for ensuring a timely outcome for all intercepted persons.[102] This normally consists of settlement or resettlement for persons entitled to refugee status and of return to the country of origin for the others. Four different models of extraterritorial reception and processing have been taken into consideration by the UNHCR, namely: third-state processing, carried out in and by a state other than the intercepting state; out-of-country processing, carried out by the intercepting state in the territory of another state or on part of the territory of the intercepting state that has been declared extraterritorial for migration purposes; regional processing, carried out jointly by several transit or destination states; and processing on board maritime vessels, which however is generally considered as not appropriate.[103]

The summary conclusions of a meeting of experts on 'Refugees and asylum-seekers in distress at sea—How best to respond?', held in Djibouti in November 2011 under the sponsorship of UNHCR, include a 'Model framework for cooperation following rescue at sea operations involving refugees and asylum-seekers',

[97] UNHCR, Protection Policy Paper, *Maritime Interception Operations and the Processing of International Protection Claims: Legal Standards and Policy Considerations with Respect to Extraterritorial Processing*, November 2010, para. 2.

[98] UNHCR, *Maritime Interception Operations and the Processing of International Protection Claims*, (n 97) para. 3.

[99] UNHCR, *Maritime Interception Operations* (n 97) at para. 23.

[100] UNHCR, *Maritime Interception Operations* (n 97) at para. 27.

[101] UNHCR, *Maritime Interception Operations* (n 97) at para. 28.

[102] UNHCR, *Maritime Interception Operations* (n 97) at para. 30.

[103] UNHCR, *Maritime Interception Operations* (n 97) at paras 36–59.

which aims at enhancing international cooperation among concerned states and other stakeholders.[104] The document is based on the assumption that:

fundamentally, a core challenge in any particular rescue at sea operation involving asylum-seekers and refugees is often the timely identification of a place of safety for disembarkation, as well as necessary follow-up, including reception arrangements, access to appropriate processes and procedures, and outcomes. If a shipmaster is likely to face delays in disembarking rescued people, he/she may be less ready to come to the assistance of those in distress at sea. Addressing these challenges and developing predictable responses requires strengthened cooperation and coordination among all States and other stakeholders implicated in rescue at sea operations. (paragraph 10)

It is envisaged that, in joining the model framework, each concerned state commits to undertake specific responsibilities which may include coordinating search and rescue activities, carrying out such activities, providing a place of disembarkation and initial reception, processing rescued persons, providing solutions for them, and providing financial support to affected states. The states concerned are also invited to establish a task force to identify according to relevant factors the most appropriate country for disembarkation,[105] to ensure adequate reception arrangements, to establish mechanisms for profiling and referral to identify and differentiate among rescued persons according to their background and needs, to process asylum claims in accordance with applicable international standards, to provide a range of outcomes to rescued persons, and to allow UNHCR to undertake a number of activities.

Regional approaches should be envisaged, where appropriate. For instance, negotiations are being held within the IMO framework for a memorandum of understanding on concerted procedures relating to disembarkation of persons rescued at sea which would apply to the Mediterranean area.[106]

E. The application at sea of human rights law

A tool used by certain states to elude international human rights law, including refugee law, is the strange theory that international human rights rules do not apply to persons found outside the national territory of the state. This theory is somehow based on a restrictive interpretation of the word 'jurisdiction'—indeed a word having a rather opaque meaning—which is understood as 'territory'.

Apart from the case of illegal migration, this strange theory has recently been applied by the United States with regard to the practice of extraordinary renditions. This is a gross violation of a number of fundamental human rights, such as the right

[104] See also the summary conclusions of an expert meeting on 'International cooperation to share burdens and responsibilities', held in Amman in June 2011 under the sponsorship of UNHCR.

[105] 'Relevant factors in identifying the place of disembarkation include: practical considerations (e.g., maritime safety; geographical proximity; the extent to which the rescuing vessel will be required to deviate from its intended voyage; the needs of rescued persons; facilities at the proposed site of disembarkation, including access to fair and efficient asylum procedures; applicable SAR and SOLAS provisions; the principle of *non-refoulement*)' (para. 4, ii).

[106] See IMO circular letter No. 3203 of 18 August 2011.

not to be subjected to enforced disappearance or torture. Some non-American nationals suspected of terrorism were kidnapped by American secret agents in states other than the United States, including several European countries with the complicity of the local secret services, and were forcibly transported to a third state where torture was carried out to extract information from them. As stated in 2006 by the United States legal advisor, John Bellinger, Article 3 CAT (no-return obligation),[107] and other human rights treaties to which the United States is a party as well, are deemed not to be binding on the US agents when they act outside the national territory.

> For more than a decade, the position of the US Government, and our courts, has been that all of those terms refer to returns from, or transfers out from the United States. So we think that Article 3 of the CAT is legally binding upon us with respect to transfers of anyone from the United States; but we don't think it is legally binding outside the United States.[108]

As has been rightly remarked, the strange theory in question leads to a situation of 'legal apartheid', according to which, if United States territory[109] and American nationals are protected from torture, foreign individuals can be tortured elsewhere under the 'sponsorship' of American agents.

> The rendition, abduction and detention of terrorist suspects have always taken place outside the territory of the United States, where such actions would no doubt have been ruled unlawful and unconstitutional. Obviously, these actions are also unacceptable under the laws of European countries, who nonetheless tolerated them or colluded actively in carrying them out. This export of illegal activities overseas is all the more shocking in that it shows fundamental contempt for the countries on whose territories it was decided to commit the relevant acts. The fact that the measures only apply to non-American citizens is just as disturbing: it reflects a kind of 'legal apartheid' and an exaggerated sense of superiority. Once again, the blame does not lie solely with the Americans but also, above all, with European political leaders who have knowingly acquiesced in this state of affairs.[110]

It must be very clearly stated that the strange theory that human rights treaties apply only within the territory of states parties is not only wrong, but it also makes a mockery of the rule of law. Human rights obligations bind states wherever their agents act. In the context of human rights treaties, the term 'jurisdiction'[111] is to be

[107] For the text see n 82, this chapter.

[108] Parliamentary Assembly of the Council of Europe (PACE), *Alleged Secret Detentions and Unlawful Inter-State Transfers Involving Council of Europe Member States, Draft Report—Part II (Explanatory Memorandum)*, Rapporteur Mr Dick Marty, Part II, 7 June 2006, para. 272. Whether or not the United States maintains the same position also today is a question that would need further research and goes beyond the scope of the present chapter.

[109] Incidentally, is Guantánamo Bay within the United States' territory? Apparently it is not. But this question also requires further research and goes beyond the scope of the present chapter.

[110] PACE, *Alleged Secret Detentions* (n 108) para. 4.

[111] The word 'jurisdiction' is often used to indicate the scope of application of human rights treaties. 'Each State Party to the present Covenant undertakes to respect and to ensure to all individuals within its territory and subject to its jurisdiction the rights recognized in the present Covenant' (Art. 2(1) ICCPR). 'The High Contracting Parties shall secure to everyone within their jurisdiction the rights and freedoms defined in Section I of this Convention' (Art. 1 ECHR). 'The States Parties to this Convention undertake to respect the rights and freedoms recognized herein and to ensure to all persons

understood as 'power or effective control', with the consequence that respect for human rights is due to any individual who is under the power or effective control of any agent of a state party, wherever he happens to act. The general rule that treaties have to be interpreted in good faith in accordance with the ordinary meaning of the terms of the treaty in their context[112] and in the light of its object and purpose (Article 31(1) of the Vienna Convention on the Law of Treaties) cannot be undermined and nullified by playing with legal devices on the territorial application of treaties.[113]

As stated in 2004 by the Human Rights Committee in General Comment No. 31 on the nature of the general legal obligation on states parties to the International Covenant on Civil and Political Rights, such states

> must respect and ensure the rights laid down in the Covenant to anyone within the power or effective control of that State Party, even if not situated within the territory of the State Party.[114]

The Committee Against Torture, established under CAT, held in its decision of 21 November 2008 on the communication *J.H.A. v. Spain*, relating to a case where Spain rescued on the high seas 369 illegal migrants and returned them to Mauritania,[115] that:

> jurisdiction must also include situations where a State party exercises, directly or indirectly, in whole or in part, de jure or de facto control, in accordance with international law.... [T]he State party maintained control over the persons on board the *Marine I* from the time the vessel was rescued and throughout the identification and repatriation process that took place in Nouadhibou. (paragraph 8.2)

The present jurisprudence of the European Court of Human Rights confirms that the ECHR binds states parties also beyond their territory[116] and in particular on the

subject to their jurisdiction the free and full exercise of those rights and freedoms' (Art. 1(1) of the American Convention on Human Rights). 'Each State Party shall take effective legislative, administrative, judicial or other measures to prevent acts of torture in any territory under its jurisdiction' (Art. 2(1) CAT).

[112] In any case the ordinary meaning of 'jurisdiction'—a word nobody knows the precise meaning of—is much closer to 'power or effective control' than to 'territory'.

[113] Under Art. 29 of the same convention, 'unless a different intention appears from the treaty or is otherwise established, a treaty is binding upon each party in respect of its entire territory'. This provision says that treaties normally do not apply to portions of the territory of a state party. But it does not say anything about the application of treaties beyond national territory.

[114] UN Doc CCPR/C/21/Rev.1/Add.13, 26 May 2004, para. 10.

[115] See K. Wouters and M. Den Heijer, 'The *Marine I* Case: a Comment', 22 *International Journal of Refugee Law* (2010) 1. On the agreements concluded by Spain with some West African States, see I. Lirola Delgado, 'España y la lucha contra el tráfico ilícito de inmigrantes por mar, in J. Pueyo Losa and J. J. Urbina (eds), *La cooperación internacional en la ordenación de los mares y océanos* (2009) 397.

[116] It seems that the Court is presently trying to get rid of the disgraceful inheritance of the decision of 12 December 2001 in *Banković and Others v. Belgium, the Czech Republic, Denmark, France, Germany, Greece, Hungary, Iceland, Italy, Luxembourg, Norway, the Netherlands, Poland, Portugal, Spain, Turkey and United Kingdom* (Application No. 52207/99), where it held that 'Article 1 of the Convention must be considered to reflect this ordinary and essentially territorial notion of jurisdiction, other bases of jurisdiction being exceptional and requiring special justification in the particular circumstances of each case' (para. 61). The result was that the applications by the relatives of a number

high seas. In the judgment of 29 March 2010 in the case *Medvedyev and others v. France*, the Grand Chamber of the Court held that the interception on the high seas by France of a Cambodian ship engaged in drug trafficking was within the jurisdiction of France for the purposes of the ECHR.[117]

In the recent judgment of 23 February 2012 in the case of *Hirsi Jamaa and others v. Italy*,[118] the Grand Chamber of the Court concluded that the ECHR applies in cases where a state party has exercised its jurisdiction outside its national territory.[119] In particular, the ECHR applies on the high seas, which cannot be seen as an area outside the law.

> Furthermore, as regards the exercise by a State of its jurisdiction on the high seas, the Court has already stated that the special nature of the maritime environment cannot justify an area outside the law where individuals are covered by no legal system capable of affording them enjoyment of the rights and guarantees protected by the Convention which the States have undertaken to secure to everyone within their jurisdiction. (paragraph 178)

The Court consequently found that also the operations of interception of illegal migrants on the high seas must be carried out in compliance with the obligations arising from the ECHR and its protocols.

> Having regard to the foregoing, the Court considers that the removal of aliens carried out in the context of interceptions on the high seas by the authorities of a State in the exercise of their sovereign authority, the effect of which is to prevent migrants from reaching the borders of the State or even to push them back to another State, constitutes an exercise of jurisdiction within the meaning of Article 1 of the Convention which engages the responsibility of the State in question under Article 4 of Protocol No. 4. (paragraph 180)

The conclusion that may also be drawn is that the obligation of *non-refoulement* provided for in Article 33(1) Refugee Convention, which is a human right specifically applying to refugees, binds states parties wherever their agents act, including the high seas. When the refugees are on board a ship, they are subject to the jurisdiction of the flag state, as if they were on the territory of that state. As stated by the UNHCR:

> The principle of *non-refoulement* does not imply any geographical limitation. In UNCHR's understanding, the resulting obligations extend to all government agents acting in an official capacity, within or outside national territory. Given the practice of States to intercept persons at great distance from their own territory, the international refugee protection regime

of Yugoslav civilians allegedly killed by bombs dropped by the air forces of states parties were found inadmissible because Yugoslavia was not a party to the ECHR. See, in general, P. De Sena, *La nozione di giurisdizione statale nei trattati sui diritti dell'uomo* (2002).

[117] Application No. 3394/03. The interception took place with the authorization of Cambodia.

[118] Application No. 27765/09. On the merits of the case see this chapter, III.F. See also F. Lenzerini, 'Il principio del non refoulement dopo la sentenza Hirsi della Corte europea dei diritti dell'uomo', 95 *Rivista di Diritto Internazionale* (2012) 721 A. Liguori, 'La Corte europea dei diritti dell'uomo condanna l'Italiaper i respingimenti verso la Libia del 2009: il caso Hirsi', 95 *Rivista di Diritto Internazionale* (2012) 415.

[119] Para. 178.

would be rendered ineffective if States' agents abroad were free to act at variance with obligations under international refugee law and human rights law.[120]

F. Some relevant instances (United States, Australia, Italy, European Union)

In international practice some instances of dubious compliance with human rights obligations at sea may be found, as the following cases show.

A) Adopted to deal with a massive flow of refugees from Haiti, Executive Order 12807 of 24 May 1992 (Interdiction of Illegal Aliens), provides that the President of the United States:

> has authority to suspend the entry of aliens coming by sea to the United States without necessary documentation, to establish reasonable rules and regulations regarding, and other limitations on, the entry or attempted entry of aliens into the United States, and to repatriate aliens interdicted beyond the territorial sea of the United States. (Section 1)

The order applies to ships flying the flag of the US, to ships without nationality and to ships flying the flag of a state with which the US has arrangements authorizing their stopping and boarding. It gives to the US Attorney General the power to decide 'in his unreviewable discretion' that a person who is a refugee will not be returned to another state without his consent.

By the judgment of 21 June 1993 in the case *Sale et al. v. Haitian Centers Council, Inc., et al.*[121] the US Supreme Court held that Article 33(1) Refugee Convention does not prohibit the return to other states of migrant aliens intercepted on the high seas without giving them the possibility to present asylum claims.[122] The general prohibition to 'return ("*refouler*")' was understood by the Court in the restricted and unwarranted meaning of a prohibition to exclude at the border. The Court did not consider that a refugee is, by definition, someone who is outside the country of his nationality and not someone who presents himself at the border of another country. The Court relied on the statements made by delegates of a few states during the *travaux préparatoires* for the Refugee Convention, without considering that recourse to the preparatory works, which is a supplementary means of interpretation, cannot change the ordinary meaning of a term used in a treaty (see Articles 31 and 32 of the Vienna Convention on the Law of Treaties). As remarked by the dissenting Justice Blackmun:

[120] UNHCR, *Interception of Asylum-Seekers*, see n 12, at para. 23. See S. Trevisanut, 'The Principle of *Non-Refoulement* at Sea and the Effectiveness of Asylum Protection', 12 *Max Planck Yearbook of United Nations Law* (2008) 205; S. Trevisanut, 'Diritto di asilo e contrasto dell'immigrazione irregolare via mare', in C. Favilli (ed.), *Procedure e garanzie del diritto di asilo* (2011) 241.

[121] 32 *International Legal Materials* (1993) 1041.

[122] For a comment see T. D. Jones, 'International Decisions: Sale v. Haitian Centers Council, Inc.', 88 *American Journal of International Law* (1994) 114.

what is extraordinary in this case is that the Executive, in disregard of the law, would take to the seas to intercept fleeing refugees and force them back to their persecutors – and that the Court would strain to sanction that conduct.[123]

The refugees attempting to escape from Haiti do not claim a right of admission to this country. They do not even argue that the Government has a right to intercept their boats. They demand only that the United States, land of refugees and guardian of freedom, cease forcibly driving them back to detention, abuse, and death. That is a modest plea, vindicated by the Treaty and the statute. We should not close our ears to it. I dissent.[124]

B) In 2001, Australia adopted the Migration Amendment (Excision from Migration Zone) Act. It provides for cutting out (so-called 'excision') certain portions of Australian territory, such as Christmas Island, the Cocos Islands, and the Ashmore and Cartier Islands, from the 'migration zone', the area where applications for protection visas may be made by people having entered Australia without lawful authority, including refugees. Refugees in the excision zone are considered 'offshore entry persons' and are prevented from applying for asylum, unless the Minister for Immigration and Citizenship exercises his discretionary and non-compellable power to allow them to apply. No judicial remedies are available to them. They can be removed to another state (so-called 'declared country'), where their applications for asylum can be processed if the Minister is satisfied that appropriate arrangements are in place to prevent their *refoulement* from the declared state.

It is doubtful whether the application of the Australian legislation complies with the obligations arising from the Refugee Convention, to which Australia is a party, and in particular with the obligation to grant to a refugee fair and efficient asylum procedures. There is no reason why this treaty should not apply to the entire Australian territory.

C) In May 2009, Italy started a new policy of intercepting migrants at sea and sending them back to the countries from which their ships sailed, in particular Libya and Algeria ('push-back policy').[125] Most of the intercepted migrants have the nationality of Eritrea, Somalia, or other African countries. In the brief period between May and July 2009, a total of 602 migrants were pushed back, or returned, to Libya, and twenty-three to Algeria, including children and pregnant women.

The report of the visit made in 2009 by a delegation of the European Committee for the Prevention of Torture,[126] established under the 1987 European Convention for the Prevention of Torture and Inhuman or Degrading Treatment or

[123] 32 *International Legal Materials* (1993) 1041, 1059.

[124] 32 *International Law Materials* (1993) 1039, 1068.

[125] The already mentioned 2007 Protocol between Italy and Libya (this chapter, II.C) generically provides that the patrolling naval units are bound to act 'in compliance with international conventions in force, according to the operational modalities to be defined by the competent authorities of the two countries'. Nowhere in the Protocol is the Refugee Convention explicitly mentioned, to which only Italy—but not Libya—is a party.

[126] Hereinafter: CPT.

Punishment,[127] casts many doubts on Italy's compliance with its international obligations. The CPT remarks that cooperation received during the visit by Italy was regrettably unsatisfactory, as documents and information were kept confidential in violation of Articles 3[128] and 8(2)[129] of the ECPT.[130] On the substance, the CPT points out that the Italian push-back operations are carried out without any concern for the identification of the migrants and their right to present asylum applications.

The Italian authorities have acknowledged officially that they do not proceed with the formal identification of migrants who are intercepted at sea and pushed back. The CPT has, however, been informed by the UNHCR that among the migrants pushed back there were persons who were registered with the UNHCR and to whom it had previously issued temporary documents. Other migrants, including persons from Somalia and Eritrea, were later interviewed by the UNHCR and found immediately to be seeking and possibly qualifying for international protection.[131]

In the specific case, Italy insisted on the circumstance that no illegal migrants made any requests for asylum. However, the credibility of such a justification totally depends on the factual conditions in which operations of interception at sea were carried out. A number of questions should be asked in this regard. Were the migrants ever given the opportunity to be in a condition to present their asylum application, if they had any?

Nevertheless, the Italian Government has affirmed that no migrant has ever expressed his/her intention to apply for asylum and that, consequently, there has been no need to identify these persons and establish their nationality. Even if what is affirmed were to correspond to reality, it must be borne in mind that persons surviving a sea voyage are often not in a condition in which they should be expected to declare immediately their wish to apply for asylum.[132]

This is particularly the case when the circumstances are such that the persons concerned are not in a position to express such a request. In this regard, a Coast Guard Admiral responsible for a large Search and Rescue area stated to the delegation that persons surviving a sea voyage were clearly not in a condition in which they should be expected to declare their wish to apply for asylum. In particular, such persons were often dehydrated, physically and mentally exhausted and their sole preoccupation at the time of rescue was to be brought to safety.[133]

[127] ETS 126. Hereinafter: ECPT.

[128] 'In the application of this Convention, the Committee and the competent national authorities of the Party concerned shall co-operate with each other'.

[129] 'A Party shall provide the Committee with the following facilities to carry out its task: . . . other information available to the Party which is necessary for the Committee to carry out its task. In seeking such information, the Committee shall have regard to applicable rules of national law and professional ethics'.

[130] 'The CPT considers that the shortcomings outlined . . . , when taken together clearly indicate that the Italian authorities have not been engaging with the Committee in a co-operative spirit in relation to the issue addressed during the visit'. Council of Europe, Report to the Italian Government on the visit to Italy carried out by the European Committee for the Prevention of Torture and Inhuman or Degrading Treatment or Punishment (CPT) from 27 to 31 July 2003, CPT/Inf (2010) 14, 28 April 2010, para. 9.

[131] Council of Europe, Report to the Italian Government (n.130) at para. 13.

[132] Council of Europe, Report to the Italian Government (n.130) at para. 14.

[133] Council of Europe, Report to the Italian Government (n.130) at para. 32.

Were the Italian officials prepared to deal with potential asylum-seekers speaking languages other than Italian?

> Further, information gathered through interviews held by the delegation would indicate that, even if a migrant were to request protection whilst aboard an Italian vessel, there is no procedure in place capable of referring him/her to a protection mechanism; nor have the competent authorities been instructed on how to identify and screen migrants. It should be noted, in this context, that intercepted migrants do not have access to linguistic or legal assistance on board the intercepting vessels, in order to express their needs.
>
> Indeed, representatives of both the Navy and the Coast Guard with whom the delegation spoke, clearly stated that they are not responsible in any way for the identification of migrants, the provision of information on how to apply for asylum, or the treatment of asylum requests; nor have they been instructed by the Ministry of the Interior in relation to these issues. The information gathered from representatives of the *Guardia di Finanza* [Italian Finance Police] also indicated that it did not proceed to individual identification of the migrants, though collective interviews may be carried out.[134]

Can a request for asylum be made in a situation where, as alleged, force is used in a disproportionate way?

> The delegation was unable to interview the migrants pushed back to Libya or, given the authorities' refusal to provide their names, the captains of the Italian vessels involved in the operation. However, reliable information collected by the delegation would indicate that, during the operation, which lasted around 12 hours, the 74 persons on the *Guardia di Finanza* vessel were provided insufficient water and no food or blankets; further, physical violence, in particular with kicks, punches and blows with an oar, was allegedly used against a number of migrants by Libyan police at the harbour in Tripoli, to force them to disembark from the two Coast Guard vessels.[135]

As regards the issues related to torture, the CPT recalls the peremptory norm of international law that prevents a state from sending a person to another state where there are substantial grounds for believing that he would run a real risk of being subjected to torture or other forms of ill-treatment.[136] It is the practice of the CPT to recommend to all parties to the ECPT

> that they ensure that migrants have ready access to an asylum procedure (or other residence procedure) which guarantees both confidentiality and an objective and independent analysis of the human rights situation in other countries. That procedure should involve an individual assessment of the risk of ill-treatment in case of expulsion of the person concerned to the country of origin or a third country.[137]

According to the CPT, states are obliged, in order to comply with the principle of *non-refoulement*, to screen intercepted migrants with a view to identifying persons in need of protection, assessing those needs, and taking appropriate action.[138]

[134] Council of Europe, Report to the Italian Government (n 130) at para. 13.
[135] Council of Europe, Report to the Italian Government (n 130) at para. 18.
[136] Council of Europe, Report to the Italian Government (n 130) at para. 26.
[137] Council of Europe, Report to the Italian Government (n 130) at para. 27.
[138] Council of Europe, Report to the Italian Government (n 130) at para. 30.

In view of the specific circumstances, the alleged absence of requests for asylum could not be taken as a justification for returning people to states where their right not to be tortured could be violated.[139]

Considering also that Libya is not a party to the Refugee Convention and that it does not have asylum legislation or procedures in place, the view of the CPT is that,

> there would appear to be a real risk . . . that persons detained in Libya, including migrants, may be subjected to severe ill-treatment and/or be sent to a country where they are at risk of such treatment.[140]

The conclusion of the CPT is that the Italian push-back policy does not meet the requirements 'to ensure that migrants are provided with appropriate treatment, are given an opportunity to apply for asylum and are not sent back to a country where they may be at risk of ill-treatment'.[141]

Yet the response given by Italy to the CPT report[142] far from improves the Italian position. Beside insisting on the existence of state secrets[143] (in a case involving torture!), Italy puts forward legal formalisms on who should first pronounce the word 'asylum':

> It is the opinion of Italian Authorities that, according to international and EU standards, there is no obligation during search and rescue operations to provide information on the possibility to apply for asylum. On the contrary, such information has to be ensured once the migrant expresses his/her willingness to apply for asylum. . . .
>
> To confirm such approach, Italian Authorities recall that when a migrant rescued at sea expresses the intention to apply for asylum or other forms of international protection on board of an Italian vessel, s/he is not returned to the country of departure/transit but s/he is brought to Italy. The same rule applies to all those who, after a medical visit, are in need of medical assistance.[144]

The Italian response sidesteps the main points. How could the interlocutors, namely the Italian official and the migrant, who spoke different tongues and who were in a situation of danger and acting at haste, understand each other? Before the

[139] 'In any event, the absence of an explicit request for asylum does not necessarily absolve the Italian authorities of their *non-refoulement* obligations under Article 3 of the ECHR' (Council of Europe, Report to the Italian Government (n 130) at para. 32).

[140] Council of Europe, Report to the Italian Government (n 130) at para. 47. 'The CPT has not itself been in a position to verify, through an on-site visit, conditions of detention and the treatment afforded to persons detained in Libya. However, according to consistent accounts from a variety of sources, overcrowding, absence of beds, poor hygiene, inadequacy of food, lack of health care and sanitation, and rampant skin infections would appear to be commonplace in Libyan detention centres. The UNHCR has recently described the conditions of detention and treatment in such centres as "appalling"'. (Council of Europe, Report to the Italian Government (n 130) at para. 42).

[141] Council of Europe, Report to the Italian Government (n 130) at para. 51.

[142] Council of Europe, Response of the Italian Government to the report of the European Committee for the Prevention of Torture and Inhuman or Degrading Treatment or Punishment (CPT) on its visit to Italy from 27–31 July 2009, CPT/Inf (2010) 15, 28 April 2010.

[143] 'Once again, Italian Authorities recall that for security reasons, they are not in a position to provide the names of either the commanders of the Units involved or the physicians. Accordingly, neither logbooks nor relating documents can be provided since they should be considered as classified material'. (Council of Europe, Response of the Italian Government (n 142) at para. A).

[144] Council of Europe, Response of the Italian Government (n 142) at para. D.

operations, had the applicable rules on refugees ever been explained to the Italian officials by their instructors?

The judgment, unanimously rendered on 21 February 2012 by the European Court of Human Rights (Grand Chamber) in the case *Hirsi Jamaa and others v. Italy*,[145] confirms that the Italian push-back policy does not comply with the obligations arising from the ECHR. The case was filed by eleven Somalis and thirteen Eritreans who were among a group of about 200 migrants intercepted at sea by Italian authorities, and summarily returned to Libya. The applicants claimed violations of a number of provisions of the ECHR, including Article 3 (Torture) and Article 4 of Protocol No. 4 (Prohibition of collective expulsion of aliens).

As regards the existence of bilateral agreements on the fight against illegal migration,[146] the Court observed that:

> Italy cannot evade its own responsibility by relying on its obligations arising out of bilateral agreements with Libya. Even if it were to be assumed that those agreements made express provision for the return to Libya of migrants intercepted on the high seas, the Contracting States' responsibility continues even after their having entered into treaty commitments subsequent to the entry into force of the Convention or its Protocols in respect of these States. (paragraph 129)

On the merits, the Court found that Italy was responsible for a violation of Article 3 ECHR, as it had exposed the applicants to the risk of being subjected to torture or inhuman or degrading treatment in Libya or in their countries of origin.

> [D]uring the period in question no rule governing the protection of refugees was complied with by Libya. Any person entering the country by illegal means was deemed to be clandestine and no distinction was made between irregular migrants and asylum seekers. Consequently, those persons were systematically arrested and detained in conditions that outside visitors, such as delegations from the UNHCR, Human Rights Watch and Amnesty International, could only describe as inhuman. Many cases of torture, poor hygiene conditions and lack of appropriate medical care were denounced by all the observers. Clandestine migrants were at risk of being returned to their countries of origin at any time and, if they managed to regain their freedom, were subjected to particularly precarious living conditions as a result of their irregular situation. Irregular immigrants, such as the applicants, were destined to occupy a marginal and isolated position in Libyan society, rendering them extremely vulnerable to xenophobic and racist acts. (paragraph 125)
>
> . . . according to the UNHCR and Human Rights Watch, individuals forcibly repatriated to Eritrea face being tortured and detained in inhuman conditions merely for having left the country irregularly. As regards Somalia, in the recent case of *Sufi and Elmi* . . . the Court noted the serious levels of violence in Mogadishu and the increased risk to persons returned to that country of being forced either to transit through areas affected by the armed conflict or to seek refuge in camps for displaced persons or refugees, where living conditions were appalling. (paragraph 150)

[145] See this chapter, III.E. Judge Pinto de Albuquerque attached to the judgment a concurring opinion in which he develops a convincing criticism of the already mentioned 1993 judgment of the United States Supreme Court in the *Sale* case.

[146] See this chapter, II.C.

This situation was well known to the Italian authorities or was easy for them to verify on the basis of multiple sources.[147]

According to the Court, irrespective of the fact that an intention to apply for asylum was manifested by the applicants—a circumstance that was disputed by the parties—Italy was under the obligation of not returning the migrants to Libya.

In any event, the Court considers that it was for the national authorities, faced with a situation in which human rights were being systematically violated, as described above, to find out about the treatment to which the applicants would be exposed after their return. . . . Having regard to the circumstances of the case, the fact that the parties concerned had failed to expressly request asylum did not exempt Italy from fulfilling its obligations under Article 3. (paragraph 133)

The Court also found that Italy was responsible for a violation of Article 4 of Protocol No. 4, which prohibits the collective expulsion of aliens. In this regard, the Court rejected the formalistic assumption put forward by Italy that an expulsion can take place only if the aliens are within the national territory and not if they are on the high seas. After having remarked that Article 4[148] does not use the word 'territory',[149] the Court interpreted the ECHR and its Protocols in a way 'which renders the guarantees practical and effective and not theoretical and illusory',[150] showing a particular consideration for the fate of migrants who risk their lives at sea.

The Court has already found that, according to the established case-law of the Commission and of the Court, the purpose of Article 4 of Protocol No. 4 is to prevent States being able to remove certain aliens without examining their personal circumstances and, consequently, without enabling them to put forward their arguments against the measure taken by the relevant authority. If, therefore, Article 4 of Protocol No. 4 were to apply only to collective expulsions from the national territory of the States Parties to the Convention, a significant component of contemporary migratory patterns would not fall within the ambit of that provision, notwithstanding the fact that the conduct it is intended to prohibit can occur outside national territory and in particular, as in the instant case, on the high seas. Article 4 would thus be ineffective in practice with regard to such situations, which, however, are on the increase. The consequence of that would be that migrants having taken to the sea, often risking their lives, and not having managed to reach the borders of a State, would not be entitled to an examination of their personal circumstances before being expelled, unlike those travelling by land. (paragraph 177)

The Court also found that there had been a violation of Article 13 ECHR (right to an effective remedy), taken together with Articles 3 and 4 of Protocol No. 4, as the applicants were deprived of any remedy which would have enabled them to lodge their complaints with a competent authority and to obtain a thorough and rigorous assessment of their requests before the removal measure was enforced.[151]

The political events of 2011 have seriously worsened the humanitarian catastrophe suffered by too many people who try to flee from North African countries, especially Libya, to Europe. United Nations Security Council Resolution 1973

[147] See judgment, paras 131 and 156.
[148] 'Collective expulsion of aliens is prohibited.'
[149] Para. 173.
[150] Para. 175.
[151] Para. 205.

(2001) of 17 March 2011, which authorized member states 'to take all necessary measures' (a wording currently used to mean the use of armed force) 'to protect civilians and civilian populated areas under threat of attack in the Libyan Arab Jamahiriya', did not consider the need to assist all those involved in the massive flow of civilians that followed. It seems that the so-called 'responsibility to protect' has stopped halfway. The military operations in Libya, combined with the lack of control over the flow of illegal migrants, had the unwanted, but foreseeable, consequence of multiplying the number of unseaworthy boats that try to reach the other side of the Mediterranean Sea, and of aggravating the tragic toll of hundreds of human lives, including women and children, lost at sea.

In this regard, the report *Lives lost in the Mediterranean Sea: Who is responsible?*, prepared in 2012 by Tineke Strik for the Parliamentary Assembly of the Council of Europe, sheds light on a tragic event. In March or April 2011 a small boat left Tripoli with seventy-two people on board and, after two weeks at sea, drifted back to Libya with only nine survivors.

> No one went to the aid of this boat, despite a distress call logged by the Italian Maritime Rescue Coordination Centre, which pinpointed the boat's position. There were also a number of alleged direct contacts between the boat in distress and other vessels, including a helicopter that dropped biscuits and water, but never returned to provide assistance, and a large military vessel which came into close contact with the boat, but ignored obvious distress signals.[152]

Apart from a number of gaps and obscurities in the applicable legal rules, which are underlined in the report, it is astonishing that it was impossible to identify any of the vessels and aircraft which entered into contact with the boat and which, by their omissions, contributed to the deaths of sixty-three people, including women and children. As the report bitterly remarks:

> the Mediterranean is one of the busiest seas in the world, and at the same time one of the best monitored. Yet, in 2011, the Mediterranean was also the sea in which the most people disappeared. I am not talking about somewhere in the middle of the Pacific, but about the Canal of Sicily which is full of ships, with many radars and with satellite imagery available. The boat could and should certainly have been rescued and not left to wash up on the shores of Libya with only a handful of survivors. (paragraph 155)

D) The discussions that have taken place in 2011 within the framework of the European Union are discouraging. The European Council seems to place at the same level the question of the 'concrete solidarity' required by the member states that are 'most directly concerned by migratory movements' and the question of the 'humanitarian emergency in Libya' and of the people 'wishing to flee the fighting' (respectively paragraphs 10 and 9 of the declaration made by the Council on 11 March 2011). Too much emphasis has been placed on the overcrowded condition of the small Italian island of Lampedusa, located midway between North Africa and Sicily, where illegal migrants and asylum seekers were often first disembarked, as if

[152] PACE, Doc. 12895, 5 April 2012, summary.

the whole territory of Italy did not unfold behind Lampedusa, and as if the whole territory of the European Union did not unfold behind Italy. In fact, the most directly concerned European Union member states should not even have to ask for forms of internal cooperation, which instead, should be spontaneously provided by the other member states. In cases of humanitarian emergencies, all European Union member states should simply be ready to provide all possible assistance to thousands of human beings, including women and children, who are in such desperate conditions as to run the risk of losing their lives at sea.

By a recent judgment, rendered on 5 September 2012 in case C-355/10, *European Parliament v. Council of the European Union supported by European Commission*, the Court of Justice of the European Union (Grand Chamber) annulled Council Decision 2010/252/EU of 26 April 2010 supplementing the Schengen Borders Code as regards the surveillance of the maritime external borders in the context of operational cooperation coordinated by the European Agency for the Management of Operational Cooperation at the External Borders of the Member States of the European Union.[153] Decision 2010/252, which supplements the Schengen Borders Code, that is Regulation (EC) No. 562/2006 of 15 March 2006 establishing a Community Code on the rules governing the movement of persons across borders,[154] was found to contain essential elements of the surveillance of the maritime external borders which go beyond the scope of the additional measures within the meaning of Article 12(5) of the Schengen Borders Code. According to the Court, such measures could have been enacted only by means of a legislative act and not by an implementing instrument adopted by the Council. The measures in question relate to the action that border guards may take against ships detected and persons on board. According to the Court:

> it is important to point out that provisions on conferring powers of public authority on border guards – such as the powers conferred in the contested decision, which include stopping persons apprehended, seizing vessels and conducting persons apprehended to a specific location – mean that the fundamental rights of the persons concerned may be interfered with to such an extent that the involvement of the European Union legislature is required.

IV. Conclusion

Migration, whether legal or illegal, often has its roots in the human suffering that too many migrants have to endure. Among the poorest people of the world, thousands have lost their lives in unsuccessful attempts to cross a border and reach a place where they would be safe from persecution, poverty, conflicts, natural disasters, or other calamities. Does it really matter if, in many cases, such attempts were illegal from the point of view of a national legislation?

[153] OJ 2010 L 111/20. The judgment has not yet been published. The Court however decided to maintain the effects of the Decision until the entry into force of new rules within a reasonable time.

[154] OJ 2006 L 105/1.

Illegal migrants have the right to be treated humanely and not as criminals. If they are also in distress at sea, they have the right to be rescued and brought to a place of safety. If they are also refugees, they have the right not to be returned to a place where they are persecuted, and to be allowed to apply for asylum (as written by Justice Blackmun, this is a modest plea, vindicated by international law).[155] Like all human beings, they have the right not to be sent to a place where they could be tortured.

But too many of the facts show that illegal migrants are the victims not only of smugglers, but also of a number of states which try to evade their legal and moral duties by resorting to shows of strength against the weakest human beings, or to barely credible legal technicalities. The very invention of asymmetrical rights undermines the merits of international law in addressing the basic needs of illegal migrants. This is the reason why, where different views were admissible, I was led to take a clear position in favour of the weaker subject, the illegal migrant, and against the stronger subject, the state. If it appears that the rules in force do not offer sufficient protection for the weaker party, the only conclusion to be drawn is that the present regime should be improved as soon as possible. The essence of law is not conservation, but change and improvement.

[155] See this chapter, III.F.

7

The Asylum/Convention Refugee Process in the United States and Canada

*Michael J. Churgin**

I. Background

Canada and the United States have much in common in their histories concerning the admission of immigrants. Both have viewed themselves as quite hospitable, but during much of the post-First World War period, both were restrictive, including when it came to admitting individuals fleeing Europe. For example, neither would permit the landing of the infamous *SS St. Louis*, which left Hamburg in May 1939 with almost 1000 Jews bound for Cuba. After Cuba refused landing, the ship sailed along the coasts of the United States and Canada, requesting permission to dock. Both nations refused.[1]

Neither nation initially agreed to sign the 1951 Convention Relating to the Status of Refugees because each wished to do nothing to limit its ability to determine who should and who should not be admitted or deported. More recently, Canada and the United States have acceded to the Convention through their signing of the 1967 Protocol Relating to the Status of Refugees, which made the terms of the convention worldwide in application.[2] During the last several decades, both Canada and the United States have admitted large numbers of refugees from abroad. Government policy is consistent in each case, favouring the ability to pick and choose among refugees from various locations overseas. Simultaneously, both nations have enacted into domestic law, as part of their respective immigration Acts, special provisions providing for the entry of individuals who qualify for what in the United States is called 'asylum' status and in

* Preparation of this chapter was facilitated by a grant from the Canadian Faculty Research Program.

[1] For a summary of the saga, see <http://www.ushmm.org/wlc/en/article.php?ModuleId=10005267>. In January 2011, a memorial sculpture by Daniel Libeskind was unveiled in Halifax, marking the incident. See 'Canada: National Role Acknowledged in Turning Back Refugees' Ship', *New York Times*, 21 January 2011; available at: <http://www.nytimes.com/2011/01/21/world/americas/21briefs-Canada.html>.

[2] The United States signed the Protocol in 1968, while Canada signed both the Convention and Protocol in 1969.

Canada referred to as 'convention refugee' status. These are persons who, because of past persecution or a well-founded fear of persecution, seek not to return to their home countries. The fear must be on account of race, religion, nationality, membership in a particular social group, or political opinion. These provisions, now part of domestic law in each country, are consistent with the Protocol and Convention, and are adjudicated in each country. In other words, individuals make their own way to Canada and the United States and once there, present their claims to the governments, seeking to remain.

While courts in both nations traditionally have been rather deferential to the executive and legislative authorities on questions of immigration, judges in both countries have been willing to review decisions concerning asylum/refugee status, particularly now that the process is part of domestic law and not treaty alone.[3] Today, there are administrative structures in both nations to adjudicate and review claims, with possible appeals to the courts. Canada has committed proportionately more resources to the process, and has been until recently more generous than the United States in awarding convention refugee status to applicants. A further factor is that there are proportionately more support groups for the applicants and lawyers who can represent the claimants in Canada than in the United States. In Canada, applicants generally are eligible for provincial legal aid. That is not the situation in the United States. In addition, unlike the United States, claimants in Canada are eligible for social welfare assistance while awaiting a decision on their applications.

This chapter will discuss various aspects of the decision-making process, reviewing some legislative and judicial activities in both nations. In addition, Canada and the United States have signed and implemented a safe third-country agreement to force individuals to present their claims in only one country, with some exceptions. Despite the rhetoric embracing comprehensive immigration reform in the United States, none has taken place during the Bush and Obama administrations, and the rather draconian legislation of 1996 remains in place as supplemented by additional restrictive amendments. In contrast, the Canadian Parliament passed a reform bill (C-11) during the summer of 2010, ultimately with support of all parties. However, subsequent legislation in 2012 has undermined the reforms and more punitive legislation has been introduced by the government.

II. United States Adjudication

After acceding to the 1967 Protocol Relating to the Status of Refugees, President Lyndon B. Johnson submitted the treaty to the Senate for ratification. The administration claimed that domestic law would not have to change, and the Senate ratified the treaty in short order. The representation was not quite accurate because the *non-refoulement* clause that had been part of domestic law was not

[3] See, eg, M. J. Churgin, 'The Role of the Courts of the United States in Asylum Cases', in B. Conforti and F. Francioni (eds), *Enforcing International Human Rights in Domestic Courts* (1997) 355.

mandatory, while the Protocol made it so.[4] However, it was not until the enactment of the Refugee Act of 1980 during the Carter Administration that the United States finally had a broad statutory basis for the admission of refugees and the consideration of asylum claims by persons who had come to the United States.[5]

After the post-Second World War Displaced Persons Acts and prior to the Refugee Act, the executive branch had acted independently of Congress. A statute authorized individual admission of persons from the Middle East or Communist nations, but there was no general refugee authorization. The administration of Dwight Eisenhower was confronted with the problem of the Hungarian refugees who had fled the Soviet invasion of 1956. Congress was not in session and the President used the so-called 'parole power' to admit refugees. This statute was designed for the admission of someone for an operation, a visit to a dying relative, or perhaps an orphan, but not for the mass admission of refugees. Being paroled did not give a person any status; the fiction was that the individual was at the border.[6] However, President Eisenhower began a trend that continued to be used by subsequent presidents as the need arose. It was used for the admission of Cubans repeatedly; as the ink was barely dry on the Refugee Act in 1980, approximately 100,000 Marielitos came to Key West. The largest use of the parole power was by President Gerald Ford with the end of United States presence in Indochina—about a million persons were allowed to come to the United States. In every instance, Congress eventually would enact special legislation (often grudgingly) to permit these individuals to become lawful permanent residents.

The Refugee Act regularized the process. There were to be annual consultations between the President and Congress about the number of refugees to be admitted and from what area of the world. Ultimately, the President would publish the allocation in the Federal Register. This governed the selection of individuals in refugee camps around the world for admission, often done in consultation with nongovernmental organizations and the United Nations High Commissioner for Refugees. In 1996, Congress explicitly prohibited the use of the parole power for the admission of any group of refugees. The Refugee Act also provided for asylees, individuals who made it to the United States to present their applications. Once admitted, both asylees and refugees could become permanent residents in due course.

Unlike other nations, the United States separated those entitled to withholding (*non-refoulement*) from those entitled to refugee or asylee status. An individual granted *non-refoulement* could stay in the United States, but the withholding of deportation (or removal as it is now called) was not a road to permanent resident status. In addition, there remained the possibility that the status could be revoked if conditions in the home country changed. Moreover, the adjudication process was different in that the claimant had to establish a probability (more likely than not) to qualify for *non-refoulement* while an asylum applicant need only prove a

[4] Formerly section 243(h) of the Immigration and Nationality Act, now renumbered as §241(b)(3).

[5] [1980] *Public L.* 96–212.

[6] The parole provision is now section 212(d)(5) of the Immigration and Nationality Act.

well-founded fear of persecution, which the Supreme Court indicated could be as low as a 10 per cent chance. However, *non-refoulement* was mandatory once the standard was reached, while an asylum grant is discretionary once the criteria have been met. The Supreme Court noted the paradox, rejecting the government's position that asylum applicants should be subject to the stricter *non-refoulement* standard. The Court said it was for Congress to change the system.[7] To date, there has been no change of the basic structure. The Court also has indicated that the Convention/Protocol only applies to individuals who have reached the United States. In the context of the interdiction programme of boats leaving Haiti bound for the United States, the United States took the position that until such time as someone landed in the United States, there was no obligation to inquire as to persecution or to provide the protection of *non-refoulement* under Article 33. The Supreme Court agreed.[8]

Today, one can apply for asylum affirmatively, and you receive a non-adversarial interview with a specially trained asylum officer. If granted, your status will be changed. If you are denied and you are not currently in a lawful status, you will be referred to the immigration court for processing. Similarly, if you are currently in removal proceedings, you may apply for asylum status. Before the immigration court, you are part of an adversarial process. The government is seeking to remove you, and you ask the immigration judge to adjudicate your asylum claim as a claim for relief from removal. The government attorney will invariably oppose the claim, cross-examine you, and seek to disprove your claim. You have the burden of persuasion that you meet the criteria for asylum: well-founded fear of persecution on account of one of the five factors and that you merit a favourable exercise of discretion. As a fallback, you might seek withholding (*non-refoulement*) or also relief under the Convention Against Torture and Other Cruel, Inhuman or Degrading Treatment or Punishment.[9] Once the immigration judge rules, either party may appeal to the Board of Immigration Appeals, an entity within the Department of Justice. If you lose there, you may petition for review by one of the twelve regional federal courts of appeals throughout the United States. The various courts have a rich jurisprudence on asylum issues. Either party may then petition for review in the Supreme Court. The Supreme Court has taken few asylum cases. However, in one broad decision, it directed the courts of appeal to defer to the Board of Immigration Appeals (BIA): '[a]nd if he seeks to obtain judicial reversal of the BIA's determination, he must show that the evidence he presented was so compelling that no reasonable factfinder could fail to find the requisite fear of persecution'.[10] Some courts of appeal seem only to pay lip-service to this maxim, and the volume of cases is such that it is unlikely that any one particular decision will be

[7] *INS v. Cardozo-Fonseca*, 480 US 421 (1987).

[8] *Sale v. Hatian Centers Council*, 509 US 155 (1993).

[9] See, eg, *Aguilar Ramos v. Holder*, 594 F.3d 701 (9th Cir. 2010).

[10] *INS v. Elias-Zacarias*, 502 US 478 (1992). See also *INS v. Ventura*, 537 US 12 (2002) (Court of Appeals should have remanded case to the BIA).

reviewed by the Supreme Court.[11] Even the government's own watchdog agency has complained about inconsistency in administrative asylum rulings.[12]

The United States has several unique features of asylum adjudication. The Illegal Immigration Reform and Immigrant Responsibility Act of 1996 (IIRIRA)[13] established a new category called expedited removal. When an immigration officer determines that someone at the port of entry or within a close distance of the border has no documents or fraudulent documents, the officer may schedule the individual for expedited removal, which means essentially no access to the adjudicatory system. To protect individuals, there is a requirement that the officer ascertain that there is no issue of persecution if returned. If there is a possibility, then there is to be a 'credible fear' interview to determine whether you should be detained for a formal immigration removal hearing at which time you may present your claim.[14] There has been considerable criticism of this process, but it remains in use. A comprehensive study of expedited removal was undertaken by the United States Commission on International Religious Freedom; its 2005 report noted repeated failures to ascertain whether there was a fear of persecution by those being examined by immigration inspectors.[15] As noted, as an initial matter, once the credible fear has been found, the applicant will be detained pending further proceedings; the period of detention can be quite extended.

Also in 1996, Congress added a requirement that the claim of asylum must be presented within a year of coming to the United States. The exceptions are for extraordinary personal situations or because of changed circumstances in the home country. In either case, the decision making on whether you fit within an exception is left to the administrative process. Under the statute, the courts of appeals may not review this decision.[16] Thus, individuals found not to fit within an exception are relegated to submitting a claim of *non-refoulement*, with its higher burden of persuasion. In addition, in 2005 Congress added a requirement that an applicant for asylum 'establish that race, religion, nationality, membership in a particular social group, or political opinion was or will be at least one central reason' for the persecution. The amendments also restrict judicial review of credibility decisions by immigration judges.[17] Some aspects of the 2005 legislation were ameliorated as a result of lobbying from evangelical Christian groups who feared that those escaping regimes persecuting individuals on the basis of religious observance would be stymied by some provisions. The United States Commission on International Religious Freedom actually inserted itself in one pending case when the government

[11] A comprehensive reference work on the subject is D. E. Anker, *Law of Asylum in the United States* (2011).

[12] USGAO, 'U.S. Asylum System: Significant Variation Existed in Asylum Outcomes across Immigration Courts and Judges', GAO-08-940 (2008). See also J. Ramji-Nogales, A. Schoenholtz, and P. Schrag, 'Refugee Roulette: Disparities in Asylum Adjudication', 60 *Stanford Law Review* (2007) 295, at 305.

[13] [1996] Public L. 104–208.

[14] Section 235(b) of the Immigration and Nationality Act.

[15] See <http://www.uscirf.gov/issues/asylum-a-refugees.html>.

[16] Section 208(a)(2)(B) and (D) and 208(a)(3) of the Immigration and Nationality Act.

[17] REAL ID Act of 2005, Division B of Public L. 109-13. See *Matter of C-T-L* (BIA 2010); available at: <http://www.justice.gov/eoir/vll/intdec/vol25/3697.pdf>.

supported a BIA decision in a federal appellate court that seemed to sanction the Chinese government's prosecution of an individual who supported the Vatican, for holding an unregistered Catholic religious gathering. The Court of Appeals affirmed the BIA decision. The Commission contacted the Department of Justice to protest; the department in turn notified the BIA, which then *sua sponte* reversed itself. The court then vacated its judgment.[18]

While the categories of race, religion, and nationality are relatively straightforward, the concepts of membership in a particular social group and political opinion have more wriggle-room. Thus, applicants for asylum have attempted to fit their claims within these categories. Interestingly, the United States domestic debate over abortion caused Congress to expand the concept of 'political opinion' to include persecution for failure to submit to abortion or sterilization. Previously, the BIA had found that China's implementation of its population control policies did not amount to persecution. Congress changed that.[19] Defining membership in a particular social group has been a difficult task. For example, in one recent case, a federal appeals court reversed the BIA on a question of whether certain family ties were sufficient.[20] The most vexing question has been claims concerning gender. One serious difference between the United States and Canada concerns the handling of gender-related claims. Canada has been in the forefront in terms of recognizing convention claims based on violence against women, while the United States has taken baby steps in comparison. The Canadian Federal Court of Appeal recognized a claim in 1992 and the Immigration and Refugee Board (IRB) promulgated guidelines a few years later.[21] In the United States, an applicant with an asylum claim based on domestic violence began her odyssey in 1995, lost before the BIA in 2009,[22] and then watched her case bounce around the Department of Justice for a decade as it was considered by successive attorneys general.[23] As the Clinton Administration left Washington, it proposed regulations on the subject, but they have languished and none has been promulgated. The claimant finally was awarded asylum in 2009,[24] but there still is no administrative precedent decision or formal regulation.

Complicating the process is the lack of counsel for most applicants. The federal statute allows counsel, but refers to it as a privilege and does not provide for the availability of free legal assistance. While there are organizations that provide counsel and pro bono programmes, this does not fill the need. Congress has

18 See: <http://www.uscirf.gov/government-relations/government-correspondence/792-chinaasylum-issues-uscirf-deeply-troubled-by-5th-circuit-decision-in-li-v-gonzales.html>; see *Li v. Gonzales*, 420 F.3d 500, vacated, 429 F.3d 1153 (5th Cir. 2005).

19 Section 101(a)(42) of the Immigration and Nationality Act, overruling *Matter of Chang*, 20 I & N Dec. 38 (BIA 1989).

20 *Crespin-Vallandares v. Holder*, 632 F.3d 117 (4th Cir 2011).

21 See, eg, *Mayers v. Canada*, 97 D.L.R. 4th 729 (1992) and IRB, *Guideline for Women Refugee Claimants Fearing Gender-Related Persecution* (1996).

22 R-A-, 22 I&N Dec. 906 (BIA 1999).

23 R-A-, 24 I&N Dec. 629 (AG 2008) (setting forth history of the case).

24 Center for Gender & Refugee Studies, Documents and Information on Rody Alvarado's Claim for Asylum in the U.S.; available at: <http://cgrs.uchastings.edu/campaigns/alvarado.php>.

prohibited the Legal Services Corporation, the underfunded general provider of civil legal services, and its grantees from serving the undocumented in immigration proceedings. While limited exceptions exist, most programmes do not service individuals in removal proceedings. Furthermore, many persons in removal proceedings are detained in facilities far from major metropolitan areas and are isolated.[25] In addition, with certain exceptions, applicants are denied access to work authorization or federal welfare programmes.

III. Canadian Adjudication

Canada was once considered the world model for convention refugee (or asylum) adjudication. In fact, the United Nations High Commissioner on Refugees (UNHCR) awarded Canada special recognition in 1986 as the recipient of the Nansen Medal for its policies—the only time a nation has been so recognized.[26] However, there have been considerable changes in the adjudicatory process and in attitudes expressed by the governments of the day. There has been increased criticism of the Canadian approach during the twenty-first century.[27] However, certain features of the Canadian process do stand out when compared to that of the United States. Provincial legal aid in most provinces extends to individuals in deportation proceedings. Detention, while increasingly used and espoused by the national government, is a pale imitation of the extensive system used in the United States. In addition, health and welfare services, although recently reduced, are available to refugee applicants. There is no limitation on when you can submit your claim for refugee status. Finally, Canada has been in the forefront of recognizing gender guidelines in adjudicating cases; as noted previously, the United States is far to the rear.

The key administrative entity has been the Immigration and Refugee Board (IRB). A person with a refugee claim is referred by Citizenship and Immigration Canada (CIC) or the Canadian Border Services Agency to the IRB. In almost all situations, the IRB case will be conducted by one person who will hear the application and render a decision. A denied applicant may seek leave to appeal to the Federal Court, which, like the Board, sits in major cities. If the Federal Court grants leave to appeal, there is the possibility of further appeal to the Federal Court of Appeal. The 2001 Immigration and Refugee Protection Act provided for an administrative appeal from the decision of the IRB, while eliminating the automatic right of appeal to the Federal Court. However, that administrative appeal provision never was proclaimed, and both Liberal and Conservative governments did not

[25] M. J. Churgin, 'An Essay on Legal Representation of Non-Citizens in Detention', 5 *Intercultural Human Rights Law Review* (2010) 167.

[26] See <http://www.irb-cisr.gc.ca/eng/media/newsnouv/2009/pages/nansen.aspx>.

[27] For example, see the website of the Canadian Council for Refugees, <http://ccrweb.ca/en/c49>, and J. Gould, C. Sheppard, and J. Wheeldon, 'A Refugee from Justice? Disparate Treatment in the Federal Court of Canada', 32 *Law & Policy* (2010) 454.

establish an IRB appeal process.[28] C-11, the Balanced Refugee Reform Act, which passed in 2010 and had been proclaimed, established for the first time a Refugee Appeal Division in 2012, later delayed to 2013.

Canada also has a safety valve process for individuals denied refugee status. One may apply for a pre-removal risk assessment (PRRA) and also submit a humanitarian and compassionate application (H&C) to remain in Canada after being denied refugee status by the Board. An immigration officer rules on these applications and one may apply for leave to have judicial review in the Federal Court. If an application is allowed, the matter usually will be referred back to a different officer for redetermination.[29] One aspect of C-11 that took effect immediately was a bar preventing denied refugee claimants from submitting PRRA and H&C applications during a year period following the Board's denial of status.

The year of 2010 began with widespread agreement that the Canadian convention refugee process was in crisis. The backlog at the IRB was significant, causing delays of years in adjudication. Refugee support groups complained that an appeal division, authorized in the 2001 legislation, had never been proclaimed. Citizenship and Immigration Canada saw the breakdown in the system enabling individuals with weak cases to be able to remain in Canada for long periods of time, thus accumulating equities that might encourage humanitarian and compassionate applications and further litigation. The delay in processing also increased costs because refugee applicants generally have access to Canadian welfare programmes.

The initial approach by the government to the situation was to submit legislation with bombastic rhetoric that seemed to echo the Tory efforts in the United Kingdom under Michael Howard and Ann Widdecombe in John Major's Cabinet. There were references to 'bogus' refugees and harsh language was used; several proposals even were modelled on the UK efforts of that era. During the spring of 2010 they had a bumpy ride in Parliamentary circles, and the provisions received sharp criticism from non-government groups, the organized bar, and the local office of the UNHCR.[30]

CIC Minister Kenney, sensing that it was unlikely that the Tory submission could be passed in its present form, entered into negotiations with opposition members of Parliament. Eventually, all parties hammered out compromises and fashioned a new bill. The new legislation moved through Commons and the Senate with unanimous support. In testimony before the senate committee, the UNHCR representative announced 'that UNHCR is pleased with the bill as amended'. A prominent refugee lawyer and author noted: '[a]t the end of the day, the positive effects of the bill far outweigh the negative ones, in my view. I think it is a compromise that should be embraced by the Senate'. Representatives from the Canadian Bar Association (CBA) and the Canadian Council for Refugees highlighted areas of concern that needed attention during the implementation process,

[28] A comprehensive treatise is L. Waldman, *Canadian Immigration and Refugee Law Practice* (2011).

[29] A representative example is *Pathmanathan v. Canada* [2010] 3 F.C.R. 395.

[30] 29 *Lawyers Weekly* No. 47 (23 April 2010), at 1.

but approved of the many changes that had taken place during the negotiations. The representative from the CBA noted that all the political parties in Parliament endorsed C-11. 'In addition to that process, various stakeholders and organizations were involved with bringing the parties together and advocating on these issues. It is something that could make all Canadians proud.'[31]

This positive activity and good faith negotiation was in sharp contrast to the actions south of the border. Early 2010 was to have been the time for Comprehensive Immigration Reform (CIR). Nothing happened. There was considerable carping and nasty press releases and statements by members of Congress on the subject of immigration. There was no mood to negotiate or compromise, and the Obama Administration never formally proposed draft legislation on CIR. Initiatives concerning improvements in the asylum adjudication system never made it out of committee.

While C-11 passed Parliament with almost uniform praise, there was much work left to be done. The legislation required significant appointments and new regulations. The good faith negotiations and spirit of compromise that accompanied passage continued initially but then soured during the months necessary to implement C-11; the law indicated that the appeal division would come into force with appropriate changes to the adjudicatory process by 29 June 2012. Questions included the level of the official who will conduct the initial interviews, the level and number of public servants who will engage in the adjudicatory process of the Refugee Protection Division of the IRB (rather than Cabinet appointees), and finally the governor-in-council appointees who will constitute the new appeal division. The government agreed that attorneys could accompany the applicants at the interviews, and of course, at the adjudication and before the appeal division. However, much was needed in the form of regulations about how the new system will work—at the interview, adjudication, and appeal level. There were provisions for expedited consideration for nationals of certain countries and those who submit 'manifestly unfounded' claims—this must be resolved in the details of the regulations. There was a promise to consult with stakeholders, which did take place. Initially, the thought was that much of the new act could be operational by early 2012; in the autumn of 2011, the government applied the brakes and indicated there would be no early date for the coming into force. Some speculated that this delay was part of the deficit reduction action plan, while others saw more fundamental changes in government direction.

Much of the good feeling evaporated when the government introduced C-49, new security legislation in the autumn of 2010 with several proposals that would seem to undercut the recently passed C-11. As a result of the landing of a ship with individuals who paid a smuggler for passage from war-torn Sri Lanka, the government proposed a special level of refugee processing that would be less welcoming. There would be a temporary status for up to five years before a person could secure

[31] *Proceedings of the Standing Senate Committee on Social Affairs, Science and Technology*, Canadian Parliament, Issue 11, 22 June 2010.

permanent residency and provisions for extended detention.[32] The minority Harper government was unable to secure support from any of the opposition parties, and the preliminary debate in Parliament showed sharp divisions.[33] The surprise election of a majority government for Prime Minister Harper in early May 2011 suggested that the government would have its way with C-49, now renamed C-4, Preventing Human Smugglers from Abusing Canada's Immigration System Act. Some commentators noted that there was more about restricting refugee rights in the proposed legislation than provisions dealing with smuggling. But more changes were to come.

There had been some prepublication of proposed regulations for C-11 implementation. The proposal concerning the timing of appeals to the newly formed Refugee Appeal Division (RAD) was quite restrictive—fifteen days for the notice as well as all submissions.[34] This would be quite difficult for denied applicants to comply with; there is a provision to extend the time on motion, but it would make more sense to allow final submissions for a period of at least thirty or forty-five days. An interview of this author with IRB staff revealed that there was an unwillingness to permit the exception of an extension of time to become the norm for operation of the appeal system. The provision of legal aid could not be completed in this time period. There would have to be some special provision for accelerated legal aid determinations for appeals or a standing legal aid system for refugee applicants funded separately by the government to make the appeal effective. In any event, it soon became apparent that the government planned to renege on some of the C-11 provisions, and the era of good feeling disappeared.

C-4 was pulled off the table, but was replaced by a more comprehensive and more regressive C-31 in February 2012, Protecting Canada's Immigration System Act. This bill took a meat clever to the progressive provisions of the Canadian refugee adjudicatory process and imitated some of the harsh provisions of the United Kingdom, the United States, and Australia asylum adjudicatory processes. So-called 'irregular arrivals' received second-class status in all stages of adjudication and administration. This included mandatory detention, a five-year bar to regularization of status once successful, inability to apply in a timely fashion for family unity, lack of appeal rights, and specified reporting requirements. In addition, access to the newly enacted administrative appellate process was cut off for some additional applicants, others were deemed ineligible for convention refugee status, detention was made more commonplace with limited review, the discretion of the Minister of CIC was broadly augmented, and the general tone of the legislation was a far cry from the final passage of C-11.

The stakeholders who praised C-11's final form all sharply condemned the new C-31. In testimony and submissions before the House of Commons committee during April and May of 2012, presenter after presenter criticized the features of the

[32] D. Harrold and D. Lussier, Legislative Summary Bill C-49, Library of Parliament (8 November 2010).

[33] See, generally, Hansard House of Commons Debates, 28 October 2010.

[34] See: <http://www.canadagazette.gc.ca/rp-pr/p1/2011/2011-03-19/html/reg1-eng.html>.

proposal. Many predicted successful constitutional challenges to C-31 for violations of various provisions of the Charter of Rights and Freedoms. The UNHCR issued a comprehensive analysis, bemoaning the changes proposed in refugee adjudication, and noting inconsistencies between C-31 and Canada's treaty obligations under a series of international conventions.[35] The Harper government made a few changes in the committee stage, providing for some IRB review of detention decisions at the two-week and six-month interval, rather than the year interval initially proposed. (It was perceived by many that prolonged detention without any review for a year would run afoul of the Charter of Rights and Freedoms as previously interpreted by the Supreme Court of Canada.) There also would be no automatic loss of permanent residence because of changed conditions in the original home country. Moving in the opposite direction, the pre-removal risk assessment for unsuccessful refugee applicants is to be barred for three years rather than the one year initially in place, making the PRRA essentially a dead letter.

Minister Kenney spoke in the House and explained that the government was committed to having C-31 pass the voting process and receive royal assent by 29 June 2012. That was the day specified in the enacted C-11 legislation passed in 2010 for implementation. C-31, when passed, removed that date. As the Minister stated: '[W]e have concluded that it is necessary to strengthen the asylum reforms.... That is why we have had to delay the coming into force of the balanced refugee reform act from the last Parliament. To be blunt, we are not in a position to implement the new system contemplated in Bill C-11 in the 40th Parliament.'[36] The new legislation is now in force, along with the new appeal division, the remnant of C-11.[37] The Harper government is not yet done. It has proposed C-43, Faster Removal of Foreign Criminals Act, which would cut off access to the appeal division for certain individuals, further restrict humanitarian and compassionate relief, and place more discretion in the minister. It passed in early 2013.

IV. The Role of the Supreme Court of Canada

The Supreme Court of Canada might end up playing a significant role with the new legislation. Traditionally, courts have been deferential to the government in matters of immigration. The watershed involvement of the Canadian judiciary took place in 1985 when the Supreme Court of Canada considered a government practice of denying claims while declining to grant a personal hearing to applicants for convention refugee status. The Court declared the practice unlawful, with several members relying on the old statutory Bill of Rights, while others embraced the language of the more recent Charter of Rights and Freedoms. Judge Bertha Wilson,

35 See: <http://www.unhcr.ca/resources/documents/RPT-2012-05-08-billc31-submission-e.pdf>.
36 Minister Jason Kenney in the House of Commons, 29 May 2012.
37 See: <http://www.ccrweb.ca/en/refugee-reform>.

speaking for the plurality referring to the Charter, used bold language that has been repeatedly quoted in subsequent refugee-related cases.[38]

> Certainly the guarantee of the charter would be illusory if they could be ignored because it was administratively convenient to do so. No doubt considerable time and money can be saved by adopting administrative procedures which ignore the principles of fundamental justice but such an argument, in my view, misses the point of the exercise under 1. The principles of natural justice in procedural fairness which have long been espoused by our courts, and the constitutional entrenchment of the principles of fundamental justice in section 7, implicitly recognized that a balance of administrative convenience does not override the need to adhere to these principles.

The Supreme Court of Canada has continued to be basically solicitous of the rights of applicants for refugee status.[39] While the number of judgments is not large, it is proportionately greater than that of the United States Supreme Court. However, there was a hint of a change of position in the wake of the events of 11 September 2001. As the Federal Court of Appeal pointed out in 2005: 'In *Suresh*, our Supreme Court acknowledged that there were indicia that the prohibition on torture had reached the status in international law as a peremptory norm from which no derogation is acceptable.... Yet, it did not close the door on a possible deportation to torture.' (The court noted that in contrast, the United Kingdom's House of Lords would not permit such a result.) However, in 2007, a unanimous Supreme Court rejected the Parliament's authorization in the Immigration and Refugee Protection Act (IRPA) of only a truncated review of security certificates for detention, while invoking the Charter. In addition, it found that foreign nationals should have the same detention review process as permanent residents.[40]

In 2008, the Supreme Court of Canada unanimously rejected a government claim that it need not divulge reports on interrogation conducted by Canadian officials of a Canadian detained by the United States in its facility in Guantánamo Bay. While in a 'normal' situation the Charter would not apply to actions by Canadian officials outside Canada, this was not such a case.

> With the benefit of a full factual record, the United States Supreme Court held that the detainees had illegally been denied access to habeas corpus and that the procedures under which they were to be prosecuted violated the Geneva Conventions. Those holdings are based on principles consistent with the Charter and Canada's international law obligations. In the present appeal, this is sufficient to establish violations of these international law obligations, to which Canada subscribes.
>
> ... The violations of human rights identified by the United States Supreme Court are sufficient to permit us to conclude that the regime providing for the detention and trial of Mr. Khadr at the time of the CSIS [Canadian Security and Intelligence Service] interviews constituted a clear violation of fundamental human rights protected by international law.[41]

38 *Singh* [1985] 1 SCR 177, 218–19.

39 See, eg, *Canada v. Ward* [1993] 2 SCR 689 and *Pushpanathan v. Canada* [1998] 1 SCR 982.

40 *Charkaoui v. Canada* [2007] 1 SCR 350.

41 *Canada v. Khadr* [2008] 2 SCR 125.

These unanimous decisions suggest that the Court is now unwilling to accept the government's mantra of security without question. However, there is some uncertainty. In November 2011, two new Harper-appointed Justices of the Supreme Court of Canada were sworn in; both had reputations as Crown supporters while serving on the Ontario Court of Appeal. That might or might not be indicative of attitudes towards convention refugee claims. In August 2012, another justice retired, giving Prime Minister Harper his fifth appointment to the high court. Several other vacancies will occur during the mandate period of the new Harper government, so it is unclear what the make-up and attitude of the Supreme Court of Canada will be like in the future. The Federal Court hears the bulk of those refugee cases that reach the courts. As noted earlier, the Federal Court has been quite deferential to decisions of the IRB. In 2012, Chief Justice Crampton indicated that in his view the Supreme Court of Canada wanted the Federal Court to act that way: '[T]hey are sending us a very strong signal that we should not intervene unless we really do think that the decision is "unreasonable" as they define it.'[42] A recent study shows tremendous variations among federal court judges concerning decisions on applications by those denied refugee status for leave to appeal.[43]

V. Safe Third-country Agreement

One interesting interaction between Canada and the United States has been the development of a safe third-country agreement. The United States and Canada have engaged in a higher level of cooperation on border control matters since 11 September 2001 than existed previously. One of the elements of the so-called 'Smart Border' plan of December 2001 was to be the establishment of a safe third-country agreement, whereby most asylum seekers would be required to have their cases adjudicated at the first country reached as between the United States and Canada. Failure to do so would mean being returned to the other country. This was one provision sought by Canada, and it was estimated that it would reduce the Canadian asylum caseload by one-third. This action by the United States and Canada was part of a larger international movement to establish some method of adjudication in sister countries which would be honoured and given full force so that each individual nation would not be 'used' and to avoid 'forum shopping' in the convention refugee adjudicatory process. (Western Europe took some steps in this direction through the Dublin convention of 1990, although largely unsuccessful, and later through the Amsterdam Treaty of 1999.) Each nation's adjudication process would be deemed fair ('safe') enough to be considered in sufficient compliance with each individual nation's own domestic law and treaty obligation under the Convention and the Protocol. An earlier effort to have such an agreement died

[42] 29 *Lawyers Weekly* No. 47 (23 April 2012), at 31.

[43] S. Rehaag, 'Judicial Review of Refugee Determinations: The Luck of the Draw?' 38 *Queen's Law Journal* (2012) 1.

when Congress passed the rather draconian 1996 immigration acts; the Chrétien government's enthusiasm for cooperation waned.

The obvious question is why the United States would sign on to an undertaking that would increase its asylum adjudication workload. A large backlog of cases already existed. The Judiciary Committee of the United States House of Representatives held a hearing on the agreement in October 2002. Before a sceptical committee, the Deputy Assistant Secretary of State Kelly Ryan suggested 'that this agreement be viewed in the context of the overall 30 point [border] action plan'. Canada had agreed to cooperate with the United States on security matters and to share information as never before. The Agreement was the carrot to encourage further integration of border enforcement. One subsequent example: in August 2003, the nations signed the Annex Regarding the Sharing of Information on Refugee Claims, and in its operations plan for 2007–2008, Citizenship and Immigration Canada announced a goal of full implementation of the annex. During the hearing, it also was revealed that there was a side agreement by which Canada agreed to accept a certain number of individuals for resettlement. It is presumed that these will be French-speaking Haitians who would go to Quebec; a small number have been admitted to date for this purpose.[44]

The Chrétien government took steps to implement the now-signed Agreement; it was to be limited to land crossings. The House of Commons Standing Committee on Citizenship and Immigration issued a report, recommending assurances and changes in the government's initial draft. The Minister's Response in May 2003 acknowledged that there are differences between the way the Canadian and United States immigration authorities handle asylum/convention refugee applications, although there was little in the way of formal changes to the implementation plan. Minister Corderre maintained that he had received assurances that the expedited removal procedure would not be used for those individuals returned to the United States under the Agreement. The final regulations promulgated by the United States Department of Homeland Security in November 2004 provide that the expedited removal process will only apply in a small group of cases. The United States also agreed to a wider definition of 'family' to reflect Canadian concerns, including grandparents and aunts and uncles; those with close family ties are not subject to transfer under the Agreement. The Agreement finally took effect on 29 December 2004. After three months, Citizenship and Immigration Canada reported a drop of 40 per cent in refugee protection claims made at Canada–United States land border points of entry. In contrast, it was estimated that perhaps 200 individuals will be returned annually to Canada from the United States—only sixty were returned in the first year. The asylum adjudication systems of the two countries are different, and there has been some concern that persons shut off from the Canadian system will be at some disadvantage. For example, as noted earlier, applicants generally are afforded provincial legal aid in Canada, welfare

[44] United States and Canada Safe Third Country Agreement, Hearing before the Subcommittee on Immigration, Border Security and Claims, Committee on the Judiciary, U.S. House of Representatives, 107th Cong., 2d Sess. (16 October 2002).

assistance, and a more generous consideration of claims, particularly those involving gender issues.

Both parties held their first consultation about the Agreement during the summer of 2005, with the invited presence of the United Nations High Commissioner on Refugees. The UNHCR issued a comprehensive report on its first year of operation, which criticized practices by both governments, particularly the use of detention by the United States.[45] In its 2006 Annual Report to Parliament on Immigration Issues, the CIC reported that of 4033 claims made at the border during 2005, 80 per cent fit into exceptions. The largest category (1577) consisted of those with relatives already in Canada, while 1218 were from countries to which Canada had suspended deportations. I have not been able to locate any comparable United States statistics and no word on any specific communications between the governments. It has been reported that the Agreement adversely affects individuals from countries that do not have nonstop air routes with Canada. In particular, the Canadian Council for Refugees has noted the impact on those from Colombia; the approval rate for claims in Canada is almost double that of the United States.

In late 2005, the Canadian Council of Churches, Amnesty International's Canadian chapter, and the Canadian Council on Refugees joined forces to file suit challenging the designation of the United States as a 'safe' country under the Agreement. The basic claim was that the implementation of the Agreement and the sending of convention refugee applicants back across the United States border without adjudication violate the Charter of Rights and Freedoms because of the ways the claims are handled in the United States. The hearing before the Federal Court involved extensive testimony about asylum practices in the United States. Some leading United States practitioners testified about the differences between adjudication in the United States and Canada, and particularly the impediments faced by asylum applicants in the United States. There also was testimony about the substantive matter of protection concerning gender issues and how the United States has yet to adopt regulations on the subject while Canada did so almost twenty years ago. The government also sought expert opinion south of the border. A former general counsel for the Immigration and Naturalization Service testified that the United States was indeed a 'safe' country for asylum adjudication. In an extensive decision in late 2007, Justice Phelan held that the Canadian government had improperly implemented the agreement without adequate review of the practices of the United States and found certain aspects of United States policy to be violative of the *non-refoulement* provisions of both the Convention Relating to the Status of Refugees and the Convention Against Torture.[46] Chief Justice Richards of the Federal Court of Appeal stayed the judgment and was one of the members of the panel reviewing the judgment. The Court of Appeal's decision focused on the manner in which the judge had reached his conclusion concerning the Agreement rather than the question of whether the United States was a safe country. In a narrow decision devoted largely to the question of standing, the Court

[45] See: <http://www.unhcr.org/protect/PROTECTION/455b2cca4.pdf>.

[46] *Canadian Council for Refugees v. Canada* [2008] 3 FCR 606.

of Appeal indicated that the lower court judgment could not stand.[47] The Supreme Court of Canada denied leave to appeal.[48] The safe third country agreement remains in force. There has been increased cooperation between the two governments on asylum/refugee matters and increased sharing of information.

VI. The Role of International Human Rights Bodies

The Canadian government also has forced applicants from the United States back across the border, independent of the Agreement, without adjudicating their claims. Officials had to know that it was highly likely that the applicants would be detained in the United States and not be able to return to Canada for further processing. This Canadian practice has been the subject of a proceeding before the Inter-American Commission on Human Rights of the Organization of American States. Canada responded to the petition and sought dismissal of the claim. There was a hearing before the Commission on 17 October 2005 at which written and oral testimony were presented in support of the petition. Canada then filed a more substantive response and indicated that in the five months after 1 January 2005, only twelve of forty-seven claimants turned back failed to show up for a scheduled interview. In addition, Canada argued strongly that it is reasonable to accept the United States asylum adjudication system as fair. In 2006, the Commission found the complaint admissible, issued a report on the case, and indicated it would proceed further.[49] Subsequently, the Commission forwarded a response by the complainants to Canada for further reply. They relied in considerable measure on the June 2006 report of the United Nations High Commissioner on Refugees on the first year of operation of the Safe Third Country Agreement, which devoted significant attention to the Canadian practice of turn-back. The UNHCR was highly critical. The Inter-American Commission process is glacial, but in 2011 it ruled that Canada had acted wrongfully in turning back three refugee applicants to the United States.[50]

The United Nations Committee on the Elimination of Racial Discrimination has also taken note of the passage of the new legislation. In its 2012 report on Canada, it recommended 'appropriate measures to ensure that procedural safeguards will be guaranteed when addressing asylum requests of persons considered coming from "safe countries" without any discrimination based on their national origin'. It also condemned mandatory detention of refugee applicants.[51]

Both Canada and the United States are signatories to the International Covenant on Civil and Political Rights (ICCPR). However, Canada also has accepted the

[47] *Canadian Council for Refugees v. Canada*, [2009] 3 FCR136.

[48] *Canadian Council for Refugees v. HM The Queen* (Case 32820, leave denied 5 February 2009).

[49] Petition of John Doe; available at: <http://www1.umn.edu/humanrts/cases/121-06.html> (2006).

[50] *John Doe et al. v. Canada*, 23 March 2011, Inter-American Commission on Human Rights Report No. 24/11.

[51] See item 15; available at: <http://www.refworld.org/cgi-bin/texis/vtx/rwmain?page=search&docid=506183642&skip=0&query=safe%20countries%20cerd&coi=CAN>.

Optional Protocol to the ICCPR, which means that Canada can be subject to proceedings before the Human Rights Committee of the United Nations. (The United States almost never agrees to such optional protocols and usually accompanies its ratifications of international conventions with reservations, understandings, and declarations as it did with the ICCPR.) As a result, Canada has been called before the Committee to respond to submissions submitted by individuals denied refugee status and denied permission to remain in Canada. For example, in 2010, the Human Rights Committee ruled against Canada twice in refugee cases involving nationals of Tunisia and Guinea, finding violations of the ICCPR.[52] In each case, the Committee essentially considered matters that already had been evaluated by the Board and the Federal Court. However, the Committee did not choose to defer to the Canadian process and found violations concerning torture and female genital mutilation, claims that had been rejected by Canada. In 2012, the Human Rights Committee considered a situation that might seem similar to that contemplated by C-31. Over the objections of Canada, the Human Rights Committee ruled that Canada had violated the Covenant on Civil and Political Rights in denying a Sri Lankan family permission to remain in Canada; the family had lost before the IRB and Federal Court on the merits after submitting an H&C application.[53] Based on a follow-up report to the Human Rights Committee in March 2012, Canada has acquiesced in the decision, and the family remains in Canada. It will be interesting to see if there is more frequent resort to international human rights bodies with the new Canadian legislation in force. Conceivably, this could lead to Canada withdrawing from several optional protocols, thus cutting off access to some of these international bodies.

VII. Conclusion

When I began this research, I envisioned a sharp contrast between Canada and the United States concerning matters of convention refugee/asylum reform. C-11 was like a breath of fresh air with stakeholders and the government of the day drawing together to reach a consensus. In the United States, there was no movement on refugee matters; the draconian legislation and policies of the Clinton and Bush years remained in place. The now majority Harper government in Canada has dampened this view with the passage and implementation of C-31, and Canada no longer stands out as somewhat different from other Western nations that have turned their backs on many seeking refugee status.

[52] See *Hamida v. Canada*, CCPR/C/98/D/1544/2007 (2010) and *Kaba v. Canada*, CCPR/C/98/D/1465/2006 (2010).

[53] UN Doc CCPR/C/101/D/1763/2008, 29 April 2011.

8

Italy and Unauthorized Migration: Between State Sovereignty and Human Rights Obligations

*Alessia Di Pascale**

I. Introduction

In Italy, migration is a rather recent, but nonetheless significant, phenomenon. Migration flows became perceptible in the mid-1970s, but have increased significantly since the first decade of the 2000s, when Italy became a country of both destination and transit for international migration.[1] Especially in 2008 and 2009, there was what has been called a 'securitization' of immigration policy, introducing 'security-package' measures to combat crime at both macro- and micro-level, in which the major changes to immigration laws were included. The relevant legal provisions on immigration also bring to light the close attention given to relations with third countries, which are increasingly considered as essential partners in efforts to reduce illegal immigration and manage migration flows better.

The Italian case appears all the more worthy of note since it may be considered emblematic of an approach to irregular migration that is gaining ground globally, and raises several theoretical issues that are a prerequisite to legal analysis. Many national laws and practices also show a process of securitization in relation to migration matters,[2] increasingly resorting to measures that eventually result in

* I wish to express my gratitude to Professor Ruth Rubio-Marín for her valuable comments, encouragement, and counsel, and Anny Bremner and the EUI staff for their support in editing the text.

[1] The foreign presence has grown both suddenly and remarkably, increasing from less than 200,000 foreigners (0.3 per cent of the population) in 1975 to 5.4 million people (approximately 10 per cent of the current population) in 2012. Until 2010, the number of individuals with non-Italian citizenship increased at an average of 431,000 a year since 1993, ie, an annual rate of 12.7 per cent, which has led to a doubling of this population every six years. V.Cesareo, 'Migrazioni 2010: uno sguardo d'insieme', in Fondazione Ismu, *Sedicesimo Rapporto sulle migrazioni* (2010) 7. The economic crisis that has affected Italy over the last years has caused a sharp reversal of this trend with a drastic reduction of new entries. See V. Cesareo, 'Migrazioni 2012: uno sguardo d'insieme', in Fondazione Ismu, *Diciottesimo Rapporto sulle migrazioni* (2012) 7.

[2] Migration is increasingly interpreted as a security problem. See J. Huysmans, 'The European Union and the Securitization of Migration', 38 *JCMS* (2000) 751; D. Bigo, 'Security and

the criminalization of irregular migrants and the restriction of their fundamental rights.[3] The most striking aspect is the attempt to identify more effective ways of controlling undocumented flows, even at the cost of undermining those fundamental rights that should be inviolable, or at least by exploiting those margins of ambiguity that are left in the process of interpretation of international law.

The UN Special Rapporteur on the human rights of migrants has described these general trends in two broad categories: criminalization of labour migration, and externalization of migration control policies.[4] In fact, over the past several years, many states have progressively chosen to criminally prosecute individuals who enter or re-enter their territory irregularly, rather than rely on administrative sanctions. We have also seen an increased attempt on the part of states to 'externalize' border controls and transfer responsibility to countries of origin and transit, by utilizing bilateral agreements and/or aid in order to involve them directly in reducing migratory pressures on receiving states.

This tendency should stimulate the debate on a basic question that will constitute the main thread of the analysis of the Italian legal framework: where is the balance to be drawn between what has traditionally been considered a prerogative of the state's sovereignty—that is, the admission and treatment of aliens in its territory—and human rights obligations?[5] As has recently been emphasized, 'the challenge for the state is to strike a proper balance between protecting the rights of all those who are inside or at its borders, and maintaining control of the borders'.[6]

An analysis needs to be undertaken to ascertain whether restricting the fundamental rights of those in a territory without authorization can legitimately be used as a tool to combat undocumented immigration. The question of the lawfulness of restrictive rules such as those that have been adopted in Italy must be evaluated in

Immigration: Toward a Critique of the Governmentality of Unease', 27 *Alternatives* (2002) 63; T. Balzacq, 'The Three Faces of Securitization: Political Agency, Audience and Context', 11 *EJIR* (2005) 2, at 171–201; D. Bigo, 'Globalized (in)Security: the Field and the Ban-opticon', in D. Bigo and A. Tsoukala (eds), *Terror, Insecurity and Liberty: Illiberal Practices of Liberal Regimes after 9/11* (2008) 5.

[3] B. Bogusz et al. (eds), *Irregular Migration and Human Rights: Theoretical, European and International Perspectives* (2004); C. Dauvergne, *Making People Illegal: What Globalisation Means for Migration Law* (2008). See also S. Palidda, *Racial Criminalization of Migrants in the 21st Century* (2011); A. Leerkes, G. Engbersen, and J. Van der Leun, 'Crime Among Irregular Immigrants and the Influence of Internal Border Control', 58 *Crime Law and Social Change* (2012) 15.

[4] Report of the Special Rapporteur on the human rights of migrants, 21 March 2011, UN Doc A/HRC/17/33. The reports received by the Special Rapporteur illustrate the practices used by states to combat irregular migration, including greater criminalization of migration offences (as opposed to treating them as an administrative offence). See para. 12.

[5] A. Brouwer and J. Kumin, 'Interception and Asylum: Where Migration Control and Human Rights Collide', 21(4) *Refuge* (2003) 4; M. Bastick and K. Grimm, 'Security Sector Responses to Trafficking in Human Beings', Geneva Centre for the Democratic Control of Armed Forces (DCAF), Policy Paper 21, available at: <http://www.dcaf.ch/DCAF-Migration/KMS/Series-Collections/DCAF-Policy-Papers>. See also the remarks contained in the report by the Special Rapporteur on the human rights of migrants, François Crépeau, Addendum, Mission to Italy (29 September–8 October 2012), 30 April 2013, A/HRC/23/46/Add.3.

[6] Council of Europe Commissioner for Human Rights, 'The Human Rights of Irregular Migrants in Europe', CommDH/IssuePaper(2007)1, 17 December 2007; available at: <https://www.wcd.coe.int/wcd/ViewDoc.jsp?id=1237553>.

light of the fact that fundamental rights, or at least a minimum core thereof, refer to any person, regardless of their legal status.

The UN Human Rights Council has expressed concern at legislation and measures adopted by some states that may restrict the human rights and fundamental freedoms of migrants, and reaffirmed that, when exercising their sovereign right to enact and implement migratory and border security measures, states have the duty to comply with their obligations under international law, including international human rights law, in order to ensure full respect for the human rights of migrants.[7] A growing number of authorities at the international level appear to respond negatively in the narrowest of terms, thus putting into question the traditional concept of state sovereignty and the limits to its discretion.[8]

This chapter will outline the evolution of immigration laws in Italy, describing both the legal framework and the main features of the practice that has developed both internally and externally in order to control and reduce irregular migration. This policy has not been without its critics, at the national level and in the wider international context, as regards respect for fundamental rights and especially the protection of the right to asylum. After defining the theoretical framework (part II), and briefly describing the evolution of Italian immigration laws, two of the most controversial changes in the system in recent years will be examined in detail: the strengthening of criminal sanctions against undocumented migrants with the introduction of the so-called crime of irregular migration, and the restriction in the enjoyment of their fundamental rights, with the stated objective of discouraging irregular migration (part III). Italian treaty practice on unauthorized migration will also be mentioned, pointing out its features (part IV), and questioning the legitimacy of this kind of practice in light of human rights obligations (part V).

II. The Enjoyment of Human Rights by Undocumented Migrants and the Criminalization of their Status

A. The status of aliens under human rights law

The recognition of the rights of foreigners is one of the most significant aspects in the evolution of international human rights law. The permeation of international human rights law through general international law has been defined as a quiet revolution,[9] a pertinent example of which is the greater consideration of the issue of foreigners' rights, particularly when traditionally, the obligation to ensure diplomatic protection

[7] HRC, 'The Human Rights of Migrants', UN Doc A/HRC/RES/18/21, 17 October 2011.

[8] Statement of the Global Migration Group on the Human Rights of Migrants in Irregular Situation, Geneva, 30 September 2011; available at: <http://www.ohchr.org/EN/NewsEvents/Pages/DisplayNews.aspx?NewsID=10396&LangID=E. See also the GA Res. 62/156, UN Doc A/RES/62/156>, 18 December 2007.

[9] M. T. Kamminga, 'Final Report on the Impact of International Human Rights Law on General International Law', in M. T. Kamminga and M. Scheinin (eds), *The Impact of Human Rights Law on General International Law* (2009) 1.

has in fact always been understood in favour of citizens.[10] The more recent approach has affirmed that in accordance with the principles and the provisions set out in the core universal human rights instruments, states have obligations to respect, protect, and fulfil the fundamental human rights of all individuals within their territory, including all migrants.[11] The situation of migrants is, however, in many respects different from that of foreigners who are only temporarily in the territory of a state other than their own. Migrants intend to reside in the countries of immigration for a long time, if not permanently. This also raises the issue of the enjoyment of a variety of positions related to stable residence in the host country.

Although there is no commonly accepted generic or general legal concept of a migrant in international law, the international community's growing attention to the issue of human rights of migrants[12] is borne out by the many initiatives that have been taken by the United Nations in recent years, such as the establishment in 1997 of the Working Group of Intergovernmental Experts on the human rights of migrants, and, in 1999, the appointment of a Special Rapporteur on the human rights of migrants, for the purpose of identifying the obstacles to the effective and full protection of the human rights of migrants.[13]

Not all rights (civil, political, economic, social, and cultural), however, have been interpreted as 'fundamental rights' applicable to the foreigner, but a certain core of basic rights has been identified that correspond to universally recognized values, for which the status of the individual is irrelevant. Political rights remain excluded, being a typical expression of the relationship between the state and its citizens (the right to vote and to stand for elections, to take part in public life and public service). Among the list of essential rights are the right to life, safety, and personal freedom,

[10] B. Nascimbene, 'Straniero (diritto internazionale pubblico)', in *Enciclopedia del Diritto* (2013). See also ILC, Draft Articles on Diplomatic Protection with commentaries, Commentary to Art. 6, *YILC* (2006), vol. II, Part Two; P. Mazzeschi, 'The Relationship Between Human Rights and the Rights of Aliens and Immigrants', in U. Fastenrath et al. (eds), *From Bilateralism to Community Interest: Essays in Honour of Judge Bruno Simma* (2011) 552.

[11] Report of the United Nations High Commissioner for Human Rights, 1 June 2010, UN Doc E/2010/89, para. 5. As far back as 1956, the Draft Articles on the responsibility of the state for the injuries caused in its territory to persons or property of aliens, prepared by the Special Rapporteur Mr García-Amador, intended to reconcile the opposing theories on the standards of treatment, on the basis of humanitarian principles enshrined in the most relevant international instruments. See 'The Diplomatic Protection of Nationals and the International Recognition of Human Rights', in F. V. García Amador, L. B. Sohn, and R. R. Baxter, *Recent Codification of the Law of State Responsibility for Injuries to Aliens* (1974) 1.

[12] As noted by the Special Rapporteur on the human rights of migrants, Ms Gabriela Rodríguez Pizarro, in her first report, UN Doc E/CN.4/2000/82, 6 January 2000, para. 28.

[13] The need to make further efforts to improve the situation and ensure the human rights and dignity of migrants was clearly stated as a purpose underlying resolution 15/1997 of the UN Commission on Human Rights. See also P. Taran, 'Human Rights of Migrants: Challenges of the New Decade' 38 *International Migration* (2001) 7; G. Rodriguez, 'The Role of the United Nations Special Rapporteur on the Human Rights of Migrants', 38 *International Migration* (2001) 73; J. Bustamante, 'Immigrants' Vulnerablity as Subjects of Human Rights', 36 *International Migration Review* (2002) 333; T. Lesser, 'The Role of United Nations Special Procedures in Protecting the Human Rights of Migrants', 28 *Refugee Survey Quarterly* (2009) 139. At the regional level, in 1997 the Inter-American Commission on Human Rights (IACmHR) established the Special Rapporteurship on Migrant Workers and their Families. Since then, the 4-year mandate has been constantly renewed.

but also, according to wider interpretations, the right not to be enslaved or to be subjected to torture or cruel, inhuman, or degrading treatment or punishment,[14] the inviolability of private life, and freedom of thought and religion.

In contrast to these rights, which are seen as fundamental, social and economic rights have been often regarded as aspirations or ideals rather than rights.[15] The position of non-citizens under the International Covenant on Economic, Social and Cultural Rights (ICESCR) appears somewhat more limited than under the International Covenant on Civil and Political Rights (ICCPR).[16]

Yet, as has been pointed out by the Special Rapporteur of the former Subcommission on the Promotion and Protection of Human Rights, Mr David Weissbrodt, in his final report, which provides a synthesis of the general principles and specific exceptions to the rights of non-citizens under international human rights law, the architecture of international human rights law is built on the premise that all persons, by virtue of their essential humanity, should enjoy all human rights unless exceptional distinctions, for example, between citizens and non-citizens, serve a legitimate state objective.[17] In recent decades, the principle of non-discrimination, which together with that of equality, represents a cornerstone of the international human rights system, appears to have played a primary role in the evolution of the status of foreigners.

B. The status of undocumented aliens under human rights law

If the emergence of the international law of human rights has expanded the safeguards due to the foreigner, which were originally conceived only in terms of diplomatic protection, the most recent development seems to emphasize that some fundamental rights apply to any alien regardless of their legal status. This section will therefore provide a reflection on the evolutive framework of the rights of undocumented migrants.

It has been affirmed that while states may expel or remove migrants who are illegally on their territory, international human rights law is clear in its requirement

[14] See, among many others, *Chahal v. United Kingdom*, ECHR (1996) Appl. No. 22414/93, judgment of 15 November 1996 (GC), at para. 79; *Saadi v. Italy*, ECHR (2008) Appl. No. 37201/06, judgment of 28 February 2008 (GC), at para. 127. Along the same lines, the ICJ has stated that 'the prohibition of inhumane and degrading treatment is among the rules of general international law which are binding on States in all circumstances, even apart from any treaty commitments', *Case concerning Ahmadou Sadio Diallo (Republic of Guinea v. Democratic Republic of the Congo)* ICJ Reports (2010) 639, at para. 87.

[15] P. Oberoi, 'Defending the Weakest: The Role of International Human Rights Mechanisms in Protecting the Economic, Social and Cultural Rights of Migrants', 11 *IJMS* (2009) 19.

[16] K. Touzenis and R. Cholewinski, 'The Human Rights of Migrants: Editorial Introduction', 11 *IJMS* (2009) 1.

[17] Report on the Rights of Non-Citizens: Final Report of the Special Rapporteur, Mr David Weissbrodt, 26 May 2003, UN Doc E/CN.4/Sub.2/2003/23. The Universal Declaration of Human Rights clearly states that '[e]veryone is entitled to all the rights and freedoms set forth in this Declaration, without distinction of any kind' (Art. 2). See also Art. 2(1) ICCPR; Art. 2(1) CRC; Art. 7 ICRMW; Art. 1(1) ACHR; Art. 3(1) Arab Charter on Human Rights; Art. 2, African Charter on Human and Peoples' Rights.

that the state should generally protect their (fundamental) rights without discrimination for as long as they remain in its territory, irrespective of their immigration status.[18] Such concern regarding the protection of fundamental rights for irregular migrants found express recognition in the mandate of the UN Rapporteur for the human rights of migrants. Since 1999, the need to recognize the particular vulnerability of women, children and *those undocumented or in an irregular situation* has been expressly underlined.[19]

Discussions on the extent of the rights of irregular migrants are of course not new. However, the issue is of growing interest and was recently the subject of some relevant decisions and declarations at the international level. Thirty years ago, states were divided on the scope of the Declaration on the Human Rights of Individuals who are not Nationals of the Country in which they live,[20] but in the end they agreed in Article 1 that for the purpose of the Declaration 'the term alien shall apply, with due regard to qualifications made in subsequent article, to any individual who is not a national of the state in which he or she is present'.[21] They stipulated however that only 'aliens lawfully residing in the territory of a state' are to enjoy the whole range of social rights.[22] Although this instrument may be considered as superseded by subsequent developments, it nonetheless reflects the tension between the principle of universal human rights protection and the practical delivery of such rights to non-nationals generally, and particularly those residing in a country without authorization.[23]

It should therefore be asked what rights are currently deemed to belong to foreigners regardless of their status. The uncertainty as to their minimum rights, ascribed to the large number of disparate instruments and the varying number of signatures and ratifications, has been acknowledged by the Council of Europe Parliamentary Assembly. It has emphasized, however, the urgent need to provide clarity on the matter, even though it is both a difficult and sensitive issue.[24] The Assembly has underlined that the European Convention on Human Rights provides a minimum safeguard and requires that its contracting parties take measures for the effective prevention of human rights violations against vulnerable persons

[18] Global Migration Group, *International Migration and Human Rights. Challenges and Opportunities on the Threshold of the 60th Anniversary of the Universal Declaration of Human Rights* (2008), available at: <http://www.globalmigrationgroup.org/uploads/documents/Int_Migration_Human_Rights.pdf>.

[19] Commission on Human Rights, Resolution 1999/44.

[20] UN Doc A/RES/40/144, 13 December 1985.

[21] G. Goodwin-Gill, 'International Law and Human Rights: Trends Concerning International Migrants and Refugees', 23 *IMR* (1989) 526.

[22] Pursuant to Art. 8, only aliens lawfully residing in the territory of a state enjoy the right to safe and healthy working conditions, to fair wages and equal remuneration for work of equal value without distinction of any kind; the right to join trade unions and other organizations or associations of their choice, and to participate in their activities; the right to health protection, medical care, social security, social services, education, rest, and leisure.

[23] R. Cholewinski, *Study on Obstacles to Effective Access of Irregular Migrants to Minimum Social Rights* (2005).

[24] PACE, Resolution 1509 (2006), 27 June 2006, Human Rights of Irregular Migrants. See also Commissioner for Human Rights, Council of Europe, 'The Human Rights of Irregular Migrants in Europe', 17 December 2007, CommDH/IssuePaper (2007)1.

such as irregular migrants. Without making a differentiation or hierarchy, a number of minimum civil and political rights, but also economic and social rights, were identified, which must be applied by Council of Europe member states in favour of irregular migrants.[25]

In addition to essential civil rights mentioned in section II.A, particularly significant in the present framework is the focus on economic, social, and cultural rights, which represents an evolution with respect to conceptions that had prevailed in the past.[26] In various recent positions the protection of these rights, including the right to health, an adequate standard of living, social security, adequate housing, education, and just and favourable conditions of work, have been incorporated in the list of fundamental rights of all persons, regardless of their migration status,[27] and the exclusion of migrants, regular or irregular, from the core content of economic, social, and cultural rights has been considered inadmissible.[28]

In this evolutive scenario, the advisory opinion of the Inter-American Court of Human Rights in a renowned case concerning the juridical condition and rights of undocumented migrants, especially in the workplace, must be mentioned. In its opinion, the Court made clear that, under the American Convention on Human Rights, the principle of equality and non-discrimination is an *erga omnes* human rights principle and pointed out that 'the migratory status of a person can never be a justification for depriving him of the enjoyment and exercise of his human rights'.[29]

[25] With respect to the establishment of a list of minimum rights for irregular migrants, the Committee of Ministers, in its reply of 18 December 2006, PACE Doc. 11111, referred to the activities of the European Committee on Migration (CDMG), and in particular to the report on 'Irregular migrants, access to social rights' published in 2005.

[26] For a detailed analysis of the evolution of migrants' social and economic rights, see Chapter 5 in this book.

[27] Statement of the Global Migration Group (n 8).

[28] Report of the United Nations High Commissioner for Human Rights, UN Doc E/2010/89, 1 June 2010, at para. 14.

[29] *Juridical Condition and Rights of the Undocumented Migrants*, IACtHR (2003) Series A No. 18, Advisory Opinion OC-18/03, 17 September 2003, paras 109, 133, and 134, respectively. As noted by S.-H. Cleveland, 'Legal Status and Rights of Undocumented Workers. Advisory Opinion OC-18/03', 99 *AJIL* (2005) 460, 'OC-18 is an important pronouncement regarding the human rights of aliens and constitutes the most extensive articulation to date of the workplace rights of undocumented workers', at 462. On that occasion, many interventions were submitted as *amici curiae,* many of which supported the application of evolutionary standards, allowing for a greater protection in favour of unauthorized migrant workers, thus confirming a changing approach. '[M]ost parties argued that unauthorized workers should enjoy greater workplace protection than they had under existing international law'. B. Lyon, 'The Inter-American Court of Human Rights Defines Unauthorized Migrant Workers' Rights for the Hemisphere: A Comment on *Advisory Opinion 18*', 28 *NYU Review of Law & Social Change* (2003–2004) 547, at 549. See also the decision issued by the European Committee of Social Rights in the case *Defence for Children International (DCI) v. Belgium*, 23 October 2012, Appl. No. 69/2011. The Committee, which is entrusted to supervise the compliance of member states' practices and laws with the European Social Charter, declared that the Social Charter applies to irregular migrants in relation to the most fundamental rights enshrined therein, despite the provision set out under para. 1 of the Appendix to the Charter which limits the Charter's scope of application to foreigners only insofar as they are nationals of other parties lawfully resident or working regularly within the territory of the party concerned. Although it pointed out that this interpretation would be justified only in the event that excluding unlawfully present foreigners from the protection afforded by the Charter would have seriously detrimental consequences for their fundamental rights (such as the right to life, to the preservation of human dignity, to psychological and physical integrity and to health) and would

The Court concluded that the state has the obligation to respect and guarantee the labour human rights of all workers, irrespective of their status as nationals or aliens, and that undocumented migrant workers possess the same labour rights as other workers in the state where they are employed.

The conventions on the rights of migrants signed in recent decades might well contribute to clarifying the position of irregular migrants. They are characterized, however, by the limited number of ratifications and a long wait before their entry into force. In particular, the UN Convention on Migrant Workers (ICRMW)[30] is also one of the core international human rights treaties: concluded in 1990, it entered into force in 2003.[31] This convention, which helps to define the status of the migrant worker in relation to a number of issues (including access to the labour market, education, health, procedural rights) does not establish specific rights, except to a very limited extent (such as the right to transfer earnings and savings, Article 47, or access to information on all phases of the migration process, Article 33), but offers a more precise interpretation of the applicable norms on human rights contained in the corpus of fundamental rights in respect of migrant workers. It also contains a list (the third part) of all the rights specifically applicable to this category of foreigners, regardless of their status, thus stating their application also to undocumented migrants.

One of the main obstacles to a wider ratification of the ICRMW is, however, precisely the common claim that the ICRMW would limit the sovereign rights of states to decide upon who can enter their territory and for how long they can remain, and that it endows irregular migrants with too many rights, and as a result would hinder both processes of social integration and the struggle against irregular movements of people.[32]

Despite the uncertainties then, all these initiatives and positions show how important the theme of the protection of undocumented migrants' essential rights is becoming, which might lead to some significant developments in the future.[33]

consequently place the foreigners in question in an unacceptable situation regarding the enjoyment of these rights, as compared with the situation of nationals and of lawfully resident foreigners (paras 28–39), the Committee's statement is a warning to states to carefully evaluate any limitations of social and economic rights of undocumented migrants.

30 Other relevant conventions are ILO Convention No. 143 of 1975 and the European Convention on the Legal Status of Migrant Workers, CETS No. 93.

31 As of 14 November 2013, forty-seven states were parties to the Convention.

32 E. MacDonald and R. Cholewinski, *The Migrant Workers Convention in Europe: Obstacles to the Ratification of the International Convention on the Protection of the Rights of All Migrant Workers and Members of their Families: EU/EEA Perspectives* (2007), available at: <http://www.unesdoc.unesco.org/images/0015/001525/152537e.pdf>.

33 In December 2011, the European Union Agency for Fundamental Rights organized an International Conference entitled 'Dignity and Rights of Irregular Migrants'. A report on *Fundamental Rights of Migrants in an Irregular Situation in the European Union: Comparative Report* (2011) was presented and discussed. In its recommendations, the Agency stated that certain EU legislation should be revised in order to better safeguard some fundamental rights of undocumented migrants. The report is available at: <http://www.fra.europa.eu/fraWebsite/attachments/FRA_2011_Migrants_in_an_irregular_situation_EN.pdf>.

C. The resort to criminal sanctions to combat undocumented migration

What has been defined as a process of criminalization of migrants concerns another aspect of this issue, which is often closely interrelated. The Italian securitization process mirrors an international context that is gradually criminalizing the irregular migrant. Aggravated by the political impact of terrorist attacks in 2001, migration policies around the world have increasingly shifted towards law enforcement, and even criminalization of irregular migration.[34] This is also evident in the new immigration rules introduced by the European Union over the past decade, with the gradual expansion of the use of criminal tools to combat irregular migration.[35]

In spite of this emerging trend towards the strengthening of criminal penalties applied to those who contravene immigration laws, not only nationally but also supranationally, some authoritative international bodies with a human rights mandate have taken a different approach. In fact, having resort to criminal law for the purpose of controlling and repressing irregular immigration cannot be qualified as 'neutral', since it involves a number of side effects, making the position of the alien most precarious.[36]

This point has been clearly stressed by the Special Rapporteur for the human rights of migrants, Mr Bustamante. He has made it clear that migration policies, plans, and programmes that aim to address solely security and border control concerns and lack human and protection approaches, impact detrimentally on the enjoyment of human rights by migrants and do not serve the purpose of deterring irregular immigration. He also pointed out the consequences of the criminalization of migration on the enjoyment of human rights by migrants and warned of the disproportionate use of the criminal justice system to manage

[34] C. Fernandez, A. Manavella, and J. M. Ortuno, 'The Effects of Exceptional Legislation on Criminalization of Immigrants and People Suspected of Terrorism' (Challenge Report 9, 2009); available at: <http://www.libertysecurity.org/article2496.html>. See also A. Edwards, 'Back to Basics: The Right to Liberty and Security of Person and "Alternatives to Detention" of Refugees, Asylum-Seekers, Stateless Persons and Other Migrants' (2011), PPLA/2011/01.Rev.01, available at: <http://www.unhcr.org/refworld/pdfid/4dc935fd2.pdf>; V. Türk and A. Edwards, 'Introductory Note to the Summary Conclusions of the Global Roundtable on Alternatives to Immigration Detention', 23 *International Journal of Refugee Law* (2011) 873.

[35] R. Cholewinski, 'The Criminalisation of Migration in EU Law and Policy', in A. Baldaccini, E. Guild, and H. Toner (eds), *Whose Freedom, Security and Justice? EU Immigration and Asylum Law and Policy* (2006) 301. See also M. Merlino and J. Parkin, 'Irregular Migration in Europe: EU Policies and the Fundamental Rights Gap' (CEPS Report, 2011), available at: <http://www.migration.etuc.org/en/docs_en/1%20Irregular%20Migration%20in%20Europe_%20EU%20policies%20and%20the%20Fundamental%20Rights%20Gap.pdf>.

[36] 'Access to social rights such as health care or accommodation is fundamentally affected by the criminalisation of foreigners. When state authorities make a decision that an individual is no longer regularly on the territory the consequences for his or her access to social rights is essentially changed'. Council of Europe Commissioner for Human Rights, 'Criminalisation of Migration in Europe: Human Rights Implications', CommDH/IssuePaper(2010)1, 4 February 2010, available at: <https://www.wcd.coe.int/wcd/ViewDoc.jsp?id=1579605>, at 25. This happens because they lose entitlement but also because they fear that applying for any of these rights will expose them to the risk of criminal penalties, as the threatened amendement in relation to access to health care in Italy has clearly shown. See following at III.B.

irregular migration.[37] His successor, Mr Crépeau, has confirmed this position, by stating bluntly that 'irregular migration is not a crime'.[38]

Referring specifically to the proposals advanced by Italy in 2008, the Commissioner for Human Rights in the Council of Europe affirmed that '[c]riminalization is a disproportionate measure which exceeds a state's legitimate interest in controlling its borders . . . Immigration offences should remain *administrative* in nature'.[39] These authoritative positions at the international level, by bodies responsible for monitoring or ensuring respect for human rights, thus all point in the same direction. While recognizing the right of states to control and regulate migration flows, they claim that the use of criminal sanctions exceeds the legitimate interest, emphasizing the need to balance potentially conflicting interests and values.

The position of the international courts is more nuanced. The case law developed in recent years in relation to the most severe criminal penalty, that is, detention, clearly shows the search for a middle position. Without questioning the legitimacy of detention of migrants with an irregular status, which within stated limits is moreover affirmed in various international instruments (see in particular, Article 5(1) ECHR and the 'Return Directive'),[40] international courts have, however, given a reading of such an afflictive measure that restricts its applicability to situations where there is a lack of alternatives, in light of the principle of proportionality, and subjects it to the respect of migrants' fundamental rights, both in relation to the right to an effective remedy and treatment conditions, and the rule of law.

In the ECtHR case law under the sub-paragraphs of Article 5(1), which permits the detention of an asylum seeker or other immigrant prior to the state's grant of authorization to enter, any deprivation of liberty must, in addition to falling within one of the exceptions set out in sub-paragraphs (a)–(f), be 'lawful'. Compliance with national law is not, however, sufficient: Article 5(1) requires in addition that any deprivation of liberty should be in keeping with the purpose of protecting the individual from arbitrariness.[41]

Lawfulness of undocumented migrants' detention, and its limits, was also examined in recent ECJ case law in relation to the scope of EU Directive 2008/

[37] Report of the Special Rapporteur on the human rights of migrants, Mr Jorge Bustamante, 3 August 2010, UN Doc A/65/222.

[38] Statement by Mr François Crépeau, Special Rapporteur on the Human Rights of Migrants to the 66th session of the General Assembly, Third Committee—Item 69 (b), (c), 21 October 2011, para. 3, available at: <http://www.ohchr.org/EN/NewsEvents/Pages/DisplayNews.aspx?NewsID=11523&LangID=E>.

[39] Council of Europe Commissioner for Human Rights, 'It is wrong to criminalize migration' (Viewpoint, 29 September 2008), available at: <http://www.coe.int/t/commissioner/Viewpoints/080929_en.asp>. Similar principles had been affirmed already in the past by the Working Group on Arbitrary Detention. See Report of the Working Group on Arbitrary Detention, UN Doc E/CN.4/1999/63, 18 December 1998.

[40] Parliament and Council Directive 2008/115/EC of 16 December 2008, OJ 2008 L 348/98, on common standards and procedures in member states for returning illegally staying third-country nationals.

[41] See *Saadi v. United Kingdom*, ECHR (2008) Appl. No. 13229/03, judgment of 29 January 2008 (GC), paras 67 and 74. See also S. Peers, *EU Justice and Home Affairs Law* (2011) 519.

115/EC.[42] The Court remarked that the Directive does not preclude the law of a member state from classifying an illegal stay as an offence and laying down penal sanctions to deter and prevent such an infringement of the national rules on residence. Also in light of the Directive's scope, national legislation is not precluded from placing a third-country national in detention with a view to determining whether or not his stay is lawful.[43] The Court has acknowledged in principle the legitimacy of criminal sanctions against foreigners who have violated the rules on entry and stay, noting nonetheless that the deprivation of personal freedom must only serve the objective pursued by the Directive, that is, the return of undocumented migrants, thus implicitly excluding a punitive intent, and that the imposition of criminal sanctions is subject to full compliance with fundamental rights, particularly those guaranteed by the European Convention for the Protection of Human Rights and Fundamental Freedoms and the principle of proportionality.[44]

At another, regional level, in 2010 the Inter-American Court of Human Rights clearly affirmed that the detention of people for non-compliance with immigration laws should only be applied when it is necessary and proportionate and only for the shortest period of time, but should never involve punitive purposes.[45] According to the Court, in a democratic society punitive power must be exercised only to the extent that is strictly necessary in order to protect fundamental legal rights from serious attacks that may impair or endanger them. States must therefore seek alternatives to detention whenever possible and those migratory policies whose central focus is the mandatory detention of irregular migrants, without ordering the competent authorities to verify the possibility of using less restrictive measures to achieve the same ends in each particular case and by means of an individualized evaluation, are arbitrary.[46]

III. The Evolution of Migration Policy and Law in Italy and the Security Approach

Many analyses of Italian immigration policies emphasize its sudden transformation from an emigration country into a country of destination.[47] Faced with the first

[42] Case C-61/11 PPU, *El Dridi*, [2011] ECR I-03015; Case C-329/11, *Achughbabian*, judgment of 6 December 2011, not yet published. For an analysis of the impact of the *El Dridi* judgment on Italian migration law in relation to criminal penalties see R. Raffaelli, 'Criminalizing Irregular Immigration and the Returns Directive: An Analysis of the *El Dridi* Case', 13 *EJML* (2011) 467.

[43] *Achughbabian*, Rec. 28 and 29.

[44] As noted by the Court in *El Dridi*, Rec. 57, according to Rec. 13 in the preamble of Directive 2008/115, the use of coercive measures is made expressly subject to the principles of proportionality and effectiveness with regard to the means used and objectives pursued.

[45] *Vélez Loor v. Panama*, IACtHR (2010) Series C, No. 218, judgment of 23 November 2010.

[46] *Vélez Loor v. Panama*, paras 170–171. The same principles have been expressed in the the Report of the Special Rapporteur on the human rights of migrants, Mr François Crépeau, UN Doc A/HCR/ 20/24, 2 April 2012, at Conclusions and Recommendations.

[47] For a detailed historical reconstruction of Italian immigration policy, see L. Einaudi, *Le Politiche dell'Immigrazione in Italia dall'Unità ad oggi* (2007). See also D. Del Boca and A. Venturini, 'Italian Migration' (IZA Discussion Paper, No. 938, 2003), available at: <http://www.econstor.eu/bitstream/

manifestations of the phenomenon of immigration, in the late 1960s and early 1970s, there was no awareness of the transformation of Italy into a country of immigration, nor a unified plan to address the phenomenon;[48] instead, there has been a tendency to consider immigration as a temporary problem and related to occasional situations and emergencies.

From a legal perspective, although a series of bills were submitted from the end of the 1970s until 1986, none of the proposals succeeded in being approved. The provisions on immigration which followed one another until the Law 40 of 1998 were incomplete, uncoordinated, and frequently ineffective and contradictory.[49] These measures had very little efficacy, and periodically resulted in regularizations to legalize illegal immigrants. Assuming, finally, that immigration could not be considered as a transitory phenomenon, the 1998 Law, known as the Single Text on Immigration,[50] appears for the first time to be inspired by a need for comprehensiveness. The rules cover all aspects of a foreigner's life (fundamental rights, family reunification, health, education, integration policies, etc.), all stages of immigration (entry, stay, and removal), and all types of entry and residence.

However, this wide-ranging regulation of the status of foreigners was strongly hampered by the failure to regulate the right to asylum properly. Article 10(3) of the Italian Constitution enshrines the right to asylum of foreigners who are denied the effective exercise of democratic freedoms guaranteed by the same Constitution in their country 'in accordance with the requirements laid down by the law'. This provision, however, has never been implemented by the adoption of a comprehensive law regulating the right to asylum and this has caused many difficulties of interpretation for courts and legal scholars.[51] Numerous bills have been filed over time in order to bridge the legislative gap and implement the constitutional stipulation, but a comprehensive law on asylum has not been adopted.

Before the security packages, the Single Text on Immigration[52] underwent some major amendments in 2002,[53] when Law No. 189, the so-called Bossi-Fini Law (named after its promoters) modified the rules on immigration in a significant

10419/20175/1/dp938.pdf>; G. Zincone and T. Caponio, 'Immigrant and immigration policy-making: The case of Italy' (IMISCOE Working Paper: Country report, 2005); available at: <http://www.imiscoe.socsci.uva.nl/publications/workingpapers/documents/country_report_italy.pdf>.

48 See P. Bonetti, 'I profili generali della normativa italiana sugli stranieri dal 1998', in B. Nascimbene (ed.), *Diritto degli Stranieri* (2004) 1. See also C. Favilli, *Migration Law–Italy, Encyclopedia of Law* (2013).

49 A. Di Pascale, 'The New Regulations on Immigration and the Status of Foreigners in Italy', 4 *EJML* (2002) 71.

50 B. Nascimbene, 'The Regularisation of Clandestine Immigrants in Italy' 2 *EJML* (2000) 337.

51 B. Nascimbene, 'Comments on the Past Ten Years of Italian Jurisprudence on the Right of Asylum', 19 *Italian YB Intl L* (2009) 159, and F. Lenzerini, 'The Evolution of Italian Jurisprudence Concerning the Relationship between the Constitutional Right of Asylum and the Recognition of Refugee Status', 19 *Italian YB Intl L* (2009) 139.

52 Legislative Decree No. 286, 25 July 1998, 'Testo unico delle disposizioni concernenti la disciplina dell'immigrazione e norme sulla condizione dello straniero' gathered and coordinated all rules on immigration contained in Law No. 40/1998, the Consolidated Laws of Public Safety, Law No. 943/1986 and Law No. 335/1995 on the reform of the social security system.

53 Law No. 189 of 30 July 2002, amending previous legislation on immigration and asylum. After 2002 and before the security packages, the Single Text was modified as a result of adaptation to EU

manner. Although the general structure of the Single Text was kept intact, it resulted in a noteworthy turning-point in Italian migration policies.[54] The main intent of the legislator was that of making the regulation of migration more restrictive to combat illegal immigration. As pointed out by the Italian Supreme Court, security 'has become the central topic with Law 189/2002'.[55]

Despite the aspirations of the 1998 Single Text on Immigration to regulate migration effectively in all its phases for the first time, the strong presence of irregular migrants on Italian territory has however remained an issue that is both difficult to resolve and fraught with controversy. Concerns regarding the struggle against illegal immigration have started to occupy an increasingly central role in political debate, due also to the public outcry resulting from some grave news items involving illegal immigrants. Insecurity attributable to irregular migration was one of the key topics of the 2008 electoral campaign. It was no coincidence therefore that immediately after being appointed, the government set the adoption of new stricter measures as a priority, with the aim of discouraging and reducing illegal flows. Although official statistics show that crime has fallen since the 1990s, the need to adopt a 'security package' was supported by the widespread perception—fuelled by politicians and the media—that Italy was facing a national security emergency, largely caused by irregular migrants.[56]

As a result, criminal law provisions were hardened.[57] The existing rules were also made more restrictive in relation to various aspects including the expulsion of foreigners, and EU citizens, detention in view of their removal, family reunification, citizenship acquisition through marriage, and the procedure for granting and

directives, especially in matters of expulsion, and of certain rulings of the Constitutional Court and the adoption of some measures to combat terrorism.

54 B. Nascimbene, 'Nuove norme in materia di immigrazione. La legge Bossi-Fini: perplessità e critiche', *Corriere Giuridico* (2003) 532; K. Touzenis, 'Migration and Human Rights in Italy: Prospects for the ICRMW', in R. Cholewinski, P. de Guchteneire, and A. Pécoud (eds), *Migration and Human Rights: The United Nations Convention on Migrant Workers' Rights* (2009) 343.

55 As the Supreme Court pointed out, 'some aspects of security and public order assumed a greater role in already in the Law 40 of 1998, but they became the central theme with the Law 189 of 2002'. Judgment of the *Cassazione Penale* Court, Third Section, of 23 January 2003, No. 3162.

56 M. Barbagli (ed.), *Rapporto sulla criminalità in Italia* (2007). See also F. Pastore, 'Se un delitto fa tremare l'Italia: Come si affronta una *security crisis*' (CeSPI Paper, 2007), available at: <http://www.cespi.it/PDF/Pastore-percent20art-Italienieuropei.pdf>.

57 The 2008 security package included a draft law (which was then adopted in its final form in the 2009 security package), a law decree and two legislative decrees. The 2009 Security Law concerns five areas: immigration; organized crime; widespread crime; road safety; urban decor. The bill on security—according to Interior Minister Roberto Maroni—is a very important step towards ensuring the safety of Italian citizens. On the matter of immigration, certain standards against the phenomenon of illegal immigration are set which will increase the results obtained with the rules of the security package already in force, as the decree converted into Law 125/08 (Press release, 2 July 2009). As mentioned by A. Lang, 'Le modifiche al decreto legislativo n. 30 del 2007 sui cittadini comunitari', 10 *Diritto, Immigrazione e Cittadinanza* (2008) 120, the 2008 security package also included a draft legislative decree aimed at introducing and integrating the provisions of Legislative Decree No. 30 (2007), (which transposed EU Directive 2004/38). With an unusual procedure, which must however be considered compatible with the objectives of EU law, the scheme had been sent by the Minister of the Interior to the European Commission for an opinion on the compatibility of the proposed amendments with EU law. The criticism by the European Commission prompted the Interior Minister to announce the withdrawal of this specific scheme.

withdrawing refugee status. In many respects, and especially those concerning the rules applicable to EU citizens, these changes have raised doubts not only as regards fundamental rights, but also their compatibility with EU law.[58]

A. The crime and the aggravating circumstance of irregular migration

One of the main, and most controversial, novelties introduced by the 2008 security package was the aggravating circumstance applicable to aliens with irregular status.[59] In 2009 the criminal legal system was further strengthened through the introduction of the so-called 'crime of illegal entry and stay'.[60] The first revision implied an aggravation of the penalty imposed for the commission of a crime by up to one-third, solely by virtue of being a foreigner not complying with immigration law requirements, whereas in the second case illegal entry and stay became an offence punishable with a fine of a criminal character from €5000 to €10,000.[61]

These amendments have met criticism and been disputed for several reasons. One critique has been in relation to the principles of subsidiarity and proportionality of criminal punishment, both of which are enshrined in the Italian legal system and which certainly represent an orientation criterion for the legislature in the field of criminal law. The restriction of rights, which is implied in criminal sanctions, should be subject to ascertaining the absence or ineffectiveness of other less coercive and afflicting sanction mechanisms. A second criticism has been made that these provisions are also questionable in view of the principle of non-discrimination, as the level of rebuke seems mainly to rely on the status of the offender. Many Italian commentators considered this to be 'a crime which is inherent in people'—that is, in irregular migrants—and therefore the cornerstone of a new criminal law, an 'author criminal law' based on geopolitical (or citizenship) discrimination.[62] Discussions also focused on whether criminal prosecution of undocumented migrants may be considered an effective measure to discourage and prevent irregular migration, and the limits of the legislature's discretion in this respect.[63]

[58] A. Adinolfi, '"Pachetto sicurezza" e violazioni (. . . sicure) di obblighi comunitari', 91 *Rivista di Diritto Internazionale* (2008) 1088.

[59] Art. 61, para. 11-bis of the Criminal Code as amended by Law No. 125 of 2008. In its original wording, the rule seemed to apply to any foreign national, including EU citizens, thus raising the profile of non-compliance with EU law. With the 2009 security package, it was made clear that this aggravating circumstance did not concern EU citizens.

[60] Art. 10-bis of the Single Text on immigration as amended by Law No. 94 of 2009. The initial draft was limited to illegal entry, but in the end the typical conduct of the incriminating rule was extended to also encompass the case of illegal stay, characterized in that the presence of foreigners in the territory, which was originally supported by a legitimate title, has become irregular at a later date.

[61] Detention initially envisaged in the draft proposal was then replaced with a fine, which is nonetheless a criminal sanction.

[62] M. Donini, 'Il cittadino extracomunitario da oggetto materiale a tipo d'autore nel controllo penale dell'immigrazione', *Questione giustizia* 1 (2009) 101. As noted by the author, at 127, about the purposes underlying the rule, this is not a law applying in light of real or abstract danger presented by the individual case, nor a true law of individual culpability, nor is it a law that can re-educate and even less promise an 'inclusion'.

[63] F. Viganò, 'Diritto penale e immigrazione: qualche riflessione sui limiti alla discrezionalità del legislatore', 12 *Diritto, Immigrazione e Cittadinanza* (2010) 65.

Not surprisingly, then, the Constitutional Court was very quickly called upon to assess the constitutionality of the two major innovations introduced by the 2008 and 2009 security packages. The Court declared the aggravating circumstance unconstitutional,[64] whereas it dismissed the objections raised against the so-called crime of illegal immigration.[65]

More generally it can also be asked on what grounds the state applies a sanction of a criminal character to a foreigner with irregular status. Breaches of immigration laws have been defined as victimless crimes, since 'to the extent that harm is done at all, it is to the integrity of the state's border and immigration control laws'.[66] As noted by the Special Rapporteur on the human rights of migrants, irregular entry or stay are not per se crimes against persons, property, or national security.[67] The Constitutional Court has specifically dealt with this issue.

1. The aggravating circumstance of irregular migration

The discriminatory nature of the aggravating circumstance was promptly denounced by commentators, who considered that it required a difference of treatment and punishment among citizens and regular and irregular immigrants, without the slightest justification. In the aftermath of its introduction, the President Emeritus of the Constitutional Court pointed out that it effectively discriminated between persons on grounds of national origin and personal circumstances, in violation of Articles 2 and 7 of the Universal Declaration of Human Rights, Article 14 ECHR and Article 26 ICCPR, as well as Article 3 of the Italian Constitution.[68] Similar doubts about the discriminatory character of the new provisions, also in the light of EU law, were expressed by supranational bodies such as the European Commission and the European Parliament, and the Commissioner for Human Rights at the Council of Europe.[69]

As the Constitutional Court emphasized in its ruling on the aggravating circumstance, the challenged provision is effectively based on a general and absolute presumption that third-country irregular migrants are more dangerous, which is reflected in the sanction being applicable to any violation of criminal law that they

[64] Constitutional Court, Judgment No. 249 of 8 July 2010.

[65] Constitutional Court, Judgment No. 250 of 8 July 2010.

[66] Commissioner for Human Rights (n 39) at 8. [67] UN Doc A/HCR/20/24, para. 13.

[68] V. Onida, 'Efficacia non scontata per il ricorso al penale', *Il Sole 24 Ore*, 22 May 2008.

[69] The Commissioner took note of the EU Commission's declaration of 23 September 2008 according to which the above-mentioned law decree 'poses problems of compatibility with Community Law, in particular concerning the rules on the automatic expulsion of EU citizens'. Report by Thomas Hammarberg, Commissioner for Human Rights of the Council of Europe, following his visit to Italy on 13–15 January 2009, CommDH(2009)16, 16 April 2009, at para. 63. Available at: <https://www.wcd.coe.int/ViewDoc.jsp?id=1428427>. On 15 September 2008, the legal service of the European Parliament delivered an opinion which stated that an aggravation of the penalty imposed for the commission of a crime based exclusively on the quality of being a non-national European citizen not complying with immigration law requirements, would be discriminatory and contrary to the principles behind Directive 2004/38 and the case law of the Court of Justice on the matter. See Masera, 'Incontro di studio sul tema: Le novità della legislazione penale in materia di immigrazione', 4–5 February 2010.

may have committed. The fact that EU citizens were subsequently expressly excluded from its scope of application was deemed to confirm this logic.

Hence, adhering to many of the critiques that had been raised, the Court confirmed that the relevant provision was contrary to the principle of equality, since it established an unreasonable aggravation of a penalty based on the unlawful presumption of undocumented migrants being more dangerous. Moreover, it was also deemed unacceptable that migrants were not punished more severely for their conduct, but for being illegal, according to the logic of personal criminal law.

> Assuming that illegal migrants are inherently more dangerous than citizens or foreign nationals with a legal status means to give them a stigma, which grounds a different criminal treatment... the qualities of the individual to be judged are reconducted to the general quality established by law, based on an absolute assumption that identifies a type of author, who is subject, always, to a more severe treatment...[70]

The Court's assessment appears to conform to certain positions taken by international bodies on the prohibition of discrimination in national legislation and the administration of justice. In particular, the Committee on the Elimination of Racial Discrimination stipulated that under the Convention, differential treatment based on citizenship or immigration status will constitute discrimination if the criteria for such differentiation, judged in the light of the object and purpose of the Convention, are not applied pursuant to a legitimate aim, and are not proportional to the achievement of this aim.[71]

2. The crime of irregular migration

Possible stigmatization of the condition of undocumented migrants was, however, assessed with a different approach in relation to the new crime of illegal immigration. The Court considered firstly that the new offence did not object to 'a way of being' of the person, but to a specific type of behaviour.[72] The Court held that the incriminating rule was not intended to penalize the conduct of life and the intentions of the irregular migrant, but rather the lack of compliance with the rules on entry and stay of foreigners in the state. The condition of irregularity is not a

[70] Constitutional Court, Judgment No. 249 of 8 July 2010, para. 9.

[71] *General Recommendation No.30: Discrimination Against Non Citizens*, 1 October 2004, para. 4. See also *General recommendation 31 on the prevention of racial discrimination in the administration and functioning of the criminal justice system*, para. 5(a).

[72] In this respect, reference can also be made to a landmark ruling issued in 2004 in the UK, which however concerned the indefinite preventive detention of foreign nationals who were suspected terrorists. The Law Lords of Great Britain found that the statute conflicted with the obligation not to discriminate against foreign nationals, an obligation found in the European Convention on Human Rights, which Britain had incorporated into its own law in the Human Rights Act. The Lords reasoned that a 'suspected terrorist' poses the same threat whether he is a British citizen or a foreign national, and therefore there is no justification for treating the two differently. *A (FC) and others (FC) v. Secretary of State for the Home Department* [2004] UKHL 56, 16 December 2004. See also D. Cole, 'The Idea of Humanity: Human Rights and Immigrants' Rights', 37 *Columbia Human Rights Law Review* (2005–2006) 627.

pre-existing and unrelated circumstance, but is instead the consequence of the same criminal conduct which is made illegal.

The Court identified the harm 'in the interest of the state to control and manage migratory flows, in accordance with a regulatory framework'. In this respect, resorting to criminal sanctions cannot be considered arbitrary, since such interest can actually be infringed by illegal entry and stay of aliens.[73] In particular, the legal control of migration necessarily involves that conduct in violation of these rules is construed as a tort.

Determining the most appropriate penalty for a violation, and whether it should have a criminal sanction rather than a purely administrative one (as was the case before the entry into force of Law No. 94 of 2009), are judged to be under the discretion of the legislature. The quality and level of repressive intervention resulting from this can vary significantly over time in relation to the changing characteristics and dimensions of migration and the significance of the different needs associated with it.

The analysis carried out by the Court raises the issue of balance between border control and the protection of fundamental rights. In this respect, the Court makes reference to its case law that 'the reasons for human solidarity cannot be established outside of the proper balancing of the values at stake'.[74] However, according to the Court, the reasons for human solidarity are not in themselves contrary to the rules on immigration aimed at guaranteeing orderly migration flows and appropriate reception and integration of foreigners. The Court also reiterated that the Italian legal framework 'provides a different regulation—even in the Constitution (Article 10(3))—for entry and stay of foreigners in the country, according to whether they are applicants for asylum or refugees or economic migrants'.[75]

These statements are all the more significant as a trend is emerging in many countries that provides for greater resort to criminal sanctions against undocumented migrants. The remark made by the Constitutional Court, and placed among the reasons of the decision, that the choice made by the Italian legislator is far from being isolated in the international scene speaks volumes in this sense. In fact, the Court has emphasized that standards of a similar nature, sometimes accompanied by penalties even significantly more stringent than those imposed by the provision in question, are present in the legislation of several European

[73] The orderly management of migration flows is qualified by the Court as instrumental to the implementation of an advanced form of protection of complex 'final' public goods (i.e. public security and health, public order, international obligations etc.), having constitutional significance, which may be compromised by uncontrolled immigration. Constitutional Court, Judgment No. 250 of 8 July 2010, para. 6.3.

[74] Constitutional Court, Decision No. 353/1997.

[75] It is undeniable, in fact, that the power to regulate immigration is a basic corollary of state sovereignty, as an expression of territorial control. As the Court had remarked earlier, 'the State cannot [...] abdicate its, inescapable, responsibility to guard its borders: the rules established on the basis of an orderly migration and an adequate reception should therefore be respected, and not be circumvented [. . .] since they are set to defend the national community and, together, to protect those who have observed and that may receive damage from the tolerance of illegal situations'. Constitutional Court, Judgement No. 250 of 8 July 2010, para. 6.3.

Union countries.[76] Criminal law sanctions in relation to entry and stay have been adopted in Germany, where irregular entry (and residence) is an offence under criminal law. The sanction for the least severe form is imprisonment for up to one year or a fine in addition to expulsion. Similar sanctions were provided for irregular entry in Greek immigration law.[77] Moreover, in recent years, the US government has also increasingly handled migration control through the criminal justice system.[78] In France, however, under the direct influence of the earlier mentioned ECJ case law (*El Dridi, Achughbabian*), and referring to the norm that provides up to one year imprisonment and a fine of up to €3750 in case of entry and stay of the foreigner in breach of immigration rules,[79] the Supreme Court affirmed that a third-country national who is only accused in relation to the crime provided for in Article L. 621-1 CESEDA cannot be placed in custody ('*placé en garde à vue*') on that account alone.[80]

In conclusion, according to the Italian court, the legislature enjoys broad discretion in limiting the access of foreign nationals to the state. This is in fact the outcome of a balancing of values that are relevant and the discretionary exercise of which are questionable only if the choices made are manifestly unreasonable, which in any event, also applies to the selection of the repressive instruments (whether of a criminal or administrative nature). Far from being universally shared, these considerations are at the heart of an issue that is of growing importance, as is the treatment of irregular migrants and the tools that can be legitimately used to discourage the phenomenon. Different international bodies have different positions on the subject, which clearly show the contrast between statements that express concerns more oriented to the development of absolute values and the need to protect fundamental rights (such as the statements of the Special Rapporteur on the human rights of migrants or the Commissioner for Human Rights), and other underlying concerns related more towards the protection of state prerogatives. At the European level, the ECJ has undoubtedly had an influence, and thus contributed to redefining the national laws on the matter. The Court ruled specifically in relation to Article 10-bis of the Italian Consolidated Text at the end of 2012. The

[76] Constitutional Court, Judgment No. 250 of 8 July 2010, para. 6.5. Regarding French legislation, see the remarks in the ECJ decision in *Achughbabian* (n 42).

[77] For an analysis of national criminal provisions and references to European national legislations, see Council of Europe Commissioner for Human Rights, 'Criminalisation of migration' (n 36). See also European Migration Network, *Practical measures for reducing irregular migration, 2012*, available at: <http://www.ec.europa.eu/dgs/home-affairs/what-we-do/networks/european_migration_network/reports/studies/results/irregular-migration/index_en.htm>.

[78] C. Chacón, *Managing Migration Through Crime*, 109 *Columbia Law Review Sidebar* (2009) 135. The author notes that since the 1980s, Congress has passed legislation subjecting more and more acts associated with migration to criminal penalties, or increasing the severity of criminal sanctions imposed for the commission of those acts. See also F. Crépeau and D. Nakache, 'Controlling Irregular Migration in Canada: Reconciling Security Concerns with Human Rights Protection', 12 *IRPP Choices* (2006) 3, available at: <http://www.irpp.org/choices/archive/vol12no1.pdf>; J. Estibaliz, *La criminalisation du trafic de migrants au Canada*, 46 *Criminologie* (2013) 131.

[79] Art. L621-1, Code de l'entrée et du séjour des étrangers et du droit d'asile.

[80] Cass., civ., 1ère, arrêt n. 959, 5 July 2012, *Le procureur général près la cour d'appel de Rennes c/X.*, n. 11–30.371; Cass., civ., 1ère, arrêt n. 965, 5 July 2012, *Le procureur général près la cour d'appel de Versailles c/X*, n. 11–30.530; Cass., civ, 1ère, arrêt n. 960, 5 July 2012, *Achraf B.*, no.11–19.250.

ruling does not consider the norm providing for a criminal prosecution which can lead to a fine for which an expulsion order may be substituted, incompatible with the principles stated in the Return Directive itself, since it has markedly different effects from those of legislation providing for a criminal prosecution which may lead to a term of imprisonment in the course of the return procedure. However, the Court has further specified the limits of its lawful application.[81]

B. The restriction of the enjoyment of fundamental rights of irregular migrants

Another important novelty introduced by the 2009 security package is the provision of a large area of activities corresponding to fundamental rights, which have been made subject to presentation of the residence permit. These restrictions concerned the applications for licences and public authorizations and the capacity to marry, while access to medical care (originally proposed) remained excluded. The significant aspect of this intervention lies in the fact that it is not a mere discrimination or limitation of rights, but was specifically aimed at irregular immigrants.[82]

In Italy, access to essential health care for disease and injury is guaranteed to any foreigner, irrespective of their legal status.[83] In 2008, the government proposed to amend the system by introducing a provision that would have required health professionals to report a suspected crime.[84] Further to the introduction of the so-called crime of irregular migration, and in the absence of a specific exemption, health professionals would have in fact been obliged to inform the public authorities if they had treated a foreigner in a position of irregularity. In the final text of Law 94/2009, this provision was abandoned, partly because of the tough stance of doctors, who strongly disagreed with the obligation to report, claiming breach of their ethical obligations. The mere rumour about the introduction of that rule had, however, caused a series of episodes that illustrate the practical consequences of an approach that deprives migrants of the enjoyment of fundamental rights.[85] The

[81] Case C-430/11, *Md Sagor*, judgment of 6 December 2012, not yet published. See also Case C-522/11, *Mbaye*, order of 21 March 2013, not yet published, where the Court has confirmed its position stating that the third-country nationals accused or convicted of the offence of illegal stay provided for by the legislation of a member state may not, on the sole crime of illegal stay, be exempted from the scope of Directive 2008/115/EC.

[82] See, in the past, M. Pluymen and P. Minderhoud, 'Access to Public Services as an Instrument of Migration Policy in the Netherlands', 16 *Immigration, Asylum and Nationality Law* (2002) 208.

[83] Art. 35(3).

[84] Pursuant to Art. 35(5) of the Single Text on Immigration, access to health care by foreigners who do not comply with the rules on residence cannot result in any type of reporting to the police authority, except in cases where it is compulsory to report on equal footing with Italian citizens. The proposed amendments would have abrogated this provision.

[85] When in the spring of 2008 there were rumours about the introduction of the 'crime of illegal immigration' and the ensuing duty for all doctors and health workers to denounce those who were in an irregular situation, refusing them any kind of care, clinics and facilities dedicated to immigrants saw a sharp decline in migrants' presence, accompanied by a widespread fear that resulted, at times, in serious incidents. A decrease of 15 per cent in immigrant presence at hospitals was recorded. See, 'Il 15% degli immigrati rinuncia alle cure', *La Repubblica*, available at: <http://www.temi.repubblica.it/micromega-online/il-15-degli-immigrati-rinuncia-alle-cure>.

right to health is in fact guaranteed under several human rights treaties[86] and a provision of the sort envisaged by the Italian Legislature, introducing a duty on health professionals to report undocumented migrants and thus using health care and services as an instrument of immigration control policy, was condemned by the UN Commissioner for Human Rights, who affirmed that it had the effect of preventing migrants from gaining effective access to health care even if there was no express prohibition.[87]

The request for licences, permits, registrations, and the like from a public authority was instead made subject to the possession of a residence permit.[88] An exception to this rule—in addition to access to health care and mandatory schooling—applies only to measures relating to sports and recreational activities of a temporary nature. Compared to the existing provision, the new wording removed two references to acts of civil status and access to public services, for which in the past a residence permit was not required. Doubts were immediately raised about the scope of this provision, particularly as regards birth registration. The question asked by many was whether this provision would prevent undocumented migrants from registering the birth of their children and a request for clarification was addressed to the government by many NGOs. A strict reading of the rule would have appeared contrary not only to the Constitution but also to Articles 7 and 8 of the United Nations Convention on the Rights of the Child of 1989, which requires states parties to ensure the immediate registration of the birth of a child, and to preserve their identity and family life. Birth registration was then later specifically excluded from the scope of the new provision.[89]

The innovation that deserves more attention is certainly the norm which linked the possibility of marriage to the demonstration of the alien's regular position, as similar rules, which set conditions and requirements to avoid situations of fraud, were also introduced elsewhere and were deemed inconsistent with fundamental rights by national and supranational courts. The amendment brought in 2009 to Article 116 of the Civil Code required any foreigner who wished to get married in Italy to present the registrar with a document certifying the legality of their stay on Italian territory, in order to prevent sham or simulated marriages. The right to marry and to found a family is in fact specifically enshrined in Article 16 of the Universal Declaration of Human Rights, in Article 12 of the ECHR and in Article 9 of the European Charter of Fundamental Rights, which is now binding on EU member states.

The new condition introduced in Italy was added to the already existing requirement which burdened the alien with the submission of a statement issued by the competent authority of his or her country, providing clearance for the

[86] See Art. 12 ICESCR and *General Comment No. 14* of the Committee on Economic, Social and Cultural Rights, in particular at para. 34.

[87] Report of the United Nations High Commissioner for Human Rights, UN Doc E/2010/89, 1 June 2010. See also V. Chetail and G. Giacca, 'Who Cares? The Right to Health of Migrants', in A. Clapham and M. Robinson (eds), *Realizing the Right to Health* (2009) 224.

[88] Art. 6 of the Single Text on Immigration.

[89] See Circular of the Ministry of the Interior of 7 August 2009, No. 19.

marriage according to the laws to which he/she is subject. A subsequent ministerial circular[90] made it clear that the 'regularity condition' only applies to non-EU foreign nationals, thus excluding EU citizens.

The rule, which makes the capacity to marry of non-EU citizens in Italy subject to the requirement of the regularity of their stay, was challenged on the grounds of its compatibility with the constitutional principles relating to freedom of marriage as a fundamental human right, and international obligations.

Similar issues had been examined in France by the *Conseil Constitutionnel*, in Switzerland by the Federal Administrative Court, and by the ECtHR in relation to UK legislation. The French Court ruled on the Law of 26 November 2003, insofar as it allowed the registrar to verify the status of the alien who had applied for marriage and refuse to proceed if there was a suspicion of irregularity, in which case he was obliged to notify the public prosecutor. The Court stated that irregularity of stay may not be an obstacle to the legal right to marry in France, but only a possible indication, if accompanied by other serious factors, of the possibility of a sham marriage. Assuming that such status would in any case be a serious indication of lack of consent violates the constitutional principle of freedom of marriage.[91]

The case of *O'Donoghue and Others v. the United Kingdom*[92] concerned a UK legislation scheme requiring that, in order to marry, persons subject to immigration control had to have either entry clearance expressly granted for the purpose of enabling them to marry in the United Kingdom or a Certificate of Approval.[93] The ECtHR ruled that the UK legislation on immigration related to the marriage capacity of foreign nationals violated Articles 12 and 14 of the ECHR. The arguments of the Court appear particularly relevant to Italian law. The Strasbourg Court first stated that the fundamental right to marry and start a family, provided by Article 12 of the ECHR, may be subject to limitations and restrictions by states, when these respond to legitimate purposes including the orderly regulation of migration flows. This may also include preventing sham marriages; that is, those designed to circumvent the regulations on entry and residence of foreigners. However, such limitations and restrictions must meet the criterion of proportionality and must not impair the essence of the right to marry. According to the Strasbourg Court therefore, the presumption of 'bad faith' of the marriage of an alien in an irregular position or holding a short-term residence permit, resulting in automatic and indiscriminate restriction on the right to marry, is contrary to the European Convention in that it goes beyond the margin of appreciation granted to states.[94]

90 Circular of the Ministry of the Interior of 7 August 2009, No. 19.

91 Decision no. 2003–484 DC of 20 November 2003. See in particular paras 95 and 96.

92 *O'Donoghue and Others v. the United Kingdom*, ECHR (2010) Appl. No. 34848/07, judgment of 14 December 2010.

93 For a detailed description of the requirements associated with the enforcement of the scheme, see the judgment, paras 5–28.

94 '[A] blanket prohibition, without any attempt being made to investigate the genuineness of the proposed marriages, restricted the right to marry to such an extent that the very essence of the right was impaired'. *O'Donoghue and Others v. the United Kingdom* (n 92) at para. 89.

This decision was followed by the Italian Constitutional Court in July 2011 in a case concerning the legality of the amendments to Article 116 of the Civil Code.[95] The Court said that while the legislature is allowed to regulate the entry and stay of foreigners in Italy, this must be reasonable and proportionate (particularly when the enjoyment of a fundamental right is at issue) and not in contravention of international obligations.

Thus, while a foreigner may be treated differently on certain grounds 'subject to the balance of various public interests', such as those concerning 'safety and public health, public order, the international and national obligations on immigration', their legal status cannot be used in order to allow a 'diversified and pejorative treatment'.[96]

In the present case, although the aim of the protection of borders and controlling migration flows is legitimate, imposing a general impediment to marriage was not proportionate to that aim, especially since the immigration law in force already contained provisions to tackle sham marriages.[97]

Similar principles have been expressed also by the Swiss courts where the revision of the Civil Code, which came into force on 1 January 2011, requires couples who want to get married in Switzerland to show that they are lawfully resident in the country before beginning a preparatory procedure for marriage.[98] In its judgment of 23 November 2011,[99] the Federal Court, hearing an appeal against a refusal of an authorization of stay in view of a marriage, examined the conformity of the Swiss legislation with the right to marry guaranteed under Article 12 ECHR and in light of the *O'Donoghue* judgment. The Court stated that the system set up under Article 98(4) of the Civil Code would violate Article 12 ECHR if the police authority were to presume conclusively that an alien deprived of a residence permit in Switzerland can only have a flawed desire to marry, regardless of the duration and stability of the relationship and any children born of it, and if it was thus brought to prohibit, in general, automatically and indiscriminately, the right to marriage for a category of persons (recital 3.5). Based on the legislature's intention as reflected in the *travaux préparatoires*, the Court held that the concerned provision is intended to prevent sham marriages and that for this measure to remain reasonable and proportionate, it is up to the competent police authority to consider, when deciding on an application for residence permit for marriage, the

[95] Constitutional Court, Judgment of 25 July 2011, No. 245.

[96] Constitutional Court, Judgment of 25 July 2011, No. 245, at 3.1, recalling Decision No 249 of 2010, para. 4.1.

[97] Constitutional Court, Judgment of 25 July 2011, No. 245, at 3.1.

[98] Art. 98(4) Swiss Civil Code, introduced by Federal Law of 12 June 2009 (Preventing the conclusion of marriages in cases of illegal stay). The revision also includes a requirement for officers of civil status to communicate to the competent authority the identity of the couple who have not showed the legality of their stay in Switzerland (art. 99, para. 4).

[99] Case 2C_349/2011, Second Court of Public Law of the Federal Administrative Court. For a comment, see F. Matthey, 'Le droit au mariage en cas de séjour irrégulier; analyse de l'arrêt du Tribunal fédéral 2C_349/2011', *Newsletter DroitMatrimonial.ch*, January 2012, available at: <http://www.droitmatrimonial.ch/uploads/tx_bailarrets/12_janv_Analyse_theme_du_mois.pdf>.

requirements linked to respect for the right of marriage and the principle of proportionality.

The question thus arises again as to what the legitimate limitations on the rights of undocumented migrants are. The principles elaborated by the courts represent an attempt to mediate between the acknowledgment of universal rights and the preservation of state prerogatives. In other words, the limitation of fundamental rights pertaining to the person requires strict scrutiny though the principle of proportionality. Similar statements can be found in landmark decisions of other national courts. Among these is Decision 236/2007 of the Spanish Constitutional Court, in relation to certain restrictions in Spanish immigration law and enacted by Statute 8/2000. The Court linked core fundamental rights to personhood and not citizenship, and affirmed that the legislator could not alter their content, nor deny them to non-citizens. Moreover, the Court affirmed that even beyond the sphere of these core rights, the legislator can subject other rights to constraints, but not totally deny them.[100]

In all these situations, it is not disputed that the national legislature, which has the power to mediate between constitutional values, can legitimately set conditions aimed at limiting cases of fraud, or more generally at regulating the entry and treatment of non-EU citizens. However, such requirements cannot have the effect of making the exercise of a fundamental right impossible. As affirmed by the Italian Court, the legislature—far from making it easier to ascertain any element 'of convenience' of the marriage—has instead created a general impediment to marriage by unauthorized third-country nationals present in the state.[101] According to the ECtHR judgment in *O'Donoghue and Others v. the United Kingdom,* the margin of appreciation granted to the states cannot extend so far as to introduce a general, automatic and indiscriminate restriction on a vitally important right.

IV. Italian Treaty Practice and International Human Rights Standards on Unauthorized Migration

Due to its location and geography, Italy has been exposed to significant immigration by sea, initially from Albania (through the Straits of Otranto), and more recently from North Africa (mainly through the Sicily Channel).[102] Precisely because of public attention, the search for suitable tools to address this has remained a priority

[100] R. Rubio-Marín and C. M. Rodriguez, 'The Constitutional Status of Irregular Migrants, Testing the Boundaries of Human Rights Protection in Spain and the United States, in M.-B. Dembour and T. Kelly (eds), *Are Human Rights for Migrants? Critical Reflections on the Status of Irregular Migrants in Europe and the United States* (2011) 73.

[101] Constitutional Court, Judgment of 25 July 2011, No. 245, at 3.2.

[102] For a reconstruction of the Italian treaty practice to contain irregular migration by sea, see P. Cuttitta, 'The Case of the Italian Southern Sea Borders: Cooperation across the Mediterranean?', 17 *Migraciones* (2008) 45; P. Monzini, 'Sea-Border Crossings: The Organization of Irregular Migration to Italy', 12 *Mediterranean Politics* (2007) 163; A. Di Pascale, 'Migration Control at Sea: the Italian Case', in B. Ryan and V. Mitsilegas (eds), *Extraterritorial Immigration Control: Legal Challenges* (2010) 281.

and, since the 'Apulian' route has been made impassable, attention has shifted to the countries of North Africa.

The effective management of the migration process is deemed to require close collaboration with the countries of origin, destination, and transit of migrants. As discussed above, this strategy has been thoroughly pursued since the early 1990s not only nationally, but also at the European level,[103] and found formal recognition in the Single Text on Immigration, being then further reinforced in 2002 by the Bossi-Fini Law. Although in recent years attention has been directed at migration by sea, the dense network of agreements concluded by Italy must be included within a broader framework which covers a variety of countries.

As noted by the UN Special Rapporteur for the human rights of migrants, the use of techniques in order to 'externalize' border controls to countries of origin and transit, whereby bilateral agreements and/or aid are utilized in order to transform these targeted countries into a potential buffer zone to reduce migratory pressures on receiving states, is increasingly diffused.[104]

Within the EU migration policy framework, the external dimension involving bilateral cooperation with migrants' countries of origin and transit is increasingly important,[105] and re-admission agreements are considered a necessary tool for the efficient management of migration flows into EU member states.[106]

A. Collective removals

Treaty practice on unauthorized migration was the subject of much criticism in 2004 and 2005, when Italy was accused of carrying out collective expulsions in

[103] For an analysis of Italian support for the EU strategy of cooperation with third countries regarding control of unauthorized migration, see A. Di Pascale, 'La participation de l'Italie à la politique d'externalisation de l'Union européenne', in A. Berramdane and J. Rossetto (eds), *La politique européenne d'immigration* (2009) 133.

[104] UN Doc A/HRC/17/33, n 4, at para. 14. For an account of bilateral cooperation on migration control enacted by Spain, France and Italy, see P. Garcia Andrade, A. Sarraj, and A. Di Pascale, 'L'importance des relations bilatérales. Une analyse de l'action extérieure de l'Espagne, la France et l'Italie et pays tiers en matière d'immigration', in P. De Bruycker and M.-C. Foblets (eds), *La dimension extérieure de la politique européenne d'Immigration* (2011) 241.

[105] In December 2005, the European Council adopted 'the Global Approach to Migration: Priority actions focusing on Africa and the Mediterranean', intended as a policy framework of coherent policies and action on migration, addressing a vast array of migration issues to be developed in partnership with third countries and bringing together the various relevant policy areas including external relations, development, employment, and justice, freedom, and security. This global approach was the subject of an assessment in the first half of 2011 through a wide public consultation and in November 2011, the European Commission adopted a Communication (COM(2011) 743 final) which put forward 'a renewed Global Approach to Migration and Mobility (GAMM)'. It must also be recalled that in October 2010, the European Commission announced the conclusion of a 'cooperation agenda' with Libya in the field of combating clandestine immigration, aimed at strengthening border control and a 'dialogue on refugees'.

[106] All agreements contain clauses allowing applications for readmission of persons who do not have the nationality of either of the Parties (including stateless persons) and who transited the territory of one of the Parties. See: Evaluation of EU Readmission Agreements, Communication from the Commission to the European Parliament and the Council, COM(2011) 76 final, of 23 February 2011.

relation to the modalities of repatriation of undocumented aliens who had arrived on its coasts. Many of the more than 10,000 people who arrived on Lampedusa in 2004 were returned by air to Libya within a short space of time, probably on the basis of an informal agreement.[107] Concern was expressed that such collective removals did not provide sufficient opportunity to make any claims about their situation, or the dangers to which they would have been exposed in case of return, or for the provision of information on the asylum procedure and the identification of those who might be in need of international protection.[108] These questions were raised explicitly by the European Parliament in a resolution[109] which called on the Italian authorities 'to refrain from collective expulsions of asylum seekers and "irregular migrants" to Libya as well as to other countries and to guarantee that requests for asylum are examined individually and the principle of *non-refoulement* adhered to', and condemned this practice, on the basis that Italy had failed to meet its international obligations.

The issue was submitted to the ECtHR, which in 2006 ruled on the admissibility of an action brought by eighty-four people—Palestinians, Iraqis, Algerians, Moroccans, and Tunisians—who arrived on Lampedusa (part of the 1200 people estimated by the Court to have reached the island in that same period, largely rejected or expelled from Italy to Libya), and had been served a decree of expulsion between March and April 2005.[110] The claim was based on Article 4 of Protocol No. 4 (prohibition of collective expulsions), and Articles 2 (right to life), 3 (prohibition of inhumane and degrading treatment), 13 (effective remedy), and 34 (right of individual recourse) ECHR. Following an analysis of international reports as well as the arguments offered by the Italian government, the position of the Court in deciding admissibility reflected a strong concern about how this externalization policy was managed, in particular regarding respect for fundamental rights.

The judgment issued in 2010,[111] however, focused mainly on formal procedural issues, noting that the representatives had lost contact with all of the applicants concerned, so the Court was unable to learn anything more about the particular situation of each one. It did not rule on the merits and thus the alleged violations were not examined and the case was struck from the list.[112]

[107] See C. Favilli, 'Quali modalità di conclusione degli accordi internazionali in materia di immigrazione?', 88 *Rivista di Diritto Internazionale* (2005) 156.

[108] See Report By Mr Alvaro Gil-Robles, Commissioner For Human Rights, On His Visit To Italy, 10–17 June 2005, CommDH(2005)9, 14 December 2005, available at: <https://www.wcd.coe.int/ViewDoc.jsp?id=948027&Site=COE>, in particular paras 170–175.

[109] European Parliament resolution on Lampedusa of 14 April 2005, P6_TA (2005)0138.

[110] *Hussun and Others v. Italy,* ECHR (2006) Appl. No. 10171/05, 10601/05, 11593/05, and 17165/05, decision of 11 May 2006.

[111] *Hussun and Others v. Italy,* ECHR (2010) Appl. No. 10171/05, 10601/05, 11593/05, and 17165/05, judgment of 19 January 2010.

[112] The ruling does not mention the context in which the defender must act in these cases, with limited time available, dealing with people of various nationalities, speaking different languages, some of whom are even illiterate. This certainly does not excuse any lightness or tampering, but would require a more complete assessment of the specific circumstances. As has been noted with respect to these cases, factual circumstances determine the outcome of proceedings more than legal issues.

The ECtHR therefore did not conduct a full review of the Italian authorities' actions. It remains the case, however, that collective expulsion is prohibited in absolute terms by many human rights treaties.[113] According to ECtHR case law, in relation to the prohibition established under Article 4 of Protocol 4, measures forcing aliens as a group to leave a country do not amount to a collective expulsion if undertaken following a reasonable and objective examination of the personal circumstances of each of the aliens forming the group,[114] also taking into account the circumstances in which the expulsion is carried out.[115]

B. Interception in international waters and push-backs

In 2009, following the entry into force of the Treaty on Friendship, Partnership and Cooperation signed between Italy and Libya on 30 August 2008, bilateral cooperation to control illegal immigration by sea took on a different form. Italian naval units carried out several operations aimed at stemming irregular flows. In particular, boats that were intercepted in international waters were sent back to their ports of departure, most notably to Libya, or the migrants were transferred to Libyan naval units operated by joint Libyan and Italian crews as provided by the 2009 Operational Protocol on joint patrolling. Based upon official figures provided by the Italian government, from 6 May to 6 November 2009, Italy carried out nine operations designed to return a total of 834 persons to the Libyan ports from where they had departed.[116]

S. Saroléa, 'A Critical Look at Direct Access to the Single Court: a Practitioner's Perspective', in *Ten Years of the "New" European Court of Human Rights 1998–2008: Situation and Outlook* (2009) 23. On the *Hussun* case, see: A. Liguori, 'Il caso Hussun e a c. Italia: sui respingimenti Italia-Libia del 2005 la Corte di Strasburgo decide . . . di non decidere', 4 *Diritti Umani e Diritto Internazionale* (2010) 452; P. Bonetti, 'Respinti e indifesi? La prima pronuncia della Corte europea dei diritti sugli sbarchi a Lampedusa', *Quaderni costituzionali* (2010) 426.

[113] The ILC Special Rapporteur on expulsion suggested that it could be reasonable to affirm that there is a general principle of international law on this matter that is 'recognized by civilized nations' and prohibits collective expulsion. ILC, Third Report on the Expulsion of Aliens, UN Doc A/CN.4/581, para. 115.

[114] *Vedran Andric v. Sweden*, ECHR (1999) Appl. No. 45917/99, decision of 23 February 1999.

[115] *Čonka v. Belgium*, ECHR (2002), Appl. No. 51564/99, 5 February 2002, at paras 59–63. In relation to the scope of Art. 4 of Protocol 4, see also *Sultani v. France*, ECHR (2007) Appl. No. 45223/05, judgment of 20 September 2007. In this case, concerning an Afghan National, the Court considered that in their decisions rejecting the asylum requests, the domestic authorities took account not only of the overall context in Afghanistan, but also of the applicant's statements concerning his personal situation and the risks he would allegedly run in the event of a return to his country of origin. Accordingly, the Court noted that the applicant's situation was indeed examined individually and provided sufficient grounds for the contested expulsion. In those circumstances, the applicant's deportation from French territory was not considered to amount to a violation of Art. 4 of Protocol No. 4.

[116] Under-Secretary of the Ministry of Interior, Nitto Franceso Palma, at the Chamber of Deputies on 24 November 2009, available at: <http://www.interno.it/mininterno/export/sites/default/it/assets/files/17/00116_palma_Soro_n._1-00260.pdf>. As Save the Children pointed out in a hearing on 19 January 2010, although consistent data are not available, there is evidence of presence of children on intercepted boats. See: <http://www.camera.it/_dati/leg16/lavori/stenbic/30/2010/0119/s020.htm>.

The Council of Europe Committee for the Prevention of Torture and Inhuman or Degrading Treatment or Punishment (CPT) was explicit in affirming that Italy's policy violated the principle of *non-refoulement*, and urged the Italian authorities to substantially review the practice. According to the CPT findings, the violations were linked in particular to the fact that migrants, including asylum seekers or vulnerable persons, were not allowed to submit an application for international protection and that their individual position was not adequately assessed by Italian authorities.[117] The Italian government contested these assertions officially, denying infringement of the principle of *non-refoulement* and affirming that the method for managing the operations was consistent both with the obligations imposed by the EU (in particular those laid down in Directive 85/2005/EC), as well as national legislation.

Requests for clarifications regarding action taken to ensure adequate aid and protection for migrants being pushed back were nonetheless addressed to the Italian government by the European Commission, the United Nations High Commissioner for Refugees, and the European Commissioner for Human Rights.[118] The Commission pointed out that while the EU law governing this matter only applies on member states' territory—including, therefore, their territorial waters—the actions of the Italian military and coastal authorities derive from the border surveillance activities envisaged by Article 12 of the Schengen Borders Code.[119]

Compared to the practice implemented in previous years, Italian authorities did not carry out expulsions of unauthorized migrants that had already arrived on its national territory, but rather pushed back boats filled with migrants that were intercepted on the high seas,[120] thus exploiting the ambiguity arising from the extraterritorial scope of the *non-refoulement* principle.[121]

[117] Council of Europe, Report to the Italian Government on the visit to Italy carried out by the European Committee for the Prevention of Torture and Inhuman or Degrading Treatment or Punishment (CPT) from 27 to 31 July 2009, CPT/Inf(2010) 14, 28 April 2010, paras 13–14, available at: <http://www.cpt.coe.int/documents/ita/2010-inf-14-eng.htm>.

[118] See B. Nascimbene, 'Control of illegal immigration and Italian-EU relations' (IAI Documents 2009), IAI0922E, available at: <http://www.iai.it/pdf/DocIAI/IAI0922E.pdf>.

[119] Parliament and Council Regulation 562/2006 of 15 March 2006, OJ 2006 L 105/1, establishing a Community Code on the rules governing the movement of persons across borders (Schengen Borders Code). In 2010, Council Decision 2010/252/EU of 26 April 2010, OJ 2010 L 111/20, supplementing the Schengen Borders Code as regards the surveillance of the sea external borders in the context of operational cooperation coordinated by the European Agency for the Management of Operational Cooperation at the External Borders of the Member States of the European Union, was adopted. In relation to EU obligations, see V. M. Lax, 'Seeking Asylum in the Mediterranean: Against a Fragmentary Reading of EU Member States' Obligations Accruing at Sea', 23 *International Journal of Refugee Law* (2011) 174.

[120] As noted by the UNHCR in its Submission by the Office of the United Nations High Commissioner for Refugees in the Case of *Hirsi and Others v. Italy* (Appl. No. 27765/09), at 3 (before the ECtHR, available at: <http://www.unhcr.org/refworld/docid/4b97778d2.html>). This policy was a departure from the previous practice where Italian naval forces had regularly disembarked such persons in Lampedusa or Sicily.

[121] E. Lauterpacht and D. Bethlehem, 'The Scope and Content of the Principle of *Non-Refoulement*: Opinion', in E. Feller, V. Türk, and F. Nicholson (eds), *Refugee Protection in International Law: UNHCR's Global Consultations on International Protection* (2003) 87. See also G. Goodwin-Gill, 'The Right to Seek Asylum: Interception at Sea and the Principle of *Non-Refoulement*', 23 *International Journal of Refugee Law* (2011) 443. For a detailed discussion on state human rights obligations on the high seas, see Chapter 6 in this book.

This point was also underlined by the Parliamentary Assembly of the Council of Europe, which in a resolution concerning the interception and rescue at sea of asylum seekers, refugees and irregular migrants, pointed out that despite several relevant international instruments which satisfactorily set out the rights and obligations of states and individuals applicable in this area, interpretations of their content appear to differ. Some states do not agree on the nature and extent of their responsibilities in specific situations and some states also call into question the application of the principle of *non-refoulement* on the high seas.[122]

V. The Externalization of Migration Control in Light of Human Rights Obligations

The practices implemented by Italy over the years raise some fundamental questions, which extend to all practices of externalization in the field of migration. As mentioned earlier, the search for more effective ways of preventing undocumented migration flows has induced many countries to develop stringent forms of cooperation with migrants' countries of origin and transit in order to involve them directly. As far as Italy is concerned, the greatest attention was directed towards North African countries, most notably Libya, considered a strategic partner, in spite of the fact that the deplorable conditions in which unauthorized migrants are detained upon return, as well as the difficulty they have in accessing any form of international protection, if available at all,[123] have been described in detail by several international agencies and NGO reports which had a wide impact.

The implementation of bilateral cooperation with a state whose respect for fundamental rights is doubtful brings us back to the fundamental question at the beginning of this analysis: how far can a state go in order to maintain its border control?

[122] The interception and rescue at sea of asylum seekers, refugees and irregular migrants, PACE Resolution 1821 (2011) of 21 June 2011. This point was also raised by the European Commission in the letter of the former EU Commissioner for Justice and Home Affairs Mr Barrot, who recalled the ECtHR case law, referring specifically to *Al-Saadoon and Mufdhi v. the United Kingdom*, ECHR (2009) Appl. No. 61498/08, decision of 30 June 2009, paras 85–88. The ECtHR ruled that actions carried out by a state naval unit on the high seas are an example of the exercise of extra-territorial jurisdiction. As such, they could result in the state concerned being deemed responsible. See also more recently the decision issued by the Grand Chamber in the case *Medvedyev and others v. France*, ECHR (2010) Appl. No. 3394/03, judgment of 29 March 2010 (GC). These critical issues were also reflected domestically, so as to prompt the Chamber of Deputies in November 2010 to approve a motion which committed the government to promote the revision of the treaty of friendship with Libya to bring it into line with the international obligations of Italy, including the right of asylum and the right to life, and to suspend the policy of push-backs.

[123] As noted in A. Di Bartolomeo, T. Jaulin, and D. Perrin, 'CARIM—Migration Profile: Libya' (2011), at 9, available at: <http://www.carim.org/public/migrationprofiles/MP_Libya_EN.pdf>. 'Like its neighbours, Libya is still without any national asylum procedure. Unlike its neighbours, its official position is to deny the existence of refugees on its territory. Yet, thousands of *de facto* refugees live in the country as economic migrants. UNHCR has been tolerated since 1991 and offers humanitarian aid to a few thousands of people under its informal mandate, with status certificates which are not always recognised by the official authorities'.

In the enactment of this bilateral cooperation aimed at stemming irregular migration flows, the concerned countries have been encouraged to toughen national legislation on emigration and residence of foreigners,[124] to improve monitoring at land borders (to avoid an influx of migrants from neighbouring countries) and sea (to prevent the departure of boats), and to extend controls both on their territories and in international waters. This cooperation has also included support for facilities and equipment to ensure effective monitoring of borders and training of officers and staff.[125]

The most critical aspects of such bilateral processes of cooperation are therefore centred on the potential serious violation of the fundamental rights of migrants, *in primis* the right to asylum, especially in light of the principle of *non-refoulement*. But it should also be asked whether this form of cooperation, based on the features described earlier and promoted by migration destination countries which do not commit fundamental rights violations directly, can give rise to international liability for complicity in a wrongful act in the most serious cases, since these countries provide facilities and equipments and cannot be said to be unaware of how migrants and asylum seekers are treated by their partners.[126]

Even if this latter hypothesis is debatable, what cannot be neglected in the evolution of the most recent Strasbourg jurisprudence is the increased importance of the attention given to protection of foreigners when there are serious indications of the risk they might incur, resulting in the lowering of the burden of proof borne by the applicant. In this respect, the protection offered by Article 3 is further strengthened around the concept of a rule which does not permit derogation and goes beyond the appearance in not just relying on the circumstances described by the state involved. It is worth mentioning the considerations of the ECtHR in the *Saadi* case: the court rejected the objection of the Italian government that the risk of being exposed to torture and inhuman treatment was not corroborated by adequate

[124] On these issues, see D. Perrin, 'The Impact of European Migration Policies on Migration-Related Legislative Activity in Maghreb Countries: An Overview of Recent Reforms', in C. Gortázar et al. (eds), *European Migration and Asylum Policies: Coherence or Contradiction? An Interdisciplinary Evaluation of the EU Programmes of Tampere (1999), The Hague (2004) and Stockholm (2009)* (2012) 251.

[125] Art. 21(4) and (5) of the Single Text expressly states that these agreements of cooperation may provide for the transfer, at no cost to the authorities of the concerned countries, of goods and equipment specifically identified, and that the Ministry of the Interior may establish one or more multi-annual programmes for the acquisition of facilities and technical and logistic equipment and the provision of assistance and other ancillary services.

[126] Italy's potential liability under Art. 16 of the International Law Commission's Articles on State Responsibility has been invoked in relation to the collaboration implemented with Libya within the framework of the Partnership agreement. See T. Gammeltoft-Hansen, 'The Externalisation of European Migration Control and the Reach of International Refugee Law', in E. Guild and P. Minderhoud (eds), *The First Decade of EU Migration and Asylum Law* (2011) 273. According to this rule, '[a] State which aids or assists another State in the commission of an internationally wrongful act by the latter is internationally responsible for doing so if: (a) that State does so with knowledge of the circumstances of the internationally wrongful act; and (b) the act would be internationally wrongful if committed by that State'. The commentary explicitly notes that this provision is also applicable in cases concerning material aid to a state that uses the aid to commit human rights violations. See ILC, Draft Articles on Responsibility of States for Internationally Wrongful Acts, with commentaries (2001), at 67, para. 9.

evidence, and relied on the reports submitted which illustrated the human rights situation in the country, bearing in mind the authority and reputation of their authors.[127] Similar assertions could be made in relation to the cooperation with Libya, where the vulnerable conditions of migrants in the country, the difficulty experienced by the UNHCR whose office was temporary closed in 2010, and the serious human rights violations perpetrated, were also documented in many international reports.[128]

These principles have been further strengthened in the case *M.S.S. v. Belgium and Greece*, where this line of protection has been applied even in an EU country, where the conditions in which unauthorized migrants found themselves were considered to fall within the scope of Article 3 ECHR and could not be ignored by another EU member state.[129] In a subsequent case, *H.R. v. France*, the Court in its ruling considered that further to the recent lifting of the emergency rule due to the recent events of the 'Arab Spring', it had no concrete evidence to refute or confirm the application in Algeria of practices of torture or treatment contrary to Article 3 vis-à-vis suspected terrorists. As a consequence, in the Court's view, the decision to send back the applicant would constitute a violation of Article 3.[130] In relation to this provision, therefore, the Court has applied the greatest possible caution.

Decisive interpretative principles with specific reference to the bilateral cooperation implemented between Italy and Libya have been provided by the ECtHR judgment in the case *Hirsi Jamaa and Others v. Italy*.[131] This sensitive and remarkable case concerned an action brought by a group of Somalis and Eritreans, who had been intercepted at sea south of Lampedusa in the summer of 2009 while trying to reach Italy on board boats from Libya, and were returned by the Italian authorities. The Italian government was accused of violating Article 3 (prohibition of inhuman and degrading treatment) ECHR, Article 4 Protocol 4 (prohibition of collective expulsions) and 13 ECHR (right to an effective remedy). The judgment was delivered unanimously by the seventeen judges who sit on the Grand Chamber, to which the case was referred in consideration of the important and sensitive problems of interpretation of the Convention and its Protocols that it raised, and is therefore final.[132] The interest and significance of the application, not only at the European regional level, are also confirmed by the many interventions made by

[127] *Saadi v. Italy* (n 14) paras 102–116 and 142–149.

[128] See Human Rights Watch, *World Report 2011: Libya*, available at: <http://www.hrw.org/world-report-2011/libya>; Amnesty International, *Annual Report 2011: Libya*, available at: <http://www.amnesty.org/en/region/libya/report-2011>; Global Detention Project, *Libya Detention Profile* (2009), available at: <http://www.globaldetentionproject.org/countries/africa/libya/introduction.html>. In the past, see also Report of the Council of Europe Commissioner for Human Rights, CommDH(2005)9, 14 December 2005; European Commission, Technical Mission to Libya on Illegal Immigration 27 November–6 December 2004: Report, No. 7753/05, 4 April 2005.

[129] *M.S.S. v. Belgium and Greece*, ECHR (2011) Appl. No. 30696/09, judgment of 21 January 2011 (GC).

[130] *H.R. v. France*, ECHR (2011) Appl. No. 64780/09, judgment of 22 September 2011.

[131] *Hirsi Jamaa and others v. Italy*, ECHR (2012) Appl. No. 27765/09, judgment of 23 February 2012 (GC).

[132] Art. 30 ECHR.

international organizations and NGOs from different regions, pursuant to Article 36(2) ECHR.[133]

The judgment emphasizes the obligations (and limits) incumbent on contracting states in relation to immigration control practices, focusing specifically on interceptions on the high seas. Reaffirming its previous case law, the Court formulated new principles and reinforced points already established in the past. The judgment is relevant for its recognition of extraterritorial jurisdiction for violations committed against persons under the continuous and exclusive control of de jure and de facto authorities of the state, regardless of the purpose and reasons for the intervention. Through a systematic and evolutionary interpretation, the Court also found that even though the push-back of migrants is carried out outside the national territory, it still remains within the notion of collective expulsion under Article 4, Protocol 4.

Consistent with the principles mentioned, the Court warned that respecting the prohibition under Article 3 is not a purely formal manner: contracting states have a duty to ensure that migrants sent back are not exposed to the risk of inhuman and degrading treatment, or to be arbitrarily repatriated by an intermediate country to places of origin where they may be exposed to similar risks. To this effect it is not sufficient to rely on (generic or specific) provisions contained in a bilateral treaty to be exempt from fulfilling the obligations under Article 3. States must verify the actual situation, especially where reliable sources document partner states' failure to comply with their obligations to protect fundamental rights.

The judgment is a clear condemnation of the 'push-back policy' enacted by Italy and a warning to Italy to comply with the principles embodied in the ruling, by adopting general measures, including legislation. Nevertheless, in addition to restoring the 2008 agreement,[134] on 3 April 2012 (that is, after the ruling was delivered) Italy and Libya reaffirmed their willingness to cooperate on migration control. Not only are previous bilateral agreements in the field of migration recalled in the premises of a new mutual covenant,[135] but the text also provides for the

[133] The President of the Court may, in the interest of the proper administration of justice, invite any High Contracting Party which is not a party to the proceedings or any person concerned who is not the applicant to submit written comments or take part in hearings. In the instant case, written observations were received from the United Nations High Commissioner for Refugees (UNHCR), Human Rights Watch, the Columbia Law School Human Rights Clinic, the Centre for Advice on Individual Rights in Europe (the AIRE Centre), Amnesty International, and the International Federation for Human Rights (FIDH), acting collectively. Observations were also received from the United Nations High Commissioner for Human Rights (UNHCHR), which had been given leave to intervene by the President of the Court. The UNHCR was also given leave to participate in the oral proceedings.

[134] The agreement with Libya was suspended during the international military intervention that took place in 2011 (see UNSC Resolutions S/RES/1970 (2011) of 26 Febuary 2011 and S/RES/1973 (2011) of 17 March 2011), following the upheavals related to the 'Arab Spring' which led to the unforeseen sharp fall of a regime in power since 1969. At the end of that year the agreement was restored with the new government.

[135] The covenant has been concluded in the form of 'minutes of a meeting', without any formal procedure. The content was not made public by the Italian government, but was published on the website of the newspaper *La Stampa* on 18 June 2012. The text is available at: <http://www.asgi.it/public/parser_download/save/1_2012_accordo.libia.pdf>. In a joint high-level meeting between the Italian Ministry of the Interior and the Libyan Foreign Ministry, held in Rome on 4 July 2013, the two

renewal of collaboration in several areas (training, monitoring of borders, establishment of reception centres, return). The parties have also agreed to coordinate activities at sea in the respective areas of jurisdiction and in international waters, in accordance with bilateral agreements and international maritime law. Despite the lack of improvement in the human rights situation in Libya, references to obligations of protection are still very generic and do not provide for any specific guarantee in favour of migrants, in defiance of the principles upheld by the Court.[136] This conduct clearly illustrates the resistance to reconciling the obligations of protection with choices made in migration policy.

VI. Concluding Remarks

The analysis of the Italian case permits the drawing of some conclusions. As already mentioned, in recent years Italy's search for tools to reduce irregular migration has focused on the use of its criminal law apparatus, or resulted in an attempt to restrict the rights of undocumented migrants. The not-so-hidden goal of this choice is the intention to 'make life difficult for undocumented aliens', in the hope that these may well be discouraged from choosing Italy as a country of destination.

The validity of this choice in pursuing the goal of reducing unauthorized presence, and the reasons behind this (such as the difficulties in programming the number of new entries, weak internal controls, and the attractiveness of the informal economy) are evaluations of migration policy that fall outside the scope of this chapter. From a legal point of view however, it seems possible to assert that the affirmation of human rights, which have gradually extended their scope to a sector traditionally considered to reside within state sovereignty, such as the treatment of foreigners, has permeated this area to the extent that state power cannot be considered absolute.

The idea that state sovereignty should be exercised in accordance with international law, including international human rights law, backed up with increasing frequency by many international authorities, seems to have had an impact on national courts. Recent analysis of many different national and supranational rulings highlights the focus on common questions and the difficult search for a balanced position: how far does the margin of appreciation of states extend? How does the principle of proportionality balance this? What limits can be set on fundamental rights and what are currently untouchable fundamental rights, regardless of the nationality and status?

countries reaffirmed their willingness to cooperate in combating irregular migration, in compliance with human rights obligations, see the press release at: <http://www.governo.it/Presidente/AudioVisivi/dettaglio.asp?d=72014>.

[136] Pursuant to section III, para. 6, of the Covenant, for migration control activities and during the stay of undocumented migrants in accommodation centres, the parties have confirmed their commitment to respect human rights, as protected by international agreements and conventions in force.

These issues were dealt with by the Italian Constitutional Court which, having been requested to assess the legitimacy of some of the most emblematic new provisions, has at least in part undermined the security-focused approach. While showing the difficulties of carrying out the necessary balance between apparently conflicting values, it has however made significant inroads in affirming that inviolable rights, in general, belong to individuals, not as participants in a given political community, but as human beings. The legal status of foreigners cannot be regarded—in relation to the protection of those rights—as justifying a diversified and pejorative treatment, especially under criminal law, which is more directly related to the fundamental freedoms of the person. It is true therefore that the Constitution allows a broad exercise of the legislature's discretion, however the balance of different interests (including the duty to safeguard fundamental rights) meets the constitutional limits imposed by the hierarchy of interests.

The same approach appears to be followed by the ECtHR. While maintaining the traditional view that a state is entitled, as a matter of well-established international law, to control the entry of aliens into its territory and their residence there,[137] the Court has consistently upheld, however, the need to strike a fair balance between the competing interests of the individual and of the community as a whole, thus tempering the state margin of discretion.

Within the EU, the need to ensure the coherence of the EU legal system, in light of its underlying principles, such as effectiveness, proportionality, and cooperation, prevents absolute arbitrariness in sectors increasingly regulated at a common level. Hopefully the binding legal effect attributed to the Charter of Fundamental Rights of the European Union under Article 6 of the amended Treaty on European Union and the future accession to the ECHR will exercise a direct influence on new legislation on the matter, becoming a specific point of reference and subsequently affecting the choices of the national legislature as further limits.

What emerges is a struggle between centripetal and centrifugal forces acting on essential values, the emblem of a conflict between different views, which will hopefully find an appropriate and satisfactory balance, always ensuring respect for fundamental rights in the implementation of any migration policy.

[137] See, among many others, *Abdulaziz, Cabales and Balkandali v. the United Kingdom*, ECHR (1985) Series A, No. 94, 34, judgment of 28 May 1985, para. 67; *Boujlifa v. France*, ECHR (1997), *Reports of Judgments and Decisions* 1997-VI, 2264, judgment of 21 October 1997, para. 42.

Index

Page numbers suffixed with *n* refer to notes.

The manufacturer's authorised representative in the EU for product safety is Oxford University Press España S.A. of El Parque Empresarial San Fernando de Henares, Avenida de Castilla, 2 - 28830 Madrid (www.oup.es/en or product.safety@oup.com). OUP España S.A. also acts as importer into Spain of products made by the manufacturer.
Printed and bound by CPI Group (UK) Ltd, Croydon, CR0 4YY
14/09/2026
02216305-0010